The Critical Response to Tennessee Williams

Recent Titles in
Critical Responses in Arts and Letters

The Critical Response to Tennessee Williams

Edited by
George W. Crandell

Critical Responses in Arts and Letters, Number 24
Cameron Northouse, Series Adviser

Greenwood Press
Westport, Connecticut • London

Library of Congress Cataloging-in-Publication Data

The critical response to Tennessee Williams / edited by George W.
    Crandell.
        p.   cm.—(Critical responses in arts and letters, ISSN
    1057–0993 ; no. 24)
      Includes bibliographical references (p.) and index.
      ISBN 0–313–29372–4 (alk. paper)
        1. Williams, Tennessee, 1911–1983—Criticism and interpretation.
    I. Crandell, George W., 1956–   . II. Series.
    PS3545.I5365Z616   1996
    812′.54—dc20   96–18345

British Library Cataloguing in Publication Data is available.

Library of Congress Catalog Card Number: 96–18345
ISBN: 0–313–29372–4
ISSN: 1057–0993

First published in 1996

Greenwood Press, 88 Post Road West, Westport, CT 06881
An imprint of Greenwood Publishing Group, Inc.

Printed in the United States of America

The paper used in this book complies with the
Permanent Paper Standard issued by the National
Information Standards Organization (Z39.48–1984).

10 9 8 7 6 5 4 3 2 1

Copyright Acknowledgments

The editor and publisher gratefully acknowledge permission for use of the following material:

Mel Gussow, "Stage: *Battle of Angels,*" *The New York Times,* November 4, 1974, p. 51. Copyright © 1974 by The New York Times Company. Reprinted by permission.

Nancy M. Tischler, "The Distorted Mirror: Tennessee Williams' Self-Portraits," *Mississippi Quarterly* 25.4 (Fall 1972): 389-403. Reprinted by permission.

Claudia Cassidy, "Fragile Drama Holds Theater in Tight Spell," *Chicago Tribune,* December 27, 1944, p. 11. ©Copyrighted Chicago Tribune Company. All rights reserved. Used with permission.

Louis Kronenberger, "A Triumph for Miss Taylor," *New York Newspaper PM,* April 2, 1945, 16.

Joseph Wood Krutch, "Drama," *Nation,* April 14, 1945, pp. 424-25. Reprinted with permission from *The Nation* magazine. (c) The Nation Company, L.P.

Henry Hewes, "Helen of Sparta," *Saturday Review,* December 8, 1956, p. 29. REPRINTED BY PERMISSION © 1956, S. R. Publications, Ltd.

Howard Taubman, "Diverse, Unique Amanda," *The New York Times,* May 16, 1965, sec. 2, p. 1. Copyright © 1965 by The New York Times Company. Reprinted by permission.

Edwin Wilson, "Fragile Laura and the Gentleman Caller," *Wall Street Journal,* December 23, 1975, p. 6. Reprinted by permission.

Frank Rich, "Theater: *Glass Menagerie,*" *The New York Times,* December 2, 1983, sec. 3, p. 3. Copyright © 1983 by The New York Times Company. Reprinted by permission.

Jan Stuart, "A *Glass* You Can See Things In," *New York Newsday,* November 16, 1994, pp. B2, B14. New York Newsday, Inc., Copyright, 1994.

Geoffrey Borny, "The Two Glass Menageries: An Examination of the Effects of Meaning That Result From Directing the Reading Edition as Opposed to the Acting Edition of the Play," *Page to Stage: Theatre as Translation,* ed. Ortrun Zuber-Skerritt (Amsterdam: Editions Rodopi B.V., 1964): 117-36. Reprinted by permission.

Julius Novick, "Honesty or merely disarming?", *Village Voice,* March 8, 1973: 58. Reprinted by permission of the author and *The Village Voice.*

Lawrence Van Gelder, "Stage: Williams's *2 Character Play,*" *The New York Times,* August 22, 1975, p. 16. Copyright © 1975 by The New York Times Company. Reprinted by permission.

Albert J. Devlin, "The Later Career of Tennessee Williams," *Tennessee Williams Literary Journal* 1.2 (Winter 1989-90): 7-17. Reprinted by permission.

Clive Barnes, "Stage: Williams's *Eccentricities,*" *The New York Times,* November 24, 1976, p. 23. Copyright © 1976 by The New York Times Company. Reprinted by permission.

Walter Kerr, "A Touch of the Poet Isn't Enough to Sustain Williams's Latest Play," *The New York Times,* May 22, 1977, sec. 2, pp. 5, 30. Copyright © 1977 by The New York Times Company. Reprinted by permission.

Gerald Weales, "Tennessee's Waltz: Familiar Williams Themes," *Commonweal,* March 16, 1979: 146-47. Reprinted by permission.

John Simon, "Damsels Inducing Distress," *New York,* April 7, 1980: 82, 84. Reprinted by permission.

Wilborn Hampton, "Tennessee Williams's Next-to-Final Finale," *The New York Times,* April 21, 1995, p. C30. Copyright © 1995 by The New York Times Company. Reprinted by permission.

Dan Isaac, "Tennessee Revisited," *Other Stages* 4.7 (December 17, 1981): 6, 8. Reprinted by permission.

Albert E. Karlson, "A House Not Meant to Stand," *Theatre Journal* 34.4 (1982): 539-42. Reprinted by permission.

Grateful acknowledgment is given to New Directions Publishing Corporation for permission to quote from the following copyrighted works of Tennessee Williams:

Androgyne, Mon Amour: Copyright © 1944, 1949, 1967, 1968, 1969, 1973, 1974, 1975, 1976, 1977 by Tennessee Williams.

Baby Doll: Copyright © 1945, 1946, 1953, 1956 by Tennessee Williams.

Collected Stories: Copyright © 1985 by The Estate of Tennessee Williams (See book for individual copyright lines).

Stopped Rocking and Other Sceenplays: Copyright © 1984 by The Estate of Tennessee Williams.

In The Winter of Cities: Copyright © 1956, 1964 by Tennessee Williams.

From *The Theatre of Tennessee Williams:*

Vol. 1

Battle of Angels: Copyright 1940, 1945 by Tennessee Williams.

The Glass Menagerie: Copyright 1945 by Tennessee Williams.

A Streetcar Named Desire: Copyright 1947 by Tennessee Williams.

Contents

Camino Real (1953)

Cat on a Hot Tin Roof (1955)

Twenty-seven Wagons Full of Cotton (1955)

Orpheus Descending (1957)

Garden District (1958)

Clothes for a Summer Hotel (1980)

Something Cloudy, Something Clear (1981)

A House Not Meant to Stand (1982)

Series Foreword

Critical Responses in Arts and Letters is designed to present a documentary history of highlights in critical reception to the body of work of writers and artists and to individual works that are generally considered to be of major importance. The focus of each volume in this series is basically historical. The introductions to each volume are themselves brief histories of the critical response an author, artist, or individual work has received. This response is then further illustrated by reprinting a strong representation of the major critical reviews and articles that collectively have produced the author's, artist's or work's critical reputation.

The scope of *Critical Responses in Arts and Letters* knows no chronological or geographical boundaries. Volumes under preparation include studies of individuals from around the world and in both contemporary and historical periods.

Each volume is the work of an individual editor, who surveys the entire body of criticism on a single author, artist, or work. The editor then selects the best material to depict the critical response received by an author or artist over his/her entire career. Documents produced by the author or the artist may also be included when the editor finds that they are necessary to a full understanding of the materials at hand. In circumstances where previous, isolated volumes of criticism on a particular individual or work exist, the editor carefully selects material that better reflects the nature and directions of the critical response over time.

In addition to the introduction and the documentary section, the editor of each volume is free to solicit new essays on areas that may not have been adequately dealt with in previous criticism. For volumes on living writers and artists, new interviews may be included, again at the discretion of the volume's editor. The volumes also provide a supplementary bibliography and are fully indexed.

While each volume in *Critical Responses in Arts and Letters* is unique, it is also hoped that in combination they form a useful, documentary history of the critical response to the arts, and one that can be easily and profitably employed by students and scholars.

Cameron Northouse

Chronology

1907	June 3: Cornelius Coffin Williams marries Edwina Dakin (Tennessee Williams's parents)
1909	November 19: Sister, Rose Isabel Williams born
1911	March 26: Thomas Lanier ("Tennessee") Williams born in Columbus, Mississippi
1918	July: Family moves to St. Louis, Missouri
1919	February 21: Brother, Walter Dakin Williams born
1929	June 13: Graduates from University City High School, St. Louis; September: Enrolls at University of Missouri
1931-35	Works intermittently for International Shoe Company, St. Louis
1935	Fall: Enrolls at Washington University, St. Louis
1937	Fall: Enrolls at University of Iowa
1938	August 5: Graduates from University of Iowa with B. A. in English
1939	March 20: Group Theatre awards Williams $100 for a collection of plays, *American Blues*; Audrey Wood becomes Williams's agent; December: Awarded $1,000 Rockefeller Foundation grant
1940	December 30: *Battle of Angels* opens at Wilbur Theatre, Boston
1943	May-October: Employed as MGM screenwriter

1944   December 26: *The Glass Menagerie* opens at Civic Theatre, Chicago

1945   March 31: *The Glass Menagerie* opens at Playhouse Theatre; September 25: *You Touched Me!* opens at Booth Theatre

1947   Meets Frank Merlo, who becomes Williams's longtime companion; December 3: *A Streetcar Named Desire* opens at Barrymore Theatre

1948   May: Pulizter Prize awarded for *A Streetcar Named Desire*; October 6: *Summer and Smoke* opens at Music Box Theatre

1951   February 3: *The Rose Tattoo* opens at Martin Beck Theatre

1952   Elected to lifetime membership in the National Institute of Arts and Letters

1953   March 19: *Camino Real* opens at Martin Beck Theatre

1955   March 24: *Cat on a Hot Tin Roof* opens at Morosco Theatre; April 19: *All in One,* featuring *Twenty-seven Wagons Full of Cotton,* opens at Playhouse Theatre; May: Pulitzer Prize awarded for *Cat on a Hot Tin Roof*

1957   March 21: *Orpheus Descending* opens at Martin Beck Theatre; March 27: Cornelius Coffin Williams dies

1958   January 7: *Garden District* (*Suddenly Last Summer* and *Something Unspoken*) opens at York Theatre

1959   March 10: *Sweet Bird of Youth* opens at Martin Beck Theatre; April 14: *I Rise in Flame, Cried the Phoenix* opens at Theatre de Lys; December 8: *The Purification* opens at Theatre de Lys

1960   November 10: *Period of Adjustment* opens at Helen Hayes Theatre

1961   December 28: *The Night of the Iguana* opens at Royale Theatre

1962   American Academy of Arts and Letters awards Williams a lifetime fellowship

1963   January 16: *The Milk Train Doesn't Stop Here Anymore* opens at Morosco Theatre; September 21: Frank Merlo dies

1966	February 22: *Slapstick Tragedy* (*The Gnadiges Fraulein* and *The Mutilated*) opens at Longacre Theatre
1967	December 12: *The Two-Character* play opens at Hampstead Theatre Club
1968	March 27: *Kingdom of Earth* (*The Seven Descents of Myrtle*) opens at Ethel Barrymore Theatre
1969	May 11: *In the Bar of a Tokyo Hotel* opens at Eastside Playhouse
1971	July 8: *Out Cry* opens at Ivanhoe Theatre, Chicago; Bill Barnes succeeds Audrey Wood as Williams's agent
1972	April 2: *Small Craft Warnings* opens at Truck and Warehouse Theatre
1973	March 1: *Out Cry* opens at Lyceum Theatre
1975	June 18: *The Red Devil Battery Sign* opens at Shubert Theatre, Boston; August 14: *The Two-Character Play* opens at Quaigh Theatre
1976	November 23: *The Eccentricities of a Nightingale* opens at Morosco Theatre
1977	May 11: *Vieux Carré* opens at the St. James Theatre; June 8: *The Red Devil Battery Sign* opens at Roundhouse Theatre, London; July 7: *The Red Devil Battery Sign* opens at Phoenix Theatre, London
1979	January 21: *A Lovely Sunday for Creve Coeur* opens at Hudson Guild Theatre; September: *Kirche, Kutchen und Kinder* performed by Jean Cocteau Repertory Company
1980	March 26: *Clothes for a Summer Hotel* opens at Cort Theatre; April 21: President Carter names Williams winner of Medal of Freedom; June 1: Edwina Dakin Williams dies
1981	August 24: *Something Cloudy, Something Clear* opens at Bouwerie Lane Theatre; November 19: Williams receives Common Wealth Award with Harold Pinter
1982	April 27: *A House Not Meant to Stand* opens at Goodman Memorial Theatre, Chicago
1983	Night of February 24-25: Williams dies, Hotel Elysée, New York City

Introduction

Tennessee Williams is generally regarded, along with Eugene O'Neill and Arthur Miller, as one of the greatest American dramatists of the twentieth century. This reputation rests upon more than forty years of critical acclaim accrued by Williams's two masterpieces--*A Streetcar Named Desire* and *The Glass Menagerie*--and by a body of works that also includes the Pulitzer prize-winning drama *Cat on a Hot Tin Roof*, and more than sixty other plays, among them *The Rose Tattoo, Sweet Bird of Youth, Orpheus Descending*, and *The Night of the Iguana.* Gifted with an empathetic understanding of the human condition and a talent for rendering incisive psychological portraits, Williams has created some of the most enduring characters on the American stage: Amanda Wingfield, Blanche Du Bois, Stanley Kowalski, Big Daddy Pollitt, Maggie "the cat," and Serafina Delle Rosa. In roles created by Tennessee Williams, actors such as Maureen Stapleton (as Serafina Delle Rosa) and Marlon Brando (as Stanley Kowalski) have launched their careers, while others, such as Laurette Taylor (as Amanda Wingfield) have delivered some of the most memorable performances of the twentieth century. Distinguished by a lyrical voice that has its origins in the rhythms of Southern speech, Williams displays a brand of "personal lyricism" that has an appeal far wider than the boundaries of the U.S. geographical region where he was born (Williams, "Williams" 3). His plays, for example, have been translated into more than thirty different languages and have been performed on stages in countries all around the world.

Emerging into prominence just as the second world war came to a close, Tennessee Williams offered theatregoers a new "plastic" theatre, more caustic than the escapist dramas of the war years, but nevertheless more engagingly sensitive than the social dramas of the 1930s (Williams, "Production" ix). Williams considered his own brand of theatre more vital than "the exhausted theatre of realistic conventions" and aimed to supplant the latter with a plastic theatre employing "unconventional techniques," offering his audiences a view of reality distilled through a "poetic imagination" (Williams, "Production" ix).

Nurtured by the tragic life and the lyric poetry of Hart Crane, Tennessee Williams initially found expression for his own poetic imagination by writing verse. During the 1930s, Williams would publish more than forty poems, most of them in small, literary periodicals, but two of them appeared in the prestigious *Poetry* magazine. Even so, Williams's growing dissatisfaction with his own verse, the dim prospect of earning enough money to support himself by writing poetry, and his discovery in 1935 of the enchantment of hearing an audience respond to his first dramatic production--*Cairo, Shanghai, Bombay!*-- signalled the beginning of Williams's love affair with the theatre and marked a significant metamorphosis in the form of Williams's artistic expression.

Williams's transformation from poet to dramatist, however, as reflected in the critical response to Tennessee Williams, was never wholly complete. Something of the poet in Williams always remained, visible to commentators who, over the years, would point to the divided nature of the artist in Tennessee Williams. Frank Durham, for example, drawing attention to the poetic elements in *The Glass Menagerie,* calls the playwright a "Theatre Poet in Prose" (3). Harold Bloom, emphasizing the influence that lyric poet Hart Crane had on Tennessee Williams, argues that Williams never became "the lyrical dramatist that Williams is supposed to have been" (3), but remained "more of a dramatic lyrist" (2). Both writers would agree, however, that the "poetry" of Tennessee Williams encompasses more than the metrical qualities of his language. As Durham observes, Williams and other practitioners of the plastic theatre eschewed the verse forms that distinguish conventional poetry, opting instead for "an eclectic but organic union of both verbal and nonverbal elements of the theatre" (3). Supporting Durham's view, Alan Downer writes:

> [T]he true poet of the theater is not necessarily concerned in the least with the traditional forms and language of poetry, but with making all the elements at his disposal--plot, actor, action, stage, lighting, setting, music, speech--unite to serve as a vehicle for his theme, his vision, or his interpretation of man's fate. (110)

Even at the beginning of his professional career, Williams was consciously aware of the struggle within himself between poet and dramatist. With a remarkable prescience, Williams observes about himself what Lyle Leverich calls "the division in his artistic personality that would become the hallmark of Tennessee Williams's writing" (334). In December 1939, Williams recorded the following lament in his journal:

> The tragedy of a poet writing drama is that when he writes well--from the dramaturgic, technical pt. of view he is often writing

badly. One must learn--(that is the craft, I suppose)--to fuse lyricism and realism into a congruous unit. I guess my chief trouble is that I don't. I make the most frightful *faux pas*. I feared today that I may have taken a distinctly wrong turn in turning to drama. But, oh, I do *feel* drama so intensely sometimes. (qtd. in Leverich 334)

By 1942 Tennessee Williams believed that he had discovered a solution to the problem of fusing lyricism and realism, "a method of presenting his passion and the world's in an articulate manner" (qtd. in Leverich 446). Considering himself an "experimental dramatist," Williams intended to fashion a new "poetic" art form called "sculptural drama" (qtd. in Leverich 446). In March of 1942, Williams first articulated the theory of dramatic structure that underlies the composition of his plays, however much in actual practice the execution differs from the design.

> This form, this method, is for the play of short cumulative scenes which I think is on its way in. I visualize it as a reduced mobility on the stage, the forming of statuesque attitudes or tableaux, something resembling a restrained type of dance, with motions honed down to only the essential or significant. (qtd. in Leverich 446)

Just as Williams's "artistic personality" may be said to be divided, so too may be the critical response to his plays, and along lines similar to Williams's self-assessment. Reviewers routinely praise Williams for the lyrical, poetic aspects of his work, while critics who find fault with Williams generally point to his failures of dramatic craftsmanship. Similarly divided between praise of Williams's lyricism and criticism of his dramatic technique, the reviews of Williams's plays may also be grouped into three broad categories that adhere to no evenly divided or strictly demarcated chronological periods: the first group includes restrained responses to a "new" playwright who is not yet in command of his dramatic skills; the second group includes estimates of Williams's greatness, which draw attention to the mastery of his craft or point to evidence of his maturity; finally, a third group of reviews notes when Williams departs in direction or quality from the standard established by Williams's own masterpieces.

From Catastrophe to Success (1940-1949)

The critical response to Tennessee Williams during the first decade of his professional career mirrors the extremes that characterize this early period represented by the initial failure of his first production in Boston, *Battle of Angels* (1940), and by the unanticipated Broadway triumph of *The Glass Menagerie* in 1945. The latter play, along with *A Streetcar Named Desire*

(1947), would elevate Williams to the status of major American playwright and assure him of a long and successful career in the theatre. Two other productions during the 1940s, *You Touched Me!* (1945) and *Summer and Smoke* (1948), suffered by comparison with what would later be acknowledged as Williams's two most successful plays.

When *Battle of Angels* premiered at the Wilbur Theatre on December 30, 1940, the Boston critics who were not offended by the play's language rejected it for its melodramatic excesses, which many felt bordered on madness. Fine performances by Miriam Hopkins and her supporting cast, the critics concluded, were not enough to save a play badly in need of revision. Although the play closed only twelve days after its opening, Williams harbored a special affection for his "first" play and would bring it to life again, revised and retitled *Orpheus Descending,* seventeen years later. Even this production, however, would not be its final incarnation. In 1974 Williams presented theatregoers with yet another version of the play, stripped of the heavy symbolism that troubled critics in 1957 and the excesses that brought about its failure in 1940. Titled *Battle of Angels* again, because it more closely resembled the original production than *Orpheus Descending,* the play earned favorable reviews. Recalling the early history of *Battle of Angels,* Mel Gussow concluded in 1974 that it could "stand on its own" (51). He added, however, that "[t]he original play," obscured by the success of *The Glass Menagerie,* nevertheless "became Williams's most neglected piece of theater, a footnote in a great career" (51).

The neglect of *Battle of Angels* contributes to the naive but commonly held belief that *The Glass Menagerie* is Williams's first play. The fact that *The Glass Menagerie* was Williams's first play to be produced on Broadway as well as his first success also gives credence to this myth. Some critics, however, even those aware of *Battle of Angels,* sometimes find the myth useful to suggest that Williams's career begins with a sudden, spectacular success. Gerald Weales, for example, relies upon this legend to argue that "Williams suffers from a familiar affliction of American playwrights--first-play afflatus" (18) and to contend that *The Glass Menagerie* is also Williams's "best play" (19). Whether *The Glass Menagerie* or *A Streetcar Named Desire* is the better play is the subject of a debate that still continues, but the high standing of *The Glass Menagerie* was by no means assured when it opened in Chicago on December 26, 1944.

The timing of the production could not have been less fortuitous--in winter, in Chicago, the day after Christmas--but the champions of *The Glass Menagerie,* among them Claudia Cassidy, Henry T. Murdock, and Ashton Stevens, implored audiences to see the show at the risk of missing a remarkable performance by Laurette Taylor. Although the Chicago critics' altruistic display of affection for the play insured its trip to New York and a Broadway opening on March 31, 1945, *The Glass Menagerie* ultimately proved that it, too, could stand on its own. Successful, if not brilliant performances by Helen Hayes and Maureen Stapleton as Amanda in revivals of the play (in 1956 and 1965 respectively), have since dispelled initial suspicions that *The Glass Menagerie* depended upon Laurette Taylor for its success. Even when *The Glass Menagerie* is performed poorly, as Stanley Kauffmann concluded after seeing the 1975 revival, "the play survives its mistreatment" (28). Succeeding revivals of *The Glass Menagerie,* including those in 1983 and 1994, apparently have confirmed Claudia Cassidy's original forecast that "*The Glass Menagerie* holds in its shadowed fragility the stamina of success" (11).

Whether or not Tennessee Williams possessed the same "stamina of success" as a playwright was a judgment withheld by many reviewers, at least until the New York production of *You Touched Me!* in 1945, when comparisons of it with *The Glass Menagerie* inevitably resulted. Actually, *You Touched Me!* had been produced at the Playhouse Theatre in Cleveland in October 1943 and again in November 1943 at the Playbox Theatre in Pasadena. This play (on which Williams collaborated with Donald Windham) might have been produced in New York before *The Glass Menagerie,* but Eddie Dowling, the director, and Audrey Wood, Williams's agent, insisted that *The Glass Menagerie* should precede *You Touched Me!* to Broadway (Leverich 574). Their decision, with which Williams ultimately agreed, significantly shaped the resulting critical response to the play. While many critics found it entertaining, more of them shared beliefs similar to Wiella Waldorf's opinion that the play suffers from "a confusion of tongues and a strange medley of dramatic styles" (38). To all those who had seen *The Glass Menagerie, You Touched Me!* seemed disappointing by comparison. Only Joseph Wood Krutch saw the humor in the plight of critics who had "gone out on a limb" and written perhaps too enthusiastically about *The Glass Menagerie* ("6 Oct. 1945" 349). Speaking in jest on behalf of these reviewers to Tennessee Williams, Krutch wrote: "'The least you could have done . . . was to write something which would have made my former enthusiasm seem prophetic'" ("6 Oct. 1945" 349).

Just as *You Touched Me!* had been compared with *The Glass Menagerie,* so too *A Streetcar Named Desire,* when it premiered at the Barrymore Theatre on December 3, 1947, invited comparisons to Williams's previous work. Likening *A Streetcar Named Desire* to *The Glass Menagerie,* a number of critics perceived a developmental improvement in Tennessee Williams, believing that *A Streetcar Named Desire* equalled or surpassed *The Glass Menagerie* in quality. Brooks Atkinson, for example, argues that *Streetcar* "is a more coherent and lucid drama," a play in which "the mood is more firmly established" ("*Streetcar*" 3). Joseph Wood Krutch agreed that while *The Glass Menagerie* is "uncertain and intermittent," *A Streetcar Named Desire* is "sure and sustained" ("20 Dec. 1947" 686). Even though *A Streetcar Named Desire* would eventually become an internationally acclaimed drama, it did not win universal approval among its first reviewers. Impatient critics thought simply that, by Broadway standards, the play was too long--by twenty minutes to be exact. More seriously, Robert Coleman excluded *Streetcar* from his classification of "top flight" plays because of its "episodic and strangely static" form (38). As *Streetcar* continued its Broadway run (lasting 855 performances), criticisms such as these faded into obscurity, but Coleman's remarks remain of interest, if only because he identifies as faults some of the defining features of Williams's sculptural drama.

Both in the initial production of *A Streetcar Named Desire* and in subsequent revivals, much of the critical attention has focused on the dynamic relationship between Blanche Du Bois and Stanley Kowalski. The performance of Jessica Tandy in the 1947 production, for example, has since become legend, but a surprising number of the initial reviewers believed that Tandy had been miscast. Among this group, Harold Clurman felt that Tandy lacked the "emotional range" to play the part (*Lies* 77). Similarly, Marlon Brando's performance seems to have gained in stature over the years, especially following his starring role in the 1951 film version of the play. Before this date, Robert Brustein argued that Brando played Stanley as "a more sensitive character than Williams created," a fault corrected, Brustein maintained, by Anthony Quinn, who in 1949 played Stanley "more like the thick-headed antagonist Williams intended" ("America's" 125).

Whether because reviewers remember the performances of Brando and Tandy as great or because, as Mimi Kramer suggests, audiences have come to perceive Stanley and Blanche as embodiments of "campy melodrama in relations between men and women" (82), actors playing these parts have since failed to satisfy the critics in revivals of *Streetcar*. Critics in 1956 almost unanimously panned Tallulah Bankhead, while in 1973 reviewers felt that the performance of James Farentino (as Stanley) was not equal to that of Rosemary Harris (as Blanche). According to the commentators, subsequent pairs starring as Stanley and Blanche--Blythe Danner and Aidan Quinn in 1988, Jessica Lange and Alec Baldwin in 1992--have all lacked spark in what is supposed to be a combustible relationship. All have failed, therefore, to ignite a positive critical response. Like *The Glass Menagerie,* however, *A Streetcar Named Desire* seems to survive mistreatment at the hands of directors and actors. Few, if any, critics would dispute the claim of Philip Kolin that *A Streetcar Named Desire* remains "one of the two or three most significant American plays on the world stage" (ix).

The same reviewers who in 1947 confidently predicted the success of *A Streetcar Named Desire,* reserved judgment about the capabilities of Tennessee Williams. In a review of *Streetcar,* Joseph Wood Krutch spoke for many critics when he observed that "[t]he extent of Mr. Williams's range is still to be demonstrated" ("20 Dec. 1947" 686). The production of *Summer and Smoke,* beginning on October 6, 1948 at the Music Box Theatre, did little to convince critics that Williams was a playwright capable of great range or diversity in characterization, theme, or method. Some critics even felt that Williams had resorted to repeating himself, even though *Summer and Smoke* has been produced in Dallas at the Gulf Oil Playhouse before the New York production of *A Streetcar Named Desire* and could have been brought to Broadway ahead of it. Just as *You Touched Me!* faded in the brilliant glow surrounding *The Glass Menagerie,* so too *Summer and Smoke* languished in the gathering critical acclaim afforded to *A Streetcar Named Desire.*

Four years later, theatre audiences were more receptive to a revival of *Summer and Smoke* at the Sheridan Square Theatre. Accounting for its modest success in 1952, Brooks Atkinson speculated that the distance in time from the production of *Streetcar* was one factor, but also surmised that the Music Box Theatre, where it was first performed in New York, may have been "too large [a theatre] for such a sensitive play" ("Second" 1). Although *Summer and Smoke* was not revived after 1952, it would, like *Battle of Angels,* be revised and retitled. Premiering as *The Eccentricities of a Nightingale* on November 23, 1976, the play received mixed reviews, most of the critics convinced that Tennessee Williams had not improved the play by revising it.

Dramatic Diversity (1950-1962)

If the earliest critical responses to Tennessee Williams's plays reflect the extremes of failure and triumph, then the responses during the twelve year period from 1950 to 1962, by contrast, describe a period of stable productivity distinguished from the previous decade by a greater display of diversity in the forms of Williams's artistic expression.

As if in response to Joseph Wood Krutch and other critics who doubted whether Williams could extend his range, Williams produced, in the space of a dozen years, three comic plays: a grotesque comedy, *The Rose Tattoo* (1951); a comic fantasy, *Camino Real* (1953); and a serious comedy, *Period of Adjustment* (1960). During the same time period, Williams continued to write serious dramas of the distinctive type for which he is best known: *Cat on a Hot Tin Roof* (1955), *Orpheus Descending* (1957), *Garden District* (1958), *Sweet Bird of Youth* (1959), and *The Night of the Iguana* (1961). In addition, three shorter works, secondary in importance to these major plays by Tennessee Williams, were staged in New York with relative success, owing both to the popularity of the playwright and a growing interest in his works written prior to his classics, *A Streetcar Named Desire* and *The Glass Menagerie.*

Of the short, minor works performed in the 1950s, *I Rise in Flame, Cried the Phoenix* (1959) garnered the most unqualified praise. Only Louis Calta objected that the work was "too brief to be of any real theatrical worth" (30). *Twenty-seven Wagons Full of Cotton,* a melodramatic work compared by many to Erskine Caldwell's *Tobacco Road*, attracted scant notice, but did afford critics an opportunity to see Maureen Stapleton (in 1955) and later Meryl Streep (in 1976) display their extraordinary talents in the role of Flora Meighan. The most unusual short work by Williams, a drama in verse called *The Purification*, was performed in New York in 1959 and again in 1975. Written in the early 1940s, *The Purification* received mixed reviews, but continues to be of academic interest, perhaps because it recalls William's uneasy transformation from poet to dramatist.

Juding by the critical response to *The Rose Tattoo, Camino Real*, and *Period of Adjustment*, Tennessee Williams's reputation as a dramatist rests more securely upon his serious works. Of the three comedies that Williams produced between 1950 and 1962, *The Rose Tattoo* fared the best in its initial production and, according to some critics, improved with age. Writing about the 1966 rivival, Henry Hewes attributed its better reception to a shift in the theatre, away "from naturalism in the direction of the grotesque" (60). Although critics in 1995 would again debate the "timelessness" of *The Rose Tattoo*, they would also conclude that Williams's comedies will never rival his best serious works.

This view was certainly affirmed by the negative reception afforded to *Camino Real* (1953), which many critics had difficulty labeling--comedy, farce, fantasy--and which even more had difficulty understanding. One critic, Richard Hayes, praised Williams for seeking "a certain mobility and freedom of form" (51), but he was joined by many others who believed that Williams had written a confusing play, made obscure by "symbolic gestures" and a "structure of embellishment" that baffled almost everyone (52). Originally published as *Ten Blocks on the Camino Real* in *American Blues* (1948), *Camino Real* was expanded to include sixteen blocks, but some believe that, during the process of expansion and revision, Williams never succeeded in unifying the work or giving it coherence. With repetition--it was revived in 1960 and again in 1970--*Camino Real* has become more accessible to critics, but has not yet been reviewed favorably.

Period of Adjustment (1960), Williams's third comedy, enjoyed a more favorable initial reception than *Camino Real*, but has since attracted little attention. Characterized by the reviewers as superficial and dishonest, *Period of Adjustment* has not been revived on Broadway.

Including the three comedies, twelve plays by Tennessee Williams appeared on Broadway or New York City stages between 1950 and 1962. From among this group, *Cat on a Hot Tin Roof*, winner of the Pulitzer Prize in 1955, has generated the most enthusiastic and sustained critical response. When it opened on March 24, 1955, reviewers knew immediately that it bore the stamp of success, yet they were reluctant to afford this play the approbation of greatness. While many agreed with Walter F. Kerr that *Cat on a Hot Tin Roof* is "beautifully written, perfectly directed, and stunningly acted" (12), some could not wholly endorse the play because of its "vulgar" language. Others wished that Williams had resolved the ambiguity or mystery surrounding Brick's character ("Is he or is he not a homosexual?" they wondered). Cognizant of the play's virtues and vices, Richard Watts expressed the view of many critics who held divided opinions about *Cat on a Hot Tin Roof*: "the final paradox of the work is that it is insistently vulgar, morbid, neurotic and ugly and still maintains a quality of exotic lyricism" (57).

To reviewers nineteen years later, *Cat on a Hot Tin Roof* seemed not at all shocking. Big Daddy's diction, considered bawdy in 1955, attracted little notice in 1974. Similarly, the critical response in 1974 reflected changing attitudes toward homosexuality, such that some critics considered Williams's treatment of the topic in *Cat on a Hot Tin Roof* somewhat dated. By 1990, other features of the play, for example, the presentation of "sexual tension" and the "hush-hush attitude toward cancer and scandal over childlessness" seemed to Linda Winer "almost quaint" (358). These differing perspectives all contribute to the ongoing debate about the stature of *Cat on a Hot Tin Roof,* including John Simon's provocative suggestion that *Cat on a Hot Tin Roof* is "a lively attention-holding, highly theatrical play: worthy commercial fare, but not art" ("Cat" 48).

Orpheus Descending, the play that followed *Cat on a Hot Tin Roof* on Broadway in 1957, shared with it the qualities of "exciting, absorbing theatre" (Keating 9), but most reviewers agreed that Williams failed in his attempt to rework the play that seventeen years ago he called *Battle of Angels.* As John Gassner noted, its "snarled symbolism" and "scrambled" mythology, serve only to obscure the meaning of the play (225). Critics of the 1989 revival, among them Robert Brustein, once again pointed to the confusing clash of symbols and mythology ("Robert" 25). Apparently, neither Williams's revisions nor the passage of time have helped to clarify the ambiguities inherent in *Orpheus Descending.*

A year later, in 1958, when *Garden District* (a double-bill featuring *Suddenly Last Summer* and *Something Unspoken*) opened, critics greeted the works with the temperance usually afforded minor works by a major artist. Quickly dismissing *Something Unspoken,* many reviewers responded to *Suddenly Last Summer* as they had to *Cat on a Hot Tin Roof,* noting its paradoxical qualities. Despite objections to the play's subject matter-- lobotomy, homosexuality, cannibalism--early critics could not easily dismiss Williams's writing. As John Gassner observed: "Williams has rarely written dialogue with such intensity of feeling and vividness of imagery as in *Suddenly Last Summer*" (228). For other critics, such as Tom F. Driver, the intensity and vividness of the play were evidence instead of Williams's reliance upon shocking material to deliver a "sensual wallop" rather than a "dramatic statement" (136). Responding to a revival of *Suddenly Last Summer* in 1995, reviewers echoed the remarks of earlier critics. In the interval between the two productions, however, the scholarly work of John Satterfield and Steven Bruhm has given support to George Freedley's contention, voiced in 1958, that Williams "enhanced his own considerable dramatic reputation with *Garden District*" (2).

If, after the production of *Suddenly Last Summer,* critics hoped that Williams would dispense with shocking material and embark upon a new direction, they would have to wait until after the 1959 production of *Sweet Bird of Youth.* When it opened at the Martin Beck Theatre on March 10, reviewers responded to it more positively than they had to *Garden District,* but with less enthusiasm than to *Cat on a Hot Tin Roof.* Many reviewers agreed with Robert Brustein that the play was "crudely melodramatic" ("Sweet" 59), and even more objected to its disturbing subject matter, but almost all admitted that it had the "sweet smell of commercial success" ("New Plays" 58). Revived in 1975, *Sweet Bird of Youth* enjoyed surprisingly positive reviews. Commenting on the play then, Douglas Watt echoed the sentiments of many earlier reviewers: while the play may be sentimental and melodramatic, it is nevertheless "effective theatre" (115).

Believing that Williams had finally put away the sensationalism and pessimism evident in *Orpheus Descending, Garden District,* and *Sweet Bird of Youth,* critics generally agreed that *The Night of the Iguana,* which opened at the Royale Theatre on December 28, 1961, represented Williams's best effort since *Cat on a Hot Tin Roof.* Whitney Bolton believed that in *The Night of the Iguana* Williams had created some of his best characters since *A Streetcar Named Desire* (2), an opinion shared by Harold Clurman, Douglas Watt, and Henry Bolton. Whatever the merits of the play or its defects, *The Night of the Iguana* marks a turning point in the critical response to Tennessee Williams. In subsequent years, as Williams's newest works shared the spotlight with revivals or revisions of older plays, critics and reviewers alike would refer to *The Night of the Iguana* as Williams's last successful play. After 1962, many of the revivals, including those of *The Night of the Iguana* in 1976 and 1988, would enjoy a more favorable reception than Williams's newly created works.

"Too Personal?" (1963-1982)

Although reviewers and critics perceived *The Night of the Iguana* as different in kind and quality from the twelve Tennessee Williams plays produced after it in New York, Williams considered it as one of many works still in progress. By the time Williams wrote *The Night of the Iguana,* which appeared in various forms on smaller stages before reaching Broadway in late 1961, he had come to view the stage as a place to fashion his works in progress, much to the dismay of reviewers. As a result, theatre audiences often witnessed his plays in various states of completion. *The Milk Train Doesn't Stop Here*

Anymore, provides an illustrative example of the process. Opening on Broadway in 1963, it closed after 64 performances, but a year later, a revised version of *The Milk Train* opened on Broadway again. It, too, failed, this time, after just four performances. Although critics appreciated the novelty of the attempt to resurrect a play after such a short interval, they did not hold Williams blameless for the faults of the play or for his unsuccessful efforts to revise it. For example, a reviewer for the *London Times* wrote that "In a theatre where recent plays are seldom revived, Tennessee Williams keeps his works alive by rewriting them" ("Mr. Tennessee" 13).

This criticism, directed specifically at *The Milk Train Doesn't Stop Here Anymore,* might have been applied to a number of dramas produced by Williams after 1962. Beginning with *The Gnadiges Fraulein* and *The Mutilated*--together called *Slapstick Tragedy* (1966)--and continuing for more than twenty years, reviewers frequently charged Williams with self-plagiarism, with deliberately repeating characters and themes from earlier plays. Wilfred Sheen, Chauncey Howell, and John Simon all called *Kingdom of Earth* (1968) a parody of Williams's earlier work. Similarly, three other plays, *The Red Devil Battery Sign* (produced in Chicago in 1975), *A Lovely Sunday for Creve Coeur* (1979), and *Kirche, Kuchen, und Kinder* (performed off-Broadway at the Jean Cocteau Repertory Company in September 1979) would also be dismissed as parodies.

If one group of the plays produced after 1962 were similar because of a parodic resemblance to previously written Williams plays, another group of plays were alike in their development from autobiographical materials. In the last decades of his life, Williams turned increasingly to work of a confessional nature. In an essay titled "Too Personal," Williams defended the practice by answering a question he posed himself:

> Is it or is it not right or wrong for a playwright to put his persona into his work?
>
> My answer is: "What else can he do?"--I mean the very root-necessity of all creative work is to express those things most involved in one's particular experience. (Williams 5)

As Williams became increasingly personal, his public audiences found his works more and more inaccessible. Speaking, perhaps, for many of Williams's followers, playwright David Mamet poignantly expressed how many felt about Tennessee Williams: "when Williams's 'life and view of life became less immediately accessible, our gratitude was changed to distant reverence for a man whom we felt obliged--if we were to continue in our happy feelings toward him--to consider already dead'" (qtd. in Bigsby 133-34).

Of five plays based loosely or extensively upon autobiographical materials, *Out Cry* (1973), later revised as *The Two-Character Play* (1975), distinguished itself from the others, owing to its affinities with works by Pirandello and Beckett. Critics noted, in particular, a similarity between *Out Cry* and Pirandello's *Six Characters in Search of an Author,* but they also agreed that Williams had not yet "mastered . . . the technique of planned confusion" (Novick 58). As a result, some critics voiced the opinion that *Out Cry* was as confused as the earlier *Camino Real.* While many critics elected to focus on the metatheatrical aspects of *Out Cry,* they had little choice but to notice the autobiographical elements in plays such as *In the Bar of a Tokyo Hotel* (1969) that offered little else for consideration. Writing about this play, for example, Harold Clurman, objected to its "unabashed confession" ("Theatre" 710), agreeing with Clive Barnes that the material in the the play was simply "too personal" (54). *Small Craft Warnings* (1972) fared somewhat better than *In the Bar of a Tokyo Hotel* and two other autobiographical works, *Vieux Carré* (1977) and *Something Cloudy, Something Clear* (1981) because it displayed some of the personal lyricism characteristic of Williams's earlier work that won him renown. In general, however, the critics concluded that Williams failed to make his personal experience either meaningful or dramatic in this group of autobiographical plays.

Differing from Williams's self-parodies and autobiographical works, *Clothes for a Summer Hotel* (1980) was based on the lives of F. Scott Fitzgerald and his wife Zelda. John Simon gave it the dubious distinction of being the only play out of the last eight or ten written by Williams that was not "embarrassing" ("Damsels" 82). Other critics who faulted Williams for revealing too much about himself in previous works, now charged Williams with revealing too little about the Fitzgeralds. Most of the information that Williams chose to tell his audiences about the famous couple, critics already knew from other published sources.

During the last twenty years of Williams's artistic career, a number of critics clung to the hope that Williams would write at least one more play equal to the standard set by either *The Glass Menagerie* or *A Streetcar Named Desire.* As documented in the critical response to Tennessee Williams, that wish was never fulfilled. Shortly before his death in 1983, Williams was at work on yet another autobiographical play. Originally presented as *Some Problems for the Moose Lodge* in 1980, it was revised and retitled *A House Not Meant to Stand* and performed on the Goodman Memorial Theatre's main stage in 1982. Like so many of the plays that Williams wrote after 1962, it was a "work in progress," the last new play produced in the lifetime of Tennessee Williams (Syse 80).

*   *   *

The selection of reviews and criticism included in this volume reflects the critical response to thirty plays by Tennessee Williams produced in New York, Chicago, or Boston from 1940 to 1982. From among the more than sixty plays written by Williams, twenty-eight were chosen, on the basis of their production on Broadway or on Off-Broadway stages in New York, as the subject of this book. Whether or not one agrees with Gerald Weales that "American drama is synonymous with New York production" (vii), the record of these performances constitutes an important part of the critical response to Tennessee Williams and the history of American theatre. Two other plays, the Boston performance of *Battle of Angels* (1940) and the Chicago production of *A House Not Meant to Stand* (1982), are also included because they represent, respectively, the first major production of a Tennessee Williams play, and the last, new play by Williams to be produced before his death on the night of February 24-25, 1983.

For each of twelve major productions, at least one review and one scholarly article is included. Each of the remaining eighteen plays (sixteen different productions) is represented by at least one review. Owing to the significant attention afforded to the New York revivals of Tennessee Williams's plays, this collection includes at least one review of the original New York production, and a review of each successive New York revival (through August of 1995).

Individual reviews and scholarly articles were selected neither because they represent the majority opinion about a particular work, nor because they articulate the view of a specific critical school or theory, but because they express a distinctively original point of view that contributes to the continuing discussion of Tennessee Williams and his works. Rather than presenting a single perspective, this selection reflects the diversity of opinion generated by the production and publication of Williams's plays. The resulting collection of reviews and scholarly articles thus provides not only an interesting commentary on individual plays, but also a documentary history of changing attitudes and differing perspectives within the critical community.

This diversity of critical opinion is also reflected in the extensive body of criticism, apart from the numerous reviews of the plays, devoted to the works of Tennessee Williams. During the 1950s and 1960s, scholars applied a variety of critical approaches to the study of Tennessee Williams, among them formalist, structuralist, mythological, biographical, psychobiographical, comparative, and textual. In the 1970s, critical interest in Williams slowed for a brief period, but in the 1980s and 1990s, especially as literary studies have become more theoretically informed, scholars have turned again to Tennessee Williams. New perspectives, addressing topics such as racism, gender issues, and ideology in Williams's plays and films, for example, are reflected in works by Philip Kolin, Anca Vlasopolous, Kathleen Margaret Lant, Pamela Anne Hanks, Steven Bruhm, John M. Clum, and David Savran. Philip Kolin's

Confronting Tennessee Williams's A Streetcar Named Desire, Essays in Critical Pluralism (1993), a collection of fifteen essays from more than ten different critical perspectives, is one example illustrating the extent to which the application of differing methodologies can be usefully employed in the study of Tennessee Williams. The selection of scholarly articles included in *The Critical Response to Tennessee Williams* represents only a small portion of the available materials, but each essay offers an insightful approach to one or more of the plays. Together with the reviews of original productions and revivals, they suggest the possibility that major as well as neglected works by Tennessee Williams may be profitably re-examined using methods as diverse as the many dramatic, fictional, and poetic compositions in the Tennessee Williams oeuvre.

WORKS CITED

Atkinson, Brooks. "Second Chance *Summer and Smoke* Put on In Sheridan Square." *New York Times* 4 May 1952, sec. 2: 1.

---. "*Streetcar Tragedy:* Mr. Williams' Report on Life in New Orleans." *New York Times* 14 Dec. 1947, sec. 2: 3.

Barnes, Clive. "Theatre: *In the Bar of a Tokyo Hotel.*" *New York Times* 12 May 1969: 54.

Bigsby, C. W. E. *Tennessee Williams, Arthur Miller, Edward Albee.* Cambridge: Cambridge UP, 1984. Vol. 2 of *A Critical Introduction to Twentieth-Century American Drama.* 3 vols. 1982-1985.

Bloom, Harold. Introduction. *Tennessee Williams's The Glass Menagerie.* Ed. Harold Bloom. Modern Critical Interpretations. New York: Chelsea House, 1988. 1-5.

Bolton, Whitney. "*Night of the Iguana* Eloquent, Moving." *New York Morning Telegraph* 30 Dec. 1961: 2.

Brustein, Robert. "America's New Culture Hero: Feelings Without Words." *Commentary* 25.2 (1958): 123-29.

---. "Robert Brustein on Theater: Orpheus Condescending." *New Republic* 30 Oct. 1989: 25-27.

---. "Sweet Bird of Success." *Encounter* 12.6 (1959): 59-60.

Calta, Louis. "Play by Williams on ANTA Double Bill." *New York Times* 15 Apr. 1959: 30.

Cassidy, Claudia. "Fragile Drama Holds Theater in Tight Spell." *Chicago Tribune* 27 Dec. 1941: 11.

Clurman, Harold. *Lies Like Truth: Theatre Reviews and Essays.* New York: Macmillan, 1958.

---. "Theatre." *Nation* 2 Jun. 1969: 709-10.

Coleman, Robert. "*Desire Streetcar* In for Long Run." *New York Daily Mirror* 4 Dec. 1947: 38.

Downer, Alan. *Fifty Years of American Drama, 1900-1950.* Chicago: Regnery, 1951.

Driver, Tom. F. "Accelerando." *Christian Century* 29 Jan. 1958: 136-37.

Durham, Frank. "Tennessee Williams, Theatre Poet in Prose." *South Atlantic Bulletin* 36.2 (1971): 3-16.

Freedley, George. "Of Books and Men." *New York Morning Telegraph* 16 Jan. 1958: 2.

Gassner, John. *Theatre at the Crossroads: Plays and Playwrights of the Mid-Century American Stage.* New York: Holt, Rinehart and Winston, 1960.

Gussow, Mel. "Stage: *Battle of Angels.*" *New York Times* 4 Nov. 1974: 51.

Hayes, Richard. "The Stage: *Camino Real.*" *Commonweal* 17 Apr. 1953: 51-52.

Hewes, Henry. "Theater--Off the Leash." *Saturday Review* 26 Nov. 1966: 60.

Kauffmann, Stanley. "Stanley Kauffman on Theater." *New Republic* 17 Jan. 1976: 28.

Keating, John. "Tennessee Williams' New Play, A Moving Drama." *Cue* 30 Mar. 1957: 8-9.

Kerr Walter F. "*Cat on a Hot Tin Roof.*" *New York Herald Tribune* 25 Mar. 1955: 12.

Kramer, Mimi. "Blanche and the Boys." *New Yorker* 28 Mar. 1988: 81-82.

Kolin, Philip. Preface. *Confronting Tennessee Williams's A Streetcar Named Desire.* Ed. Philip Kolin. Westport, Connecticut: Greenwood P, 1993. ix-xi.

Krutch, Joseph Wood. "Drama." *Nation* 6 Oct. 1945: 349-50.

---. "Drama." *Nation* 20 Dec. 1947: 686-87.

Leverich, Lyle. *Tom: The Unknown Tennessee Williams.* New York: Crown, 1995.

"Mr. Tennessee Williams's Two Steps Back." *London Times* 6 Feb. 1963: 13.

"New Plays on Broadway." *Time* 23 Mar. 1959: 58.

Novick, Julius. "Honest or Merely Disarming?" *Village Voice* 8 Mar. 1973: 58.

Simon, John. "A Cat of Many Colors." *New York* 12 Aug. 1974: 48-49.

---. "Damsels Inducing Distress." *New York* 7 Apr. 1980: 82, 84.

Syse, Glenna. "Tennessee Williams' *House* of tremors and quiet terrors." *Chicago Sun-Times* 2 Apr. 1981: 80.

Waldorf, Wiella. "*You Touched Me!* Is Not As Touching as It Sounds." *New York Post* 26 Sept. 1945: 38.

Watt, Douglas. "Worth Superb in *Sweet Bird.*" *New York Daily News* 4 Dec. 1975. Rpt. in *New York Theatre Critics' Reviews.* Eds. Joan Marlowe and Betty Blake. Vol. 36. New York: Critics' Theatre Reviews, 1975. 115.

Watts, Richard. "The Impact of Tennessee Williams." *New York Post* 25 Mar. 1955: 57.

Weales, Gerald. *American Drama Since World War II.* New York: Harcourt, Brace & World, 1962.

Winer, Linda. "In *Cat* It's Kathleen's Show." *New York Newsday* 22 Mar. 1990. Rpt. in *New York Theatre Critics' Reviews.* Eds. Joan Marlowe and Betty Blake. Vol. 51. New York: Critics' Theatre Reviews, 1990. 358.

Williams, Tennessee. "Production Notes." *The Glass Menagerie.* New York: Random House, 1945. ix-xii.

---. "Too Personal?" *Small Craft Warnings.* New York: New Directions, 1972. 3-6.

---. "Williams: Person-to-Person." *New York Times* 20 Mar. 1955, sec. 2: 1, 3.

The Critical Response to Tennessee Williams

Battle of Angels (1940)

Miriam Hopkins at Wilbur: *Battle of Angels* Is Full of Exciting Episodes
Anonymous

As the New Year's offering, the Theatre Guild presented the attractive Miriam Hopkins in a new play, *Battle of Angels,* the work of Tennessee Williams, at the Wilbur Theatre last night.

Although New Year's Eve was still some 24 hours away, many in the audience wondered if the happenings on the stage were not the aftermath of the glorious celebration in the imaginative brain of a genius who celebrated gaily but a little too well and was removed for quiet to that famous ward at the Bellevue Hospital.

And there he could have dreamed the tale that was acted out last night by a charming actress, aided by a gifted leading man, Wesley Addy.

For 120 minutes furies pursued Miss Hopkins, and when they were not chasing her up and down a steep flight of stairs into a mysterious backroom, the three ugly old fates sat by, placing the evil sign on her white forehead.

There have been other nights of wild drama in the American theatre, but to the young playwright, Mr. Williams, must go the credit for furnishing Boston and later New York, if the play is not considered too much of a shock for the nervous system of Manhattan, for the maddest night of melodrama.

Doris Dudley, a beautiful and competent actress is, unfortunately, miscast as the other woman, the too finely bred, aristocratic, rich and wild girl of the town. It may be that her acting throws the play off its key in her scenes with Miss Hopkins and Mr. Addy, but whatever it is, in those hysterical, fantastic moments, the play sinks to amateurishness that leaves Miss Hopkins and her leading man, standing out apart and removed. The vagrant, half mad with fear of fire in which he was once scarred as boy [*sic*], conceives himself a genius, about to write the great American novel, but always women and fear of fire dog his steps.

Others in the cast are Marshall Bradford, the sick husband; Dorothy

Peterson, Edith King, who play the neighbors; Charles McClelland, the sheriff; Katherine Raht, Eva Temple and Blanch Temple.

Boston Post, December 31, 1940: 8.

Play Must Have Lines Taken Out: *Battle of Angels* Cut After Council Demands Probe--Denial by Miriam Hopkins of Offence
Anonymous

Viewing last night's performance of the Theatre Guild play, *Battle of Angels,* at the Wilbur Theatre, after City Councillor Michael J. Ward of Allston had denounced it as "putrid" and demanded it be shut down, Police Commissioner Timilty and Assistant City Censor Joseph Mikolajewski decided the show could continue provided certain lines were deleted.

Commissioner Timilty said he found a few lines objectionable and the management agreed to take them out of the play.

Councillor Ward said his opinion, based on six complaints he received, was that the play--which stars noted Miriam Hopkins--should be shut down and that "the police should arrest the persons responsible for bringing shows of that type to Boston."

The councillor has not seen the play himself, but he declared, "this show is a crime to be permitted to run in the city of Boston."

If other cities want plays "of this kind," he told the council, let them have them. But they don't, in his opinion, belong in Boston.

As a result of Councillor Ward's heated denunciation of *Battle of Angels,* which he did not mention by name, but which he referred to as "the show at the Wilbur Theatre," the council passed an order, unanimously, asking the city censor to investigate the play.

Councillor Maurice A. Sullivan, who offered no specific charges against *Battle of Angels,* told the council at the same meeting that something should be done about the burlesque shows in this city. "There are more burlesque shows operating here than in New York, or any other city of comparable size in the country," he declared, and when the members of the council seemed amused at his remarks, commented "It's serious. It isn't a laughing matter of boys."

There is, according to Councillor Sullivan, a "regular Barbary Coast of burlesque theatres, all the way from Dock Square to Dudley Street" and these should be "banished from the city." If the law will not permit such action, then legal ways and means should be devised, he declared.

The attack led by Councillor Ward brought a promise from City Censor John J. Spencer, who has been ill, to begin an investigation today and sent Police Commissioner Timilty on a personal trip to the Wilbur Theatre, last night.

Censor Spencer was away at the Sugar Bowl game when *Battle of Angels* had its first performance on any stage, at the Wilbur, one week ago last night. On his return, he was ill and has been unable to work since.

Battle of Angels is a first play by a 24-year-old native of Mississippi, a young man named Tennessee Williams, who is little known in the theatre. The play has not been a success and the members of the sponsoring Theatre Guild announced last Thursday that the end of the Boston engagement on Saturday night would mark the end of the play, until a collaborator could be found for young Mr. Williams.

The locale of the play is the Mississippi Delta and the characters are all pretty low grade, suggesting something like *Tobacco Road* to some playgoers. Miriam Hopkins, making her first stage appearance in Boston after seven years of movie success, takes the role of an unhappy storekeeper, who falls in love with a small town Romeo, while her own husband lies ill.

Another woman, a character of less than spotless kind, takes away the Romeo. The wife is killed by the husband. A mob pursues the "other woman" for her misbehavior with a colored man. Doris Dudley, the actress who replace [*sic*], then was replaced by Elaine Barrie, in the John Barrymore play, *My Dear Children,* is the "other woman."

Miss Hopkins, noted for her outspoken ways, indignantly denied last night that the play is dirty. "That's an insult to the fine young man who wrote it," she said. "It's not a dirty play. I wouldn't be in it if it were a dirty play. I haven't got to the point where I have to appear in dirty plays.

"The dirt is something in the minds of some of the people who have seen it. They read meanings into it according to their own suppressed feelings.

"As far as the City Council goes, I'll bet they haven't even seen the play. I think it would be a good idea if the City Council should be flung into your Boston harbor, the way the tea once was," she laughed.

Mr. Williams and members of the directorate of the Theatre Guild, producers of the play, visited here for the premiere, but have since returned to New York.

Miss Hopkins declared that the play was a disappointment to her from the dramatic point of view, but that it had seemed brilliant in the reading.

"If the police close it," she said, "I'll be glad I don't have to play it any more. But it's not a dirty play."

Boston Post, January 7, 1941: 1, 8.

Stage: *Battle of Angels*
Mel Gussow

Battle of Angels, Tennessee Williams's first produced play, opened in Boston on Dec. 30, 1940 and closed in two weeks. Seventeen years later it finally came to New York in a vastly altered version, *Orpheus Descending.* It ran for only 68 performances, and--in its third incarnation--became the Marlon Brando-Anna Magnani movie, *The Fugitive Kind.* The original play became Williams's most neglected piece of theater, a footnote in a great career.

For its first production in its new theater--the former Off Broadway Sheridan Square Playhouse--the Circle Repertory Company, one of the cornerstones of modern Off Off Broadway, last night presented the New York premiere of *Battle of Angels.* It was an evening of renewal and reclamation.

First of all, the play can stand on its own, irrespective of its later versions. *Battle* and *Orpheus* share characters (some of the names change), sections of dialogue and a central situation. But the spirit is vastly different. *Battle* is clearly a young man's play. The tone is wistful and lyrical, in contrast to the portentous symbolism of *Orpheus.* This is a play of atmosphere and mood, despite the melodramatic ending.

Williams has described his hero, Val Xavier, as a "wild-spirited boy who wanders into a conventional community of the South and creates the commotion of a fox in a chicken coop." In *Battle,* he is a gentle fox "chased by the hounds" of womankind. He is not, like the Val of *Orpheus,* rapacious.

The first play, less ambitious and bold than later Williams, has a redeeming sweetness and sensitivity. In it we can see the threads and tones that have sustained the author's career--from the ironic humor of the small-town gossips to the moth-into-flame compulsiveness of his heroines, here exemplified by Cassandra, the rich aristocrat who is the object of both envy and scorn.

Marshall W. Mason's production appears to take its key from the phrase "lonesomeness carved in people's bodies." Val, Cassandra and, particularly, Myra--the older woman who takes Val into her life and into her bed while her husband is dying upstairs--are locked inside themselves. They never touch each other at the same time.

Wisely, the script--reworked by Williams--has omitted the published prologue and epilogue and also the conflagration that apparently helped to devastate the original Boston production. All this would have added a false note of portent to a wispy, realistic play.

Physically the production has the Circle's customary concern with detail. The Torrance Mercantile Store is reproduced down to the juke box, pinball machine and shoeboxes filled with dowdy shoes.

There are a number of first-rate performances in subordinate roles--

Conchata Ferrell, as a religious visionary, Sharon Madden as a boisterous gossip, Mary Ellen Flynn and Berrilla Kerr as spinster sisters. But the three leads are less effective in conveying their characters.

Tanya Berezin accents the pathos of Myra, but misses her pent-up passion. An actor named Max, as Val, lacks excitement--we wonder why the women are so drawn to him.

When Trish Hawkins as Cassandra groups the two of them as "the fugitive kind" and suggests that "we live in motion," Max looks stolid, as if nailed to the ground. Of the three leads, Miss Hawkins comes closest--almost turning her characters into a whirlwind.

It was good to see this play--finally. The Circle Repertory Company is to be applauded for rediscovery--not just of a play but also of a theater. The newly restored playhouse has never looked better.

New York Times, November 4, 1974: 51.

The Distorted Mirror: Tennessee Williams' Self-Portraits
Nancy M. Tischler

Tennessee Williams, like any talented playwright, has written a number of bad plays. The most interesting of these is his first major play and the one he continues to love best--variously named *Battle of Angels, Orpheus Descending, The Fugitive Kind, Something Wild in the Country,* etc. The endless revisions with their repeated, repaired, and fresh flaws reveal Williams' blindness to his own strengths and weaknesses. The much simpler and much greater plays that have served as interludes between the revisions of his perennial play contrast sharply with the grandiose failure of his favorite. Many of the same characters, the same themes, and the same images are used to much better advantage in *The Glass Menagerie* or *A Streetcar Named Desire,* but Williams' talent is apparently sufficiently unconscious that he cannot see why his story sometimes succeeds and sometimes fails. He is reported to have commented that *The Glass Menagerie* was better received than *Battle of Angels* because it is safer to write about mothers than about sex. Such a theory could hardly explain *A Streetcar Named Desire.* In all of his revisions of *Battle of Angels,* because of his limited capacity in self-criticism, he has perpetuated the same flaw--a flaw that is instructive in an analysis of Williams' other failures, of his successes, and of that form of Romanticism he so clearly exemplifies. He is in love with an idealized self-portrait, which he understandably continues to garb more elaborately while failing to comprehend more fully. So long as he allows the self-portrait to reveal himself without authorial interference, he succeeds; whenever he tries to intellectualize and explain and universalize that portrait, he fails.

The first version of *Battle of Angels,* written when he was still an unknown, itinerant youth, living the bohemian life, supported by occasional odd jobs and stipends from home, won him a Rockefeller Grant of $1000 and brought him to the attention of John Gassner. With the help of Gassner and Theresa Helburn, he polished the play for presentation as the first play of the Theatre Guild's 1940 season. The play's hero, Valentine Xavier, is an adolescent vision of the artist in the modern world, a compendium of Williams' own brief life and that of those alienated young artists he had come to know in his travels. Val is a young author whose single volume comprehends both his thought and his life, but is too sacred to share until it is complete. In his early days, Williams frequently followed the Romantic creed that equates art and life, insisting that Truth is more valuable than art and there is no truth except that a man experiences for himself. Like Williams, Val elevates the rights of the individual above the demands of society, but also like Williams, he is defensive about his lack of roots or responsibility. Insisting that a man can fulfill himself only when unencumbered, he wrenches free of the clutching hands that try to retain him and the proffered love that would entrap him. There is a price implied in the nomadic life: Val says, "I was tired of moving around and being lonesome and only meeting with strangers. I wanted to feel like I belonged somewhere and lived like regular people." But an inner need to discover what he labels "the secret of life" drives him from job to job and place to place. His real need is for self-fulfillment, not for love or security. Even the desert, he tells the hysterical heroine as she tried to hold him, would be crowded should he share it with her.

The theme is recurrent in Williams' work. His archetypal artist (in "The Poet," a short story, for example) is a solitary wanderer, a Pied Piper who appeals to children and those who can come to him as little children, and who is a threat to the adults. He rejects home, family, job, and organizations for freedom. Always Williams' sympathy and admiration go out to the "lonely exiles" of Greenwich Village or the Vieux Carré. The portrait is clearly an apology for his own rootless life. His background and his strong emotional ties with his home make this justification essential. As a result, there is no solution for Val any more than there is later any clear solution for Tom. To fall in love or to accept the role imposed by society is to die. But to cut the vital cords that bind man to his society and his family is to destroy something in himself. Myra, love, biology, conscience, and society all conspire to murder the non-conformist, disengaged poet.

Val Xavier, the saint of the tale, is thus the modern poet in the typical Romantic fusion of art and religion. Aping Williams' personal poet-hero, Hart Crane, he rejects the middle-class American dream while he fixes his vision on the Holy Grail of pure art and intense experience. Like both Crane and Williams, he has arrived at the threshold of middle-age (thirty in Williams' world), when he appears less the youthful rebel than the aging ne'er-do-well. With blasted dreams and unfinished manuscript, he contemplates a return to the world and momentarily replaces his snake-skin jacket with the blue serge suit of the conformist and finally the white coat of the servant. But at the end of the story, he makes Williams' own decision: he must remain a solitary wanderer and must consequently continue to appear an enemy of the people. He may even--and usually does in Williams' stories--become their victim. (It is, of course, the portrait we see again as Chance Wayne in *Sweet Bird of Youth.*) In a sense, Val insures his own sacrificial death by rejecting the safe exit for the more perilous but more honest one. It is for Williams a satisfying approximation of the Hart Crane image.

In these points, the play closely parallels *The Glass Menagerie,* where the author is again the hero. Here also love and societal pressures are the enemies of art. To leave home and Amanda is to insure self-preservation, but at the same time to kill something vital within the self. It is when Williams extends the poet image that he destroys credibility. Rather than being satisfied with a fairly obvious justification of bohemia, he insists on giving his poet a mysterious origin and a visionary capacity so that he becomes more of a prophet-hero and less of a modern dislocated artist. This pattern is accentuated in the later revisions of the play so that he is transformed into the archetypal hero in search of truth and beauty.

In *Orpheus Descending,* a play some seventeen years later than *Battle of Angels,* Val is nearly thirty and has exchanged his boyish charm for a weary disgust at his own corruption. Instead of the bright young animal who seeks an epic answer to his epic questions, we see a tired roué suffering from the effects of the endless party. (In this much of the portrait, Williams is apparently chronicling his disillusionment with bohemia as a post-adolescent way of life, but is still too distressed with the alternative path to reject it outright.)

Although disgusted with the flesh and the world, Val has found in art a means of cleansing and sanctification. His guitar is his sacred symbol, evidence of an immortality and a transcendence of the flesh achievable in art. (Curiously, it also seems to be a phallic symbol, clutched at by sexually undernourished wives of "small planters," stroked by the doomed aristocrat seeking death through sex, and threatened by the penis-envying husbands of the community.) Now Val is Orpheus with his magic lyre, able to charm even Death for a moment. The harpies appear to be those malevolent women who pursue him after he has lost Eurydice and who destroy him in a Bacchic orgy. Thus, he is the archetypal artist in search of truth and beauty, hoping to bring life back to the sterile land (the dry-goods store). He does briefly cause a false Spring--an orchard blooms in the confectionery and life stirs in Lady's womb--but Pluto comes to reclaim his wife and to destroy human happiness.

Val or Orpheus is sacrificed as a scapegoat, cleaning the town of its anger and guilt, but the death seems to be the result more directly of his sexuality than of his artistry. Certainly his occasional renditions of "Heavenly Grass" on the guitar are not adequate motivation for lynching. Williams undoubtedly feels that the artist suffers for his break with social codes of behavior and thought, but he fails here to convince the audience that Val is much of an artist. Undoubtedly too Williams believes that art has had the effect of cleansing and justifying his life: he has used writing as a Catholic uses confession. But in Val's case, it is his capacity for compassion rather than his ability with the guitar that brings Lady's rebirth.

Tennessee Williams, in fact, runs into untold confusions as he continues to rewrite this painfully overwrought play. Seldom does his vagrant hero justify the grandiose claims the playwright makes for him: his life is hardly an idealized quest, an engraved guitar is at best an inadequate symbol for art that justifies all aberrations and all irresponsibilities, and foxes do not make good scapegoats.

The repeated appearance of the fox image (fox and hounds, fox in the henhouse) is the clue to another flaw in this play which is a characteristic flaw of this playwright. The image is D. H. Lawrence's and is characteristically the manner in which Williams refers to Lawrence and the Lawrence hero. Lawrence's effect on Tennessee Williams is at least as important as Hart Crane's, and much less natural. To the rebel in a Puritan family, Lawrence served as a symbol of freedom. In *The Glass Menagerie,* the mother would censor Tom's reading if she could, and underlines this by returning the D. H. Lawrence book to the public library before her son has read it. In *I Rise in Flame, Cried the Phoenix,* the play that dramatizes Lawrence's death, the hero is seen as the foe of all petty feminine restrictions and demands, the old, primitive, independent male principle. The play that was to follow *Battle of Angels,* an adaptation of a Lawrence short story entitled *You Touched Me!,* included much of the same enthusiastic endorsement of fleshly, sexual love. But in the later play, the mood is more clearly Lawrence's, for sex proves indeed to be a cosmic solution. Williams has several times toyed with this notion--notably in *The Rose Tattoo.* Even so late a play as *The Night of the Iguana* continues to use Lawrence (now a decadent, defrocked Christ figure) as muddling along toward a sexual salvation while simultaneously coveting a "voluptuous crucifixion" in much the same manner as the old D. H. Lawrence dies in *I Rise in Flame.* Clearly, Williams has not relinquished the idea that sex is the path to salvation, at least for a few people. Myrtle keeps descending to the kingdom of earth to find her happiness among the lusty living, just as Myra did in that first Lawrencian vision of the sexual Beatrice.

Williams makes the Lawrence figure very clear in *Orpheus Descending,* even to the point of using the trail of sexual salvation as the reason for the crucifixion. Sexuality is equated with vitality and identified with art is its capacity for enriching, sensitizing, and fertilizing human life. Val is a kind of

Prince Charming in snake-skin jacket who awakens the Sleeping Beauties, but does not linger to live happily ever after with them. Val certainly brings life back to Lady, who blossoms and prepares to bear fruit like the little fig tree she describes. And the sexual envy by the sterile residents of this wasteland community is adequate motive for watering the soil with Val's blood. But this excessively sexual prowess (idealized as is his poetic sensitivity) draws the attention away from the real question and brings an almost irrelevant death. Williams' hero is more honestly sacrificed for nonconformity than for animal vigor.

Williams is consistently more effective when he develops his natural images rather than combining all possible ideals to make his hero a man for all seasons. The characters that are the more successful self-portraits incline toward but eventually reject sexual solutions. Tom in *The Glass Menagerie,* Brick in *Cat on a Hot Tin Roof,* and Shannon in *The Night of the Iguana* all find sex appealing, but nothing more than a temporary narcotic for forgetting the real anguish of existence. The women who also appear in some way to be self-portraits personify the same tensions. Even the nymphomaniacs (Cassandra in *Battle of Angels* and Blanche of *A Streetcar Named Desire*) realize that sex is little more than a way of forgetting about death. Val says that he once believed people could communicate through touch, but he has come to reject his answer. So do most of Williams' more sensitive people.

His real poet is an asexual wanderer, like Hannah Jelkes in *The Night of the Iguana,* who has learned to rise above the human condition and tolerate the awful solitude of the solitary imprisonment that is life. In fact, Williams' most sincerely felt ideal is the homosexual poet, finding rare moments of love in a world that sees him as an anarchist and an outcast. Thus, the Lawrencian image (no matter how intensely affirmed intellectually) is not germane to Williams' psyche. Norman Mailer may believe that happiness is one great heterosexual bed, but Tennessee Williams merely wishes he believes it. The play is thus, in part, a failure because Williams insists on listening to his conscious rather than his unconscious mind, to other men's answers rather than to his own--a cardinal sin for the Romantic iconoclast.

Among those portions of his world he tried to put behind him in his journey from the St. Louis apartment to the New Orleans flop house was that form of Puritanical Christianity he had assimilated in his youth and hated in his adolescence. Thus Christianity, along with the Puritan sexual ethic and the legalistic behavioral code, became a primary villain in his early plays. His pastors are fools and his church pillars are hypocrites. The honestly religious people in his stories are frustrated by the fare they find at the church social and end by painting red church steeples or running off for a life of prostitution. Vee in *Battle of Angels* offers us a foretaste of the extremes to which the rebellious Puritan will be driven in *Summer and Smoke* and *The Night of the Iguana.* But the more sinister religious figure in *Battle of Angels* is Jabe, the cancer-stricken husband whose rot has gone too deep for the knife and who is doomed. This death-in-life figure, surrounded by his symbols of impotence, sits like the dead hand of historical Christianity, warping the human life below his death bed. This superannuated Jehovah thumps his cane in fury at the forbidden vitality flowering on the earth below his sterile heaven. When he fails to thwart the love of the rebellious angels, he casts them out of the world that he still controls--murdering one and causing the lynching of the other. This cruel God is a heartfelt part of Williams' visceral philosophy. He puts people into this jungle world, afflicts them with loneliness, decay, and the awareness of impending death, and allows pleasure only to make that death more bitter by contrast with life. Williams may have chosen to reject Christianity in his flight from this youthful world, but he found he could not escape it. This venomous old Jehovah continues to be an underlying theme in play after play.

His natural response was to construct an alternative in his "savior," a god-man who is the very antithesis of the dying God he hated. Thus Val is by contrast the symbol of human compassion, in love with life and with all things human. His name relates him to the Christ symbol, but his actions equate him more with Lucifer, the rebellious angel. Like many an author, Williams finds it far easier to record the philosophy that has blighted his life than to construct the ideal that would save it. While Jabe can be a fairly consistent symbolic presentation, Val must represent a cluster of values that appear here and there in Williams' personal religious, literary, and psychological history. As a result, he becomes more of a pastiche than a character.

In the more drastic revision of the play, he becomes Orpheus to Jabe's Pluto. But Williams could not resist holding onto the Christian mythology as well, so that the Orphic dimension served only to complicate further the already fantastic symbolism. In addition, the author found that he had to telescope the Orpheus myth so that the later death scene overlaps the Eurydice story. Actually, using either Christian or Greek mythology involved Williams in deep trouble. On the one hand, the story alienated those few who followed its Freudian study of Christian symbolism; and on the other it failed to make sense of the vestiges of the Christian story when translated into a Greek context. As he continues to clutter his play more and more in hopes of salvaging it, he makes it increasingly fascinating to the psychologist and the anthropologist, and diminishes by each stoke that much of its tragic stature. His first audience in Boston was outraged by the play, his more recent audiences have been amused.

All that is wrong with *Battle of Angels* makes increasingly obvious all that is right with *The Glass Menagerie*. In Williams' own terms, he is now being honest instead of artificial, writing from his heart rather than his head, using his own life as his book. Again basing the story on a self-portrait, he is this time less mythic and intellectual and defensive and pretentious. Instead of Valentine Xavier, he is simple Tom Wingfield, hardly an elaborate mask for Tom Williams. The problem basic to the play is a gain the hesitation to cross a threshold--this time between adolescence and youth, dependence and independence. The trap of love is again sprung by an older woman, but this time she is honestly the mother, not Venus, the Virgin Mary, Proserpine, and Eurydice. Again the young man escapes and must escape from the tender trap in order to live. But this time all of the social world need not lumber after him to destroy him for his apostasy. The punishment lies not in a lynch mob but in the pain of his memories. The love Tom feels for his mother and his sister is much more real and much more demanding than the combination of sex and compassion Val feels for Lady and the other lost females. The simple tale of a supper for a gentleman caller and an anguished leap for freedom needs no mythic undergirding because it is true and natural and universal. Amanda is by her very nature not merely Tom's mother: she is everyone's mother.

The circumstances are much less disguised and idealized than in *Battle of Angels*. The apartment parallels Williams' somber memories of St. Louis, the girl polishing her glass animals closely follows his portraits of his sister Rose before her mental breakdown, and the mother is clearly Williams' own mother with her memories of Mississippi and of youth and springtime and happiness. The major change is his removal of his hated father, who is now but a smiling picture symbolic of the love of long distance. But this change is useful in allowing Williams to avoid a portrayal he was not yet prepared to encounter, to simplify the story, and to intensify Amanda's demands, her paranoia, and to help explain Tom's guilt. The alteration of Rose's infirmity to a physical one does not change her role drastically from that she has played in his life; and she still retains some of that withdrawal from reality that was the clue to her increasing schizophrenia.

Thus, in *The Glass Menagerie,* Tennessee Williams used the very antithesis of the method he had employed for *Battle of Angels.* Instead of constructing this play, he revealed and slightly ordered his own memories. In a sense, he found this easier because he was dealing with his past in *The Glass Menagerie,* while in *Battle of Angels* he had striven to justify and idealize his present and his future. Where he strove to make *Menagerie* more significant by relating it to the Depression and the growing violence abroad, his prose sound ponderous and irrelevant to the play's tone. His sentimentality at the end is effective enough because it grows out of the deliberately ironic tone Tom has been using as a defense in most of the story. But the excessively arty stage directions reveal the same tendency toward overemphasis so glaringly evident in *Battle of Angels.*

It is far easier to understand Tom's need to escape Amanda and her smothering motherhood than it is to see the archetypal poet's need to escape love and society. The terms of *The Glass Menagerie* are more concretely stated and the conclusions more acceptable: a man of imagination seldom finds fulfillment in a shoe factory; a boy seldom becomes a man under the watchful eye of a domineering mother; the break with the past is always painful for the sensitive man; and there is health in this drive to preserve one's integrity and develop to one's maturity regardless of the demands of the family.

Williams has used the tension between self-fulfillment and contribution to the family as the core of several of his plays. Apparently he has found that a man who loves his family never really escapes it. Bad plays like *Moony's Kid Don't Cry* and *The Rose Tattoo* are built on this theme, but good ones are as well (*A Streetcar Named Desire* and *Cat on a Hot Tin Roof*). He finds a resolution of sorts in *Night of the Iguana,* where the grandfather and the daughter can make a home in one another's hearts without demanding permanence or needing to escape (as he and his grandfather did). But even as late as *The Seven Descents of Myrtle,* the mother continues to rule the son, here to the extent that he becomes a transvestite in his effort to accept her personality.

This eternal struggle to cut the umbilical cord, underlying almost all of Williams' work, explains a number of his related ideas. The separation from the mother-figure parallels the separation from society and its values. Amanda represents the ideals of the Old South, the Puritan tradition, and a kind of meaningless conformity that destroys the individual without the consequence of enriching the world. In seeing Amanda, we understand the real reason for the angry attacks on conformists, church people, and small-town tyrants. Val is obviously the Romantic ideal that Tom pictures as he makes his escape out of ugliness, censorship, repression, and stifling love into a world of adventure, rootlessness, and moral anarchy. The artist, as he perceives him, lives in a world of polarities: masculine and feminine, past and present, conformity and non-conformity, control and chaos. He also discovers his world is full of paradoxes: love is a weapon women use to unman the male; compassion is a virtue but involvement is a peril; freedom demands cruelty. The world comprehends instinctively that the artist, the fanatic, the lover of beauty, the anarchist are its enemies. Thus it must work to control, to pervert, to tame, and to castrate what it senses to be its enemy. *The Glass Menagerie* understates these discoveries, paralleling the covert way in which life itself reveals them. But *Battle of Angels* intensifies them into hyperbole, alienating the sympathetic viewer by the stridency of the complaint and the exaggeration of the terms. Poets may be fired from jobs or manipulated by mothers, but are seldom blow-torched by red-necked mobs.

The generalization that would grow naturally out of this contrasted analysis of two extremely different Williams plays is clearly that Williams should restrict himself to slightly altered reminiscences. However, another powerfully written play suggests more interestingly the boundaries of Tennessee Williams' talents. *A Streetcar Named Desire* uses many of these same materials with astonishing and effective variations. The story is again one of family tensions, the demands of the past impinging on the present, culture facing barbarism, sickness threatening health, man fighting woman. Yet, while it is much more violent that *Glass Menagerie, Streetcar* is much more real and much more tragic than *Battle of Angels.*

The wanderer entering alien territory is again sensitive and artistic and morally suspect. But it is a woman who takes the role of guardian of human values this time. Her age, her accent, her memories, and her demands on those who love her remind the reader of Amanda. But Blanche contains within her character much that reminds one of Tom as well. She too finds the past stifles her, she too searches for a new life that has beauty and adventure. And she is more forthright in the admission that one is never free of the past. It is always part of one's luggage. Blanche contains more of Williams' self than does Amanda. While the playwright saw the earlier character with sympathy and irony combined, he more fully identifies with the later character. Critics have frequently noted Williams' remarkable ability to create fully rounded female characters. The reason is largely that it is in the woman or the effeminate man that Williams most often reveals himself. Blanche, like Williams, lives briefly in New Orleans, her accent and her manners contrast grotesquely with those about her, her love of romance seems ludicrous to the world she can never quite bring herself to enter. In the feminine personality, Williams has found his satisfying parallel to the Romantic poet; in our culture, love of beauty is seen as a weakness in a man, excessive sensitivity as a fault.

The antithesis is Stanley Kowalski--all that society worships in the male. He is virile, loud, smart, aggressive, ambitious, and independent. He is in fact the sum total of those characteristics Williams resented in his father, and his portrait explains the omission of the father from *Menagerie.* Stanley's view of Blanche parallels society's view of the artist. He resents the implicit judgment on his own habits of mind and life. He resents the intrusion into his world of this alien voice. And he feels threatened by the strength behind the veneer of weakness. Therefore he attacks her with his natural weapons, stripping her of her illusive surface; he turns the naked bulb on her to reveal her physical weaknesses. He isolates her from her lover and her sister, and then rapes her and sends her off to the madhouse. His role is essentially the same as that of the men in *Battle of Angels.* This time, though, the brutality is more effective because of the difference in sex. Rather than attributing the men's hatred of the Romantic to some mystique of sex envy that forces the actor playing the sensitive poet to flex his muscles and lounge suggestively around the stage while stroking his guitar, Williams allows the more complex antipathy between the lover of the ideal and the lover of the real to be his motive for destruction.

Rape is a more effective image for what society does to the artist than lynching. In *Orpheus Descending,* the characters toy with the idea of castration, and in *Sweet Bird of Youth,* they carry out their threat. Williams here points out that this is what life and time do to all of us, but to the most sensitive first. Rape is an effective term for what the Romantic believes the world does to him and his art. It robs the artist of his dreams and then uses him for its own diversion. In Holden Caulfield's terms, it prostitutes the artist.

Madness is also a good image for Williams' Romantic ideal, for the world must look on the poet's retreat from its vision of reality as madness. It is not surprising that Williams so often cites Don Quixote as one of his literary heroes. Their theories of madness are remarkable similar.

In *Streetcar,* Williams is able to present in Blanche, even more effectively than earlier in Tom, certain features of his self-portrait. The mask releases him from his pugilistic stance and allows him to admit partial acceptance of his mother's values. Now he can show sympathetically the doomed beauty of the past contrasted with the gross vitality of the present, and the baroque rhetoric of the South compared with the grunts of the animalistic realist. He can confess his love of fragility without sounding sentimental. And he can insist (perhaps protesting overmuch) that his moral "corruption" has a reason and a history, and he can show that it carries with it consequent tortures. He can also admit an ambiguity in his relation to Stanley and his virile world of poker, drink, raw meat, and raw sex. Blanche's flirtation is as real as her disgust. She courts her own disaster; the death-wish, a need for punishment, for self-destruction may be a partial explanation. But the later love-hate between Brick and Big Daddy suggests still another: that the artist secretly admires and even loves the caveman who threatens his existence.

The most curious point of all seems to be a confession that Blanche's world and his are doomed. One can escape only into death, madness, or chaos. In *Camino Real,* his heroes are all diminished but still undefeated Romantics--Byron, Don Quixote, Camille--who have found that the Royal Road turns into the Real Road at the border. Like the Princess in *Sweet Bird of Youth,* they are now in Ogre Country, where their defeat, though inevitable, can yet be heroic. Williams clearly damns the real world, but he find no escape from it that lasts for long.

Blanche's story is less believable than Tom's, but her character is much more fully realized. Williams' real talent lies not in construction, but in understanding, in characterization rather than in plotting. *Streetcar* contains many of the ambiguities discovered in *Battle of Angels,* but a character study needs less consistency and clarity than does a sermon. Blanche is no idealized heroine. Williams allows the real person to carry the burden of the meaning. Her quest is for love and beauty, as was Val's, her weariness with corruption echoes his, but Williams does not outfit her in outlandish mythic garb, idealize her journey, or insist on her apotheosis. As a self-portrait she is more natural, more honest, and more tragic than any Williams character before or since. She embodies his sense of isolation, his concern for cruelty, his dread of death, and

his disgust with his own flesh. She may be dypsomaniac [*sic*] and nymphomaniac and psychotic; she may be as defensive as he is and as full of confused
drives and self-hatred, but she is also the Romantic in an unromantic land.

The Romantic imagination may construct myths or enlarge them in the
manner of Shelley and Keats, but there is a form of Romanticism which works
more effectively within the bounds of its own literal reality--a Wordsworthian
pattern. Here the intellect is useful only in analysis and aesthetic formation,
not in generalization and extension. Curiously, Williams, like Wordsworth,
also seems unable to judge his own capacities. *Battle of Angels* (like *Camino
Real*) sums up so much of his thought, brings together so many of his favorite
images and myths and heroes and situations that Williams loves it for its
portrayal of his conscious art. *The Glass Menagerie* and *A Streetcar Named
Desire* are less conscious, less intellectualized portrayals of a deeper, more
emotional experience. They are so true and so simple that he is tempted to
dismiss them as obvious. But in their composition lies the key to Williams'
greatness--nature rather than art. His later plays have proven most effective
in those moments of self-revelation: where Hannah and Shannon are portions
of his own psyche perceiving their affinity and their inability to live in
harmony for long, or where Brick and Big Daddy acknowledge that their anger
grows out of a jealous love and a wish that they could understand one another.
His moments of self-justification--Chance Wayne insisting that he is us all or
Brick attacking mendacity--are strident and unconvincing by comparison.

Williams is clearly a latter-day Romantic, by nature and by education.
He encompasses the typical tensions of this type: love of both the universal
and the particular, of art and of naturalness, of anarchy and of order. He is a
visceral rather than a cerebral Romantic, gifted with sensitivity rather than with
the philosophic mind. It is a tribute to his ingenuity and to his artistry that he
has discovered so many powerful dramas to be dredged from his own
emotional experience. His worst plays are inclined to be those that are the
most self-aware, most defensive, most idealistic. When he drops the mask and
the particular for the archetype, his exaggerated lyricism and overwrought
imagery dominate the play. But when he can lose himself in a character and
allow Blanche or Brick or Alma to speak his thoughts in their own voices, he
is controlled by the demands of the characters and of their situations. When
he reveals his truth instead of pronouncing it, letting it evolve rather than
constructing it, feeling it rather than thinking it, he is a powerful playwright.

Mississippi Quarterly 25.4 (1972): 389-403.

The Glass Menagerie (1944)

Fragile Drama Holds Theater in Tight Spell
Claudia Cassidy

Too many theatrical bubbles burst in the blowing, but *The Glass Menagerie* holds in its shadowed fragility the stamina of success. This brand new play, which turned the Civic Theater into a place of steadily increasing enchantment last night, is still fluid with change, but it is vividly written, and in the main superbly acted. Paradoxically, it is a dream in the dusk and a tough little play that knows people and how they tick. Etched in the shadows of a man's memory, it comes alive in theater terms of words, motion, lighting, and music. If it is your play, as it is mine, it reaches out tentacles, first tentative, then gripping, and you are caught in its spell.

Tennessee Williams, who wrote it, has been unbelievably lucky. His play, which might have been smashed by the insensitive or botched by the fatuous, has fallen in to expert hands. He found Eddie Dowling, who liked it enough to fight for it, Jo Mielziner, who devoted his first time out of army service to lighting it magnificently, and Laurette Taylor, who chose it for her return to the stage. He found other people, too, but ah, that Laurette Taylor!

I never saw Miss Taylor as Peg, but if that was the role of her youth, this is the role of her maturity. As a draggled southern belle who married the wrong man, living in a near-tenement, alienating her children by her nagging fight to shove them up to her pathetically remembered gentility, she gives a magnificent performance. The crest of her career in the delta was the simultaneous arrival of 17 gentlemen callers, and her pitiful quest in this play-- as often funny as sad--is the acquisition of just one gentleman caller for her neurotically shy daughter, the crippled girl played by Julie Haydon. Her preparations for that creature, once she has heckled her son into inviting him, his arrival in the hilarious extrovert played by Anthony Ross, and the aftermath of frustration--these are not things quickly told in their true terms. They are theater, and they take seeing.

Fortunately, I have been able to hang around the Civic at previews and

I have seen *The Glass Menagerie* twice. Mr. Dowling was good last night in the double role of the son and narrator [who says the first narrator was the angel of the annunciation], but he is twice as good as that when he is relaxed and easy. He had strokes of brilliance last night, but the long easy stride of his earlier performance is on a plane with Miss Taylor's playing and gives the play greater strength.

Mr. Ross enters late, but leaves an impression as unforgettable as his green coat and his face, which is perilously close to being a mug. Late of *Winged Victory,* this stalwart actor does a superb job as the gentleman caller who finds his visit a little more than he bargained for. Which leaves only Julie Haydon and there, frankly, I'm puzzled. At times she has the frailty of the glass animals of the title which are her refuge from reality. But I couldn't quite believe her, and my sympathy went to her nagging mother and her frustrated brother--because whatever the writing, acting is the final word, and they acted circles around her.

Chicago Tribune, December 27, 1944: 11. (Review of Chicago production.)

A Triumph for Miss Taylor
Louis Kronenberger

After creating a minor furore in Chicago, *The Glass Menagerie* finally reached Broadway Saturday night. Here, too, it should create something of a stir. As a play, I think there is a great deal wrong with it. But I recommend it without qualms, because it makes interesting and sometimes absorbing theater, and because Laurette Taylor is giving in it one of the most remarkable and fascinating performances in many seasons. She has always been one of the few really distinguished actresses that we have; she has probably never offered more convincing proof of her distinction.

The play which she dominates and enlarges is in essence a fairly simple portrait of a family, though in effect rather a pastiche of dramaturgical styles. Miss Taylor plays the mother of the family--a Southern woman in late middle age who has come way down in the world, been deserted by her husband and been left with rankling memories of a much-courted, magnolia-petaled youth. Her son is a lackadaisical dreamer, fond of the bottle and fretting against his home life; her daughter Laura is a shy, painfully withdrawn cripple. The burning desire of the mother's broken-down life is somehow to get Laura married, and she is forever plaguing the son to bring "gentlemen callers" to the house. At length the son brings one--to a dinner full of Alice-Adamsish mishaps and desperate gaieties, and an after-dinner session with Laura from which the caller escapes as soon as he decently can.

Miss Taylor's acting aside, there is enough that is human, touching, desolate and bitterly comic about this family picture to keep one steadily interested. Moreover, Mr. Williams has told much of his story in telltale little scenes that can be far more effective than conventional "big" ones; he is capable, when he remains relatively straightforward, of very good dialogue; and far from sentimentalizing the mother, he has shown up all her nagging, her pretenses, her small snobberies, her Southern foolishness.

So far as this is true, *The Glass Menagerie* is unhackneyed, unhokumed theater. But Mr. Williams has fancied things up in other ways, has rather jumbled his technique and forced his tone. Eddie Dowling commutes between being the son in the play and a narrator who stands outside it: the second role seems to me both pretty otiose and pretty arty. To be sure, Mr. Dowling acts as commentator because the play is conceived as a "memory"; and it is further projected as a memory by much use of atmosphere music and dim lights. All this may make, here and there, for unusual theater; but beyond the fact that Mr. Williams isn't really master of his rather showy (and derived) devices, I think he has asked oddity to do work that simple artistry can do far better. If *The Glass Menagerie* aims (rightly in my opinion) at something different from straight realism, at becoming a kind of mood play, then the mood and tone must be begotten from within it, not built up all around it. I have no desire to see anybody writing like anybody else; but instead of tinkling at various little Saroyanesque, Barrie-esque, Wilderesque whatnots, Mr. Williams might at least have found suggestive the whole method of Chekhov. For in its mingled pathos and comedy, its mingled naturalistic detail and gauzy atmosphere, its preoccupation with "memory," its tissue of forlorn hopes and backward looks and languishing self-pities, *The Glass Menagerie* is more than just a little Chekhovian. But Chekhov worked from within, as Mr. Williams does not; and successfully on more than one level, as Mr. Williams does not quite; and in such a way that his comedy and pathos coalesced, where Mr. Williams'--except where Miss Taylor makes them blend--emerge separately.

If Miss Taylor's Southerner is not quite a great characterization, it is because the materials do not exist for one. But hers is at least a great performance, which out of many small bits contrives a wonderful stage portrait. She nags, she flutters, she flatters, she coaxes, she pouts, she fails to understand, she understands all too well--all this revealed, most of the time, in vague little movements and half-mumbled words, small changes of pace, faint shifts of emphasis, little rushes of spirit. It is so fascinating as acting that it hardly needs to be (though it generally is) convincing as portrayal. It represents a personal style, but it is never just that mark of lesser actresses-- "personality." It is acting.

Mr. Dowling always has a quiet ease on the stage, and he has it here; but in neither of his roles does he seem to me quite satisfactory. Julie Haydon gets the shy, scared side of Laura, but little of the locked-up intensity that the role seems to suggest. As the Gentleman Caller, Anthony Ross hasn't an easy role to handle, but on the whole does very well with it. Paul Bowles' music is agreeable, and Jo Mielziner's set and lighting do most effectively what they are asked to do.

New York Newspaper PM, April 2, 1945: 16.

Drama
Joseph Wood Krutch

It is not often that a first play--indeed, it is not often that *any* play--gets such a reception as *The Glass Menagerie* (Playhouse Theater) got from audience and from press alike. After the final curtain had descended, the unfamiliar cry of "Author! Author!" rang through the auditorium, and next morning the reviewers staged what is commonly called a dance in the streets. Undoubtedly some of this enthusiasm was for the acting and the production, especially for the performance of Laurette Taylor, who got everything that was to be had from the character of the pitiful and terrible old woman who is the central figure. But undoubtedly the enthusiasm was also and in almost equal measure for the playwright, a young man named Tennessee Williams previously known chiefly to prize committees and to the editors of avant-garde magazines.

In his first Broadway play Mr. Williams has chosen to set forth a powerful and arresting, if somewhat abruptly truncated, situation in an elaborate and highly fanciful manner. The action begins with a pretentious and inflated speech delivered in front of a blank wall by Eddie Dowling, who is several times in the course of the play to step out of his role to act as a usually unnecessary "narrator." Then the lights behind the wall go on and we see into the dismal interior of a slum flat in St. Louis presided over by an ex-Southern belle long ago deserted by her irresponsible husband and now striving desperately to arrange some sort of future for her crippled, neurotic daughter and her restless son, about whose neck the two female millstones are hanging. In her dreams this mother, now shabby and old and fat, still relives the days when she led the cotillion at the Governor's Ball and entertained seventeen callers at one time. All her vocabulary, all her standards, all her plans are in the terms of that dead past. "Gentlemen callers," "widows well provided for," and "young men of character and promise" are the figures of the mythology from which she cannot escape. She is vulgar, nagging, and unreasonable. But she is also desperate, pathetic, and gallantly hopeless in a fight against overwhelming odds--altogether, at least at Miss Taylor plays her, unforgettable as well as almost unbearable.   She finally induces her son to entice a "gentleman caller" from the warehouse where he works; the gentleman caller charms the sickly daughter, and then, at the end of his first and only visit, announces his approaching marriage to someone else. The son leaves the house forever to join the merchant marine. His mother runs out after him to denounce his desertion and to show that she nevertheless is strong enough to go on with the fight. Then the lights go out, and the narrator steps again to the front of the stage. That, he announces, is the end of all the author has to tell. The imagination of the audience must supply for itself the rest of the story.

I have already said that the central character is unforgettable, and I must add my opinion that the fact is due at least as much to the writing as it is to the acting. Moreover, nothing which I am about to say should be taken as denying the fact that *The Glass Menagerie* is a remarkable play and its author a man of extraordinary talent. But there is not use failing to mention that his weaknesses are as patent as his gifts, or that very good writing and very bad writing have seldom been as conspicuous in the script of one play. It has a hard, substantial core of shrewd observation and deft, economical characterization. But this hard core is enveloped in a fuzzy haze of pretentious sentimental, pseudo-poetic verbiage which I can compare only to the gauze screens of various degrees of filmy opacity which are annoyingly raised and lowered during the course of the physical action in order to suggest memory, the pathos of distance, and I know not what else. How a man capable of writing as firm as is some of that in this play can on other occasions abandon himself to such descriptive passages as that in which a young man is described--in Oscar Wilde's worst style--as "like white china" is a mystery. Moreover, the incongruity is almost as conspicuous between personages as it is between passages. The insubstantial, unconvincing wisp of a Little Nell whom Julie Haydon is compelled to interpret simply does not belong in the same world as the one her mother so solidly inhabits.

The limitations of a good writer are sometimes best passed over in silence. One accepts them, and one can do nothing else. But when defects are of a corrigible sort, when they seem the result of a sort of self-indulgence which is likely to grow and grow if encouraged or even tolerated, then they ought to be reprehended in some downright manner. And the defects of Mr. Williams's manner are defects of that sort. Probably he admires most in himself what is least admirable there. At the moment no doubt many agree with him. But they will not continue to do so for long. He is one of those writers who had best heed the advice: whenever you have written a line you like especially well, strike it out.

Nation, April 14, 1945: 424-25.

Helen of Sparta
Henry Hewes

The current revival of *The Glass Menagerie* is a glorious reminder of our growing theatre heritage. The moment the curtain goes up on Jo Mielziner's drab St. Louis alley an era both of stage history and of life is back with us. And instead of seeming outdated Tennessee Williams's words about America and the world in the late Thirties have more force when spoken with ten more years distance between them and the events.

Director Alan Schneider has approached the work boldly and has steered his production in the direction of logic and humor. Helen Hayes's portrayal of Amanda Wingfield has an aggressive, non-dreamy quality that perfectly fits Amanda's statement "Life calls for Spartan endurance." Her performance is consciously and deliberately comic. At one point she uses the inflections of a minstrel show interlocutor. And at another she allows herself to caper delightedly in a peppy jig. No one admires the late Laurette Taylor's desperation-filled performance more than Miss Hayes, but in cases like these the most honest thing another great performer can do is to make the role her own. Miss Hayes does, though she stops short of heartbreak.

James Daly's Tom also seems less of a dreamer and more of a practical and wise young man. Lois Smith's Laura is full of resignation to the social disadvantages of being a cripple, but equally full of a beautiful sensitivity which expresses itself in consideration for others. She puts across exquisitely her concern for Tom's domestic entrapment, and her terror at testing her private romantic dreams. Lonnie Chapman brings an intentional surface vulgarity to the gentleman caller, and the moment he explains away Laura with the term "inferiority complex" nicely demonstrates the native lack of subtlety in American culture.

There are minor defects in this City Center production: broadness of performance that tends to distract the audience's attention from the emotional core of the play; a pace that does not permit enough time for reaction to situations. These may both be dictated by having to perform in a large auditorium. Yet, even as it is, the play, which is to Williams as *Long Day's Journey Into Night* is to O'Neill, emerges less as a vehicle for a fabulous and unforgettable actress than as one of the truly marvelous works in our American dramatic album.

Saturday Review, December 8, 1956: 29.

Diverse, Unique Amanda
Howard Taubman

The durability of *The Glass Menagerie* is substantiated once again in the admirable revival at the Brooks Atkinson Theater. Tennessee Williams's first success stands up impressively 20 years after its introduction to New York. Of its four characters, all caught with sympathy and honesty, the most compelling remains Amanda.

Amanda's indestructibility is astonishing. If you first encountered her two decades ago in the magical performance of Laurette Taylor, you probably thought, as I did, that no one would ever dare the role again. Who could approach Miss Taylor? Had she not done more for Amanda through the alchemy of her art than the author?

In the intervening years I have seen a number of Amandas in productions scattered across the land, and I know now that Mr. Williams's Amanda, indeed Amanda herself, endures. She's credible, she is true. She is specifically American, and her truth transcends national traits.

Her essential lineaments remain fixed. She still clings stubbornly to memories and appearances of unforgotten elegance and irretrievable social glamour. Yet she does not really delude herself, for she faces up to the bitter reality of her situation. She fights to sustain her pride but can drain the sour cup of humiliation. She is fussy and meddlesome, shrewd and sharp-tongued, presumptuous and sensitive, embarrassing and infuriating, funny and pathetic. She is, in short, an indomitable creation.

No matter how different actresses of divergent gifts and temperaments recreate Amanda in their own images, the essential woman prevails. No matter how one or another trait is stressed or predominates in any performance, the powerful leverage of the character remains. Could there be more convincing proof of how truly Mr. Williams wrought?

But a role in a drama to an actor, like the notes in a symphonic score to a conductor, is the basic source material, not the finished product. The speeches and instructions provided by the playwright, however precise, are the potter's clay. The task of shaping remains for the actor, guided by the director. Different tastes and intuitions can produce marked differentiations in a character.

Recalling a number of Amandas, I am struck by the diversity she has assumed. From Miss Taylor, the first, to Maureen Stapleton, the latest, each Amanda has been not only the mother of Mr. Williams's imagining but also uniquely individualized. Each interpretation has found new lights and shadows in the role; each has made subtle distinctions in the play.

Miss Taylor, more than any Amanda I remember, bathed the character in the muted glow of lost, aching illusions. No one has ever matched her in evoking a sense of the faded past. She did not merely cloak herself in a remembrance of vanished gentility. It shone from her in a kind of brave, though dimming radiance. She did not need to adorn herself in her old-fashioned party dress to conjure up the fond, foolish atmosphere of a happy girlhood in a graceful, magnolia-scented south. The inflections of her speech, her looks, her gestures and movements created mood as well as character.

Underneath the airs and pretensions of Miss Taylor's Amanda, there was the necessary and irreducible core of fierce determination. Her fussing over her son, Tom, was a compulsive habit. Her sentimentality about her daughter, Laura, and her nostalgia for her own youth as a Southern belle were self-indulgences of which she was aware. She might pretend to helplessness and hope to appeal to gallantry as of yore, but she left no doubt that she would seek to command the situation.

You believed with all your heart that her claim to social refinements was not vainglory. This Amanda had once been what she said she was. The charm she wore so readily was an old accomplishment, and the swiftness with which she assumed it is a trying or painful moment was a perfect reflection of what one remembered of gracious, calculating Southern ladies one had known.

Some years later I saw the Amanda of another famous actress. A familiarity with Southern coquetry was in this performance as well as a grasp of the woman's basic toughness. But these elements had not been fused into a cohesive interpretation. There was too much effort to emphasize the amusing contradictions in Amanda. One felt after a while that the role was being played too hard for laughs, as if the performer unknowingly was mocking Amanda.

The effect on the balance of the play as a whole was not salutary. Yet the essential brooding atmosphere was not forfeited completely. Somehow Amanda survived the misinterpretation. The half-lights of *The Glass Menagerie*, though distorted, cast their haunting spell.

A third actress made more of the iron in Amanda's will than any other player I had seen. The laughter implicit in her was almost suppressed, replaced by implacable rigidity and drive. The reasons for Tom's urge to escape and for Laura's pathological need for self-effacement were cruelly transparent. Again the balance was wrong. Nevertheless, Amanda had force.

Miss Stapleton brings probing values of her own to Amanda. The womanliness and motherliness take on a new significance. The spirit of Southern gentility is not noticeable. The troubling sense of genteel decay is there, though the geography is not distinctly identified. The laughter is tinged by despair. A strain of tenderness runs through the woman. She is divertingly and sadly domineering, but not monstrously.

She is still Amanda, the pivot of the family. But because this is an Amanda of subtly different facture, the relationships around her fall into new textures. Thus the nature and caliber of actors modify the fabric of a play.

It no longer is any secret that in the original cast there were hidden hostilities between Miss Taylor and Eddie Dowling, who played Tom, and the result was a brittleness and antagonism between mother and son. Miss Stapleton and George Grizzard do not conceal the abrasiveness, but one never doubts their mutual affection.

Pat Hingle's splendidly decent and commonplace Gentleman Caller confers a fresh significance on the long, affecting scene with Piper Laurie's Laura. Here is another vivid example of the special illumination a gifted actor can bring to a familiar role. The play takes on new strength from his insights.

New York Times, May 16, 1965, sec. 2: 1.

Fragile Laura and the Gentleman Caller
Edwin Wilson

Like many noteworthy theater pieces, there are strains of both tenderness and toughness in Tennessee Williams' *The Glass Menagerie.* Some aspects are as fragile as the tiny glass animals which Laura, the crippled young woman of the play, loves and protects, while other elements have the strength of Amanda Wingfield, the mother who claims to be bewildered by life but who manages nevertheless to badger her children night and day and to survive whatever life throws in her path.

A successful production will recognize both strains, but that requires a range few directors and performers possess. It is not entirely surprising, therefore, that the new revival at the Circle in the Square Theater concentrates almost entirely on the stronger, more obvious elements in the play and lets the others suffer a sad neglect.

As most people know, the play is a tale of a former Southern belle, now living in reduced circumstances, who tries to maintain the illusion of what life was like in the Old South. Her obsession is to find a Gentleman Caller for her daughter, the assumption being that a husband will solve all their problems. She pursues her goal in clear defiance of the reality of their situation and her daughter's condition. Not only is Laura a cripple, she is shy to the point that she becomes physically ill when forced to meet strangers.

To Tom, her son, Amanda assigns the task of producing a Gentleman Caller. Tom is an aspiring poet forced to work in a shoe factory, but because of the pressures of his job and his mother's persistence he has ideas of following in his father's footsteps. His father, the play informs us, was a telephone man who "fell in love with long distance and skipped the light fantastic out of town." Before Tom goes, he produces a Gentleman Caller who has a scene with Laura--where she is built up to hope for love only to be suddenly let down. It is one of the most poignant scenes of the modern stage, and also one of the most sure-fire dramatically.

As played by Pamela Payton-Wright and Paul Rudd, the scene comes to life again in the present production; it never fails to move us no matter how many times we have seen it. Also in this production, Maureen Stapleton, a formidable actress in virtually any part she plays, makes clear in her portrayal of Amanda how indomitable is the spirit of this misguided woman. For anyone who has never seen *The Glass Menagerie,* the Circle in the Square production provides the broad outlines and the inevitable high points which any thoroughly professional production affords.

But there is another aspect to the play, which, like Laura's spirit or one of her glass animals, is subtle, sensitive, and almost transparent. It could be called the music of the piece. Behind the blaring clash of wills in the play there is another melody, not nearly so loud, but unmistakable and absolutely essential to a true rendering of one of Mr. Williams' major plays.

Mr. Williams is a Southerner by birth and upbringing and he frequently writes in a Southern idiom. People mistakenly think that a Southern accent is a matter of pronunciation: that if you say the word sugar as if it were spelled "shugah," you have rendered a phrase correctly. But pronunciation is the least important part of it. The way the words are strung together--the inflections, the words emphasized, the rise and fall in the melody as the sounds are spoken--is the key as much as mere pronunciation. In the present revival there are four separate "Southern accents" and not a single one comes close to the real thing, although it must be admitted that Miss Payton-Wright tries her darndest.

But there is another kind of music in *The Glass Menagerie,* as there is in most successful drama, and that is the underground rhythm of the scenes. Action in drama does not proceed at an even pace or at the same peak of excitement. Scenes move slowly, then swiftly; an argument becomes heated, then levels off. Also, there is the way one scene blends into the next. All of this is akin to changes in tempo and volume in a musical performance, and no one incorporates it is his writing more than Mr. Williams.

The Gentleman Caller scene in *The Glass Menagerie* provides a perfect example. In a room illuminated by candlelight, the young visitor begins to build up Laura's confidence; slowly she lets go her inhibitions. Bit by bit the two come together, culminating in a hesitant dance, followed by a declaration by the young man of how pretty Laura is. Then a kiss. Abruptly he breaks away; he has gone too far. Fumblingly he tells her that he is engaged to another woman. Her hopes are destroyed.

The same careful modulations, the same nuances are present throughout the play. It is these modulations, these nuances--the music, if you will--that is missing so often from this production. Both Rip Torn who plays Tom and Theodore Mann who directed the play seem totally tone deaf to the tune Williams sings or to those subterranean sounds beneath the surface. Instead of the caressing softness and flow of Southern speech, Mr. Torn has a hard, jagged delivery, pouncing on certain words arbitrarily, like a man tearing into a concrete pavement with a jack hammer. (This character, by the way, is supposed to be a poet.)

For his part, Mr. Mann has coached none of his actors in the right sound and he has directed the action by fits and starts. The notes are there, but played mechanically, by rote.

Referring to an understanding of music, the legendary Louis Armstrong was quoted as saying that "there are some things if people don't know, you can't tell them." Obviously Mr. Torn and Mr. Mann don't know about Mr. Williams' music--so much so that one wonders if they would have the slightest idea what you were talking about if you told them.

Wall Street Journal, December 23, 1975: 6.

Theater: *Glass Menagerie*
Frank Rich

The new Broadway revival of *The Glass Menagerie* leaves much to be desired, but that fact doesn't diminish the largest aspect of the event. The spirits of Tennessee Williams and Jessica Tandy have been reunited for the first time in a generation, and their partnership, now as in legend, is one of the most fundamental in the history of the American theater. Perhaps some theatergoers will want to hold out for a better *Glass Menagerie* than the one at the O'Neill Theater, and no doubt it will eventually arrive. But you pass up Miss Tandy's Amanda Wingfield only at your own peril: You may turn around one day to discover that, in Mr. Williams's phrase, the past has turned into everlasting regret.

Along with *Long Day's Journey Into Night, The Glass Menagerie* is in a class apart among autobiographical American plays. "The play is memory," says Tom, Mr. Williams's alter ego and narrator--and so it is. What lifts this work above so many other family living-room dramas is its author's insistence on refracting the past through a complex and vulnerable sensibility: A remembered reality is rearranged to express the music, both sweet and discordant, of a young poet's soul. It is Miss Tandy's ability to ascend to that same realm--to give us not just the simple truth, but "truth in the pleasant disguise of illusion"--that makes her performance a piece of music that lingers in our minds as persistently as Amanda lingered in the author's.

The simple truth of Amanda is plain enough. A woman who has long since been deserted by both her husband and her genteel Southern youth, she lives in shabby circumstances in Depression-era St. Louis; she fights incessantly for her children's happiness even as she nearly smothers them to death. But if that were the sum of Amanda, Mr. Williams wouldn't have written about her. Within the exasperating nag, there is still the coquettish plantation belle. Within the woman battered on all sides by the painfulness of existence, there is still the indomitable fighter who clings to her faith in "the superior things of the mind and the spirit."

Miss Tandy, trim and in blond curls, wraps all these Amandas together in a portrayal of prismatic translucence. One second she is hectoring her son for his selfishness in a raspy Southern drawl, then she is all maternal good will, quietly tightening a muffler around Tom's neck. A second after that, she is a calculating flirt, cajoling the young man into finding his sister, Laura, a gentleman caller. When Tom takes the bait, she skips buoyantly about her drab apartment, clapping her hands in childish delight.

As always with this actress, delicate precision is all. When Amanda tells her daughter to aspire to "charm" and then remembers that charm was also her husband's fatal attribute, the word descends from a cheery highnote to a death rattle in the same sentence. When Amanda trudges home defeated by the discovery that Laura has abandoned business college, Miss Tandy enters in a moth-eaten cloth coat, looking aged and weary; then, by the mere dignity with which she removes her gloves, she reasserts the pride and determination of a woman who perseveres in the face of any defeat. Later on, while reminiscing about her marriage to her son, the actress clasps her arms to her chest on the line, "There are so many things in my heart I cannot describe to you." Her eyes tell us those indescribable things, and one of them is the unmistakable red-hot fever of sexual passion.

Miss Tandy brings one other strong asset to this role--beauty. When she puts on her yellow-linen cotillion dress to greet Laura's gentleman caller, there is nothing campy or self-parodistic about the mother's retreat to her vanished past. Sashaying about the room with a bouquet of jonquils in her hand, the actress just turns back the clock as magically as she did in *Foxfire*. Yet when disappointment sets in afterward, the same woman in the same dress withers like a leaf: the glow is gone, and we're left with a ghost floating through the lurid red shadows cast by the Paradise dance hall next door.

Unlike so many Amandas, Miss Tandy doesn't refrain from making the audience despise her--and that's how it must be, if we're to believe that she will ultimately drive her son, like her husband, out the door forever. This Amanda is tough, and even her most comic badgerings leave a bitter aftertaste. John Dexter, the British director of this production, follows the same severe tack in the rest of the revival--even to the point of using some of the distancing, slide-projected title cards that Mr. Williams calls for in the published text (but are rarely seen in performance).

Though the notion of fighting against a maudlin *Glass Menagerie* is laudable, the execution has gone astray. The exemplary designer Ming Cho

Lee has created a set that appropriately serves the abstraction of memory rather than kitchen-sink reality, but it is too big, too contemporary and too icy in its austere high-tech design. Even Andy Phillips's evocative, pointillist lighting can't always prevent it from combatting the play's intimacy.

The supporting cast, though populated by accomplished actors, is frequently playing at a routine level. Though she works hard, Amanda Plummer is miscast as Laura: as you'd expect, she captures the pathological shyness of a young woman who lives in a fantasy world of glass figurines, but a gleaming smile alone can't convey the inner radiance that is waiting to be unlocked; we just don't believe that she would haunt her brother for the rest of his life. Bruce Davison's Tom has a Williamsesque accent that comes (in the narration) and goes (in the scenes proper)--and the performance is in and out too. A cagey opponent for Miss Tandy in their fights, the actor gives an exaggeratedly actorish delineation of a dreamy poet battling for salvation.

John Heard comes off much better as the Gentleman Caller: He mines the low-key generosity of the man, thereby keeping total disaster at bay in his long scene with the almost resolutely ungiving Miss Plummer. But his flights of Dale Carnegie-style self-boosterism are accompanied by artificial and anachronistic gestures--as if he and Mr. Dexter were guessing blindly at the manners of a bygone American prototype.

That the play is often absorbing and affecting, if imbalanced, in spite of these considerable drawbacks is a testament to the enduring pull of the writing and to the flame of Miss Tandy. The wrong notes are there to be heard, but so is the voice of our cherished, departed poet, pouring directly out of one of the few incandescent theater artists he has left behind.

New York Times, December 2, 1983, sec. 3: 3.

A *Glass* You Can See Things In
Jan Stuart

Is it possible to see *The Glass Menagerie*--a work that should be second nature to anyone with a high school diploma--and experience what an audience felt at its Chicago premiere in 1944?

I wouldn't presume to speak for that opening night audience, but I had enough epiphanies at the Roundabout Theater the other night to last me a lifetime. For *The Glass Menagerie's* 50th anniversary, wizard director Frank Galati (who knows his way around an American literary icon from Steppenwolf's *The Grapes of Wrath*), has summoned together a visionary setting by Loy Arcenas and an ensemble who say the lines as if the playwright's ink had barely dried. The result is a production that reinvigorates an American landmark and redoubles the play's mythic hold on our hearts.

That said, we can't conceal our disappointment that the redoubtable Julie Harris is something less than luminous as Tennessee Williams' mother of mothers, Amanda Wingfield. Harris' Amanda is resolutely life-sized, as if the spark of vivacity had long ago drained away form one too many mornings pushing advice and Farina on reluctant children and magazines on resentful phone customers. The actress doesn't allow us to laugh at the woman's excesses, because nothing seems excessive beyond a southern talent for manipulating the English language in novel ways.

Harris' grimly realistic performance has the effect of shifting focus onto Amanda's beleaguered offspring and the playwright's stunningly modern stylizations. Most of the Wingfield charisma seems to reside in the bristling Tom of Zeljko Ivanek whose plush southern drawl (a bit thick for St. Louis, perhaps) and punch-drunk way with words convey something of his errant daddy's alleged charm. Ivanek dances his way through the role bending, swaying and darting around the apartment like a caged leopard itching to make the break. This tomcat has been pent up with mamma too long: Every elegant utterance cuts with an extra undercoating of bile. He's altogether extraordinary.

Kevin Kilner's handsome gentleman caller, by contrast, is a study in masculine poise, exuding the relaxed confidence of a onetime high school heartthrob who has sewn his last wild oat. Kilner brings out Jim's self-help instincts; there's a mildly vacuous ring to his buck-up sermonizing that suggests some cross between William Hurt's preening journalist in *Broadcast News* and a Course in Miracles guru. When he autographs an old *Pirates of Penzance* program, Calista Flockhart's breathy Laura flutters like Zasu Pitts. But for a Quasimodo-sized limp, Flockhart seems subtly less breakable than usual; you get the feeling this Laura will prevail after her misbegotten meeting with Jim. That does nothing to undercut the heartstopping power of Jim and Laura's encounter, measured out with aching precision by Kilner and Flockhart till we almost turn blue from holding our breath.

For those who only acquaintance with the play comes from the 1987 film directed by Paul Newman or the made-for-TV version with Katharine Hepburn, the evening's revelation is in the eloquent use of slide projections, which flash traces of dialogue and giant images of roses, gentleman callers and Daddy Wingfield. The blown-up words float over the players' heads like whispers from the past that come and go; the effect is gorgeously resonant and strikingly contemporary.

How stunning, then, to realize that these multimedia splashes, which look like a director's jazzing up an old melody, are actually a director's shrewd obeisance to a playwright's innovations. In his calculated antinaturalistic strategy, Williams prescribed magic-lantern slides down to the word, instructions Galati follows with the evocative addition of some set description at the outset and the wise deletion of some obvious titles in the second half. Williams' expressionistic touches are amplified by Loy Arenas' angular collision of gray walls and platforms, accented with a snatch of lace curtain and towers of steel scaffolding that suggest "the sinister latticework" of alleys and fire-escapes.

Everything conspires to eclipse Harris' Amanda, who lacks the manic ferocity to send both of her men running from the family. She comes to life in the gentleman-caller moments, upstaging Laura with a lavish outfit and mindless prattle that approaches the baroque. More often, she's just an exasperating old biddie. It's a testament to the play's rich textures and a director's fidelity to the playwright's vision that *The Glass Menagerie* remains so poignantly shatter-proof.

New York Newsday, November 16, 1994: B2, B14.

The Two Glass Menageries: An Examination of the Effects of Meaning That Result From Directing the Reading Edition as Opposed to the Acting Edition of the Play
Geoffrey Borny

Part I FROM PAGE

The Glass Menagerie was rescued from possible oblivion in December 1944 by the almost unprecedented efforts of the Chicago critics who cajoled audiences to go and see the play. Since its rather faltering first appearance, the play has gone on to become a classic of American theatre. Like all classics it has had built up around it a body of criticism which has done as much to obscure the meaning of the play as to elucidate it. King (1973, p. 207) rightly claims that ". . . . *The Glass Menagerie*, though it has achieved a firmly established position in the canon of American plays, is often distorted, if not misunderstood, by readers, directors, and audiences."

One of the most enduring, and least endearing, critical standpoints that has guided generations of readers into seeing the play from a point of view different from that intended and created by the playwright has been the almost constant, and often unquestioned, assumption that Williams' strength lies in his ability to depict *realistic* characters and situations. Not surprisingly this same standpoint leads to a devaluation of the "plastic" or "expressionistic" elements of his playwriting.[1]

The major results of such a view of Williams would not have been quite so harmful had they stayed within the covers of books and articles about Williams. Unfortunately many directors seem to be influenced by the pro-realism critics, and often downplay or cut many of the more overtly expressionistic staging devices suggested by Williams as important for the play's production. Understandably audiences can appreciate only what is presented to them, and what is most often presented by directors of *The Glass Menagerie* is a kind of sentimental soap opera. An anonymous reviewer (1965, p. 92) of the Broadway revival of the play succinctly sums up the result of ignoring the plastic/expressionistic elements of the play when he claims of Williams that:

> . . . his plays are seldom performed with the force, subtlety and imaginative risk-taking they require. Instead they have [been] . . . pushed toward realism, their complex truths dealt with as so much emotional merchandise to be peddled.

I am convinced that any downplaying in production of the expressionistic elements in Williams' *Glass Menagerie* results in a trivialization of the play. I wished to see whether or not my thesis could be sustained and the acid test had to be a production of the play. Some of the hoary old critical clichés about the so-called weaknesses of Williams' expressionistic staging devices immediately come under close scrutiny the moment one examines the play in the theatre rather than simply in the study. Long revered critical judgments concerning *The Glass Menagerie* which appear on the face of it to be incontestable, turn out to be either of dubious validity or downright unworkable, when tested in the laboratory of the theatre.

Leacroft (1982, p. 120) came to a similar conclusion concerning the famous drawings for the Tragic, Comic and Satyric scenes that appeared in Serlio's *Achitettura* (1545). When Leacroft tried to move from page to stage he found that the drawings were inconsistent with each other, a thing that no one had noticed before because no one had previously tested them.

> As is so often the case the preparation of a reconstruction--whether in the form of a drawing or a model--draws attention to discrepancies between drawings *which have been reproduced many times by historians without comment.*

Leacroft's comment certainly applies mutatis mutandis to the judgements of critics concerning Williams' use of nonrealistic staging techniques. Gassner's (1954, p. 741) early attitude that " . . . *The Glass Menagerie* was marred only by some preciosity, mainly in the form of stage directions, most of which were eliminated in Eddie Dowling's memorable Broadway production" is echoed, and echoed uncritically, by as important a critic as Styan (1981b, pp. 18-19) in his recent three volume work on Modern Drama:

From the German director Erwin Piscator he had borrowed the idea of scattering through the play titles and images projected on a screen, and Williams certainly thought of his episodic method as expressionistic. "Expressionism and all other unconventional techniques in drama have only one valid aim, and that is a closer approach to truth." Such devices were not an attempt to escape from reality, but to find "a more penetrating and vivid expression of things as they are." He also believed that they were a step towards "a new, plastic theatre," one replacing "the exhausted theatre of realistic conventions." This was the familiar tune, but in the event, the screen device got in the way of the direct impact of the play's action, and was wisely abandoned.

Styan's dismissive attitude towards those plastic expressionistic elements of Williams' dramaturgy is based on his theoretical predilection for dramas employing realistic techniques of both staging and dramaturgy. Styan (1981a, p. 137) thereby "saves" Williams from himself by transforming the American dramatist into a copy of Anton Chekhov:

> . . . the non-realistic framework of the play, in which the son of the family, Tom Wingfield, plays chorus to the scenes of his memory, and even the Piscator devices of expressionistically projected titles and images (dropped in the New York production without damaging the fabric of the play), scarcely disturbed the Chekhovian detail of the main action.

Weales (1979, p. 62) has taken into account the importance of both the realistic and nonrealistic elements of Williams' work:

> [Williams] has never been a realistic playwright . . . but he has always been capable of writing a psychologically valid scene in the American realistic tradition--the breakfast scene in *The Glass Menagerie* for instance. . . . However grounded in realistic surface, the events in Williams' plays . . . take on meaning that transcends psychological realism. . . .

Ten years earlier however, even Weales (1969, p. 920) had implied that Williams' use of nonrealistic techniques was the weaker part of his work and specifically pointed out that it was realism that was central to the American theatrical tradition:

> In the Production Notes to *The Glass Menagerie* he [Williams] makes quite clear that he believes that poetic truth can best be depicted through a transformation that escapes the appearance of reality. Despite his

aesthetic stand, he is enough in the tradition of the American theater to ask his characters to move and speak realistically when he wants them to.

Weales's slighting reference to Williams' "aesthetic stand" and Styan's even more dismissive reference to "the familiar tune" echo Gassner's charge of "preciosity." Each of these important critics recognizes that Williams has claimed that he is not a realist, yet all of them undervalue precisely those nonrealistic elements in Williams' work that lie outside the mainstream of the American theatre tradition. Williams is praised whenever his work fits the realistic tradition that Corrigan (1977, p. 380) has called "the theater of verisimilitude [where] the settings, props, and lighting provide an environment for the action." Even as perceptive a critic as Eric Bentley (1953, p. 85) asserts that "Williams can write very well when he writes realistically, when, for example, he writes dialogue based on observation of character; in fact, all his dramatic talent lies in that direction."

In my production of *The Glass Menagerie* I did not wish to challenge the obviously correct view that Williams did in fact write fine realistic dialogue and create convincing characters. Rather I wished to see whether or not the nonrealistic plastic/expressionistic elements so often dismissed by the major critics did have theatrical validity. In effect I wished to test who was the better judge of the play, the critics or the playwright himself.

When embarking on the production I accepted a directorial standpoint that assumed that there is such an entity as *the playwright's play*. With this in mind I tried to follow Williams' stated instructions as closely as possible. I fully accepted the relationship between director and playwright that is so lucidly expressed by Corrigan (1963, pp. 183-184):

> In the theatre, the playwright must be the primary creator. His intention *must* be expressed in every aspect of production. . . . The chief aim of all the artists of the theatre must always be to realise that attitude toward life expressed by the playwright in his play.

I believe that it is only when a director utilises Williams' specified nonrealistic staging techniques in combination with actors creating their characters through the use of a realistic acting style that the audience can actually experience the play that Williams wrote.

The first thing that faces a director of *The Glass Menagerie* is that there are *two* published versions to choose between. The script that Eddie Dowling used in Chicago and later New York is not the version that is published in Williams' collected works. It is not true as Styan claims that Williams "wisely abandoned" the screen device and the other nonrealistic elements. The truth is that Williams wrote a more "acceptable," because more realistic, version of his play in order to get it performed. He in effect wrote an adaptation of *The*

Glass Menagerie for the original performance *but* he chose to have his original play published in his collected works.[2]

The version used by Eddie Dowling in the original production is the so-called Acting Edition published and commented on by the Dramatists Play Service Inc. (1948, p. 5). This version

> . . . differs from the book of the play as first issued by Random House: the dialogue itself has to some extent been revised by the author, and the stage directions likewise. The latter have been drastically changed in order to guide the director and actor.

The Acting Edition certainly is different from the Reading Edition. The director and actors are given a play that is much more realistic than the one published as the Reading Edition and republished in Williams' collected plays. To begin with in the Acting Edition, unlike the Reading Edition, there is no summary description of the characters preceding the play; the expressionistic stage devices are dispensed with; the expressionistic lighting plot is made more realistic; the transition between scenes is made less obviously artificial. When one adds to this the fact that, as Beaurline (1965, p. 142) noted, there are "1100 verbal changes" that transform the characters, we can see that we are dealing with two markedly different plays.

I chose to direct the Reading Edition both because Williams seems to prefer this version and also because I think it is a much finer play than the Acting Edition. The critics who prefer the Acting Edition usually do so because that version is more realistic. Rowland (1967, p. 338) who made a study of the two versions of *The Glass Menagerie* using the character of Amanda as the focus of his examination, claims that the Amanda of the Acting Edition is

> more gentle, more loving and understanding . . . more conversational, more human, more realistic. . . . We see a more humble and practical Amanda in a more depressing and realistic world. . . . [She speaks] lines that are full of life and realism.

Ultimately Rowland (1967, p. 335) rests his case concerning the "superiority" of the Acting Edition over the Reading Edition on the grounds that the Acting Version is more lifelike:

> . . . the "reading version" gives Laura and Tom a stage companion. The "acting version" gives them a mother.

I don't contest that the Acting Edition may be more lifelike--more realistic or that that version was well received by audiences. What I do contest is the assumption that dramatic art is better the closer it gets to verisimilitude. More precisely it seems to me that the harder one pushes Williams' play towards realism the more one confuses art with life and falsifies the vision of reality that he wished to dramatize. In his production notes to the play Williams explicitly defends expressionism and attacks realism, as a means of expressing reality. Williams (1971a, p. 131) while vindicating the artist and denigrating the photographer, argues strongly that

> . . . reality is an organic thing which the poetic imagination can represent, in essence only through transformation, through changing into other forms than those which were merely present in appearance.

Williams does not see his function as an artist simply in terms of putting life on stage. He follows Aristotle's (1965, pp. 43-44) view that "poetry [art] is something more philosophical and more worthy of serious attention than history; for while poetry is concerned with universal truths, history treats of particular facts." Williams does everything in his power to transcend the particular by using all the nonrealistic techniques he can to break the illusion of reality which is so beloved in the tradition of American realism. The mere accurate description of "a mother" is trivial for Williams (1971c, p. 4) who has always claimed that his concern as a dramatist was to master the "necessary trick of rising above the singular to the plural concern, from personal to general import."

Because Williams is so adept at writing realistic dialogue and creating convincingly real characters there is a great danger that the director and actors will emphasize these realistic elements at the cost of the nonrealistic ones. We need constantly in a production of *The Glass Menagerie* to remind ourselves that it is a work of art and not a slice of life. A play is, as Hethmon (1965, p. 96) succinctly puts it, "in its very nature a symbolic representation of an individual action in relation to a system."

There seems to be little problem for critics and directors when dealing with either overtly realistic or overtly symbolic dramas. It is only in plays like *The Glass Menagerie* where realism and non-realism are mixed, where, as Wimsatt (1965, p. 53) puts it, "the order of images . . . follows or apparently follows the lines of representational necessity or probability, though at the same time a symbolic significance is managed . . ." that problems of interpretation seem to occur.

It should be clear why I chose the Reading Edition in preference to the Acting Edition as the version I wished to direct. The Reading Version has within it a realistic story that is life like and has individual significance but because it is seen through a filter of nonrealistic staging devices and metafictional elements which draw attention to the fact that the play is a play, not a slice of life, the realistic story is made symbolically significant. It moves from the particular to the universal, from history to philosophy, from a representation of men to a representation of an action.[3]

In directing *The Glass Menagerie* Reading Edition I did not undervalue the realistic characterization because any attempt to make symbolic puppets of characters like Amanda, Tom or Laura would be to make a travesty of the play. However, by equally emphasizing the nonrealistic and metafictional elements,[4] I hoped to avoid the trap noted by Juneja (1963, p. 16) when he accurately pointed out that "in *The Glass Menagerie* it is the warm flesh and blood humanity of three dimensional characters that tends to mask the philosophic import of the play."

Part II TO STAGE

Tom, the narrator, immediately sets up the metafictional nature of the play. Williams (1971a, p. 144) gives the actor playing Tom the stage direction: "He addresses the audience." This immediately breaks the fourth wall convention so central to realism. The fact that this is a "memory play" also means that historification takes place inducing a kind of alienation effect which controls the possible empathetic response that would otherwise occur. Empathy is inappropriate because it leads to an identification between the audience and the hero or heroine. What Williams requires is a degree of "distance" to allow the audience to see beyond the particular problems of his characters in order to perceive the symbolic truth of the action of the play. It is for this reason that Williams makes Tom both a character in the play and the narrator of the play. In his stage instructions Williams (1971a, p. 144) points out that "the narrator is an undisguised convention of the play. He takes whatever licence with dramatic convention is convenient to his purposes." In my production presented in a small proscenium arch theatre,[5] I emphasized this conventional use of the narrator figure by having Tom enter through the audience, click his fingers as a signal for the curtain to rise, and then climb up the fire-escape steps onto the stage itself. The aim of this entrance was to immediately establish for the audience that the theatre, including the auditorium in which they were sitting, was a world that they shared with the narrator. The characters in the play, who are figments of the narrator's memory, all existed only on the stage and so they never entered the auditorium or played directly to the audience. The characters in Tom's "memory play" becomes distanced and objectified no matter how realistically they are played by the actors because they are seen through the mediating sensibility of the often ironically humorous narrator. (King 1973; Cluck 1979).

Having Tom click his fingers and "magically" having the curtain rise helped to overcome the first problem of the play. Tom's opening line (Williams, 1971a, p. 144)[6] is difficult for an actor to justify as it appears to be an answer to an implied question from the audience:

TOM: Yes, I have tricks in my pocket, I have things up my sleeve.

The "trick" of raising the curtain and then the immediate turning to the audience to explain this behaviour overcomes this problem. Immediately the rules of the theatre game that is being played are established. Williams has Tom point out that although he does have all the "tricks" of the theatrical trade he is "the opposite of the stage magician." He gives you illusion that has the appearance of truth. "I give you truth in the pleasant disguise of illusion." (p. 144). Realism, which attempts to create an illusion of reality, has only the surface appearance of truth, but through employing nonrealistic theatrical fictions Williams, through his alter-ego Tom, will depict the truth. This opening speech is a direct attack on the inadequacies of realism and therefore anything that can be legitimately used in actual production to stop audiences reading the play as a slice of life is justifiable. Tom's preference for non-realism as a mode for embodying truth echoes what Schlueter (1977, p. 3) has called ". . . the phenomenon of self-consciousness which characterizes so much of modern art." She outlines what Williams as an artist dramatizes, namely the bankruptcy of realism as a mode for expressing anything truthful about life:

> While the great tradition of Western literature willingly accepts fiction as reality, the "other tradition" bases itself on the logical possibility that, since fictions are not real--a work of art comes closer to the truth of reality when it does not pretend to be what it is not, but rather declares itself to be what it is.

So Tom begins *The Glass Menagerie* by saying what the play *is,* not life but art. In life time goes relentlessly forward. The world of the play is not bound by such limitations. As Tom points out: "To begin with I can turn back time." (p. 145). What is important to note here is that, in production, the audience is aware of two time scales--the present in which they and the narrator exist and the past in which the other characters exist. Spectators are also made aware that they are present in two places: in a theatre in Armidale and in a slum apartment in St. Louis. In life one cannot be in two places at once nor in one place at two times. In art which does not try to be life but draws attention to its own artifice, both things are possible.

In life events are not normally accompanied by music but in Williams' play music not only occurs but, as if to emphasize the artifice of such a convention, Tom is made to draw attention to its use:

> (*Music begins to play*). The play is memory. Being a memory play, it is dimly lighted, it is sentimental, it is not realistic. In memory every-thing happens to music. That explains the fiddle in the wings. (p. 145).

We all of us have seen films where the music which we are largely unaware of carries us along on a tide of emotion. We might also remember the effect in Mel Brooks's *Blazing Saddles* where the music's typical emotional evocation of the wide open prairies is undercut when the camera forces us to see the whole of the Count Basie band playing in the middle of the Wild West! Williams' use of music is closer to the Mel Brooks variety. I chose extremely sentimental romantic music for Amanda in several phrases taken from Paganini's Violin Concertos. The idea was to back up Amanda's reveries but at the same time to allow Tom and the nonrealistic stage devices to function as Williams intended them to do by ironically undercutting the scenes in which Amanda waxes lyrical.

In scene one we have a perfect example of Williams' ability to give his audience a twofold perspective. He allows the actress playing Amanda to play the character's own reality with honest sentiment while at the same time having Tom as the narrator, and the stage devices reduce this sentiment to sentimentality.

> [*She addresses* TOM *as though he were seated in the vacant chair at the table though he remains at the portieres. He plays this scene as though reading from a script.*]
> My callers were gentleman callers--all! Among my callers were some of the most prominent young planters of the Mississippi Delta--planters and sons of planters!
> [TOM *motions for music and a spot of light on* AMANDA. *Her eyes lift, her face glows, her voice becomes rich and elegiac.*]
> [Screen legend: Où sont les neiges d'antan?] There was young Champ Loughlin. (pp. 148-149).

The first important thing that I noticed in production was that the metafictional elements and expressionistic stage devices paradoxically allowed the actors to play their own roles totally realistically. They had no need to supply any ironic comments on their own behaviour as these were supplied by the narrator and his bag of theatrical tricks. When the play is presented without the ironical undercutting, it either becomes unbearably sentimental or the actors themselves have to include in their own performances some ironical undercutting.

In the scene just quoted I had Tom as the narrator resignedly mouthing a couple of Amanda's lines as she spoke them to indicate that he had heard this "script" so many times that he knew it by heart. The spotlight and romantic music should not come in unnoticed. I had Tom click his fingers again to "magically" produce these theatrical effects. All the while the actress playing Amanda was asked to play the truth of her character. She certainly does not see herself as ridiculous. The screen image is the final, and to my mind perfect, means of deflating Amanda's pretensions. We take the same ironical view of Amanda as Tom does in his memory. These much maligned screen legends are not, as some critics seem to suppose, ponderously serious captions supplying some sort of Brechtian "gestus" for each scene. In this scene the screen legend has a humorous deflating function allowing an audience to see the pathetically romantic pretentiousness of Amanda as Tom remembers her. "Où sont les neiges d'antan?" is a cliché of Romanticism and is intentionally "over-the-top." Amanda's slightly ridiculous behaviour both in the scene quoted and in her later "jonquil" speech reminded me of the histrionic performing of actresses like Lilian Gish in the early silent films. This gave me the idea of presenting the screen legends in the form of silent film subtitles. While neither the acting style nor the conventions of silent film subtitles were originally meant to be funny, time has made them so. In "memory" they appear laughable. Certainly audiences in Armidale found the use of these legends amusing and therefore were induced to see Amanda in the ironic light of a silent film heroine! The use of silent film subtitles also seemed to reflect Tom's obsession with the movies.[7] When Williams' stage instructions are read without awareness of their ironical overtones they do indeed appear banal. Once one moves from page to stage however their theatrical power is easily realized. A few examples should suffice to illustrate the subtlety of Williams' use of screen legends. In scene six Laura learns that the gentleman caller is none other than Jim O'Connor, the boy she has silently loved from schooldays! Now if this is played realistically without any ironic comment it becomes the most clichéd piece of coincidental nonsense. This is precisely what happens in Williams' (1948, p. 44) Acting Edition:

> LAURA: Mother!
> AMANDA: What's the matter now? (*Re-entering room.*)
> LAURA: What did you say his name was?
> AMANDA: O'Connor. Why?
> LAURA: What is his first name?
> AMANDA: (*Crosses to armchair R.*) I don't remember--Oh yes, I do too--it was--Jim! (*Picks up flowers.*)
> LAURA: Oh Mother, not Jim O'Connor?

There is not a note of irony here--all we have is soap-opera. In Williams' (1971a, p. 194) Reading Edition we have the following:

> LAURA: (*With an altered look.*) What did you say his name was?
> AMANDA: O'Connor.
> LAURA: What is his first name?
> AMANDA: I don't remember. Oh yes, I do. It was--Jim! [LAURA *sways slightly and catches hold of a chair.*]

[Legend on screen: "Not Jim!"]
LAURA: [*Faintly*] Not--Jim!
AMANDA: Yes, that was it, it was Jim! I've never known a Jim that wasn't nice! [*The music becomes ominous.*]

In this version the soap-opera cliché is not made at all realistic. Rather Williams heightens the level of cliché to a point where it is parody. This is the ironic parodic view of Tom's memory and we experience both its pathos and its bathos. "Not Jim!" like the later legend "Terror!" are so overtly melodramatic that they almost certainly cause a chuckle and the ominous music is a perfect parodic "gilding of the lily."

Laughter is constantly encouraged by Williams' stage devices. A most obvious example occurs when Tom groans:

You know it don't take much intelligence to get yourself into a nailed up coffin, Laura. But who in hell ever got himself out of one without removing one nail? [*As if in answer, the father's grinning photograph lights up. The scene dims out.*] (pp. 167-168).

In Armidale we used the larger than life picture of the "telephone man who fell in love with long distance" and when the spot on the picture came up on the otherwise darkened stage, it was always greeted with a sympathetic laugh. Often the stage devices that Williams employs are to make the audience laugh in order that they may not weep. Tom's ironic defence against the pain he feels at Laura's situation is almost always laughter. He knows that there is no solution to Laura's problems. No gentleman caller will save her. To emphasize this, in my production I cast an actress who could play Laura as physically not very attractive and as mentally slightly retarded. The brace on her leg was really only a symbol of her being a psychic cripple like Williams' sister Rose who was the model for Laura. No magic "adjustment" as occurred in the film of *The Glass Menagerie* was possible for this Laura. The scene where this Laura, replete with "gay deceivers" padding her brassiere and overdressed in one of Amanda's old ball-gowns examines herself in a mirror, would have been a total tear-jerker without the irony supplied by both the screen legend and the sound effects:

[Legend on screen: This is my sister: Celebrate her with strings! Music plays.] (p. 193).

Tom's voice, heard through the caption, holds back the pain and possible tears by the use of rather bitter irony.

Perhaps the most effective stage device that Williams uses to prevent his audiences from empathizing too readily with the characters from Tom's past is The Screen Image. The finest example of this relates to Jim, the gentleman caller. The device allows us to see Jim's character in relation to the whole action of the play which concerns man's need for "illusions."

In scene five Amanda and Tom have discussed callers in general and Jim in particular. Amanda has checked him out as a prospective suitor for Laura. Despite Tom's attempts to control Amanda's fantasies this "nice, ordinary, young man" (p. 129) with freckles is turned by her into an ideal suitor for her daughter. His going to night school means for Amanda that

> . . . he has visions of being advanced in the world! Any young man who studies public speaking is aiming to have an executive job some day! (p. 187).

Scene five ends with an uncomprehending Laura being asked by an elated Amanda to wish on the moon. A romantic moon is projected as a screen image and the scene dims out to the accompaniment of a violin! Every signal to the audience presages disaster for Amanda's plan. Tom's honest description of Laura's psychic limitations has already shown the audience that she lives "in a world of her own." (p. 188). The screen image of the moon and the sentimental violin, when juxtaposed with Tom's view of Laura, ironically emphasize the fantasy world of Amanda with her pathetic wish for "Happiness! Good Fortune!" (p. 189). At the end of this scene everything is set up for the catastrophe of Jim's visit. It was at this point that I placed the Interval. The idea was to keep the audience in suspense.

Scene six begins with Tom giving another of his narrator speeches. As this mirrors the opening of scene one, I again had him enter from the auditorium. He immediately begins to talk about Mr. O'Connor and a screen image of the expected gentleman caller appears. This is a picture of Jim, the high-school hero. The audience has by now almost come to know Jim, partly because of Tom's description of him but mainly because they have seen pictures of him before. The first picture was in scene two at the point when Amanda first gets the idea of marrying Laura off to some unsuspecting gentleman caller:

[Screen image: Jim as high school hero bearing a silver cup.] (p. 156).

In this early picture the actor attempted to show some of the "tremendous Irish good nature and vitality with the scrubbed and polished look of white chinaware" (p. 190) that Tom refers to at the beginning of scene six.

The second picture of Jim that the audience sees occurs at the beginning of scene three when Tom humorously observes:

Like some archetype of the universal unconscious, the image of the
gentleman caller haunted our small apartment. . . . [Screen image: A
young man at the door of a house with flowers.] (p. 159).

The audience in Armidale immediately recognised that the young man was the
same fellow who had earlier appeared carrying silver cup.

The third picture of Jim appears in scene five. The scene has opened
with the gently blasphemous legend "Annunciation" which of course presages
a visitation. Jim may not be God-Almighty, but he does later state: "I'm
Superman!" (p. 210). In scene five the picture of Jim is a repetition of the one
in scene three:

TOM: We are going to have one.
AMANDA: What?
TOM: A gentleman caller!
[*The annunciation is celebrated with music.* Amanda *rises.*]
[Image on screen: A caller with a bouquet.] (p. 181).

The picture of Jim, the high-school hero that opens scene six is therefore the
fourth time we have seen this confident young man. Before his actual arrival
however there is one more image of him that ironically cuts this walking
example of the American Dream down to size. As someone who "was
shooting with such velocity through his adolescence that you logically expect
him to arrive at nothing short of the White House by the time he was thirty"
(p. 190) Jim has in fact not lived up to his dreams of success. Tom points out:

His speed had definitely slowed. Six years after he left High School he
was holding a job that wasn't much better than mine. [Screen image: the
Clerk.] (p. 190).

The image we had of Jim in my production was of a harassed looking clerk
checking off a clipboard list amid row upon row of shoeboxes. This image,
following the four earlier pictures of Jim in his glory always produced laughter
from the audience and prepared the way for them to see that Jim's image of
himself which occurs later in scene six:

[Image on screen: Executive at his desk.] (p. 199).

was as laughably inflated as Amanda's earlier view of him as an executive.
The effect on the audience of Jim's actual "visitation," having seen five
pictures of him, was electrifying. With one audience of high-school students
the appearance of Jim produced excited muttering on the theme of "Here he
is!" What the screen images had done was to make Jim become what

Williams intended him to be, namely "the long-delayed but always expected something that we live for." (p. 145). Instead of being the Redeemer, Jim turns out unintentionally to bring hell rather than heaven to the Wingfield home. The stage devices--the nonrealistic use of lighting, the music, the legends and the screen images, all combine to help the audience to realize that Jim is just as much a dreamer as either Laura or Amanda. As Stein (1964, p. 152) has delightfully pointed out:

> Jim's attempt to play the modern saviour is an abysmal failure. In the after dinner scene, he offers Laura the sacrament--wine and "life-savers," in this case--and a Dale Carnegie version of the Sermon on the Mount--self-help rather than divine help--but to no avail.

The film version and the Acting Edition of *The Glass Menagerie* are both pushed toward realism. Often in productions of the Reading Edition directors follow the critical objections of writers like Gassner and Styan and cut the expressionistic/plastic staging devices from the script. The result is that a realistic portrayal of a particular family is produced. The play becomes a sensitive portrayal of the plight of a few pathetic individuals. This leads to a devaluation of Williams' work. It leads critics like Falk (1958, p. 177) to see Amanda as "an escapist like her daughter . . . [who] also lives unhappily in her cocoon of dreams."

What Williams' nonrealistic stage techniques help an audience to see is that there is in the play no one single absolute reality to which characters can adjust. Jim O'Connor, who in the film version clearly represented reality and helped Laura snap out of her inferiority complex, is shown in the Reading Version to be living in his own Glass Menagerie world. His belief in the illusions of the prevailing American Dream with its success myth are undermined by his actual achievement. He is not an executive but a clerk. It is only in fantasy that his beliefs succor him.

> JIM: *Knowledge--Zzzzzp! Money--Zzzzzp! Power!* That's the cycle democracy is built on. (p. 222).

The action of Williams' play then is not about a group of misfits who fail to adjust to reality. Jim is "an emissary from *a* world of reality" (p. 145) not *the* world of reality. All the characters in the play live in private illusionary worlds. Williams is presenting an action that is making a universal statement about what he sees as the human condition. Amanda lives "vitally in her illusions" (p. 129) of a past age of jonquils and gentleman callers; Laura lives in a world of glass animals and old records; Jim lives in an illusory world of hopes of success and even Tom lives in the world of art. He escapes to the movies and into the world of writing.

What Esther Merle Jackson (1966, p. 1) has called "The Broken World of Tennessee Williams" can only be realized on stage if the idea of a single absolute and "normal" reality is rejected. This is especially true of *The Glass Menagerie.* Each character in the play creates his or her own subjective reality as a defense against the "horror at the heart of the meaninglessness of existence" (Williams, 1962, p. 56). The only absolute in Williams' (1971b, p. 262) dramatized vision of reality is death: "There is no way to beat the game of *being* as against *non-being,* in which non-being is the predestined victor on realistic levels." Against the awfulness of this absurd reality, symbolized in *The Glass Menagerie* by the alleys outside the Wingfield apartment,[8] the individuals give their lives meaning by using their imaginations to create fragile glass menagerie worlds--worlds that are "truth in the pleasant disguise of illusion." (Willaims [*sic*] 1971a, p. 144).

Given that Williams (1978, p. 88) believes in a vision of reality that is so highly relativistic, in which "no man has a monopoly on right," it is not surprising that he had rejected realism as a means for expressing his vision. The solid mirror of external reality is suitable for expressing a vision of reality where truth is absolute, but not where there are as many truths as there are people. (Kernan 1958; Albee 1967). What is surprising is the way that so many critics and even more importantly, so many directors reject, or neglect to follow, "Williams' stated nonrealistic intentions. Williams (1971a, p. 131) has argued that ". . . truth, life, or reality is an organic thing which the poetic imagination can represent or suggest, in essence, only through transformation, through changing into other forms than those which were merely present in appearance." It seems wilful distortion on the part of critics and directors to neglect the use of the nonrealistic staging devices that facilitate the "transformation" Williams desires, in favour of producing a realistic slice-of-life that presents aspects of reality "merely present in appearance."

NOTES

1. Larson (1977, p. 416) points out the importance to Williams of these plastic elements in his dramaturgy. She claims that: "'plastic' is Williams' terms [*sic*] for the antirealistic theater that he described as long ago as 1945 in his production notes for *The Glass Menagerie.*"

2. For similar reasons Williams agreed to Elia Kazan's request for an alternative ending to *Cat on a Hot Tin Roof.* Williams now has the play published with both his original last act and the Broadway version that he wrote in order to get his play performed.

3. To Aristotle (1965, p. 39) tragedy was "a representation, not of men, but of action and life." I believe that what he meant by this was related to his claim that tragedy is more philosophical than history. He seems to have understood history as being factual-- a recounting of life--of what actually happened. Tragedy could make up its stories and

could thus shape them in such a way that moral lessons could be drawn from them. Similarly a representation of men would be like history, purely factual, whereas the representation of an invented action could lead to the possibility of some universal significance being perceived.

Raymond Williams (1964, pp. 20-21) while discussing the tendency toward realism in much modern drama uses Aristotle's idea to clarify the dilemma of those whose pursuit of verisimilitude has led them to confuse art with life. "The action of a play, for example, is often only incidentally important in itself. Its interestingness, its truth, cannot be judged as if it were an action in real life. Similarly with characters, the important dramatist is concerned, not necessarily to simulate 'real, live people,' but rather to embody in his personages certain aspects of experience. That this will frequently result in the creation of characters which we feel we can accept as 'from life itself' is certain; but the result will not always be so, and we must be careful that our judgement depends not on whether the characters are lifelike, but on whether they serve to embody experience which the author has shown to be true. All we are obliged to remember, for ordinary purposes, is that character and action, in any good play, are ordered parts of a controlled expression, and that the author's control over their presentation ought to be final."

4. By "metafictional" I mean all of those elements which break the dramatic illusion of reality by reminding the audience that they are watching a play not life.

5. The Arts Theatre, University of New England, Armidale, N.S.W. A 300 seater proscenium-arch theatre.

6. All following quotations are from this edition (Williams 1971a)--unless stated otherwise--and only page numbers are given in brackets.

7. Although Williams has had most of his plays butchered in their film versions, and this is especially true of the film of *The Glass Menagerie,* he has always been interested in the cinema. He was once an usher at a cinema and according to Brandt (1967) the influence of cinema on his theatrical work is strong.

8. That the alleys are meant to symbolize the absurd conditions of life is most clearly shown in the short story which serves as the source of the play. In "Portrait of a Girl in Glass," there is only one alley, but it is a cul de sac where cats are cornered and destroyed by a vicious chow. Both Tom and Laura "called this area Death Valley." (Williams 1965, p. 64).

REFERENCES

Albee, E. (1967) "Which Theater is the Absurd One?" *in* A. B. Kernan (Ed.). *The Modern American Theater,* Prentice Hall, New Jersey.

Anon. (1965) *Newsweek 69,* 92.

Aristotle (1965) "On the Art of Poetry," *in* T. S. Dorsch (Trans.), *Classical Literary Criticism,* Penguin, Harmondsworth.

Beaurline, L. A. (1965) "*The Glass Menagerie:* From Story to Play," *Modern Drama 8,* 142-49.

Bentley, E. (1953) "Better than Europe?" *In Search of Theater,* Random House, New York.

Brandt, G. (1967) "Cinematic Structure in the Works of Tennessee Williams," *in* J. Brown and B. Harris (Eds.), *American Theatre, Stratford-upon-Avon Studies 10,* Edward Arnold, London.

Cluck, N. A. (1973) "Showing or Telling: Narrators in the Drama of Tennessee Williams," *American Literature 51,* 84-93.

Corrigan, M. A. (1977) "Beyond Verisimilitude: Echoes of Expressionism," *in* J. Tharpe (Ed.) *Tennessee Williams: A Tribute,* University Press of Mississippi, Jackson.

Corrigan, R. (1963) "Stanislavski and the Playwright," *in* R. Corrigan (Ed.), *Theater in the Twentieth Century,* Grove Press, New York.

Dramatists Play Service (1948) "Staging the Play: Practical Suggestions by the Publisher," *in* Tennessee Williams, *The Glass Menagerie: Acting Edition,* Dramatists Play Service, New York.

Falk, S. (1958) "The Profitable World of Tennessee Williams," *Modern Drama 1,* 172-80.

Gassner, J. (1954) *Masters of the Drama,* Dover Publications, New York.

Hethmon, R. (1965) "The Foul Rag-and Bone Shop of the Heart," *Drama Critique 8,* 94-102.

Jackson, E. M. (1966) *The Broken World of Tennessee Williams,* University of Wisconsin Press, Madison.

Juneja, M. M. K. (1963) Vision and Form in the Plays of Tennessee Williams, Ph. D. thesis, University of Leicester.

Kernan, A. B. (1958) "Truth and the Dramatic Mode," *Modern Drama 1,* 101-14.

King, T. L. (1973) "Irony and Distance in *The Glass Menagerie,*" *Educational Theatre Journal 25,* 207-14.

Larson, J. B. (1977) "Tennessee Williams: Optimistic Symbolist," *in* J. Tharpe (Ed.), *Tennessee Williams: A Tribute,* University Press of Mississippi, Jackson.

Leacroft, R. (1982) "Serlio's Theatre and Perspective Scenes," *Theatre Notebook 36,* 120-22.

Rowland, J. L. (1967) "Tennessee's Two Amandas," *Research Studies of Washington State University 35,* 331-40.

Schlueter, J. (1977) *Metafictional Characters in Modern Drama,* Columbia University Press, New York.

Stein, R. (1964) "*The Glass Menagerie* Revisited: Catastrophe Without Violence," *Western Humanities Review 18,* 141-53.

Styan, J. L. (1981a) *Modern Drama in Theory and Practice: Realism and Naturalism,* Vol. I, C. U. P., Cambridge.

Styan, J. L. (1981b) *Modern Drama in Theory and Practice: Expressionism and Epic Theatre,* Vol. III, C. U. P., Cambridge.

Weales, G. (1979) "Tennessee Williams," *in* J. Vinson (ed.), *Great Writers of the English Language: Dramatists,* St. Martin's Press, New York.

Weales, G. (1969) "Tennessee Williams," *in* J. Gassner and E. Quinn (eds.), *The Reader's Encyclopedia of World Drama,* Thomas Y. Crowell Co., New York.

Williams, R. (1964) *Drama from Ibsen to Eliot,* Penguin, Harmondsworth.

Williams, T. (1978) *Where I live: Selected Essays,* New Directions, New York.

Williams, T. (1971a) *The Theatre of Tennessee Williams,* Vol. I, New Directions, New York.

Williams, T. (1971b) *The Theatre of Tennessee Williams,* Vol. II, New Directions, New York.

Williams, T. (1971c) *The Theatre of Tennessee Williams,* Vol. III, New Directions, New York.

Williams, T. (1962) "Angel of the Odd," *Time 79,* 56.

Williams, T. (1948) *The Glass Menagerie: Acting Edition,* Dramatists Play Service, New York.

Williams, T. (1965) *Three Players of a Summer Game,* Penguin, Harmondsworth.

Page to Stage: Theatre as Translation. Ed. Ortrun Zuber-Skerritt. Amsterdam: Editions Rodopi B. V., 1984. 117-136.

You Touched Me! (1945)

Poetry, Passion and Politics, *Broadway in Review*
Rosamond Gilder

After the usual seasonal false start--a week or two devoted to the most incredible balderdash and nonsense--Broadway made a real effort to emerge from its wartime preoccupation with the trivial. In rapid succession, first-nighters were given a comedy, a tragedy, a problem play and a musical, each one of which sought to explore, in its particular field, some of the less trodden paths of theatre. That none of them was completely successful is of less importance than that the attempt was made.

The first play to break the deadlock of inanity in which the theatre has been gripped since last spring, was Guthrie McClintic's production of *You Touched Me!*, Tennessee Williams' and Donald Windham's "romantic comedy" which stemmed from a story by D. H. Lawrence. It should be noted that Lee Shubert is billed as co-producer (in association with, to be exact), that Mr. McClintic directed and Motley set the stage, that the cast is gathered, as are most on Broadway, from England, America and Hollywood. These disparate items, though they add up to a very typical Broadway picture, are in this case pertinent, for they contribute to the weaknesses as well as the virtues of the production. *You Touched Me!* is Tennessee Williams' second play on Broadway, but it was written (and produced in Cleveland and Pasadena) before *The Glass Menagerie.* Very properly, the deserved success of last year's Critics' Circle prize-winner has set Mr. Williams' stock high. He suffers in his second play from comparisons with his first, a possibly unjust but quite inevitable experience. Since the second is actually the first, the situation becomes slightly involved and makes it the more advisable to concentrate on the play in hand and on the various elements of production which bring it to life on the stage of the Booth, rather than on relative merits.

The authors of *You Touched Me!* deal not only with "Life and Growth amid all this mass of destruction and disintegration", as the quotation from D. H. Lawrence on the program indicates, but also with the tragic and lonely separateness of human beings. The key of the play lies in its title; plot, characters, comic situations, excursions into fantasy, all these give flesh and body and laughter to that moment when separateness is bridged. The people involved are an old British sea-captain forcibly retired for drunkenness, living out his years in a world of memories and alcoholic escape. His only friend is a charity boy he adopted years before who, a man grown, has returned from years spent in Canada and as a fighter-pilot in the war. There is also the captain's spinster sister, as isolated in her frigidity and denial of life as her brother is in the uncongenial surroundings of a strait-laced parish. The third member of the family is the captain's daughter who has been molded externally in the image of her aunt. Sensitivity and its obverse, fear, hold her spellbound, drive her in panic from the approach of passion, but she can still be saved if the fighter-pilot can get through to her. It is an age-old fable-- Brunnhilde, Andromeda, the Sleeping Beauty--but presented here, for all the lightness of touch with which the authors handle it, with overtones of urgency directly related to our own day. We must reach one another with sympathy and understanding, we must "touch" one another, or we will all indeed be utterly destroyed. All this is conveyed in a plot that does not take itself too seriously, that is halting and occasionally flat. But it has moments of tenderness and intensity that lift it above the average.

Mr. McClintic has directed the play for comedy, an approach which some of his actors have taken as license to play in terms of farce. There is, in consequence, a clash between the poetic realism of the play, its tenderness touched with humor, and the straight theatricalism of this type of acting. The set itself is also marked by this duality. Half of it is a cluttered provincial drawing room, half a mock ship's cabin where the captain drinks and dreams his life away. The action moves from one to the other with arbitrary changes of light to focus attention and establish mood. The dialogue also is unhampered by too strict an adherence to the probable. As in *The Glass Menagerie,* Mr. Williams uses a diction that is fresh and arresting; his people speak with the license granted the poet, not in the idiom of the dictaphone.

The performances of Edmund Gwenn as the captain and Catherine Willard as the domineering spinster, however, are not touched by the poetic mood. Both are entirely conventional, though they range in treatment from the techniques of parlor comedy to those of the vaudeville stage. Mr. Gwenn makes felicitous use of the latter method in his interpretation of the fantastic "set-pieces" with which the authors have embroidered the play. He is particularly engaging, for instance, in his delivery of the absurd speech about the lady porpoise who flirted with him when, a shipwrecked mariner, he was floating on a raft fifty miles off the coast of Nicaragua. He is less happy in some of his other story-telling and, by an almost constant overemphasis and exaggeration, he deprives the captain of the stature which a more considered interpretation of the part might give. Catherine Willard is also guilty of treating her role exclusively for its surface values and in a hard and obvious farce-comedy style.

It remains for the young people to sound a lighter and subtler note. Marianne Stewart is still too inexpert to meet the demands of a role which is perhaps not as clearly defined by its creators as it might be. But Montgomery Clift as the young pilot brings the needed intensity and flashes of poetic feeling to his part. Mr. Clift is a sensitive and talented actor, but he needs to discipline--and also liberate--his speech. His words have a way of running together in moments of crisis. His performance would benefit by a certain breadth and repose, but he brings so much aliveness to the scene, he conveys so vividly the sense of the fiery core of youth, its eager seeking for contact and understanding and for a better world to come, that certain of his scenes are deeply moving. The passage, for instance, where he looks into the future toward the "new countries of the mind" that must be explored and the scene at the breakfast table between the two young people are among these moments. In the latter episode the fighter-pilot is trying to force Mathilda to listen, to top denying life:

HADRIAN. . . . You see, you're amazingly--gentle. . . . Nothing else in the world is as gentle as you are. Why, you're as delicately put together, as easily torn apart, as--one of those misty little white cottony things that drift around in the sunlight, scarcely see-able, they are so fine and soft! Touch them? You wouldn't dare. They'd dissolve at your touch, to a million pieces. It's almost too much to look at them. (*softly*) When I escaped from the prison camp, I had to stick a knife in a guard. As he went down, I saw he was only a kid and just as--gentle--as you are. The life in him yielded as softly as tissue paper. It wasn't my wish to kill him--the wrong, deceitful past of the world forced it on me! I knew very well that gentle things, such as that boy and you, are made to be gently treated. Barely touched, hardly breathed upon, even! Look! (*He raises his hands before her.*) Do these impress you as being *dangerous* fingers? Do they look to be fierce and cruel?
(*She dumbly shakes her head and looks away from him.*)
No, no, no, they're not. They wouldn't dare to touch you without your permission. . . . . They'd be more frightened than you are of using too much pressure--of bruising--or burning or leaving the tiniest scar! I'm a gentle person.

It is inevitable that Tennessee Williams and Dan Totheroh whose plays opened the same week, should be compared. Both are poets, both are determined to use the theatre as their own creative impulses direct, both are moved by the essence of being rather than by the class of event. At that point their similarity ceases, for each writer's idiom is sharply his own, especially as manifested in their current plays. . . .

Theatre Arts, November 1945: 618-21.

A Streetcar Named Desire (1947)

Streetcar Tragedy: Mr. Williams' Report on Life in New Orleans
Brooks Atkinson

By common consent, the finest new play on the boards just now is Tennessee Williams' *A Streetcar Named Desire*. As a tribute to the good taste of this community, it is also a smash hit. This combination of fine quality and commercial success is an interesting phenomenon. For if the literal facts of the story could be considered apart from Mr. Williams' imaginative style of writing, *Streetcar* might be clattering through an empty theatre. It is not a popular play, designed to attract and entertain the public. It cannot be dropped into any of the theatre's familiar categories. It has no plot, at least in the familiar usage of that word. It is almost unbearably tragic.

After attending a play of painful character, theatregoers frequently ask in self-defense: "What's the good of harrowing people like that?" No one can answer that sort of question. The usual motives for self-expression do not obtain in this instance. There is no purpose in *Streetcar*. It solves no problems; it arrives at no general moral conclusions. It is the rueful character portrait of one person, Blanche Du Bois of Mississippi and New Orleans. Since she is created on the stage as a distinct individual, experiences identical with hers can never be repeated. She and the play that is woven about her are unique. For Mr. Williams is not writing of representative men and women; he is not a social author absorbed in the great issues of his time, and, unlike timely plays, *Streetcar* does not acquire stature or excitement from the world outside the theatre.

These negative comments are introduced to establish some perspective by which *Streetcar* may be appreciated as a work of art. As a matter of fact, people do appreciate it thoroughly. They come away from it profoundly moved and also in some curious way elated. For they have been sitting all evening in the presence of truth, and that is a rare and wonderful experience. Out of nothing more esoteric than interest in human beings, Mr. Williams has looked steadily and wholly into the private agony of one lost person. He supplies dramatic conflict by introducing Blanche to an alien environment that brutally wears on her nerves. But he takes no sides in the conflict. He knows how right all the characters are--how right she is in trying to protect herself against the disaster that is overtaking her, and how right the other characters are in protecting their independence, for her terrible needs cannot be fulfilled. There is no solution except the painful one Mr. Williams provides in his last scene.

For Blanche is not just a withered remnant of Southern gentility. She is in flight from a world she could not control and which has done frightful things to her. She has stood by during a long siege of deaths in the family, each death having robbed her of strength and plunged her further into loneliness. Her marriage to an attractive boy who looked to her for spiritual security was doomed from the start; and even if she had been a superwoman she could not have saved it.

By the time we see her in the play she is hysterical from a long and shattering ordeal. In the wildness of her dilemma she clings desperately to illusions of refinement--pretty clothes that soothe her ego, perfumes and ostentatious jewelry, artifices of manners, forms and symbols of respectability. Since she does not believe in herself, she tries to create a false world in which she can hide. But she is living with normal people who find her out and condemn her by normal standards. There is no hope for Blanche. Even if her wildest dreams came true, even if the rich man who has become her obsession did rescue her, she would still be lost. She will always have to flee reality.

Although Mr. Williams does not write verse nor escape into mysticism or grandeur, he is a poet. There is no fancy writing in *Streetcar*. He is a poet because he is aware of people and of life. His perceptions are quick. Out of a few characters he can evoke the sense of life as a wide, endlessly flowing pattern of human needs and aspirations. Although *Streetcar* is specific about its characters and episodes, it is not self-contained. The scenes of present time, set in a New Orleans tenement, have roots in the past, and you know that Mr. Williams' characters are going on for years into some mysterious future that will always be haunted by the wounding things we see on the stage. For he is merely recording a few lacerating weeks torn out of time. He is an incomparably beautiful writer, not because the words are lustrous, but because the dialogue is revealing and sets up overtones. Although he has confined truth to one small and fortuitous example, it seems to have the full dimensions of life on the stage. It almost seems not to have been written but to be happening.

Streetcar deserves the devotion of the theatre's most skillful craftsmen; and not entirely by accident, it has acquired them. Elia Kazan, who brilliantly directed *All My Sons* last season, is versatile enough to direct *Streetcar* brilliantly also. He has woven the tenderness and the brutality into a single strand of spontaneous motion. Confronted with the task of relating the vivid reality of *Streetcar* to its background in the city and to its awareness of life in general, Jo Mielziner has designed a memorable, poetic setting with a deep range of tones.

The acting cannot be praised too highly. Marlon Brando's braggart, sullen, caustic brother-in-law, Karl Malden's dull-witted, commonplace suitor, Kim Hunter's affectionate, level-headed sister are vivid character portraits done with freshness and definition. As Blanche Du Bois, Jessica Tandy has one of the longest and most exacting parts on record. She plays it with an insight as vibrant and pitiless as Mr. Williams's writing, for she catches on the wing the terror, the bogus refinement, the intellectual alertness and the madness that can hardly be distinguished from logic and fastidiousness. Miss Tandy acts a magnificent part magnificently.

It is no reflection on the director and the actors to observe that Mr. Williams has put into his script everything vital we see on the stage. A workman as well as an artist, he has not only imagined the whole drama but set it down on paper where it can be read. The script is a remarkably finished job: it describes the characters at full length, it foresees the performance, the impact of the various people on each other, the contrasts in tone of their temperaments and motives.

In comparison with *The Glass Menagerie*, *Streetcar* is a more coherent and lucid drama without loose ends, and the mood is more firmly established. *Summer and Smoke*, which has not yet been produced in New York, has wider range and divides the main interest between two principal characters. If it is staged and acted as brilliantly as the performance of *Streetcar*, it ought to supply the third item in a notable trilogy. For there is considerable uniformity in the choice of characters and in the attitude toward life. That uniformity may limit the range of Mr. Williams' career as a playwright; so far, he has succeeded best with people who are much alike in spirit. In the meantime, he has brought into the theatre the gifts of a poetic writer and a play that is conspicuously less mortal than most.

New York Times, December 14, 1947, sec. 2: 3.

Drama
Joseph Wood Krutch

Two years ago when Tennessee Williams was being hailed as the best new playwright to appear in a decade I was among those who were inclined to wait and see, but *A Streetcar Named Desire* (Barrymore Theater) is amply sufficient to confound us doubters. In mood and manner it is, to be sure, strikingly like *The Glass Menagerie*. Indeed, the theme and even the story might be said to be the same, since both dramas are concerned with the desperate, unsuccessful effort of a female character to hang on to some kind of shabby gentility. But the new work is sure and sustained where the former was uncertain and intermittent. Gone are all the distracting bits of ineffectual preciosity, all the pseudo-poetic phrases, and all those occasions when the author seemed about to lose his grip upon the very story itself. From the moment the curtain goes up until it descends after the last act everything is perfectly in key and completely effective. The extent of Mr. Williams's range is still to be demonstrated. He may or he may not have much to say, and it is quite possible that sickness and failure are the only themes he can treat. But there is no longer any doubt of his originality, or of his power within the limits of what he has undertaken. Since 1930 only three new talents which seemed to promise much have appeared in our theater, and of Mr. Williams one must say what one said of Odets and Saroyan. Only time can tell just how far a young man who begins like this may possibly go.

Considered merely in terms of the story it had to tell, *The Glass Menagerie* was bleak enough, but the story of the new play is both bleaker and more frankly pathological. Its central figure is a young school teacher, daughter of a decayed Southern family, who has lost her job because she is--technically and not in the loose popular sense of the term--a nymphomaniac, and who has come, as the play opens, to seek refuge with a married sister in New Orleans. At the beginning we know nothing of the past of this central character, and we have nothing except a few intriguing, unexplained incongruities in her behavior to suggest that she is anything more than the shabby, desperately refined, and respectable young woman she seems to be. We share her distraction at the discovery that her sister has complacently accepted a descent into the blowsy happiness of a misalliance with a coarse, violent husband of frankly proletarian habits; and then, as the action proceeds, the dreadful truth about the heroine emerges until, in the terrible but finely conceived final scene, she begins what she believes is a flirtation with the attendant who has come to conduct her to the insane asylum. That the play is not merely the ugly, distressing and possibly unnecessary thing which any outline must suggest is due, I suppose, in part to its sincerity, even more to the fact that the whole seems to be contemplated with genuine compassion and not, as is the case with so much modern writing about the lower depths, merely with relish. It remains, as there is no point in trying to deny, morbid enough. The mood and the atmosphere are what really count, and both are almost unrelievedly morbid, even, or perhaps especially, in those moments when a kind of grotesque comedy emerges. Yet despite the sensational quality of the story neither the atmosphere nor the mood is ever merely sensational. The author's perceptions remain subtle and delicate, and he is amazingly aware of nuances even in situations where nuance might seem to be inevitably obliterated by violence. The final impression left is, surprisingly enough, not of sensationalism but of subtlety.

Comparing, as one inevitably does, this play with its predecessor, the difference in merit between the two seems to be almost entirely the result of the author's vastly increased mastery of a method which is neither that of simple realism nor of frank fantasy. Obviously Mr. Williams is a highly subjective playwright. His stories are not told primarily either for their own sakes or in order to propound a merely rational thesis, but chiefly because they enable him to communicate emotions which have a special, personal significance. Already one begins to take it for granted that his plays will be immediately recognizable by their familiar themes and a sensibility as unique as that of a lyric poet. Yet he never quite abandons dramatic objectivity as a method. To go one step farther in the direction of subjectivity would inevitably be to reach "expressionism" or some other form of non-representational art. But though there is in the plays as written a certain haunting dream-like or rather nightmarish quality, the break with reality is never quite made, and nothing happens which might not be an actual event. Even the almost dadaist suggestion of the title is given--and more meaningfully than in the case of *The Glass Menagerie*--a rational explanation.

Though the new play is superbly directed by Elia Kazan and beautifully performed both by Jessica Tandy and by the other principal actors, the fact that the author has achieved so firm a mastery of his own technique will forestall the tendency to raise again the question so persistently raised in connection with *The Glass Menagerie*--the question, that is to say, whether or not it was the acting and the direction which "made" the play. *A Streetcar Named Desire* could easily be ruined by inadequate production. Everything in it depends upon the ability of a director and his actors to realize a subtle intention. One may even go so far as to say that if it had been given a bad performance, the spectator might easily have been misled into supposing, not that the production was bad, but that there had been nothing to produce. But to say that is by no means to say that the play was "made" by the director or the actors. It was made in the first instance by Mr. Williams himself, a playwright who demands much but who gives even more.

Nation, December 20, 1947: 686-87.

Two Views of the South
Wolcott Gibbs

The notable thing about the revival of Tennessee Williams' *A Streetcar Named Desire* at the City Center is, of course, the fact that Tallulah Bankhead is appearing in the role of the broken and desolate Blanche DuBois. This is a courageous undertaking, and I wish I could say that it was a success, but the truth, I'm afraid, is that the whole thing is one of this great woman's rare mistakes. The performance is spectacular, and often brilliant, Miss Bankhead being capable of no routine effects, but for various reasons it is far less satisfactory, less in key with the fundamental spirit and purpose of the play, than that given by Jessica Tandy in the original production.

The principal difficulty is that of personality. The story of Blanche has to do with the final stages in the destruction of a Southern gentlewoman. Some of the things that have happened to her were terrible--the long years spent watching old women die in a house that is crumbling into ruin, the suicide of the young homosexual who was her first and only love--but later on, when there was nothing left but the need for some retreat from loneliness, her life has been just a succession of mean and shameful defeats. Back in the little Mississippi town she came from, she was thrown out of a third-rate hotel for bringing men to her room, and dismissed from her teaching job for seducing a seventeen-year-old boy. In the end, in her sister's tenement apartment in the French Quarter of New Orleans, she loses her last hope when the good, stupid man who might have saved her is driven away by his discovery of her past, and her mind ultimately gives way when her brother-in-law takes her, drunkenly and contemptuously, in the back room of the seedy flat. Altogether, Blanche is one of the most tragic figures in the modern theatre, but there is no grandeur in the remnant we are now permitted to see. There is nothing, in fact, except desperate affectation, terror, and weak and futile rage. Miss Bankhead has resolutely discarded most of the mannerisms that have made her famous, but she remains incapable of acting without a certain majesty, and pathos is surely no part of her equipment. I think she is very effective in some scenes, particularly those in which she goes on about the lost glories and gathering horrors of Belle Rêve, but most of the time her behavior is nearly fatal to the play. Even in her most depressed moments, there is a sort of unconquerable arrogance about her, and it is almost impossible to believe that any circumstance could have brought such a warlike spirit low. The Blanche we meet at the City Center would, I suspect, have burned both the hotel and the schoolhouse to the ground, and her subjugation by a slow-witted, blustering Pole seems ludicrous.

This brings me to the second problem Miss Bankhead has to face, which is that the cast surrounding her is barely more than adequate. This isn't too important in the case of the heroine's suitor or her sister, but it is close to being a disaster in that of the actor who plays Stanley Kowalski. Gerald O'Loughlin, who has the role, has borrowed the externals of his performance from the one given by Marlon Brando in the original production, but somehow all the fire is missing from the core. As nearly as his interpretation can be described, it has substituted petulance for ferocity and drunken bravado for brutal vitality. He might still be a suitable opponent for anybody except Miss

Bankhead. With her, he seems cruelly mismatched.

The third, and final, handicap the actress is up against stems from her own reputation for unusual vivacity in private life. On opening night, sustained and imbecile laughter greeted every line that could conceivably be taken as a reference to the star's career outside the theatre. While this had no visible effect on her composure, which is, of course, a legend of our era, it relentlessly destroyed, time after time, whatever mood she was struggling to create. There is, I suppose, no cure for this kind of vulgarity and stupidity in an audience, except possibly the brisk employment of a machine gun. I would have been delighted, and not especially surprised, if Miss Bankhead had had recourse to just that.

New Yorker, February 25, 1956: 90, 92-93.

Another *Streetcar* Happily Comes Along
Douglas Watt

Whether or not you feel, as I certainly do, that *A Streetcar Named Desire,* which is now being given a superior revival at the Vivian Beaumont, is Tennessee Williams' finest play, it is unquestionably a masterpiece. And I don't think any of us who were present that night over 25 years ago when it opened at the Ethel Barrymore have forgotten what a shattering experience it was and how, afterward, we tumbled out onto the sidewalk still stunned by its impact and unwilling to talk about it until many minutes has passed and we were, perhaps sitting at Sardi's and groping for words.

Such evenings are relatively few in a lifetime of theatergoing, even if one limits oneself to considering just the brighter occasions. For there had just occurred one of those rare confluences in dramatic history in which a young, but already experienced, playwright (Williams was 33) had achieved complete mastery of his form, to be joined by an inspired director, Elia Kazan, and two incandescent leading players, Jessica Tandy and Marlon Brando. The result was electrifying. Kazan had addressed himself to Williams' script in a white heat of creativity, galvanizing the players to elicit a wrenching, incomparable performance of Blanche Du Bois by Miss Tandy and a blazingly original one by Brando which he soon thereafter repeated (opposite Vivien Leigh) for the movies, from which he has yet to return.

Streetcar could never again play as it did then (good as Miss Leigh and Brando were in the film, something had already been lost), but it has stayed with us over the years. Composers were anxious to convert it into an opera, Helen Tamiris used it as the subject of a flashy ballet, and it has been revived countless times (a Los Angeles production with Faye Dunaway and Jon Voight recently opened). Whether one leans toward the tender beauty of, say, *The Glass Menagerie* or the abrasiveness and shock of *Cat on a Hot Tin Roof* (the play the author seems fondest of), I think it must be conceded that in no other work of his have the poetry and savagery that exist side by side in so much of Williams been so perfectly combined.

And just listen to *Streetcar* in its present revival. Listen to the strength, imagery, and economy of the dialogue, always striking precisely the right note as it builds to create a structure of awesome power and beauty. Williams was in marvelous control of his art at the time. Among other things, it is interesting to see how he cannibalized the characters of the Daughter and Gentleman Caller in *The Glass Menagerie* to create one of the more touching scenes, between Blanche and her shy beau, in *Streetcar*. I can't think of a false or wasted moment in the play, unless it is the momentary interruption of the street vendor with his flowers for the dead.

As sound a piece of playwriting as *Streetcar* is, it's not the surefire "property" so many would assume it to be. It requires, demands, two great performances, not to mention two insightful supporting ones in its cast of 12. To stretch a point, just as only an Olivier could startle us into encountering Oedipus face to face, fresh and true, in our time, so it takes uncommon insight--some special quality having nothing to do with intelligence, though that is necessary, too, of course--on the part of the actress impersonating Blanche. It would be nice to have a supply of mercurial new Brandos around to play Stanley, too, but we can at least get by with a forceful Stanley. Blanche must sing.

Rosemary Harris sings, but coolly. She is a fine actress, one of our best, with a mysterious beauty that has served her well in a variety of roles both comic and dramatic. As the Blanche of this new revival, she understands the character, and she tellingly reveals the woman's plight bit by bit, in speech (though her voice was a little hoarse opening night) and gesture. But she is always the intelligent observer, the constantly aware interpreter, never the trapped and achingly lonely figure that Blanche is. We are not purged by this performance, as we must be.

Again, James Farentino is a strong, incisive Stanley, but the strangeness that clings to this character, the unpredictability of his nature, is not quite there.

This Blanche and this Stanley quicken our interest, excite us, and reveal to us the excellence of Williams' writing in such a way as to command our full respect. But the quicksilver is missing.

Ellis Rabb's staging is--except for his (to me) annoying use of the full, huge Beaumont stage to include "street" activity behind Douglas W. Schmidt's fine central set that often crates the impression of stagehands at play--sensitive and controlled. I didn't care much for Patricia Conolly's Stella, which was more successful in emphasizing the ladylike background of Stanley's wife than her earthy present. But Philip Bosco's Harold, the shy laborer who becomes infatuated with Blanche, is one of the season's best-realized characterizations by a leading member of a company that is, with this production, terminating its long tenure at Lincoln Center.

Just one of the many fascinations of *Streetcar* lies in the fairness with which Williams approached both Blanche and Stanley. Though our hearts go out to Blanche, one is left unable to take sides between her and Stanley. He may be brutish, but he and Stella have a marriage that works, and Blanche's interference with it is real and unjust, as great as her need is. In this way, the play, while unerring in writing, development, and resolution, possesses the ambiguity of truth, of the world beyond the stage. It is a stroke of genius that gives *Streetcar,* I believe, a classic stature.

The magic of the original production, a magic beyond recall, may be missing here, but that's hardly reason for not rushing to this one.

New York Sunday News, May 6, 1973, sec. 3 (Leisure): 3.

Danner and Quinn In a New *Streetcar*
Frank Rich

"We've had this date with each other from the beginning," says Stanley Kowalski to his sister-in-law, Blanche DuBois, just before he sweeps her away to bed in *A Streetcar Named Desire.* That line--wholly in character for Stanley and yet a classic expression of tragedy's inexorable pull--sets off what is still among the most shocking acts of human destruction the American stage has known. In the collision of Stanley, the working-class stiff, and Blanche, the frayed Southern belle, Tennessee Williams gave life to forces than run far deeper than his play's specific place (New Orleans) and sociological context (the postwar 1940's). *A Streetcar Named Desire* is not a morality tale about a brutal man victimizing a frail woman but a terrifying plunge into the madness that afflicts anyone, male or female, brute or sensitive, who submits to his own personal executioner--the passion so incendiary that it consumes the self.

It says everything about Nikos Psacharopoulos's new production of *Streetcar* at the Circle in the Square that when its Blanche and Stanley, Blythe Danner and Aidan Quinn, keep their "date," we don't witness the promised thunderclap of self-immolation. Their date really looks more like a date than a rape. As the lights fade, Mr. Quinn leads Miss Danner into a necking session--in more ways that one an anticlimax. So it goes in a staging that may not deface Williams's masterpiece but often sanitizes it. Mr. Psacharopoulos's production demonstrates how a director can provide an intelligent, entirely respectful rendition of a classic text--and still miss the streetcar.

In this instance, that streetcar is indeed named desire. What is most absent from the evening, and not just in Blanche and Stanley's showdown, is sex. Miss Danner and Mr. Quinn--both fine actors, both erotic figures in other circumstances--shed no sparks here. As they circle each other in scene after scene, submerging their increasingly torrential passions in household bickering, we never feel the magnetic undertow, the smoldering combustion that should make their ultimate mutual conflagration both inevitable and frightening. Defused, *Streetcar* becomes instead a domestic comedy--the intrusive in-law irritating the macho king of his castle. That's part of the story, but hardly the whole of it.

Miss Danner's performance is a particular disappointment, especially to an admirer who has felt that this actress had an inevitable rendezvous with the role of Blanche. To her credit, she doesn't make the mistake of playing the dispossessed Mississippi schoolteacher as a madwoman from the outset; this Blanche is initially pretentious and ridiculous, deservedly funny as she too strenuously refuses drinks and too grandly brags of the vanished traditions of her lost plantation, Belle Reve. And we get glimpses beneath the airs and coquetry, too. When, early on, Miss Danner scoops up the cherished papers, "poems a dead boy wrote," that Stanley has manhandled, she does so with a tremulous delicacy, as if in picking up the poems she were gathering up their author's ashes. At the end of Act I, when Blanche delivers her monologue describing the suicide of that "boy"--her homosexual husband--Miss Danner starts to make the transition into psychic collapse. Her pale bony hands fly to her eyes in horror as the confronts the memory of her own guilty role in hastening the death of the man she loved.

But that scene proves to be the peak of the performance. After intermission, Miss Danner lapses into the fey eccentricity of her Elvira in *Blithe Spirit* rather than sinking into desperation. When Blanche's would-be protector, Mitch (Frank Converse), holds her face to the hanging lightbulb, the harsh light exposes no ravages or secrets we haven't seen before. Miss Danner's sobs in response to Stanley's first efforts to evict her have a phony ring. Her later cry of panic--"Fire! Fire! Fire!--is fueled by pumping arms, not by a volcanic outpouring of hysteria rising from within. No wonder Miss Danner's final exit to the insane asylum is so unmoving. This Blanche needn't depend on the kindness of strangers because her illusions haven't convincingly crumbled, she never actually has snapped.

As Miss Danner pumps her arms, so Mr. Quinn pumps up his voice. It's hard to blame him. This actor provides some ambiguous qualities appropriate to Stanley--his masculinity has its androgynous side, his boorishness its leavening humor--yet he is nonetheless miscast. A compact man of bantam stature, he cannot provide the simian animal force that must rule the play's first half. The problem isn't that Mr. Quinn is not Marlon Brando but that he does not fit Stanley, as described and reacted to by the other characters. While Stanley is no abject villain, there must be an aura of danger about him--sexual danger with Blanche, physical danger with his poker-laying cronies. Even Mr. Quinn's showiest preliminary flights into rage--the hurling of a radio, the smashing of dinner dishes--seem tame. The actor must bellow to simulate a menacing presence that simply is not among his many gifts.

The rest of the cast and staging are of a piece with the stars. Frances McDormand's hearty, fleshy Stella and Mr. Converse's sincere Mitch have promise, yet we realize how underdeveloped they are when their grief-stricken reactions to Blanche's final destruction seem to come from nowhere. John Conklin's set calls attention to the awkwardness of the arena stage and substitutes nondescript tackiness for French Quarter tattiness, Williams's crucial "atmosphere of decay." The sizzle of a fetid New Orleans summer is not to be found in Curt Ostermann's Act I lighting. Michael O'Flaherty's languorous incidental jazz music and a hokily costumed, excessively malingering Mexican flower vendor serve to emphasize the lengthy, clunky waits between scenes.

"I don't want realism," says Blanche. "I want magic!" It's a formulation that can serve as a prescription for a Tennessee Williams production, if not necessarily for a life. What we have here is a *Streetcar* without that magic, without the poetry. Though one can still find the play, not only are what the Kowalskis call the "colored lights" of passion missing, but so are the shadows of what Blanche identifies as the opposite of desire, death. What falls between those two poles of existence is the ordinary stuff of realism--a genteel theatrical evening in place of a tragedy forced to rip through the night.

New York Times, March 11, 1988, sec. 3: 3.

A *Streetcar* Without Desire
Linda Winer

The photo in the ads for *A Streetcar Named Desire* has Alec Baldwin's hairy chest and arms pressed against Jessica Lange's plunging white gown, his face smashed against her neck so hard he has Brando's nose. Her head is thrown back, with her mouth slightly open and her eyes half-closed in animal ecstasy.

In truth, it never happens. The scene in the photo never happens and, more important, the passion never happens between them onstage. Although the mere proximity of the names Lange, Baldwin and Tennessee Williams seems hot enough to make smoke, the wildly anticipated revival that opened last night at the Barrymore is tasteful, reticent, and almost shockingly dull.

Gregory Mosher, in his first work since leaving the Lincoln Center

Theater, seems so determined to avoid cheap emotional cliches [*sic*] that he lets the tension drain away altogether. There are some effective moments in this handsome and stubbornly leisurely production, especially from Amy Madigan, as Stella. But we get more chemistry between her and Lange than between this Blanche DuBois and Stanley Kowalski--and the accents are somewhere between weird and downright willful.

Blanche marks Lange's stage debut. And, despite all the obvious intelligence at work here, she remains, thus far, a cinematic creature. Her voice doesn't project and, until she lets loose for the crushing climax, her acting is so internalized we keep wishing for a camera close-up.

She is, of course, fabulous looking, but her beauty seems more conventional up there--more sculpted and frozen than the unpredictably lusty one on film. This is not a fragile Blanche, which may be an interesting modern gloss on a woman Williams described as "a moth," but she's also not a terribly communicative Blanche. It's one thing to underplay and make the audience come to her; it's another to make us strain to hear her lines.

Then there is Stanley. Baldwin, so good onstage here in *Prelude to a Kiss* and *Loot,* may have gone out of his way to obliterate the memory of Marlon Brando in the role. But he has gone too far out. For starters, he has a Bronx accent--as if Stanley maybe had been raised in New York and moved to New Orleans? This is a more humorous Stanley that we've seen before-- Kowalski Lite?--reminiscent of Baldwin's comic gangster in *Married to the Mob* and a little Fred Flintstone.

Playfulness can be fun when Stanley explains the "Napoleonic code" to his wife's high-and-mighty sister Blanche, or when he fights with a stuck drawer in his dresser. Without sensual menace and animal magnetism, however, the shattering scene between Stanley and Blanche--the struggle between brute reality and fading civilization--is reduced to any old drunken rape.

Worse, this Blanche passes out before Stanley carries her to the bed, a decision that destroys any suggestion of complicity in the relationship--and undermines any grander interpretations of Blanche as the disintegration of both a woman and a society. When Stanley growls his famous "We've had this date with each other from the beginning!," there should be some hint of inexorable truth, awful as it is, to elevate the violence beyond the merely sordid. Williams, in his stage directions, said Stanley then picks up her "inert" figure. Inert is not the same as comatose--and Blanche, with her disturbing history, deserves to be appreciated as someone more than a victim.

In almost all other ways, this a doggedly straightforward production. Ben Edwards' set--an evocatively squalid apartment with New Orleans streetlife streaming through the tattered shutters--is familiar from photos of the Jo Mielziner original. Jane Greenwood's '40s costumes are flattering without being excessively retro chic. Lange and Madigan get to wear slips a lot, which both do very well.

Of the three main characters, it is Madigan's Stella who seems the most on target--almost viscerally torn between her gracious upbringing and the sexual appetites she has discovered. Madigan is the only one with a southern accent--Lange only tends to use one when flirting--but, even here, Madigan's Stella sounds more hillbilly than semi-aristocracy from a Mississippi plantation named for beautiful dreams, Belle Reve.

Madigan's too skinny to justify Blanche's comment about her being plump, just as Timothy Carhart is too slender to have been an obvious choice for Mitch, the gentleman caller who describes his massive physique. Despite that credibility glitch, Carhart is engaging as the man who almost saves Blanche from destruction. In smaller roles, James Gandolfini and Lazaro Perez are aptly raucous as Stanley's poker buddies, Matt McGrath is sweetly uneasy as the young delivery boy whom Blanche desires.

Lange's scene with the boy is deliciously neurotic and seductive, finally acknowledging a Blanche who is more than merely a sensible woman who has run out of options. Her scenes with Mitch, too, have desperation and a secret smile of coquetry--though, until her touching breakdown and acceptance of "the kindness of strangers"--she seems too hearty to be a fading flower afraid of the light.

Although Mosher is best known in New York for his biting productions of David Mamet satires, his productions of the classics at Chicago's Goodman Theater were notable for their lean, almost translucent clarity. In the lush, overripe world of Williams' poetic New Orleans, unfortunately, that impulse comes out lethargic and bland. There is atmosphere, but not much mood. Williams called this great play "a tragedy of incomprehension." Unfortunately, that has new meaning today.

New York Newsday, April 13, 1992: 45, 48.

Critical Reception
Thomas P. Adler

Within a quarter century or so of its first appearance on Broadway, *A Streetcar Named Desire's* status as one of the handful of classic works of American dramatic literature had been firmly solidified. In *A Theater Divided* (1967) Martin Gottfried, for example, would rank it along with Miller's *Death of a Salesman* "as one of the two American masterpieces of the postwar years. . . . perhaps the most romantic, poetic and sensitive play ever written for the American theater"; a few years later Jordan Miller would call it quite simply "a work as important as any other ever written for the American stage."[1] The prominent position that *Streetcar* would come to occupy could almost have been guessed, not just from the reviewers' opinions--though these were not unanimous raves without hint of criticism--but especially from the unusual seriousness and care with which they attended to Williams's second success. Finding it a richer and subtler drama than the gentler and more elegiac *The Glass Menagerie* of a few seasons earlier, they generally heaped praise upon every aspect of the production--acting, directing, design--and upon its author, whom they described as a "lyric poet" in prose (the phrase is Joseph Wood Krutch's but the judgment was echoed by others), writing in a mode that fellow playwright and novelist Irwin Shaw termed "heightened naturalism."[2]

What criticisms the early reviewers did register centered on three issues: the potentially shocking nature of Williams's material, the seemingly loose way in which he structured it, and the apparently pessimistic stance he took toward human existence. A fourth, the question of Williams's ambiguous attitude toward his two central characters, what to Brooks Atkinson was the dramatist's refusal to "take sides" and to John Mason Brown a hesitancy to pass "moral judgment"[3] at least on his heroine, was variously recorded on both the credit and debit side of the ledger; Williams undoubtedly considered it a virtue, since in his essays he recurrently praises ambiguity in characterization as one of the hallmarks of great drama. What Richard Watts saw as a deterministic point of view that hopelessly "doomed" the heroine, perhaps Williams saw as a realistic understanding of how pragmatic and utilitarian modes of thinking stand ready to dampen artistic sensitivity and condemn any hint of deviation from societal norms.

The use of a succession of cinematic scenes rather than longer acts prompted a number of early critics, such as Ward Morehouse and Robert Coleman, to conclude that the play's movement was "jerky" and "episodic"; a few others, including Louis Kronenberger, even judged it "somewhat static" and lacking in forward momentum.[4] If Williams had been self-conscious about the potential for audience disorientation over the episodic quality of *The Glass Menagerie*--to the point where he proposed that legends and images be flashed on a screen in the manner of Bertolt Brecht to help them keep their bearing-- with *Streetcar* he trusted completely in the directorial skill of Elia Kazan to blunt the episodic structure, to keep it "on the tracks in those dangerous, fast curves it made here and there."[5] Nothing he could do, however, short of totally distorting his vision, could prevent a puritanical reaction against what some saw as an undue emphasis upon the purely sensational elements in the lives of his characters. Even such a normally astute critic as George Jean Nathan, one of the chief proselytizers for Eugene O'Neill's plays, judged *Streetcar* "a theatrical shocker" rather than particularly enlightening or spiritually elevating; his demure was mild compared to that of novelist Mary McCarthy, who railed against Williams for capitalizing on "the whole classic paraphernalia of insult and injury" in the search for box-office success.[6]

Each director's interpretation of a playscript is, in a sense, an exercise in critical analysis, and the drama as realized in its initial production thus becomes the first instance of interpretive criticism of the play. Reviewers, then, are commenting not on the text itself as a literary entity but on a single version that is but one of many potential realizations of the text. In the case of *Streetcar,* Kazan's interpretation was available not only in the production as seen on stage, but also in his extensive and extremely enlightening private notebook entries written as he prepared the text for production and later published. In these, he thoroughly analyzes each of the four central figures, attempting to discover what he calls the "spine" that motivates their behavior. He also delineates what he sees as the work's theme ("the crude forces of violence, insensibility and vulgarity" crushing the representative of "light and culture"); its style (a revelation of the "subjective" or "inner life" of a character); its mode ("poetic tragedy"); and the means of maintaining a focus throughout an episodic arrangement of action ("keep each scene in terms of Blanche").[7] In *Against Interpretation* (1966) Susan Sontag takes issue with the way she feels Kazan enforced a meaning upon the text that Williams did not intend; Eric Bentley in *In Search of Theater* (1953) finds that Kazan's direction of Brando as Stanley--which has come to be seen as perhaps the most famous stage performance ever by an American actor--distorted the text by making the "tough talk" of the "brutal" Stanley simply "the mask of a suffering human soul."[8] Even Jessica Tandy, the original Blanche, came to believe that Kazan's initial production was tilted too much toward the "Stanley side of the picture."[9]

That audiences tended to identify strongly with Stanley during the first part of the play, as Kazan intended they would, is one of the points addressed by Harold Clurman, himself a renowned director of the Group Theatre, which, during the thirties and particularly in its presentations of works by Clifford Odets, came as close as perhaps any American theatrical organization ever has to reaching an ideal of ensemble acting. Clurman concluded that because of the directorial conception of Brando's role, "the play becomes the triumph of Stanley Kowalski with the collusion of the audience." Indeed, Clurman's seminal essay review, which sagely recognizes that Williams's "beautiful" and "original" work "stands very high among the creative contributions of the American theatre since 1920" and ranks "among the few worthy of a permanent place" in our national repertory, catalogs virtually all of the issues that have since concerned critics and scholars: Williams's thematic emphasis "that aspiration, sensitivity, departure from the norm are battered, bruised and disgraced in our world today"; Blanche's characterization as an artist figure, both flawed and victimized, and the necessity for audiences to be convinced of "the soundness of her values"; and finally Stanley's role as a brutish, energetic "unwitting antichrist of our time, the little man who will break the back of every effort to create a more comprehensive world in which thought and conscience, a broader humanity are expect to evolve from the old Adam."[10]

Within less than a decade and a half of the initial reviews, the high position and continued importance of *Streetcar* as an American literary/dramatic text was signaled by the publication of John Hurrell's *Two Modern American Tragedies: Reviews and Criticism of "Death of a Salesman" and "A Streetcar Named Desire"* (1961). If Hurrell's title begged the question of whether or not--and, if so, in what ways--Williams's play might be considered an example of tragic drama, Jordan Miller's introduction to *Twentieth Century Interpretations of "A Streetcar Named Desire"* (1971), a collection whose weight and substance reflect ten additional years of commentary, approaches the issue head-on. Because of Blanche's "defiant courage" in the face of an inevitable defeat brought about by "trying to survive with some shred of human dignity" in an inhospitable and even hostile world, the audience experiences, according to Miller, a sense of "tragic waste" that brings *Streetcar* "as close to genuine tragedy as any modern American drama."[11]

Although scholars such as Mary Ann Corrigan, Bert Cardullo, and Henry Schvey have, over the years, expertly addressed *Streetcar's* stylistic devices and visual imagery, in the interval between Clurman's lengthy review and now, the majority of the most substantial articles (those by Leonard Berkman and Leonard Quarino, among others) have focused on the plight of the play's heroine. Moreover, with the eighties have come a number of specifically feminist approaches, most notably in studies by Kathleen Hulley and Avea [*sic*] Vlasopolos. Hulley's semiotic reading of the text sees the two central figures in the play as writing and directing mutually exclusive theatrical texts that the other characters (and the audience) must then choose between: to privilege Stanley's text over Blanche's is to exclude everything in life "which makes art and love possible."[12] Vlasopolos's argument follows somewhat similar lines but focuses more specifically on the realm of language: Stanley's factual "language of power," though "impoverished," embodies "the dominant discourse of patriarchy." Blanche poses a threat to his "interpretive authority" by actions that are subversive of the traditional social order that victimizes and tries to render her powerless. She finally submits to another authority, this one scientific, represented by the male psychiatrist.[13]

Two of the most worthwhile book chapters on *Streetcar,* separated by twenty years, offer quite diverse mythic readings of the work, one cultural, the other classical. In *Myth and Modern American Drama* (1969) Thomas Porter focuses on Williams's handling of the dying out of the Old South through his character study of Blanche, who is both the alien "intruder" upon an "established way of life" as well as the traditional "heroine of romance." This tension is further exacerbated by the playwright's ambivalence about sex, which, to Porter's way of thinking, helps account for the play's final lack of resolution, with Williams's "Southerner . . . caught between two worlds, one gone with the wind, the other barely worth having."[14]   More recently, in *Tennessee Williams's Plays: Memory, Myth and Symbol* (1987), Judith Thompson examines in great detail allusions to classical, literary, and biblical mythology.   She discovers analogues for Blanche in Persephone, Psyche, Delilah, and Camille, and for Stanley in Dionysus; and because a curse seems to have befallen the DuBois ancestral house, a once Edenic spot has been lost and the golden age has degenerated.   Any inclusive reading of *Streetcar* will necessarily confront many of the issues raised by the earliest critics of Williams's masterwork and carried on by their successors.

NOTES

1. Martin Gottfried, *A Theater Divided: The Postwar American Stage* (Boston: Little, Brown, 1967), 250; Jordan Y. Miller, ed., *Twentieth Century Interpretations of "A Streetcar Named Desire"* (Englewood Cliffs, N. J.: Prentice-Hall, 1971), 9.

2. Joseph Wood Krutch, "Review of *Streetcar Named Desire,"* and Irwin Shaw, "Masterpiece," both in Miller, *Interpretations,* 40; 45.

3. Brooks Atkinson, *"Streetcar* Tragedy--Mr. Williams' Report on Life in New Orleans," and John Mason Brown, "Southern Discomfort," both in Miller, *Interpretations,* 32; 43.

4. Ward Morehouse, "New Hit Named *Desire,"* Robert Coleman, *Desire Streetcar* in for Long Run," and Louis Kronenberger, "A Sharp Southern Drama by Tennessee Williams," all in *New York Theatre Critics' Reviews* 8 (1947), 250-251.

5. Tennessee Williams, *Where I Live: Selected Essays,* ed. Christine R. Day and Bob Woods (New York: New Directions, 1978), 93. Hereafter cited by *Essays* and page number within the text.

6. George Jean Nathan, "The Streetcar Isn't Drawn by Pegasus," in Miller, *Interpretations,* 37; and Mary McCarthy, *Theatre Chronicles 1937-1962* (New York: Farrar, Straus, 1963), 131-35.

7. Elia Kazan, "Notebook for *A Streetcar Named Desire,"* in *Directors on Directing: A Sourcebook of the Modern Theatre,* ed. Toby Cole and Helen Krich Chinoy (Indianapolis: Bobbs Merrill, 1976), 364-66. Hereafter cited by "Notebook" and page number within the text.

8. Eric Bentley, "Better than Europe?" in *In Search of Theater* (New York: Knopf, 1953), 87.

9. Jessica Tandy, "Letter 2 November 1948," in *Tennessee Williams, Dictionary of Literary Biography Documentary Series,* vol. 4, ed. Margaret A. VanAntwerp and Sally Jones (Detroit: Gale Research, 1984), 105. Hereafter cited by Letter and page number within the text.

10. Harold Clurman, "Tennessee Williams," in *The Divine Pastime: The Theatre Essays* (New York: Macmillan, 1974), 11-12; 13-14.

11. Miller, *Interpretations,* 11-12.

12. Kathlenn Hulley, "The Fate of the Symbolic in *A Streetcar Named Desire,*" in *Themes in Drama* 4 (*Drama and Symbolism*), ed. James Redmond (Cambridge: Cambridge University Press, 1982), 96.

13. Anea [*sic*] Vlasopolos, "Authorizing History: Victimization in *A Streetcar Named Desire,*" *Theatre Journal* 38 (October 1986): 325, 326, 328, 332.

14. Thomas E. Porter, *Myth and Modern American Drama* (Detroit: Wayne State University Press, 1969), 176.

A Streetcar Named Desire, The Moth and the Lantern. Boston: Twayne, 1990: 10-15.

Summer and Smoke (1948)

Theatre: Man with a Problem
Harold Clurman

It is comforting to realize that Tennessee Williams is not a writer of hits, but a writer with a problem. His problem rises from the conflict between the quality of his sensibility and the objective material of his plots.

In *Summer and Smoke* at the Music Box (written at about the same time as *A Streetcar Named Desire*), Williams appears torn between a character and a theme. The character is observed with delicate sympathy, but the theme--too consciously articulated without being mastered--disturbs both the characterization and the play's dramatic clarity. It remains nevertheless a play whose very faults are interesting.

Alma Winemiller, the daughter of a Mississippi minister and his insane wife, is a spiritually energetic girl in love with her lifelong neighbor, Dr. John Buchanan. The young doctor is attracted by the girl's idealism, but he expresses his tenderness toward her by a harsh insistence on its sexual aspects. Shocked, the girl tries to pit her idealism against the boy's boastful sinfulness. ("You're no gentleman!" she cries--and she is right.) Alma wins the "argument" only when John's father is killed in an accident brought about by John's soiled companions. Now redeemed from his carnal course, John does not turn to his savior Alma, but instead marries a buxom little female of coarser background. Alma, in turn, converted to the doctrine of the senses (reversing the pattern of ladies from Thaïs to Sadie Thompson), now seems prepared to indulge in casual affairs.

One of the springs of Williams' inspiration is his fascination with the opposition between the old Adam which tends to keep us mired in a kind of primitive inertia, and our impulse to transcend it. In *A Streetcar Named Desire* this fascination led him almost unconsciously to a social theme: the "animal" in that play is identified with the "ordinary" American. The naturalistic details of portraiture in *Streetcar* are so right that the audience accepts and enjoys them on their own terms whether or not they follow the author's ideological intention, which, to begin with, is intuitive rather than analytic. In *Summer and Smoke* so much time is given to a conscious exposition of theme that Williams loses the specific sense of his people and to a dangerous extent our concern as spectators.

The thematic base of *Summer and Smoke* is rendered ambiguous by being stated through characters that do not properly embody the forces the play is supposed to pit against each other. Is Alma Winemiller "sexually repressed" because of her overreliance on her spiritual nature? Not really, for she loves John Buchanan with an eagerness and a shyness that are both entirely normal in themselves. That she should be repelled by his crudity is also normal. That she should be presented as the champion of the "soul" and he as advocate for the "flesh" is a confusion that derives from the author's inability to know when he is creating character and when he is interfering with the characters by talking--sometimes a little foolishly--in their stead.

The ancient dispute about the polarity of body and soul is mostly a Puritan obsession and a consequence of the abuse of words induced by faulty religious education. Of the two characters in the play, the man, who rationalizes his promiscuity on intellectual grounds, is surely the more Puritan, one might even go so far as to say the more "repressed" and the less normal. His sexual activity does not strike one as a manifestation of natural exuberance but of moral defiance.

It would have been perfectly proper for Williams to present the situation in this light. In that case the play might have suggested that so many American men are Puritans in revolt against themselves that they drive their women to licentiousness. But perhaps a residue of Puritanism in the author prevented him from knowing this.

As a result the play alternates between psychoanalytic hints (never artistically convincing) and what becomes--aside from several fine passages which reveal his natural endowments as a poet-playwright--an almost trite and at moments badly constructed plot line. Fragments of true feeling have been attenuated and vitiated by the author's failure to find a proper form for them, to think his problem through.

It is the function of the director of a play as subtly difficult as *Summer and Smoke* to articulate a coherent interpretation which the audience can actually *see*. It is evident that such an interpretation never existed in regard to this play. The production, in fact, provides an example of how a group of talented people, when there is not firm hand to guide them, may contribute to a play wholeheartedly but without valid effect. As Alma Winemiller, Margaret Phillips, an actress of considerable quality and ability, has been permitted or encouraged by the director, Margo Jones, to overstress such secondary characteristics as a nervous laugh, an affected speech, super-refinement of manner, at the expense of the main motive of the character, which should be her innate womanly instincts. Tod Andrews as John Buchanan is earnest as well as handsome, but he has been given no real characterization.

Jo Mielziner's setting is not only as pretty as can be, but an honest attempt to capture the play's special style. The setting is none the less dramatically unsuccessful because it restricts the free movement essential to the play, and its stylization ends by being almost more confining to the imagination than a realistic set. What would be best would be practically no set at all.

New Republic, October 25, 1948: 25-26.

Second Chance, *Summer and Smoke* Put On in Sheridan Square
Brooks Atkinson

Thanks to the persistence of the Loft Players in Sheridan Square, Tennessee Williams' *Summer and Smoke* is having a second chance. This is a dispensation devoutly to be wished for both the play and the players. During the past two seasons the Loft Players have been performing the rites of drama in what used to be known as the Greenwich Village Inn, where for years the public valiantly tried to escape boredom at night. Circle in the Square, as the premises are now described, is an arena theatre three-quarters round. That is, the audience sits on three side of the playing area.

Although Mr. Williams did not write *Summer and Smoke* for central staging, it stirred the hearts of audiences most completely in Margo Jones' Theatre in the Round in Dallas, where it was first produced in 1947, and it may very well have the same success now in Sheridan Square. A poignantly intimate play that penetrates deep into the souls of two bewildered young people, it burns with a small flame that is most illuminating and melting in a small area where people come together on an informal basis. As Al Hirschfeld, the bearded caricaturist, remarked on the opening night: "It seems to be written for each person as an individual." The communication between the characters and the theatregoer is direct and immediate, like a letter marked "personal."

No one knows exactly why *Summer and Smoke* did not succeed on Broadway in 1948. Although Jo Mielziner's abstract setting was beautiful and in accordance with the author's instructions, perhaps it was too elaborate. Perhaps the characters never really inhabited it, as they did the simpler, cozier setting for *A Streetcar Named Desire.* Perhaps the Music Box Theatre was too large for such a sensitive play. The audiences may have been expecting something bolder and more violent.

For *A Streetcar Named Desire* was on the boards at the same time, pitilessly chronicling the torture and madness of Blanche du Bois and the shattering brutishness of Stanley Kowalski. That play, as well as the performance of it, was overpowering. The clash of characters was shrill and shocking. In point of fact, Mr. Williams wrote *Summer and Smoke* and *A Streetcar Named Desire* coincidentally--dropping one to work on the other when he struck a snag. But *A Streetcar Named Desire* was produced in New York before *Summer and Smoke*; and when *Summer and Smoke* came along about ten months later, it may have suggested to Broadway audiences that Mr. Williams was trying to follow a strong play with one that was weaker. These are some of the intangibles that may have contributed to the financial failure of *Summer and Smoke* four years ago.

But to some of us it remains the finer piece of work. It contains one violent episode when the senior Dr. Buchanan is fatally shot by a drunken gambler. That is a harrowing, gratuitous episode which vividly epitomizes the carelessness and injustice of the universe. It reverses the twin themes of the drama. But in contrast with the people of *A Streetcar Named Desire,* the chief characters of *Summer and Smoke* are gentler and more aware. Although they are unable to change the course of history, they know what is happening to them. They are helpless, but they are also intelligent and perceptive.

Some theatregoers complained that *A Streetcar Named Desire* could not be a genuine tragedy because Blanche Du Bois lacked the spiritual stature of a tragic figure. To see *Summer and Smoke* again is to realize that the complaint is well founded. For Alma Winemiller, the minister's daughter and the singing teacher of Glorious Hill, Miss., is a person of real stature. In terms of the narrow life she has had, there is more than a touch of nobility in her spirit.

Some of the townsfolk regard her as silly and affected. She is very serious about culture; her social manners are conventional and insipid. But her experience accounts for her timid gentility. Ever since her mother became a malicious imbecile when Alma was still in high school, Alma has had to manage the rectory and take over the social and household duties that would normally belong to the minister's wife, and she has also had to put up with her mother's tantrums and crotchets. To have done all this and at the same time to have preserved her ideals, self-respect and sweetness of character is the measure of her stature as a person.

She has great spiritual strength. All her life she has been hopelessly in love with Dr. Buchanan's son next door--young Dr. John, the neighbors call him. He is extraordinarily brilliant, but he has no character. Alma's unswerving devotion to him puts her in a humiliating position, she is so pallid by comparison, her education has been so meager and her ideas are so stuffy. She is a small-town spinster foolishly eating out her heart for a dazzling man of the world. But before the play is over he knows that she is the stronger and the more enlightened of the two and that her maidenly ideals are the working principles of civilized people. Her personal strength and her personal faith triumph in him.

If *Summer and Smoke* were a romance, it would end happily, for Alma remakes young Dr. John in the image of her dreams. But Mr. Williams as a writer does not believe in formal literary solutions. His experience and observation have not convinced him that life conforms to literary patterns. Some nebulous fate has hung over the heads of his two chief characters since they were children, and Mr. Williams does not intrude on it. Writing with understanding and compassion, and yet from a cool distance, he has composed a deeply moving tone poem that shows characters going through a slow rigadoon against the indifference of nature. Out of the most humdrum materials, he has created a piece of memorable tragic literature.

On the whole, the performance at the Circle in the Square is admirable. Keith Cuerden's austere settings, reduced to bare essences, convey the detached point of view of the play; and the lighting by Noah Kalkut and Robert Randall evokes the same fond though impersonal mood. To one theatregoer, José Quintero's direction, especially in the preliminary scenes, might be still more contemplative and reserved. It is a little restless at first, marred with irrelevant motion, as though Mr. Quintero did not quite have the courage to look on from Mr. Williams's distance.

But Mr. Quintero has formed the essential parts of the story into a coherent, tender performance. Lee Richards' gentle but willful portrait of young Dr. John, headstrong but rational, is a first-rate piece of acting. And Geraldine Page's portrait of Alma catches Alma' valor and nobility under the nervous exterior of a small-town spinster. From every point of view, *Summer and Smoke* is a beautifully wrought drama. It cuts sharply into the essence of the truth. Theatregoers deserve this second chance at a noble work of art.

New York Times, May 4, 1952, sec. 2: 1.

Tennessee Williams and Jo Mielziner: The Memory Plays
Harry W. Smith

Yes, I have tricks in my pocket, I have things up my sleeve. But I am the opposite of a stage magician. He gives you illusion that has the appearance of truth. I give you truth in the pleasant disguise of illusion.

--*The Glass Menagerie*

The conventional reliance upon "memory," the lyric subtleties of both writing and scenery, and the ubiquitous mood of emotional despair characterize three early Tennessee Williams plays--*The Glass Menagerie, A Streetcar Named Desire,* and *Summer and Smoke*--and set them apart from the less "poetic" currents in the Williams canon. The plays are remarkably similar in organic configuration; their shape and texture reveal a theatrical form of considerable distinction. Although they gained articulate theatrical expression under three different directors, the scenery for all three was designed (in the "Broadway" productions) by Jo Mielziner, whose ideas have continued to influence subsequent productions. The unique fusion of the Williams-Mielziner artistry has give the American drama a consummate theatre aesthetic: a vision of dramatic life most subtle in its use of human values and most articulate in its visual definition of mood. This study is an effort to examine and perhaps codify some elements of that aesthetic, and to consider their contributions to the ultimate dramatic effect.

The Glass Menagerie is set in Tom Wingfield's memory, and the memory of each participant plays a significant part in defining the dramatic action. Tom tells the story with all the selective lapses of his own guilt-ridden memory. Amanda is living largely in the world of her memories of Blue Mountain. The memory of Jim O'Connor's high school accomplishments exacerbates Laura's traumatic encounters with reality. Furthermore, memory, both as a motive in the characterization and as a dramatic convention of presentation, is a significant element in the play's structure.

"The play is memory," says Tom Wingfield, and "being a memory play, it is . . . not realistic."[1] The motive for the Williams-Mielziner style is rooted in its disavowal of "realism." The "plastic theatre" hailed by Williams in the introduction to *The Glass Menagerie* suggests his scenic approach, an approach his designer considers "the most sensitive" of any American, playwright,[2] but beyond an almost casual use of the word "poetic," Williams is not very specific about labeling his scenic concepts. The concept of memory appears to be the key to a convention. According to stage directions, "The scene is memory and is therefore nonrealistic. Memory takes a lot of poetic license. It omits some details; others are exaggerated, according to the emotional value of the articles it touches, for memory is seated predominantly in the heart. The interior is therefore rather dim and poetic." The use of the word *therefore* implies that the concepts of *memory, nonrealistic, dim,* and *poetic* are related, if not equated, in the Williams aesthetic hypothesis. The scenery, as designed by Mielziner, reflects all four of these concepts. It presents visual images of the St. Louis tenement apartment and its shabby surroundings as if lifted right from the memory--with memory's selection, distortion, and diffusion--of Tom Wingfield. The images strike a largely emotional response--"seated predominantly in the heart"--and when collected, create an impression of Williams' dramatic world of illusion.

In the beginning of the play, Tom Wingfield addresses the audience directly, setting the play in the larger world context. As his opening speech develops, the world of the play is abridged progressively to the limits of the slum apartment where Tom's story takes place; the grim tenement wall becomes transparent, then disappears entirely into the flies, not to be lowered again until the end of the play. Beginning with this first transparency, poetic license is manifest in the selection and diffusion of visual scenic elements. Only those elements pertinent to Tom's recollections are translated into scenery and light. Irrelevant details are eliminated; more important ones are exaggerated. The most important furnishings described are the glass menagerie of the title, the phonograph, and the larger-than-life-size portrait of the long departed father. All these items have a strong emotional connection with the members of the family, and are used to underscore peaks of emotional intensity in the development of the play's action. The first such peak occurs when Tom is leaving the house after the "El Diablo" speech in Scene Three: Tom throws his jacket into the menagerie, scattering glass animals all over the floor. Used here to symbolize the rift that Tom will bring to the family, the animals enhance a tender pathetic moment in the relationship of the characters. Further, the menagerie is used spatially as a frequent point of refuge and identification for Laura. Later in the play, when Laura suggests to Jim that the broken unicorn should be happier now that he is no longer "different," it is a pointed reference to her own emotional situation.

The illuminated portrait of the elder Wingfield, a living, grinning, statement of the escape theme, is used in the play as a visual *leitmotif* for the dread specter of inevitable family disintegration: Tom's ultimate departure from the scene in the manner of his father. The portrait is described by Tom in his opening monologue: "There is a fifth character in the play who doesn't appear except in this larger-than-life-size photograph over the mantel. This is our father who left us a long time ago." Williams wanted exactly that: a larger-than-life-size photograph. The designer felt that such a large portrait might tend to monopolize the audience's attention, and that the dramatic point could be made just as effectively with a picture of smaller size.[3] Ultimately, a highly retouched photograph of the actor playing Tom, slightly smaller than life size, was used. These two properties, together with the phonograph, are important elements in the play's scenic texture, as well as in its formal structure.

The texture of *The Glass Menagerie* might be described as opalescent. Its form is fluid. The episodes flow into one another like a lap dissolve in the movies, and the "language flows with carefully selected images of light and shadow arranged in rhythmic prose."[4] The delicate highlights, such as the menagerie and portrait, are accented in the gloom. The use of highlight and shadow enhances the images of the characters. Laura is suffused with a light of "pristine clarity" similar to that emanating from her little glass animals; her glass unicorn "loves the light," the light "shines right through him." The general lighting is "dim," says the playwright in the stage directions, "in keeping with the atmosphere of memory." Laura's light is compared to the saintly radiance of an El Greco painting, and is in shimmering relief against the tawdry darkness of the apartment and the alley. The intent is undoubtedly to make Laura as out of place visually as she is emotionally.

At the end of the play, scenery and light again combine to form an emotional image. When Tom leaves the apartment after the Gentleman Caller episode, he grips the rail of the fire escape as if it were a ship headed into the wind, his face in a tiny spot of light which isolates him in the darkness. Simultaneously, Amanda and Laura silently console each other in a pool of flickering candlelight, imprisoned within a harsh perimeter of reluctant self-perception. Near the end of Tom's speech, the transparent tenement wall comes down, and Tom is irretrievably separated from his mother and sister. Laura extinguishes the candles and vanishes from sight, remaining only as a frequently recurring guilt symbol for the fleeing Tom.

The realization on the stage of the play's formal unity was accomplished largely through its visual imagery. The concepts of *memory, nonrealistic, dim* and *poetic,* in Williams' stage directions, are realized by Jo Mielziner in the scenery and lighting. The visual economy of the design contributes greatly to the mood and the absence of fussy detail in decoration suggests the process of memory. The pattern on the wall is barely discernible. The stage is generally dark except for the shafts of light illuminating specific areas, and the only properties visible on the stage are those actually used or referred to. Since the play is being presented through Tom's memories, the audience sees only that which happens to be impressed on Tom's reflective consciousness. The audience sees and hears some elements in much detail--the activity of the Paradise Dance Hall, for example--which have little to do with the play's story, but for some reason are remembered by Tom and serve dramatically only to enhance the mood. Other elements are left almost wholly to imagination.

The design offers more to the form of the play, however, than an acute sense of visual aesthetics and clever effects. There are two devices inherent in the dramaturgy which are interesting in view of their effect on the theatrical form of this play. The first device is the portrait of the father already mentioned. The second device is a Brechtian projection arrangement which was originally written into the script but never used in production. Mielziner felt that the screen, like the oversize portrait, would be distracting; acknowledging its redundance, Williams avers that "the extraordinary power of Miss Laurette Taylor's acting made it suitable to have the utmost simplicity in the physical production."[5] The organic contribution to the drama (in the form of the deletion of the screen and the reduction in scale of the portrait) is as typical of Mielziner's work for the theatre as the visual style of his designs.

And his visual style is nowhere better assimilated than in the dramatic shape of *The Glass Menagerie*. The layers of gauze provide veils of memory through which the audience sees the play. The texture of the scenery is the texture of the play: a hazy, dreary, gloomy ground, patterned by limpid emotional highlights. The purity of the glass animals, the brilliant grin of the father's portrait, the shafts of light piercing the dull suspended gloom highlight the patina which defines the play's form. The delicate images with which the characters are defined and the emotional interrelationship evolved by them state in word and action the play's basic form, a mood of exquisite pathos. The precision with which the mood is defined on the stage in scenery and lighting serves to suspend that form visually--and to lend fundamental eloquence to the play's method of communication. The attempted theatrical effect is obvious: under the terms of Williams' artistic aims and objectives, the psychological and emotional place of the drama (Tom's memory) is more important than any more literal interpretation of locale.

In *A Streetcar Named Desire*, the South emerges very definitely as the place of the drama; the South in *The Glass Menagerie* was present only as a point of view and in Amanda's dreams of Blue Mountain. The specific location of *A Streetcar Named Desire* is interesting for its curious blend of the old and the new elements which contribute to the shape of the modern South. Desire and Elysian Fields are real New Orleans streets. The neighborhood in which the Kowalski apartment is located is newer than the Old Quarter familiar to tourists, older than the more elegant, more "modern," suburban areas. Its people belong neither to the Creole culture of old New Orleans nor to the American aristocracy of suburban "middle" and professional classes. It is a near-slum neighborhood, a nether-land of railroad tracks, warehouses, and other shabby elements of a commercial culture. Such a juxtaposition of aesthetic values is a major element in this play's formal unity, and the point is made in the scenery. According to the stage directions, "It is first dark of an evening in May. The sky that shows around the dim white building is a peculiarly tender blue, almost a turquoise, which invests the scene with a kind of lyricism and gracefully attenuates the atmosphere of decay."[6]

Both the description of the setting by Williams and the scenery designed by Mielziner invest the dilapidated neighborhood with a lyric charm not always observable in this particular district of New Orleans. Such otherwise prosaic scenic elements as the back alleys in St. Louis and the L. & N. tracks in New Orleans are elevated almost to the level of elegance when seen through the veils of memory or illusion, or through the scrim of a Mielziner setting. The scenery for *A Streetcar Named Desire* was made almost entirely of scrim. The environment was established by using three levels of transparency: The upstage wall of the apartment, backed by a scrim drop depicting the street area, and further upstage, a painted drop illustrating the L. & N. tracks. The apartment of *The Glass Menagerie* was represented with a modicum of

architectural logic (straight lines, square corners, and the like) and a considerable degree of aesthetic selectivity. The Kowalski apartment in *A Streetcar
Named Desire* reveals even less strict adherence to physical principles. The
architectural detail is frankly distorted. No attempt is made to suggest that
walls and windows are real. The lines are wavy and indistinct, contributing
to the effect of shabbiness and squalor. John Mason Brown speaks of the set's
"physical grubbiness which remains a match for the emotional dilapidation of
some of the characters it houses."[7]

The aesthetic contrast here assumes a broader scope than had similar
effects in *The Glass Menagerie*. The heroine is given a saintly halo. The
psychological harassment of Blanche by her pitiless "varsouviana," the
physical violation of a tender, fragile creature, and the vulgarity of an alien
social *milieu* are all dramatically couched in a lyricism of language and visual
style. "The final impression," says Joseph Wood Krutch, "is, surprisingly
enough, not of sensationalism but of subtlety."[8]

Between the beginning of the play with its first dark turquoise sky and
the beginning of Scene Three, the mood and atmosphere of the play have
changed--according to the stage directions--from one of lyric beauty to a mood
much more harsh:

> There is a picture of Van Gogh's of a billiard-parlor at night. The
> kitchen now suggests that sort of lurid nocturnal brilliance, the raw colors
> of childhood's spectrum. Over the yellow linoleum of the kitchen table
> hangs an electric bulb with a vivid green glass shade. The poker players
> . . . wear colored shirts, solid blues, a purple, a red-and-white check, a
> light green, and they are at the peak of their physical manhood, as coarse
> and direct and powerful as the primary colors. There are vivid slices of
> watermelon on the table, whiskey bottles and glasses.

The development of action in the first two scenes in the play exposes an
essential quality in each character which subsequently leads to the emotional
crisis: Stella's submissiveness to her husband, Stanley's monumental self-
interest, and Blanche's hysterical instability. The visual environment in which
they are brought together is defined by the poetically-rendered transparent
walls; the walls make a statement about character as they underscore the
fragile inability of Blanche to exist in her new surroundings.

The lighting in *A Streetcar Named Desire*, more than in *The Glass
Menagerie*, is used as a function of the design, and as an element in the
overall visual form of the play. The "dramatic" use of the light in *The Glass
Menagerie* is primarily that of underscoring, emphasizing, or isolating other
dramatic values; a visual portrait of a psychological or emotional moment, a
particular speech, or a specific piece of business. In *A Streetcar Named
Desire*, however, lighting assumes a dramatic function of its own, not only in

support of other elements but also as comment on theme-statement in itself. The "raw, lurid" atmosphere of the kitchen and the reflections on the walls in Scene Eleven are visual images of Blanche's transition into complete insanity. Her final neurotic development is heralded specifically in images of light: Stanley rips her oriental lantern (the symbol of her illusions) from the light fixture, leaving a bare bulb, and bluntly extends the tattered lantern to the stunned Blanche. When her anxiety subsides, the lurid reflections fade from the walls. The symbolic value of Blanche's follow spot serves further to isolate her from her environment. Blanche's own announcement to Mitch in Scene Five that "soft people have got to shimmer and glow" is but a verbal reinforcement of the luminous isolation which is her image throughout the play. The isolation is not merely for visual emphasis, like the star's follow spot in a musical, but rather a part of her characterization--a visible statement of her spiritual isolation, her ostracism from the world of reality. Her memory speeches in Scene Six are spoken in a spot of intense blue light, light as intense as the yellows and red of the poker night had been. The lurid yellow poker light returns at the beginning of Scene Eleven, as if the contrast in lighting were deliberately mocking Blanche's own tragedy.

The lighting in *A Streetcar Named Desire* is further contrasted with that of *The Glass Menagerie* in that it is harsher, richer, more vivid. *The Glass Menagerie* had been expressed in values of tenuous clarity superimposed on a ground of hazy darkness, almost pallid in its definition of Laura's purity. Of *A Streetcar Named Desire,* however, Mielziner has said that "the play is colorful and vivid: there is nothing pallid about it in characterization or action and it therefore could not be pallid in the lighting."[9] The delicate transformation of violence and brutality into the subtle dramatic values so much appreciated by the critics is due in great part to the handling of light both as a design element itself and as a catalyst in the synthesis of others. Mielziner speaks of the rape in Scene Ten: "Back lighting was used to soften the shock and reduce the effect of violence; the lighting thus both revealed and concealed form and action alternately, and in so doing decreased the brutality and heightened the artistry of the scene."[10] Similarly, other scenes of violence and action more or less extraneous to the plot itself are revealed in the corridor upstage of the apartment's transparent wall. These scenes are etched in sharp cross-lighting which provides extreme plasticity and contrast punctuated by deep shadows. Even the more languid scenes of repose depend to a great extent on sharp contrasts of light and shadow. Scene Eight is introduced with these stage directions: "The view through the big windows is fading gradually into a still-golden dusk. A torch of sunlight blazes on the side of a big water-tank or oil-drum across the empty lot toward the business district which is now pierced by pinpoints of lighted windows or windows reflecting the sunset."

The view just described, of course, is seen through the transparent apartment wall at least one scrim drop. The outlines of architectural detail appear overlaid on the colorful picture in a romantic delicacy of line. The patterns of the wrought iron detail work, the curves of the spiral staircase, and the loosely sketched windows with shutters akimbo, seen in strong chiaroscuro relief, establish the visual effect of a filigree in black. The overall image of the world of the play is one of contrasts between the lyric of illusion and the cacophony of reality. The subject matter of the play--both literary and visual subject matter--is almost unbearably unpleasant. It is expressed, however, in a style of communication described as subtle and lyrical. The style invests the play with a charm and delicacy not inherent in the subject matter, and the play is therefore more valid as theatrical expression. It is an intense, poetic heightening of the reality of Williams' dramatic world.

"The concept of a design," says the playwright, "grows out of reading a play."[11] A reading of *Summer and Smoke* reveals a series of scenic images similar in concept to those in *The Glass Menagerie* and *A Streetcar Named Desire,* but more universal in dramatic scope. Where the portrait of Mr. Wingfield and the glass menagerie had been specifically and personally related to Amanda, Tom, and Laura, and had little or no relationship to anyone outside the family, the *Summer and Smoke* symbols are much broader and more inclusive of the state of man. The stone angel named "Eternity" and the illuminated anatomy chart transcend the particular problems of John and Alma. Moreover, the texture of this play is the most highly refined, the most completely distilled in the Williams canon. It reveals a more intricate pattern of emotional filigree than the translucent tissue of *The Glass Menagerie* or the gaudy kaleidoscope of *A Streetcar Named Desire.* There is a certain regularity, or formality, to the characterization and the action. The action of the play is, in fact, a ritual pattern described by Alma in Scene Eleven: "Like two people exchanging a call on each other at the same time, and each one finding the other gone out, the door locked against him and no one to answer the bell!" By the end of the play, John has given up his "evil ways" and settled down; Alma has decided to investigate the pleasures of the flesh. The ritual pattern is accomplished, complete with accompanying character mutations, and Alma has gone the way of all Williams heroines. This ritual is the primary progression of action in the play and it is symbolized by the two major scenic devices: the stone angel and the illuminated anatomy chart.

Summer and Smoke was first produced by Margo Jones in her arena theatre in Dallas, virtually without scenery. When a Broadway production was contemplated, Mielziner was dispatched to Texas to decide whether or not the play could survive the journey to New York. At least one critic had definite reservations. Brooks Atkinson, staunch Williams defender, was afraid that the play's "buoyant loveliness might disappear into the flyloft" when translated to a Broadway proscenium style. Mielziner's problem in Dallas was therefore to appraise the value of scenery to a play whose first production has been conceived without it.[12] The play, according to some critics, did not travel well.

Mielziner's scenery, however, won unanimous critical acclaim in the New York production.

The structural definition of the scenery underscores the form of the play. As Williams had likened certain moments in *A Streetcar Named Desire* to a painting by Van Gogh, his stage directions suggest that the skeletonized walls of the *Summer and Smoke* set resemble Chirico's painting "Conversation Among the Ruins." These fragmentary walls are to be set against the sky of intense blue (compared by Williams to a Renaissance religious painting) which is obviously intended to be the most important scenic element. The sky is always visible. The statement in the stage directions that "in fact there are no really interior scenes" expresses a fundamental scenic concept of the play: the constant, unvarying relationship of the two houses, watched over by the angel. This is the play's visual frame of reference. While each house may be darkened or illuminated many times during the action for dramatic or theatrical reasons of emphasis, there is always a broad expanse of sky, encompassing both houses and the angel (and once, even a secluded arbor on the banks of Moon Lake) in a visual pattern which frames and emphasizes the emotional patterns in the play.

On an emotionally symbolic as well as theatrically symbolic level, John and Alma just *pretend* to open doors for each other. There are no doors between them, just as there are no doors in the Mielziner setting. The play represents sixteen years in the lives of the participants during which they attempt sincerely to establish some mode of communication. But the attempt is vain, for the anatomy chart and the stone angel maintain a stoic indifference to each other, as if they were the alter egos of the characters they represent.

In Scene Eleven, when Alma addresses the anatomy chart in a prayerful stance (eyes closed, hands clasped), it is too late for her to appreciate the real invisibility of the rectory walls--for years she had etched them on her soul as clearly as Mielziner had etched them against the sky. At the end of the play, when Mr. Kramer appears and invites her (at her suggestion) to Moon Lake Casino, it is as if her prayers to the anatomy chart had been answered. She salutes the angel and then the audience in a valedictory gesture of fatal accomplishment. The scene fades and the light lingers, for a while, on the angel.

With this production, the development of the Williams-Mielziner style becomes fully apparent, although it had been three productions and four years in the making. The affinity between the two men's aesthetic expression seems to have taken visible shape; Mielziner had designed for this production a "glorious setting of lightly penciled lines as curved and airy as the writing."[13] The play's "buoyant loveliness," rather than being lost in the flyloft, is very carefully drawn into the scenery.

As the texture of *Summer and Smoke* is the most highly distilled, so is its scenery the most mannered of the three memory sets. The logical values of

The Glass Menagerie's setting which had given way to the loosely sketched erratic tracing of *A Streetcar Named Desire* now progress to a highly mannered filigree of definite regularity. The form is delineated in the same manner: skeletal outlines of architecture in silhouette against a background of subtle lyric beauty. The style with which the Victorian Gothic houses are drawn is one of meticulous refinement; the lines are ordered, regular, and impeccably clean. They gleam with the metallic glint of purity.

The three memory plays possess certain basic scenic similarities once referred to an "Mielziner tricks."[14] Mielziner states that his use of translucent and transparent walls was not just a "trick," but a true reflection of the contemporary playwright's concern for the "inner Man."[15] Mielziner further elaborates on Williams' eye for the visual elements of the drama--suggesting that all scene design students study Williams' production notes for *Summer and Smoke*. It appears that Mielziner, who is closely identified with the use of scrims and transparencies, found inspiration in Williams' stage directions. He complimented Williams' understanding of the stage, in terms of the technology: If Williams had written before the development of transparent and translucent scenery, he probably would have invented it. Writers now can count on "free, unconfined staging of their stories."[16]

These three Williams plays were written in final form before submittal to producers, directors, and designers. And in these plays, Williams has described the *place* of the drama, more than the stage setting. The design process in these plays moves from the author's concept in the writing through the processing by a designer whose visual and technical style is particularly suitable to the concept.

In subsequent plays, particularly when dealing with Mielziner and director Elia Kazan, Williams began to offer his collaborators earlier drafts of his plays. The well-known instance of *Cat on a Hot Tin Roof,* with its two last acts, is a case in point. The designer's influence on the final form was significant; the open, or thrust stage was *not* a literal translation of the descriptions in the early drafts. Moreover, some Williams plays of his fifties period were designed by others. In both cases, the visual style of the stage productions changed perceptibly from that of the first three plays.

Largely through Mielziner's growing interest in a new style--"thrusting" the plays out into the audience--such plays as *Cat on a Hot Tin Roof, Sweet Bird of Youth,* and *The Milk Train Doesn't Stop Here Any More* [sic] relied less on the "memory" style characterized by layers of scrim and took on a more "open" arrangement, with the use of thrusts and raked platforms.[17]

Beyond specific changes such as those in *The Glass Menagerie,* Mielziner's influence on the form of Williams' plays was a symbiotic one: Williams could write disappearing walls and multiple layers of illusion because Mielziner could deliver them. The abstract terms used by Williams in his early plays could find capable stage expression in Mielziner's scrims and lights.

NOTES

1. Tennessee Williams, *The Glass Menagerie* (New York: New Directions, 1949), p. 3. Unless otherwise indicated, all subsequent references to dialogue or stage directions are to the New Directions editions of Williams' plays.

2. Interview with Jo Mielziner, November, 1970.

3. Alva Johnston, "Aider and Abettor," *The New Yorker,* October 30, 1948, p. 38.

4. Allan Lewis, *The Contemporary Theatre* (New York: Crown Publishers, 1962): p. 290.

5. Williams, *The Glass Menagerie,* x.

6. Williams, *A Streetcar Named Desire* (New York: New Directions, 1947), p. 9.

7. John Mason Brown, review of *A Streetcar Named Desire, Saturday Review,* December 27, 1947, p. 22.

8. Joseph Wood Krutch, review of *A Streetcar Named Desire, Nation* December 20, 1947, p. 686.

9. Jo Mielziner quoted in Randolph Goodman, *Drama on Stage* (New York: Holt, Rinehart, and Winston, 1961), p. 313.

10. *Ibid.*

11. Williams, *Summer and Smoke* (New York: New Directions, 1948), p. 9.

12. Nancy M. Tischler, *Tennessee Williams: Rebellious Puritan* (New York: The Citadel Press, 1961), p. 156.

13. Brooks Atkinson, review of *Summer and Smoke, The New York Times,* October 7, 1948, p. 33.

14. George Jean Nathan, *Theatre Book of the Year: 1948-49* (New York: Alfred A. Knopf, 1949), p. 115.

15. Mielziner, *Designing for the Theatre* (New York: Athaneum, 1965), p. 124.

16. *Ibid.*, 141.

17. Jo Mielziner, letter to the author, November 1970.

Theatre Survey, 23 (1982): 223-235.

The Rose Tattoo (1951)

The Rose Tattoo
William H. Beyer

We eagerly awaited the opening of Tennessee Williams's new play, *The Rose Tattoo,* since with three of his earlier plays, *The Glass Menagerie, Summer and Smoke,* and *A Streetcar Named Desire,* Williams has revealed himself to be an original theatre artist with a unique technical approach and a dramatic flair for incisive, illuminating character portrayal and absorbing narrative. The veracity and pertinence of his characterizations permit him to expand his themes to the point where a significant social comment is implied, which, like his characters, is inevitably psychologically sound, dramatically logical, and instrumental in giving his plays stature. However, his leading women have all been neurotics of the decadent Southern aristocracy, and so we had begun to wonder whether the man had but one string to his fiddle. *The Rose Tattoo,* we are happy to report, insofar as sheer entertainment goes, in Williams at his best. Once more he has created stunning characters that vibrate with life completely within their respective theatrical dimensions. He has given the narrative warmth, vigor, lusty comedy, tenderness, and poignance in the subtleties of human relations. In fact, the vitality of his people and their emotional snarls and peccadillos are of such intensity that they considerably overcome the play's footloose, rambling dramatic structure. It opens in an aimless and awkward manner, most insecure and unskilled, swings suddenly into a compelling sequence, and achieves form and impact when the plight of the characters automatically brings the much belabored Aristotelian unities into play, then bogs down in the climactic last-act scene of the telephone, resolving itself to an unnecessarily gauche note in conclusion. However, by this time we have become so captivated by the leading woman, her lover, and the two young people, as well as by Williams's fun, fervor, and fancy in dialogue, that the obvious technical shortcomings seem of little moment.

The Rose Tattoo--what is it? The rose is here used as a symbol of the physical love of lovers realized to the point of idealization. The play is laid in a Sicilian-American Gulf Coast colony, and the story centers on Serafina Delle Rose. Serafina is an uneducated widow of peasant origin, a lusty, vain, and thoroughly female primitive, who strives valiantly though unkempt and in deshabille [*sic*], for three years to preserve the glory of love-life memory with which her husband has blessed her, and only her--her false but fond delusion. The women of the neighborhood wink, smirk, and whisper that this is all nonsense, but they dare not intrude on the obsession which isolates her in her self-imposed retirement. Worshipfully she enshrines the urn containing her husband's ashes beside her beloved Madonna. Likewise she cherishes the memory of the rose tattooed on her husband's chest, and a matching rose, a vision, which appeared on her breast the night she conceived the child she loses at the time of her husband's fatal motor accident. He, while ostensibly a banana-truck driver, was engaged in transporting illicit goods, the bananas serving only as a "front." While struggling as a seamstress to support herself and her fifteen-year-old daughter, Rosa, Serafina is equally devoted to preserving Rosa's virtue when she falls blindly in love with a local sailor home on leave. Serafina instinctively distrusts the sailor, corners him, and forces the lad to swear by the Virgin he will respect Rosa's virtue. When he shamefacedly confesses that he, too, is a virgin, it is a matter of indifference to the skeptical Serafina and, later, to the palpitating Rosa. She, like Mama, is whole hog or nothing, and brashly insists that nature take its course. It does--with Rosa and her sailor, and with Mama and a second truck driver-- another banana man, not illicit, this one. The man appears at the psychological moment when Serafina's unwillingness to concede her husband's infidelity drives her into an hysterical frenzy verging on madness. He is a vigorous, ingratiating, and awkward fellow, without a woman of his own and beset by three resolutely wacky dependents. The two are a pair, being mutually volatile and of mercurial temperament. His desperate loneliness and honesty bemuse and finally overpower the frustrated Serafina, and, convinced at last of her husband's faithlessness, she smashes the urn containing his ashes, accepts her new lover, and is restored to normalcy. He succeeds with her largely because he hurries off to get a rose tattooed on his chest which he uses as a decoy, and most successfully. Once more Serafina has a new vision and knows she has conceived again, so they will be married and en rapport morally, too, thus satisfying everyone. Early in the play, her husband's inamorata, not to be outdone, had had a rose tattooed there, too. However, it develops she works at a night-joint on the waterfront, and so here the rose's significance is obviously literal--not visionary--as quite possibly will be that of Rosa and/or the sailor--we never learn.

Well, here we have Williams writing a folk comedy in which he brings the same devotion and understanding to his characters he brought to the psychopathic women of his earlier plays--a redeeming factor, for it made these social misfits sympathetic and their struggles for adjustment pitiful and moving.   Serafina is a terrific role and is roundly played by Maureen Stapleton--both literally and technically--with wonderful skill, cordiality, and conviction.   Do not think for a moment that Williams has abandoned his study of the abnormally obsessed.   In this ignorant, often stupid, peasant woman, with all her loyalty, sensuousness, and earthy preoccupation with natural rhythms, plus her slovenly femininity and her conflict with primitive superstition and the mores of the church, she is another obsessed Williams leading woman.   Her fixation forces her masochistically into a false evaluation of facts and a self-inflicted isolation which constitute the core of the drama. While beset with her delusions she is an irrational combination of shrew, saint, slattern, and nuisance, always primitively feminine in her vanities and amoral possessiveness.   In Serafina, Williams has not struck a new string on his fiddle; he has switched to another instrument--say, to the viola--and has composed strikingly on the theme of a fanatical, deluded peasant.   Since he still has the whole string section in the orchestra of obsessed humanity before him to pluck into tune we anticipate more stirring sonorities, especially when he tackles the bass fiddle. Here, in his viola playing, Williams has brought the rich, harum-scarum and volatile life of the Sicilian community, with its garrulity, superstition, irreverence, and tempestuous high jinks into singing life. While his characters are naïve, his approach is not; especially is this so in his raffish treatment of the rose tattoo. He has gone beyond the naïve and juvenile adoration of the rose as a sentimental symbol by capriciously tossing it about to the point where it achieves the sophisticated slant of the fetish. This artistic sophistry is entirely consistent with the psychology of the peasant mind, for all the symbols Serafina arranges--the urn, the Virgin, the deshabille [*sic*] she affects--are actually fetishes and consistent with the primitive emotions that motivate her every act. She never has a thought--just brainstorms.

The immediate success of *The Rose Tattoo* is largely due to the high-powered, agile direction of Daniel Mann, and he deserves special credit for elevating Miss Stapleton to the front rank of actresses today. Miss Stapleton has heretofore appeared only in minor parts on Broadway. Since Serafina is on the stage, practically continuously, the role demands terrible stamina, great flexibility, and a high emotional tension, as well as mental perceptivity and a flair for comedy, all of which Miss Stapleton projects with fidelity and punch. Eli Wallach, as the lover, gives an ingratiating performance, playing with a virile buoyancy and comic gaucheness that are as convincing as they are compelling. The two youngsters, Phyllis Love and Don Murray, are winsome and lyrically touching and form a perfect foil to the coarse-grained adult lovers. The opening love scene of these two is a gem of tenderness, but the concluding one is of a fumbling tastelessness. In fact, from the awkward device of the telephone scene on, used apparently to speed the play to its conclusion, the play lets down considerably. Mention must be made of Boris Aronson's delightful setting--the cottage in the marshes. It has just the right touch of the exotic, romantic, and realistic to frame the play in colorful perfection. . . .

School and Society, 24 March 1951: 181-83.

Theater--Off the Leash
Henry Hewes

As a theatergoer who thought the 1965 revival of *The Glass Menagerie* disappointing, I now find it a happy surprise that the present revival of *The Rose Tattoo* is so richly rewarding. And while these rewards were apparent at City Center, they emerge even more strongly at the more intimate Billy Rose Theater to which the production has been moved.

That this 1951 Tennessee Williams play should seem even more effective now than in its original presentation is mainly attributable to the maturing of its star, Maureen Stapleton, who played the role of Serafina in both productions, and to the fact that our theater has pulled away from naturalism in the direction of the grotesque. Thus the symbolism of the roses, which originally attempted to represent the sacredness of the sexual communion between man and woman, now becomes a detail that emphasizes the grotesquerie, rather than a possibly too obvious poetic conceit of the author. To accomplish this, director Milton Katselas has concentrated on creating the wild and irrational surroundings in which Mr. Williams's fable can be the center. And everything that happens is ironic--so that we laugh at the ridiculousness of the events at the same time that we recognize the characters' agonizedly sincere involvement in them.

Near the beginning a woman who looks like Zero Mostel in drag punctures Serafina's romantic notions about love by handing her an aphrodisiac with the advice, "Be sure you put it in his coffee at supper and *not* at breakfast." Then a pedantic priest is shocked by the heretical but rather sublime notion that the primitive people of his parish "find God in each other." But the supreme irony is that the healthy lust of Serafina's household exists side by side with pretentious symbols of purity. One of the most telling moments in the play is Serafina's berating of the madonna statue for forgetting her, at the very moment that she is being restored to health and life through the godsend of Mangiacavallo, a naïve laborer who will make a good husband for this run-down widow.

Now it very probably was not Mr. Williams's intention to write *The Rose Tattoo* as a grotesque comedy, but that is what this new presentation seems, and that is why it appears not the least bit dated. Furthermore, it is the ideal style for Miss Stapleton.

For it is this rundown quality and despair that Miss Stapleton here catches so much more fully than she did fifteen years ago. Moreover, the actress has a unique capacity for confronting pretension with practical considerations. Her Serafina deludes herself with poetic euphemisms to describe her own passions, but is hilariously carthy in appraising the same passions in others.

As she tells the sailor who is dating her fifteen-year-old daughter, "My daughter is a virgin--" she stops short to face the practical truth, and exclaims with devastating gallows humor, "She is or she was." And throughout the play Miss Stapleton keeps a magnificent balance between her impulsive and direct recognitions that the worst usually happens and her desperate hopes that it won't.

This balance is also present in the performance of Harry Guardino as the gauche Mangiacavallo. He is particularly entertaining as he blithely wipes off a dropped icecube on the shirt he has just a few minutes before used as a handkerchief. Christopher Walken fits right in as the young sailor, giving us a sense that he, too, is overwhelmed by the contradictions of the situation in which he finds himself. And Maria Tucci manages to grow from Serafina's awkward pigtailed child into a radiantly beautiful woman during the course of the evening. Behind all this, director Katselas has suggested an omnipresent potential for earthiness with rowdy neighbors and a music that sounds Greek, but which we accept as Sicilian, just as we accept Miss Stapleton's delivery as Italian even though it is not. This production constitutes a thrilling triumph for director and actress that opens up a green territory in which Tennessee Williams might profitably exercise his talent.

Saturday Review, November 26, 1966: 60.

Upbeat Williams, for a Change
Ben Brantley

The spumante wine that is brought out to inaugurate one of the funniest seductions in theater history isn't the only thing bubbling in the revival of *The Rose Tattoo* that opened last night at the Circle in the Square Theater.

Led by that seeming embodiment of solar energy known as Mercedes Ruehl, this production finds a giddy, disarmingly sweet effervescence in Tennessee Williams's tale of the sexual salvation of a Sicilian widow. And as directed by Robert Falls, the play has an earthy eroticism leavened by a sense of lightheaded, improbable innocence that turns the evening into an intoxicating fairy tale for grown-ups that matches Williams's own description of the play as a "celebration of the inebriate god."

The Rose Tattoo is singular in the Williams canon. While its theme of the self-deluding woman versus the man who is Id incarnate abounds in the writer's work, the clash typically ends in disaster: you know, castration, arson, nervous breakdowns.

But after the darker *Streetcar Named Desire* and *Summer and Smoke,* Williams decided to suspend his romantic fatalism. And in *Tattoo,* first staged in New York in 1951 in the production that made Maureen Stapleton a star, he for once allowed passion to redeem rather than destroy. The play is, in a sense, the flip side of *Streetcar,* with the Stanley and Blanche figures turned into equally matched peers of comparable psychic (and for that matter, physical) strength.

Most people know *Tattoo* from the 1955 film version, which starred the magnificent, defiantly unglamorous Anna Magnani, for whom the role of Serafina was originally written. The actress's fiercely naturalistic presence, underscored by the movie's gritty black-and-white location photography, gave the film a neo-realist aura. And the fact that its subject matter was, frankly and unabashedly, the female libido tends to make people think of it as a sweaty slice of life.

In fact, the play is as poetic and wistful a work as Williams ever composed, as much of a pipe dream in its way as *The Glass Menagerie.* It is also willfully simple-minded in its laborious symbolic structure and its optimistic view of carnal love as a cure-all. And to present it today as straightforward kitchen-sink theater would make audiences laugh for all the wrong reasons.

The great strength of Mr. Falls's production is its rendering of *Tattoo* as an airy erotic fable that gives equal due to the work's broad comedy, its organically emotional depths and its more artificial lyricism. Accordingly, Santo Loquasto's charming rose-colored valentine of a set and John Kilgore's antic use of brazenly sentimental music turn the play's location, an immigrant town on the Gulf Coast, into a dreamy, slightly surreal neverland of desire.

That land is governed with flash and assurance by Ms. Ruehl as Serafina, the stormy Sicilian seamstress who sequesters herself from life in a haze of memories of her late husband's sexual prowess. Magnani may forever own this part, but while Ms. Ruehl has it our on loan you should be able to forget her predecessor.

Magnani's Serafina was indeed, as comparisons at the time had it, a Vesuvius, given to volcanic eruptions but as seemingly invincible as a mountain. Ms. Ruehl is closer to a rushing river: also a force of nature, but more fluid, kinetic and easily diverted.

While she finds the humor in Serafina's imperiousness (watch what she does with the interrogation of her daughter's suitor), she also brings to the part a childish spontaneity that is winningly at odds with its forbidding matronly side. Her face can go instantly from contorted belligerence to an achingly vulnerable openness that makes her final transformation inevitable.

And who cares if her accent is a tad too close to Gilda Radner's Roseanne Rosannadana to be entirely credible? As Kenneth Tynan observed, *Tattoo* is "the product of a mind vitally infected with the rhythms of human speech." And Ms. Ruehl hammers home those rhythms with the reflexive precision of a veteran carpenter. She finds the poetic weight in key repeated words like "heart" and "facts," and in her bizarrely poignant imitation of a ticking watch, without ever losing her visceral connection to the character.

The entire work, though, is infused with musical cadences that Mr. Falls usually makes the most of. Irene Selznick, the original producer of *Streetcar,* rejected *Tattoo* because she felt it was more like opera than like a play. And it is indeed like an opera buffa, with its soaring arias, spiky recitatives and a chorus of chattering villagers, who are appropriately sated with an almost ritualistic formality in this production.

There are also, of course, duets: the lyric, slightly sappy exchanges between Serafina's teen-age daughter, Rosa, an [*sic*] the callow sailor who is courting her (charmingly played by Cara Buono and Dylan Chalfy), and the contrastingly knotty, more combustible dialogues of Serafina and Alvaro Mangiacavallo (Anthony LaPaglia), the virile, amiable dim-witted truck driver who delivers the widow from abstinence.

In the movie, Alvaro was played, with embarrassing strain, by a miscast Burt Lancaster, and Magnani had to work overtime to make their scenes together fly. This version faces no such problems. As this buffoon with the soul of a bard, Mr. LaPaglia displays a fiery energy and sense of timing that easily matches, and occasionally surpasses, Ms. Ruehl's. They seem genuinely made for each other by sheer force of metabolism, and their erotic wrestling match becomes, as it should, the play's triumphant comic center.

A few scenes go soft in the wrong places. The choicest example of verbal foreplay in American theater--when Serafina says to Alvaro, "And now we can go on with our conversation"--is thrown away here. The supporting cast members have moments suggesting the self-consciousness of high school productions (although Philip LeStrange is a scene stealer in the small role of a traveling salesman). And I could have done without Mr. LaPaglia's overextended drunken belly dance and the goofy twanging music that accompanies it.

But more often, the production's hokeyness and exaggerations simply add helium to the proceedings. And this fable of rejuvenation, very appropriately, gives a much-needed boost to the newly reopened Circle in the Square, which by rights should finally have the popular hit denied by this season's wan productions of *The Shadow Box* and *Uncle Vanya.*

When Alvaro, whose first act of chivalry is to capture the goat that has been rooting among Serafina's tomato plants, leads the animal on-stage followed by two delighted children and an old woman, you may indeed feel a swelling of what Williams wrote he was trying to convey in this play: "the

Dionysian element in human life." I can't think of a better way for New York audiences to celebrate the rites of spring.

New York Times, May 1, 1995: C11, C15.

"Sentiment and humor in equal measure": Comic Forms in *The Rose Tattoo*
Philip C. Kolin

When *The Rose Tattoo* made its Broadway appearance on 3 February 1951, Tennessee Williams did not have a reputation as a comic writer. Quite to the contrary, his two hits, *The Glass Menagerie* and *A Streetcar Named Desire,* had, according to *Life,* established him as a dramatist who "could write only about doom-ridden damsels." For his comic efforts in *The Rose Tattoo,* Williams was promptly whipped. As the reviewer in *Newsweek* put it, "there is an uneasy feeling that his new play is sometimes funny without quite intending to be." Williams' humor was labeled in the basest terms. The more serious events in act one "descend into cheap farce which must be seen to be believed," wrote Margaret Marshall in *The Nation.* The reviewer for *Time,* contemptuous of the rapid changes of mood, renamed the play Banana Truck Named Desire. F. W. Dupee ("Literature on Broadway," *The Partisan Review,* May 1951, p. 334) quickly summarized the critical opinion of Serafina and much else in the play when he said it was "farced-up."

In the 1966 revival of *The Rose Tattoo,* Williams' comedy had evidently changed for reviewers--it had become appropriately grotesque. If they could not assent to it as it was, they could at least praise the absurdist elements, in vogue in avant-garde theater both here and abroad. Williams' play had been acceptably reclassified through making virtues of its earlier vices. Absurdity by any other name is just as meet for neurotically-conditioned audiences. Henry Hewes offered an explanation for the approval: "Now it very probably was not Mr. Williams's intention to write *The Rose Tattoo* as a grotesque comedy, but that is what this new presentation seems, and that is why it appears not in the least bit dated" (*Saturday Review,* November 1966). Jan Kott, who has found Shakespeare so relevant to our "absurd" world, would readily have approved of the change. Yet, regardless of the revival, and perhaps because of it, critics, with a few exceptions, have dismissed *The Rose Tattoo* as one of Williams' lesser accomplishments, better left on the rose heap. Ruby Cohn has given the play its death-knell: "He probably intended *The Rose Tattoo* to be something of a saturnalia, a joyous celebration of sex, but (when we are not simply bored) we tend to laughed *at* rather than *with* the celebrants (p. 110). To his credit, though, the play was and is still good box office.

Why in 1950-51 did Williams write a work which seemed in so many ways to differ from his previous, and successful, plays? Biography provides a few clues. Williams had just returned from a sojourn in Italy, the land of warm sunshine and fiery passions, and said, "I have never felt more hopeful about human nature as a result of being exposed to the Italians" (quoted in *Saturday Review,* March 1951). While in Sicily Williams must have soaked up enough local culture to write knowledgeably about the folklore, language, and characters of the region and create the Dionysian elements he claims to have captured in the play (*Vogue,* March 1951). Birds, children, goats, sky, fruit, earth, sun, and air--all are found in *The Rose Tattoo.*

Biography aside, Williams' neglect yet strong flair for the comic is found not only in *The Rose Tattoo* but elsewhere in his work. In a provocative article ("The Comic Tennessee Williams"), Charles Brooks calls Williams "an essentially comic playwright" whose "greatest power and appeal derive from a comic vision which he seems unwilling to trust fully" (p. 275). In his review Hewes had said that comedy--even the more grotesque variety--could "open up a green territory in which Tennessee Williams might profitably exercise his talent." Classifying Williams' play by genres--tragedies or comedies--is gross oversimplification. Comedy is as difficult to define as tragedy. Socrates long ago said (in *The Symposium*) they were similar, often reaching the same ends; and Aristotle unfortunately never discussed that tragedy which, like a comedy, has a happy ending. *The Rose Tattoo* is easier to type than other Williams' plays because of both its virtues and its faults. It successfully dramatizes the fulfillment of hope and love. The play is an experiment in comedy, a potpourri of comedic forms, sometimes blended and sometimes juxtaposed. Comic forms range from slapstick humor, including farce, music hall antics, and vaudeville to folk, satiric, and romantic comedy, and, occasionally, tragicomedy. Even sadness is assimilated into the comic vision.

The Rose Tattoo has characteristics of low comedy or farce. But within this broad category are elements of vaudeville, Chaplinesque humor, and vestiges of the commedia dell'arte. Though dissatisfied reviewers and critics have lampooned Williams for his cheap and unsophisticated displays, jests and clowning are part of his stagecraft from his early works to his middle ones (*Camino Real*) to his late ones (*Gnädiges Fräulein*). Williams is a shrewd man of the theater, keenly aware that laughs as well as tears sell tickets. He incorporates many comic gags, verbal and physical, to entertain and cajole his audience, and, at times, make them feel superior to his characters.

One of Williams' greatest achievements as a comic dramatist is his use of dialogue, though Ruby Cohn observes: "Larded with Italian phrases and locutions, the English is surprisingly grammatical, the vocabulary extensive, and the emotions self-consciously expressed" (p. 111). Regardless of

Serafina's regular syntax, the play is fastmoving, speeded along by a series of one-liners that are the classic tool of the comedian's art. These are hurled at and by Serafina, some of them as cutting as the knife she will use on Estelle, others as sharp as a courtier's rapier.

These one-liners are well-suited to the Italian temperament. Angered by Serafina's delay in sewing their daughters' graduation dresses, local mothers pounce on her. One of them exclaims: "Listen, I pay in advance five dollars and get no dress. Now what she wear, my daughter, to graduate in? A couple of towels and a rose in her hair?" (II, 295). She thus makes sport of both the Delle Rose name (and emblem) and Serafina's impoverishing profession. When Rosa stands naked in the window, her clothes hidden by her suspicious mother, Williams demonstrates his agility with an Italian pun when a neighbor says: "In nominis padri et figlio et spiritus sancti. Aaahh!" (p. 294). *Figlio,* the child of naked vulnerability, such as Rosa is judged to be, replaces the *filio* of the invocation. Later, Rosa catches her mother in an embarrassing lie when Serafina explains Alvaro's presence by saying he was chased by the police. Rosa shrewdly inquires: "They chased him into your bedroom?" (p. 410). And the disarray in which Serafina finds herself after her boisterous fight with Father De Leo gives rise to even more humor because of the sham politeness with which the salesman addresses her: "I see directly to merchants but when I stopped over there to have my car serviced, I seen you taking the air on the steps and I thought I would just drop over . . . (p. 348).

Serafina's verbal assaults match her muscular defenses. At the start of the play, Serafina can counter the potion-selling Assunta's attempts to bring aphrodisiacs when they are not wanted by observing that it is not the sound of Venus that the old woman hears: "Naw, them ain't the star-noises. They're termites, eating the house up" (p. 275). To those who say she is improperly, scantily dressed, Serafina proclaims: "I'm dressed okay; I'm not naked!" (p. 301). Her invectives are charged by her shrewish wit. High school for her is as "high as that horse's dirt out there in the street!" (pp. 300-301). Equally facile retorts face Jack Hunter, as Serafina, punning on his name, asks: "What are you hunting?--Jack?" (p. 326). But Serafina reveals her own narrow limits and calls down laughter on her head when she utters the understatement of the play: "But we are Sicilians, and we are not coldblooded" (p. 329). Serafina's claim to recognize religious denominations in body types is of course ridiculous. Yet she bounces back into control when she plays a game with Alvaro. When he tells her of his previous amorous mishap because he gave the girl a fake diamond (a zircon), Serafina responds that she too would have slammed the door in his face. Williams see the folly of his characters' lives and captures it in their dialogue as well.

With Alvaro, Williams invents another comic portrait in prose. Alvaro's description of this family and their petty vices sounds almost as if it came from Eudora Welty's pen: "One old maid sister, one feeble-minded grandmother, one lush of a pop that's not worth the powder it takes to blow him to hell.--They got the parchesi habit. They play the game of parchesi, morning, night, noon. Passing a bucket of beer around the table . . ." (p. 364). Alvaro's wry detachment from his inherited handicaps fills out the picture of his family. He asks Serafina what in his heritage as the grandson of a village idiot he has to be thankful about: "What have I got to respect? The rock my grandmother slips on?" (p. 366). Williams is at his best in these comic vignettes, as the comments exchanged between Bessie and Flora well illustrate. The two prigs, eager for some sexual titillation, discuss one such prank that may promise pleasure: "I heard, I heard that the Legionnaires caught a girl on Canal Street! They tore the clothes off her and sent her home in a taxi!" (p. 370). Of course they disavow any interest in this nonsense, but they obviously enjoy it.

The Rose Tattoo also shows a mastery of other standard comic conventions, including physical deformities. Serafina's exaggerated ego and passion ma ch the rotundity of her shape. Hers is a big, often stricken body, described as a "heavy, sagging bulk" (p. 297). Her hips have exceeded their girlish limits, suggesting a comparison to a "parading matador" (p. 301). Moving to the other side of the ring, Williams labels her a bull (p. 338). She is like a "strange beast in a cage" (p. 337). All these remarks suggest that Serafina is like an animal in heat, her plump body always charging her enemies or her lover. Her struggles with her girdle call attention to the incompatibility of her form and the restraint she seeks to impose on it. In these pantomimes, Serafina is both laughable buffoon and frustrated lover. The girdle represents an impediment to her passions; and the more she struggles, the funnier are her attempts. Nor has Williams spared other parts of her anatomy. Her hair is wild, greasy, always out of control like Serafina herself. No make-up, it seems, will help. Rosa's "cosmetic enterprise" (p. 321) does not improve her mother; it leaves her only with a "dazed look." Serafina's deprecatory gestures, signs of her ethnic background and feverish anger, also make her look ridiculous.

Her new lover, Alvaro, and his body are also exploited for comedy. This clown seems like an appropriate visitor to the carnival booth (p. 269) that is Serafina's house. He is as awkward as Serafina is accusatory. His ears stick out, he is short, and he hitches his shoulders--traits that certainly call attention to his comic torso. Williams refers to him as one of the "glossy young bulls" (p. 348) as if to emphasize his sexual powers. Alvaro is doubtless the bull in the dress shop. He is so clumsy that he drops everything from ice cubes to condoms. His trance after his first night with Serafina has "the pantomimic lightness, almost fantasy, of an early Chaplin comedy" (p. 405). Like the silent movie star, Alvaro finds mischief where he least expects it. He collides with Serafina's furniture and, finally, her daughter. Thinking he is raping her daughter, Serafina lunges at him, beating him all the way out of the house. Alvaro scurries around the house with "his shirttails out" (p. 408) much as

Chaplin tries to evade the comic Furies hounding him.

The fight and the ensuing chase--the two most common and oldest comic tricks--fill up much of the action in *The Rose Tattoo*. Serafina tells Alvaro that "I had two fights on the street" (p. 353), but she underestimates the number of her quarrels. She battles with her daughter, jerking her away from the window; she does much the same with her clownish customers, except she chases them out of the house with a broom (p. 314). She is forever fighting with the Strega whom she orders "Getta hell out of my yard!" (p. 341). Not even the clergy is exempt; with Father De Leo Serafina is "on the point of attacking him bodily" (p. 346) when he is rescued by her neighbors. On stage these incidents elicit laughter. Yet they also point to the turmoil inside Serafina. She is out of control, as her anger and the shrewishness arousing it demonstrate. One beating, though, which does not fit with the rest is that given Estelle early in the play by Serafina's neighbors. As she comes to see Rosario's body, "The bouquet of roses is snatched from her black-gloved hands and she is flailed with them about the head and shoulders" (p. 291). Though not comic, this incident precipitates and parallels other quarrels. Serafina's revenge lasts so long and is so violent that we automatically seek a cause: The community punishment of Estelle anticipates Serafina's punishment of the community. The difference between the two beatings shows how funny Serafina's struggles have become.

These quarrels often result in chases among objects with people falling down or being torn apart. The slapstick humor is transparent; the angrier characters become, the less successful are their attacks. But when Serafina gets into the act, all discord follows. At first she locks Rosa in the house; then a little later Rosa is locked out of it, having to run around outside. The neighborhood children often flee in panic when Serafina threatens them. In her fury, she pursues her customers, Bessie and Flora, turning over a table. The most obvious flight, however, is the goat chase, a sign of Serafina's passionate dilemma. Next comes Father De Leo, who is hounded by the widow. Then another goat chase. The pattern--chase after chase--characterizes the comic deception befalling Serafina and pinpoints Williams's hilarious if conventional source of comedy. The opportunities for improvisational comedy are unlimited here.

Alvaro's arrival brings more chases and even greater damage. His precursor, the salesman, signals further debasement for Serafina. The new product he offers "explodes in Serafina's face" (p. 349). The scene recalls Punch and Judy antics, but it prefigures the eruptions with Alvaro. While talking to him about vicious rumors, Serafina hurls a glass to the floor. Twice, in a few minutes, she explodes at Alvaro, both times chasing him for his life and crushing anything in her way. First, "she springs up and runs into the parlor. He pursues. The chase is grotesquely violent and comic. A floor lamp is overturned. She seizes the chocolate box and threatens to slam it into his face if he continues toward her" (p. 386). After a few calm moments, Serafina disrupts the peace when she hurls the phone to the floor (p. 392). She even addresses the Blessed Virgin with "explosive gestures" (p. 395). The second time, the termagant flies at Alvaro "like a great bird, tearing and clawing at his stupefied figure" (p. 407) in retaliation for his bumping into Rosa. Alvaro is the butt; even when he walks he "topples over" (p. 406).

But this rampage provides no release for Serafina; nor was it meant to. These chases only increase her frustration and rekindle the fires of her anger. For it is herself Serafina chases most often. She lunges, plunges and trounces all over; but, as Williams deftly points out, "she swiftly and violently whirls about in distraction." In desperation for clothes, she grabs at her dummies, one of which collapses. She tears things apart and threatens death to those who cross her. But she can have no honest release until she breaks the urn holding Rosario's ashes. All the other acts may be gratuitous, there for the laughs pure and simple, but when she "seizes the marble urn and hurls it violently into the furthest corner of the room" (p. 394), she finally can escape from the whirligig of the time past and confront the love Alvaro has to offer. She can break away from the comic captivity of her previous actions; she can stop being "dressed in the rags of a convict" (p. 341). Inserted among the other humorous acts, destruction of the urn may at first seem to be the result of Serafina's rage. But Williams has juxtaposed this act with other slapstick gestures to suggest how it differs from them and how, in effect, it points to the climax of the play. Within Williams' slapstick comedy is more serious business, but an appreciation of the relationship between events, however foolish, reveals the unity.

Among the most obvious but, surprisingly enough, least valued elements in *The Rose Tattoo* is the folk comedy. The passions of Rosa Gonzales, her revengeful father, and the symbolic cock fight of *Summer and Smoke* are examples of Williams' use of folk habits. Natives appear in both *Camino Real* and *The Night of the Iguana*. And insofar as his plantation caste in *Cat on a Hot Tin Roof* or *Sweet Bird of Youth* comprise separate, regional and rural subcultures, Williams reveals some knowledge of folk drama, twentieth-century style. Because of their obvious "foreignness" and importance, the Italians and Sicilians of *The Rose Tattoo* stand out most distinctly in Williams' use of folk materials. Their language, religion, and superstitions give the play its zest and shape its humor. Their music permeates the play, since a folk player appears at all the major breaks. Although living in the American South, Serafina and her neighbors lost not a whit of their native hopes and fears in steerage. They are close to the earth and to the animals and the children bred on it.

The lingo of these southern Europeans--the patois of the peasant--is liberally sprinkled throughout *The Rose Tattoo*, often adding to both the romantic and the humorous depiction of Serafina and her neighbors. Born of "contadini," Serafina becomes a "baronessa" even if her estate is no more than the sewing shop which is also her house. The Sicilian vocabulary makes Serafina's ire even more passionate and her love more earthy. Alvaro is a "cretino," a "buffone," or, even worse, a "maleducato" when he alarms her, but he is her "amore" at the end of the play; and her once intractable daughter is her "carissimo." The small house on Front Street, with the highway before it, is closer to Palermo than to New Orleans.

This language also reflects the many superstitions and taboos that prey so humorously on Serafina's psyche. Her goattending neighbor is always addressed as the Strega, the witch. So foolish is Serafina that she believes this spindly, hairy-legged creature possesses evil powers. She has "malocchio," an evil eye according to Serafina, though to the less impressionable Rosa it is only a cataract. When the Strega touches Rosa, Serafina at once supplies a folk cure--the girl must "wash [her] face with salt water and then throw the salt water away!" (p. 286). The Strega takes her place alongside Williams' other hags, comic and serious. She is part of the tradition which produced the blind woman selling flowers for the dead in *A Streetcar Named Desire* and Leona in *Confessional*; they serve as reminders of impending doom. The Strega, moreover, infrequently serves as the play's narrator, pointing out comically Serafina's excesses--"The Wops are at it again" (p. 296)--while she and her rampaging goat are also grotesque. The "little procession" of her and the goat home really begins in her having let him loose in the first place. The superstitions associated with her must be judged against those of Assunta, the "fattuchiere" with her miraculous aphrodisiacs, and the more prosaic powers of the "imported Sicilian spumanti." The artifacts of this culture--goat, potions, wine--are among the leading stage symbols, however much they are abused through repetition and obviousness. From them Williams tries to create a comic (and folk) atmosphere; they are the legerdemain of his dramatic artifice.

Even the plot of *The Rose Tattoo* reads like a series of folk motifs, many of them documented in the Stith Thompson index. A duped widow who strikes out at all around her because of their mockery of her love finds a solution to her problems with another man who, in many ways, is the muscular though comic reincarnation of her deceased husband. At first, Serafina is attracted to Alvaro because, as she claims, he has "My *husband's body,* with the head of a *clown!*" (p. 354). Alvaro is the lover disguised as a fool, and old motif that Williams adopts for his own purposes by fusing suitor and fool into one role. Alvaro's disguise is laughable to Serafina who at first fails to see the love he brings.

The mysterious attraction is demonstrated through the rose symbolism. The rose appears in folk beliefs as a magical love-producing object. In fact, it is the talisman which often draws a lover to a woman, though Williams uses it to draw the woman to the man. The sexual bonds between Rosario and Serafina need little comment. But an even more interesting folk motif about roses is associated with Alvaro. Even though Serafina is already aroused by Alvaro, when he has the patronymic emblem of her first husband emblazoned on his chest, she finds Rosario Delle Rose again, or a more faithful though less attractive version of him. In essence, her "rose" has been transformed into a human being, a folk motif which is at the center of Serafina's discovery of self and the audience's demand for comedic harmony. Folklore also associates sexual powers with roses. By eating a rose, according to one superstition, a woman could conceive. Serafina's pregnancy by Rosario and her conception after sleeping with his humorous incarnation, the tattooed Alvaro, recall the motif. As long as Serafina has a rose in her life, she does not need the sexual stimulation promised by Assunta's potion.

Much in *The Rose Tattoo* derives from the conventions of romantic comedy. Williams, who elsewhere is the frustrated romanticist or the rebellious puritan, here successfully gives the upper hand to the forces of love and nature. The fecundity of nature and man, and the desire, voiced by all romantic comedies, to unite every eligible female with every suitable man, frequently appears. Williams' pastoral setting--on the Gulf Coast between the magic city of New Orleans and the port of Mobile--displays a territory of passion and a land of sexual fulfillment. References to vegetation are numerous, and fruitful. The "Author's Production Notes" call for "palm trees," "tall canes with feathery fronds and a fairly thick growth of pampas grass" (p. 269). Rosario hauled bananas for the Romano Brothers; and Alvaro arrives with "a great golden bunch of bananas" (p. 373). The shape of this fruit leads Henry Popkin ("The Plays of Tennessee Williams," p. 59) to see it as a phallic symbol, which seems appropriate for the context. Estelle Hohengarten's last name, which literally means a high garden, likewise suggests the fruitfulness of sex. The young Jack Hunter gives Rosa a bunch of roses for her graduation. And Serafina more than once breaks open a bottle of spumanti, highly suitable for the Bacchic entertainment serving as a preamble to love. Above the fertility of the earth shines Venus, "the female star with an almost emerald luster" (p. 273), and this star appears above Serafina's porch near the end of the play "still undimmed" (p. 405).

The surge toward fertility--and reproduction--is even stronger among the characters for whom this vegetation serves as a background. The play begins and ends with Serafina pregnant, once by her unfaithful husband and once by her foolish paramour, Alvaro. Serafina's rejection of the creative rhythms of life brings only reminders of how fruitful she should be. Father De Leo cautions her: "You are still a young woman. Eligible for--loving and--bearing again!" (p. 341). Later in the play, Alvaro tells her, in his awkward proposal, that his old maid sister wants nephews and nieces (p. 387). Serafina can be happy only when she is loved and loving--whether it is every night with Rosario or not quite so often with Alvaro. Serafina's comic problem rests in acknowledging and triumphing over obstacles to love. She must ignore

Estelle's illicit affairs and forgive Alvaro's fumbling attempts to use contraceptives.

If the specific pastoral location lends itself to romantic comedy, so too does the particular time of the action. It is June, near mid-summer, the time of love passion, fulfillment, weddings. It is a highly festive day on the calendar. Even the clowns Bessie and Flora are eager to see the Veterans Parade in New Orleans. But it is also a highly symbolic day--Rosa's graduation day and Serafina's as well. This occasion suggests Rosa's development, her commencement of sexual maturity. As Rosa tells Jack, "Just think. A week ago Friday--I didn't know boys existed!" (p. 318). It is her initiation, so to speak, receiving the *Digest of Knowledge* and Jack Hunter's pristine love on the same day. Their trip to Diamond Key (the place name suggesting some kind of engagement) in a sense charts their rite of passage into sexual maturity, soon to be concluded in a New Orleans hotel room. But on this very special day, Williams reminds his audience, they are the quintessence of young love. As Brooks Atkinson said in a *New York Times* review of the original production, their affair "has all the lyric rapture and sincerity of young poetry. As sheer writing, it is one of the finest things Mr. Williams has done."

But as in so many other romantic comedies, the young lovers are frustrated in meeting and marrying. Usually, a blocking figure, some pitiful and laughable parent, stands in their way. This is one dimension of Serafina's role. She is the obstacle to their love as well as a blatant contrast to it. It is hard to agree with Charles Brooks who sees Serafina as "the healthy one in the play" and Rosa as the "sentimental" embodiment of her mother's faults who "weakens an otherwise fine comedy" (p. 277). If nothing else demonstrated how wrong this view of Rosa is, Serafina's reactions to graduation day would certainly be enough. To the embittered widow, the festive day brings only anxiety and fear. She tries to spoil the holiday at first by locking her daughter up; the celebration, she thinks, is the public declaration of all the wrong things the high school did to Rosa. Even when Rosa is released through the intervention of Miss York [*sic*], Serafina still cannot participate in the ceremonies. She tries to attend, but she never does, for she is detained by her customers. And the music she hears does more to annoy than uplift her. When Rosa returns, elated by her honors, Serafina tries to fight off the future she brings with her diploma by saying: "Va bene.--Put it in the drawer with your father's clothes" (p. 324). Serafina hopes to keep Rosa in the stagnant past with the memory of Rosario. Rosa's youthful innocence and Rosario's faithfulness are tied together. Serafina does not want change. As she tells Jack Hunter: "Two weeks ago I was slapping her hands for scratching mosquito bites. She rode a bicycle to school. Now all at once--I've got a wild thing in the house" (p. 330). Graduation day has caused all of Rosa's problems and most of Serafina's trouble.

But Serafina, like so many other foolish parents in comedy, has problems both more serious and more comic than those she anticipates. She tries to protect Rosa from sexual abuse and dishonesty. Yet she herself is the victim of one of the oldest and funniest deceptions of romantic comedy. She has been cuckolded by Rosario and refuses, until shown otherwise, to believe it. In setting up a shrine to her late and beloved husband, she makes a mockery of her injunctions to Rosa not to trust a boy. Her religious fanaticism is, therefore, not without humor. Even her name suggests some comic duplicity. Not only does it imply her own nocturnally amorous ability ("sera fina"--"fine nights"), as Ruby Cohn has pointed out (p. 111), but Williams may have had an actual Saint Seraphina in mind when he decided to name his heroine. *The Catholic Encyclopedia* states that Saint Seraphina was a virgin who "led a religious life in her parental home and was an example of piety, charity, mortification, and patience during a long serious illness . . ." (p. 105).

The Saints: A Concise Biographical Dictionary (ed. John Coulson, New York, 1958) says she was associated with white violets, which "were found to be growing on the board on which she had lain" (p. 183). The widow Delle Rose is hardly a young, suffering virgin, and the contrast between her activities and those suggested by her holy namesake emphasize the folly of her devotion. Her wifely piety and the shrine she erects come in for constant comic attacks. Her house is noted more for brawls than prayers. In fact, at one point it even turns into a kind of "casa privata" (p. 385).

But it is her opposition to Rosa and Jack that makes Serafina a foe to love. Only when she relents and sends her daughter off with a blessing does she overcome her own ignorance and accept love herself. Breaking Rosario's urn and honoring Rosa's desire to love Jack indicate the change. She moves from hostile enemy to confidant, from a blocking figure to a woman who can see the world romantically. Serafina graduates by throwing off the bonds of the past, which enshackled her in buffoonery, and accepts the love and promise of the future.

The use of festivity in *The Rose Tattoo* derives from some of the major elements of romantic comedy. These include the so-called "green world" which the lovers inhabit, the opposition of the parent to their love, the easy comic deception of the parent, the hypocrisy of the parent's advice, and the holiday occasion giving rise to these opposing views. Unlike other comic butts, though, Serafina finally joins the lovers' cause. Williams' tone of satire is replaced by a strong and unmitigated sense that harmony will finally reign.

Much in *The Rose Tattoo* does not quite fit into the categories of vaudeville, farce, or romantic comedy. The serious moments of grief early in the play, the agony Serafina encounters in act two, and the union of Serafina and Alvaro at the end of the play amidst tears and laughter, defy comic label. Shifting tones and modes, many of them branded as Williams' faults, suggest that *The Rose Tattoo* is a tragicomedy, a genre that allows comedy full and varied play, even giving it the last word, while acknowledging the undercurrent of tragic love and pain.

The playwright's inability to write pure comedy throughout the play may explain why *The Rose Tattoo* is a tragicomedy. Williams may have explained his play as a Dionysian celebration, a dream of life's juices flowing through herbs, children, and lovers, but his preface on "The Timeless World of the Play" turns the reader's eye in another direction. There Williams speculates about "plays in the tragic tradition" and discusses his own version of catharsis by which "our hearts are wrung by recognition and pity" (p. 262), a strange introduction for a saturnalian comedy. But perhaps these autobiographical assessments to some extent explain the work. Williams wants us to laugh and suffer with Serafina; she is both the dummy bride and the dummy widow. He wants "sentiment and humor in equal measure" (p. 270), an almost impossible feat in an age grotesquely divorcing the two and a difficult task for a playwright whose comedy usually reflects irredeemable futility. Still, as Henry Hewes recognized when seeing the 1966 revival, "we laugh at the ridiculousness of the events at the same time that we recognize the characters' agonizedly sincere involvement in them." Laughter may provide a better catharsis than either pity or fear.

Coarse, vulgar, foolish love exists alongside more noble kinds. The Strega, Estelle, and the taunting children get billing with Alvaro's shrewd recognition that Serafina laid her "heart in the marble urn with the ashes" (p. 372) and Rosa's advice that "Everybody is nothing until you love them" (p. 319), perhaps the topic sentence of the play. Serafina is likewise the nothing turned to everything, comic scapegoat and sympathetic heroine. Williams debases and enthrones her, often at the same time. She sinks into "comic desolation" (p. 300), and her appearance is at once "comic and shocking" (p. 321). Her former beauty is often mentioned, nowhere more poetically expressed than in Father De Leo's description of her as being "like a lady wearing a--piece of the--weather!" (p. 341).

But his view is challenged by her present appearance; she has become a hobgoblin scaring the children away. Williams seems to transfer some of his former heroines' problems to Serafina. Starnes ("The Grotesque Children of *The Rose Tattoo*") has concluded that, "In terms of Williams's typical character deployment, Serafina is actually a direct descendant of Laura Wingfield in *The Glass Menagerie* and of Alma Winemiller in *Summer and Smoke*" (p. 368). Although Serafina lives in her own world, a victim of her own dreams, the affinity with Williams' earlier female characters is tenuous. Serafina is much more adaptable than, say, Blanche DuBois. Serafina throws off the deception in time to marry Alvaro. But it is too late for Blanche and her Alvaro (Mitch), whom she loses too soon and wants too late. In short, Serafina is a complex, often contradictory figure whose failures and successes in love combine farcical comedy with tragic implications. The rapid changes, especially after

Alvaro reveals his rose tattoo in act three, are characteristic of and suitable for a tragicomedy.

Another major feature of tragicomedy is surprise, the unexpected resolution of the tragic dilemma that leads to a happy ending. Poorly used, this deus ex machina, the manipulation of events, can descend to cheap melodrama. But Williams has made some attempts to prepare his audiences, and characters, for the unexpected comedic resolution of events. The numerous references to the Blessed Mother, whom Serafina at first worships, then rebukes, then adores, suggest that these Sicilians feel providence can work out their problems. And Williams cautioned his crew and cast not to scoff at the "religious yearnings" (p. 270) these people feel. Everywhere, Serafina looks for signs. In sympathy with her, the audience should too. It is significant that the play begins and ends with Assunta saying that "it is impossible to tell me anything that I don't believe" (p. 414). The appearance of Alvaro is just that strange event which, on the face of it, seems incredible, for as he tells Serafina: "If strange things didn't happen, I wouldn't be here. You wouldn't be here. We wouldn't be talking together" (p. 361). Some have dismissed *The Rose Tattoo* as a contrived work, with Williams pulling all the strings in open view of the audience. And while there is some truth to the stricture that Alvaro is clumsy, and even stupid, his gift of love to Serafina does bring her out of despair and back into the world of love. Just as Serafina is filled with joy waiting for her first husband when the play begins, she is flowing over with excitement and love when running to meet her second husband as the play closes. That they rush to meet each other on the embankment signals their ascendancy over the neighborhood and the individuals who ridiculed and railed at them Alvaro's strange and comic visit to Serafina's house results in the triumph of love.

The theme of time adds to both the tragic and the comic dimensions of the play. In his preface to *The Rose Tattoo,* Williams says that if time is arrested the events on stage acquire more tragic worth and contribute to the dignity of the characters. Were *The Rose Tattoo* pure tragedy, such observations might clearly apply. But the cessation of time for Serafina is both cause and effect of her comic debasement and our sympathy for her. When she is bound by time, or restlessly fights its pull, she is most pathetic and least likely to accept a new and fruitful life.

The time of the play may be the present, but for Serafina it is, until Alvaro's successful wooing, always the past. Before she learns of Rosario's death, she rapturously recalls her previous nights of love. All time is measured by and included in her husband's embrace. "Each time is the first time with him. Time doesn't pass . . . " (p. 280), she tells Assunta. But when Assunta reminds her of time's witness, the clock, Serafina has only contempt for it: "No, the clock is a fool. I don't listen to it. My clock is my heart and my heart don't say tick-tick; it says love-love!" (p. 280). The action reveals both how foolish and how sad Serafina's sense of time is when Estelle imposes another interpretation on the same hours: "Tomorrow's the anniversary of the day we met . . . " (p. 282), she tells Serafina, who is of course unaware of Rosario's infidelity.

Serafina is not concerned with the future, despite reminders of time's passing. She tells Assunta that Rosario will no longer conceal drugs under his load of bananas. "Tonight is the last time he does it! Tomorrow he quits hauling stuff for the Brothers Romano" (p. 279). Tomorrow never comes, even though Williams manipulates stage time so as to make years pass between scenes three and four of act one. All of a sudden, it is "a June day, three years later" (p. 293). (One recalls the passing of sixteen years between acts in Shakespeare's tragicomedy *The Winter's Tale.*) Williams admits that "The diminishing influence of life's destroyer, time, must be somehow worked into the content of . . . [the] play" (p. 263), but Serafina's struggle against it or imperception of it causes her grief. Williams' critical views are at odds with his dramaturgy, not an unusual conflict considering that sometimes his dramatic criticism fails to provide the most trusty guide to the work it discusses. When Serafina understands and appreciates time's changes, she is saved. Until then, she has only memories, views of the past which remove her from time's obligations and successes. As she tell Alvaro, "The memory of a love don't make you unhappy unless you believe a lie that makes it dirty" (p. 363). She clings to the lie because it protectively confines her in a beautiful past. She dwells on the social honors of the past. Rosario's uncle was a baron; she is a baronessa. But this claim brings only ridicule. She forestalls giving the mothers their daughters' dresses, promising them "Domani-domani-domani" (p. 293), even though, ironically enough, the dresses are done. In front of Bessie and Flora, she speaks of her previous work for them but spurns future jobs. When Serafina snarls at Flora that she is "late for the graduation of my daughter," the angular prig cruelly retorts: "You got plenty of time" (p. 305). Serafina has plenty of time except that all of it is recounted in her past sexual feats.

It is with Rosa that Serafina's distorted sense of time is more carefully treated. So harassed is Serafina that she never attends the graduation exercises; instead, she sits in the gloomy shadows of her house, surrounded by the manikins of both bride and widow, images of time past and time present. Ironically, the time-fettered Serafina buys Rosa a Bulova watch for her graduation present. But as Rosa leaves, the "gift still ungiven" (p. 411), the action means Serafina's sense of time cannot be transferred to her sexually unhindered daughter. That the watch does not work properly to begin with is further proof that this present represents Serafina's own limits; she has been frozen in time and must be unlocked from the past. Starnes has argued that when the watch does work, "time's passing and the transience of all meaning are now all she can see"; and that when the watch ceases ticking "Time has been arrested for her again, and is significant of Serafina's spiritual rebirth" (p. 369). This view runs counter to the unfolding of events, for it is only when Serafina gives up on the defective watch that she can run to Alvaro who offers her a new love which relieves her from her past folly.

In this role as time's new man, the new watchman of Serafina's heart, some of Alvaro's silliness vanishes, and much of his thematic significance is stressed. Though an awkward lothario, Alvaro plans for the future. Although his dreams are not as grand as Jim O'Connor's, Alvaro seeks security in the household of an older, financially stable and physically developed woman. But his youth and sexual prowess make him attractive to Serafina; he can offer her new hours of pleasure in bed while granting her wish not to be saddled with "some middle-aged man, not young, not full of young passion, but getting a pot belly on him and losing his hair and smelling of sweat and liquor" (p. 312). With Alvaro, Serafina's heart will again be in step with the fluidity and fruitfulness of time. Licking the chocolate from her fingers, Alvaro reminds Rosario's widow that "You're as old as your arteries, Baronessa. Now set back down. The fingers are now white as snow!" (p. 383). This ridiculous gesture is symbolically an act of purification, or a preview of sexual delights awaiting Serafina. When she protests his advances, Alvaro says, "Is it my fault you have been a widow too long?" (p. 388); and he even agrees to "go out and come in the door again" (p. 389) if the day is wrong. Timing is important for Alvaro, for he is conscious of his past failures in love. Once Serafina exorcises the lie from her memory, comes back into time, and accepts Alvaro's youthful love, she can escape the sadness of the past and the follow of the present. Giving assent to the passing of time shifts characters and audience away from tragedy and into the joy of comedy.

The Rose Tattoo is not one of Williams' best plays, but it does show his ability to write fulfilling comedy, comedy which is indebted to a number of different dramatic traditions. From farce and slapstick humor, Williams takes the lively action of his play--fights, chases, one-liners, grotesque characterization. But he dignifies, or at least tones down, some of these antics by incorporating elements of romantic comedy. Rosa's attempts to run away with Jack Hunter are successful only when Serafina finds love herself. That recognition is placed within a tragicomic frame, allowing Williams to introduce more serious moments into the play. All this action is set within a folk community from which Williams derives further comedy. If the play never won critical approval, possibly Williams was too ambitious, too eager to make sure his play left no comic form untouched.

Tennessee Williams, A Tribute. Ed. Jac Tharpe. Jackson: University Press of Mississippi, 1977. 214-231.

Camino Real (1953)

Theater
Harold Clurman

Whatever the precise moment of its composition (the copyright date of the one-acter from which the present version was made is 1948), Tennessee Williams's *Camino Real* (National Theatre) should be regarded as a work of the author's nonage. Though this is what I sensed immediately as I watched it in the theater, I could not help feeling irritated with it. As I sit down to write about it a day later, I am inclined to view it more sympathetically. The "history" of this change may constitute the main point of my notice.

Being essentially a youthful work, *Camino Real* is immature. But like the youthful and immature work of most artists, *Camino Real* is significant of its author's seed thoughts, impulses, and ambitions. Far from being obscure, the play reiterates its intention and meaning at every point. In fact, it is too nakedly clear to be a sound work of art.

Kilroy, typical of the "natural" young American of little education, is presented more or less out of time, though the language is sharply contemporary, and out of space, though the atmosphere is the sultry one of Latin American "bohemia" with its ambiguous tone of varicolored lights, strange intoxicants, hybrid excitements, roguish pursuits, and appetizing danger. With this there is a kind of literary afflatus characteristic of the man who feeds his dreams with the color of foreign cultures. Kilroy is bewildered and innocent, seeing a haven in a world corrupt to the core, gasping for security and love in places where he can find nothing but humiliating adventures. The rich are smug and cruel; officialdom is heartless and blind; all, save the heroic poet who is willing to take action, shrink from the nobler exploits of the spirit. Kilroy is doomed to die young because he is honest, ignorant, and without guile. His redeeming feature is aspiration--not without a touch of puritanism-- an unconscious idealism which makes him brother to other errant knights who have sinned, suffered, and still believed in the inherent magnificence of life. "The violets in the mountain will break the rocks"--the dream will conquer crass reality. Don Quixote bids the boy not to pity himself, forever to seek the uncharted paths of the more exalted quests even if the ultimate destination is never to be known.

This is the mystique of romanticism, with a special stress on pity for the insulted and injured, the persecuted minorities, the victims and outcasts. Considering the times we live in, I am entirely cordial to these sentiments-- particularly since they are no longer intellectually fashionable. Williams also hankers for an unfettered theater, a theater free of the bonds of workaday naturalism, a theater where the poet in him can speak more personally and with a greater degree of self-revelation that the usual prosy play permits. Thus *Camino Real* discards the routine props of logic, exposition, and straight story line. Though there is a certain juvenile impatience in this, I can embrace Williams on this count too. His crimes have a healthy source.

What is less fortunate is that his play, instead of being the surrealist phantasmagoria it intends to be, is far too literal--in almost every respect far less poetic than *The Glass Menagerie* or *A Streetcar Named Desire*. To say, "We're all of us guinea pigs in the laboratory of God," or to have street cleaners represent death or an airplane named Fugitiva stand for escape, is far less imaginative than to have the hapless Blanche du Bois of *Streetcar* go off to an insane asylum depending on the kindness of strangers. The most successful moments of *Camino Real* are the sardonic vaudeville of the gipsy- fortune-teller scene and, even better, the boy-and-girl love scene--a sort of wrily [*sic*] sentimental comic-strip ballet of courtship--which is almost as specific as the Gentleman Caller scene in *The Glass Menagerie*. In other words, Williams, like Sean O'Casey and many others, is less suggestive and poignant when he aims point-blank at his aesthetic, poetic, or symbolic target than when he employs the concrete means of a real situation. Poetry cannot be captured by direct assault; beauty cannot be won unless we woo it first through the beast.

As with the play's poetry, so with its "philosophy." It is too blunt. It does not matter in art whether or not one is a pessimist or an optimist. To say that life is lovely is no more correct, convincing, moving, or significant than to say that it is horrid. It is the substance--not the conclusion--of an argument that gives it validity. Its *living matter*--the images, forms, characters, incidents, evocation of experience, life-content--give a work of art its power, meaning, and value. If these are rich, then the work is creative no matter how white or black the summation of the whole may be. When Kilroy repeats, "I am sincere, I am sincere, I am sincere," he is touching even in the poverty of his speech, but on the ideological level *Camino Real* is negligible because its fabric, for all its fancy patterning, is "general issue."

Yet I am loath to be harsh with it. When people on the first night are puzzled because the play seems cryptic to them, I am astonished at the paradox which makes them believe they understand the much subtler *Streetcar*--the theme of which they are hardly ever able to state; when people at the second night "love" the play in protest against what they consider a backward press, I am distressed that they are not really seeing or thinking about it so much as expressing an ill-defined and frustrated resentment against something.

That "something" is not the press. The sad fact of our theater is that a play like *Camino Real* with all its faults ought to be produced, listened to, criticized with measure and affection, but that this is difficult when its production costs a fortune, when it is forced to become part of the grand machinery of investment, real estate, Broadway brokerage and competition for reputation. A play like *Camino Real* should be produced--as it might be in France, for example--with modest means in a small theater where it would be quietly seen, enjoyed, and judged for what it is--a fallible minor work of a young artist of important talent.

Elia Kazan's production adds to the script's flaw by being conceived in a major key. It is scenically too heavy; it is vocally too noisy. It is too punchy, forthright, and "realistic." It stampedes where it should float; it clamors and declaims where it should insinuate. It has much less humor than the text. There are, none the less, good actors in it--too many to list here.

Nation, April 4, 1953: 293-94.

Revival of *Camino Real* At St. Marks Playhouse
Judith Crist

Credit Jose [*sic*] Quintero and his company with lending sporadic fascination to a hodge-podge of symbolism, giving momentary meaning to a jargon that aspires to poesy but stumbles on prose, and making the Turkish-bath atmosphere of the St. Marks Playhouse intermittently bearable.

This is a major accomplishment in a revival of *Camino Real*. Tennessee Williams' redoubtable failure of seven seasons ago, a failure that even today the playwright himself finds beyond glib understanding--or explanation. But so skillfully has Mr. Quintero directed it on an open stage, so brilliantly do his performers undertake a passing part, that it is only at the end of an impassioned speech or a sharply etched scene that the hollowness of word and action is apparent.

The re-staging has made it difficult to gauge the re-writing Mr. Williams has done since the Broadway production. The play now emerges in the framework of a dream of Don Quixote, who finds on the Camino Real--the royal road of romantics who approach the road of reality--the fellowship of loneliness.

Indeed, described perhaps aptly by the gypsy-madame as "a funny paper read backwards," the Camino Real is filled with symbols and allegories: Camille deceiving Casanova in their weary loveless love affair; Kilroy, the Golden Glove champ with "a heart as big as the head of a baby," claiming his sincerity and individuality; Lord Byron, declaiming that "there is a time for departure even when there is no place to go"; the gypsy's daughter, re-virginized at each fiesta, seeking the true lover; the garbage-collectors looking for corpses; the two hotel keepers--Gutman and A. Rat [sic]--imprisoning and luring their customers.

But Mr. Gutman, in one of his philosophical dissertations, considers the probing of the human heart: "We look into ourselves and say, 'Is this all there is?'" And we look at Mr. Williams' symbols and allegories and echo the question. There is no ultimate sum thereof.

But we look--and cannot, for long moments, turn away. Nan Martin is a desperate, caged Camille, tearing briefly at our hearts--but tearing--as she screams for escape to anywhere; Addison Powell gives Casanova a dignity that somehow escapes the pathetic; Lester Rawlins soars in speech and conscience as he Byronically mourns the cremation of Shelley. There's a fierce vulgarity and humor in Charlotte Jones' gypsy, a startling virginity in Collin Wilcox's gypsy daughter, a touching sincerity--beyond his profession thereof--in Clinton Kimbrough's Kilroy, and a twisted-mouthed top-sergeant cynicism to David Doyle's Gutman.

They bemuse--they fascinate--they almost lend an over-all meaning and depth to what too often seems childish, superficial, on a basic-English morality play level. That "brother" is the forbidden word in a captive state; that Kilroy's heart (and in this production we are, fortunately, saved the concrete sight thereof) is--repulsive image--as big as a baby's head and solid gold to boot--these are first-grade symbols.

Suddenly words stick in the craw--"and that's what curdles my blood like milk left on the doorstep of someone who's gone for the summer" or "Money wasn't legal tender--I mean it was legal bit [sic] it wasn't tender" or "Humanity is just a work in progress." And the jargon takes over and we are on no road at all.

But the dream-like atmosphere, the emergence of characters momentarily beyond their symbol, a mounting tempo that reaches fervent passions for the moment--even though these are of the moment they bear testament to the craftsmanship of director and cast. For these this revival of *Camino Real* merits attention but for little else.

New York Herald Tribune, May 17, 1960: 22.

On Stage: Tennessee Williams' Dream World
Dan Isaac

Camino Real, Tennessee Williams' masterpiece that has never been mastered, was revived January 8 at Lincoln Center. But what might have been a great moment for the American theater became instead a mixed bag of beautiful effects and blurred readings.

When it premiered on Broadway in the pre-Beatnik '50s, the play was greeted by incredibly hostile reviews and stayed alive only long enough to leave a wistful memory of its passing. That was 1953--the same year that *Waiting for Godot* was first performed in Paris. The coincidence of timing is not without significance, inasmuch as both works are a response to the exhaustion of a tradition: *Godot,* presenting the dry bones of minimal drama, represented an act of profound resignation and a first step toward silence; while *Camino Real,* flooding the stage with a fatty, rich overflow of literary symbols and metaphorical conceits, tried to recapitulate the romantic tradition in a desperate last-ditch attempt to effect its resurrection.

Replete with simulated sex, comic fake rituals and magical incantations to make the dead land fertile again, *Camino Real* was Williams' shot at writing "The Waste Land." The angry confusion major critics professed to feel when they play first opened stands now only as an index to the traumatized sensibility of that scared generation of repentant radicals. A parable of the individual in the fascist state, *Camino Real* today obviously means so much that it almost sinks under the weight of its own significance.

Written at a pivotal point in the playwright's career, *Camino Real* somehow achieves the stature of a *last* play. It rightly belongs to the rank and genre of Sophocles' *Oedipus at Colonus,* Shakespeare's *The Tempest* and Ibsen's *When We Dead Awaken*--visionary, twilight works in which the aging dramatists felt they had earned the right to forsake a traditional structure in order to express the dark poetic yearnings of a more private muse. The chief concerns of such testaments are always the immanence of death and religious transcendence.

Employing the Strindbergian mode of a dream play in *Camino Real*--an elastic form for getting everything in--Williams in his prologue posits the entire dramatic action as a dream inside the head of Don Quixote, the archetypal questing hero. But it is with this very opening that the Lincoln Center production, directed by Milton Kastelas [*sic*], commences to unravel and go awry.

Lumbering down one of the side aisles toward the marvelously imaginative set--its most prominent and functional feature, a futuristic stairway that curves grandiosely toward nothing in particular--Patrick McVey as Don Quixote begins speaking in a weary, sarcastic W. C. Fields voice. Cruelly undercutting the framing action that contains the play, this fuzzy piece of mimicry supplants the requisite image of heroic endurance. And when Quixote speaks of the blue ribbon at the end of his lance as a reminder to an old knight of the distance he has come and the distance he has yet to go, McVey feels compelled to touch the ribbon and wave it toward us to make sure we all see and know what he is talking about. It is precisely this sort of underlining that turns the play into slowly dripping maple syrup, transforming its poetry into rhetoric.

In this very uneven production that alternatively irritates and excites to pleasure, Victor Buono successfully maintains a sinister narration from the dark side of the moon, freezing the blood as he announces each scene. Ominously obese--recalling Sydney Greenstreet--Buono creates an evil presence that the playwright neglected to describe fully. For Williams too much wants goodness and the workings of the heart to win, and arranged a fictive world to make sure they do.

It is not, however, Williams' excessive sentimentality so much as Al Pacino's Kilroy that really whacks up this production. In a directorial stunt that is dramatically startling, Pacino enters by descending from the top of the auditorium, riding down on a wrecker's sky hook right into the middle of the audience. All well and good. Yet once on stage, he archly mugs his way through a role that asks a special kind of restraint.

Looking like a late graduate from the Dead End Kids, Pacino does an imitation of Leo Gorcey imitating Ruth Gordon. Eyes moving lasciviously, tongue darting in and out as a sign of savvy, his Kilroy swaggers around the stage like a stand-up comedian letting the world know that Dolly's back in town. Making instant electric contact with the audience at the expense of the play, Pacino sacrifices both the innocence and pathos implicit in Kilroy's character. What we get instead is a striking example of a director's inability to control the trademark style of an actor struggling to become an established star.

Filled with messianic longings, Kilroy is the protagonist of *Camino Real,* the young hero whom Don Quixote will choose to accompany him when he awakes from his dream. The embodiment of the mythic, ubiquitous soldier of American Fortune, Kilroy finds himself in the company of such legendary figures as Casanova, Camille and Esmeralda--Williams' way of saying that the American solider, and the middle-class culture that produced him, is the end of the line for the romantic tradition.

There is an affecting nobility about this ex-prize fighter with a bad heart. After hocking his most precious possession--his Golden Gloves--to escape the Camino Real, he impulsively decides to remain and participate as the Chosen Hero in a local ritual: taking the virginity of a Gypsy's daughter, a maiden-hood annually restored by the rising of the moon at festival time. But in Williams' dream world the hero is asked to surrender both his sex and his life. When the street cleaners come to cart him off as garbage, Kilroy shadowboxes these surrealistic emissaries of the state, collapsing finally like Cyrano from the fatigue and futility of doing battle with the gods of death.

A major fault in the construction of *Camino Real*--and the Lincoln Center production inadvertently calls attention to it--derives from Williams' expanding the work from an original one-act version into a full-length play. He left Kilroy to wander somewhere off-stage in the second act while the affairs and fortunes of the literary characters occupy our attention. These two separate strands, however, were never properly welded together, having in common only a thematic congruence. Ironically, it is just here, in the inflated middle, that the acting is at is best.

Jessica Tandy as an aging Marguerite Gautier beginning to frighten at the thought of death, delivers a performance of classical dimensions--aware, as others are not, of the speeches as arias that require the range and inflection a singer brings to song. Clifford David's Byron also reveals a moving sensitivity for vocalic coloration. In a lengthy declaration describing the burning of Shelley's body and how Edward Trelawney plucked the poet's heart from the midst of the fiery rib cage, Byron at last begins to look within himself to find the private point of failure in the romantic quest. The play reaches its most heroic pitch as he cries out: "*Make voyages!--Attempt them!--* there's nothing else. . ." (This powerful speech, which culminates with Byron's determination to sail for Athens, serves also as an apology for playwright Williams' life--as in a much larger sense does the entire play.)

It is in the last act, which treats of sex and resurrection, that Katselas' direction is at its worst. Kilroy's comically ineffectual seduction of Esmeralda should result in frenzied awkward rhythms, climaxing in the agony of meaningless orgasm. Instead, this scene is rushed through without allowing the dramatic energy implicit in perverted pleasure to emerge. Like bad sex, the flow of action freezes; and then suddenly, the director begins desperately cutting large chunks from crucial scenes.

Unhappily, it is Kilroy's resurrection that suffers most damage. As written, it is a triumph of visual poetry and contrapuntal music: While state doctors perform an autopsy on Kilroy, searching for his golden heart, the blind Madrecita keens over his body and brings him back to life with a touch of a flower.

But what does director Katselas do with this scene? He removes the autopsy from the stage altogether, and cuts Madrecita's choral lines, substituting an incomprehensible Spanish translation that is chanted and moaned in a false show of agony. The result is the most muddy, awkward moment of the play, a mangling of *Camino Real's* key scene.

If this were not bad enough, Susan Tyrell as Esmeralda is turned into a freaky fractured China doll. When it comes time for the last grand aria (a speech that is fortunately included in the program on the page opposite the cast listing), Miss Tyrell chops it up into so many little meaningless pieces that one wonders if Lincoln Center will ever be able to put Tennessee Williams together again.

Yet, with all these faults, this is in some respects a valuable production. Peter Wexler's costumes and set, as well as John Gleason's lighting, are superior conceptions. And Jessica Tandy gives a performance that I will be talking about years from now.

Camino Real, after all, is a great but nevertheless immensely difficult play. It will take much trial and error before we learn how best to force this work to surrender both its secrets and its power. Lincoln Center has at least bravely followed Lord Byron's advice: *"Make voyages!--Attempt them!"*

The New Leader, January 19, 1970: 32-33.

Time and Tide on the *Camino Real*
James Coakley

Among the plays of Tennessee Williams *Camino Real* remains an enigma. A failure on Broadway, subjected to drastic revision as if its author refused to let it ever congeal into some finished form, and regarded by critics as no more than the reworking of a jeu d'esprit, it received, Williams tells us, "more conscious attention to form and construction than . . . . any work before" (II, 420). Well and good, we might say, but after decades of exposure to European experimentalists, audiences are still baffled by, indeed scornful of, this fascinating and demanding play.

One need not invoke esthetics, literary theory, or that tiresomely incantatory phrase "avant-garde" to see that *Camino Real* is a different kind of play. Its persistent dramatic method is via the sharpest possible contrast and juxtaposition of style. Indeed, stylistic disparity promotes the play's bold efforts to break loose from the stage and spill into the house, enhancing the dramatic action's reliance upon theatricalist conventions (mime, dance, and lavish technical effects) as the source of the drama's attempts to plunge the audience directly into its reality. Yet, this eclecticism of method does not mean that the piece's structure is loose, flimsy, or haphazard. On the contrary, in no play of Williams before or since does his sense of form, of where he is going and how he is going there, serve him more faithfully.

Camino Real is nonlinear in structure, and the use of such a pattern immediately prescribes hard and fast rules: (1) to relinquish forward movement of narrative and action is to lose the easy tension in the rigidly selective organization common to linear drama where one event plunges irreversibly onto the next; (2) to deny the melodramatic core of such an action is to reject what Ionesco (see *Victims of Duty*) calls, for example, the "detective story" nature of drama; (3) and, finally, to deal in episodic units (Williams calls them "blocks," or, more familiarly, French scenes) is to present experience as fragmented, often seemingly aimless or ambiguous. This fragmentation of experience (common to films, but risky business in the theater) suggests the momentary focus on the instant, the episode caught in time and frozen in space, in which we are permitted to discover in vertical movement layers of personality often impossible to consider in the linear form's horizontal progression. In theory, at least, the nonlinear mode chooses to linger in the hidden corners of human motivation, where behavior has the clarity of true complexity. Finally, the most serious challenge of this play is its refusal to accept time either as sequential or an the fundamental common denominator of human affairs. To achieve this immediacy it presents time as discursive, arbitrary, and above all subjective. This particularly modern notion of time is the organizing principle of *Camino Real,* a method perfectly suited to the presentational production style which should, as Williams insists, aim for the freedom of improvisation in performance. It should give that sense of the "perpetual present" where the play is poised, in the words of Thornton Wilder, on a "razor-edge, between past and future, which is the essential character of the conscious being."

So restless a method as fluidity, however, requires control over the diffuse vignettes sprawling across the stage. To absorb an audience in a free association of disconnected images invites chaos or, worse, the private vision of a dilettante. Williams is too shrewdly in control of his materials, however, too aware of the dangers of excessive fragmentation, to allow his play to wander off in meaningless montages. To be sure, time interiorized and discontinuous provides unity, but *Camino* resides paradoxically in the best of two possible worlds: bracketed by Don Quixote's dream, its interior plunges ceaselessly across the country of the mind revealing a completely subjective spectrum of colors, shapes, and images, while retaining a semblance of direction in the adventures of its three quasiheroes, the Don, Kilroy, and Lord Byron. Melodramatic considerations suggesting progressions and resolutions bristle within the play's busy frame, but the truth is that while, much in the fashion of Chekhov, the arrivals and departures of characters imply movement to a destination, they really lead to perpetual wandering (the Don and Kilroy), or to death (Lord Byron). This trio is as rootless and spiritually displaced as any who are trapped forever on the Camino.

The effect of this calculated disorder upon characterization, however, allows for the play's most remarkable achievement. Normally, theatricalism robs character of dimension and consistency; tends, in fact, to dehumanize. In *Camino,* it seems to me, Williams withstands any impulses to present his people as mere style with no matter. Avoiding traditional treatment of his gallery of familiar literary types, he does rely on overtones, the suggestions of myth surrounding them, but in no way are they simply dusted off, refurbished, and reused. They are deployed and developed solely in terms of their perception of time. The persistent contrast is what they once were with what they are now: Quixote is an old desert rat, Casanova an impoverished, seedy roué, and Marguerite Gautier a frightened and lonely woman, addicted to drugs. Here, indeed, is the nub of the drama: the stasis of the present vs. the motion promised by the future, both of which are frustrated by the past's refusal to disappear. For time halted does not erase memory; it encourages the reflection proper to dimensioned characterization. The characters can be understood only by what we might call reflexive reference, their passions and problems darting back and forth; and, like the heroes of Pirandello, condemned to the limbo of the present, they are able to summon nonsequential, past experiences on the instant.

Three groups inhabit the Camino: the outcasts--the bums and drunks of a flophouse; the decadents--Marguerite Gautier, Jacques Casanova, and the Baron de Charlus; and the idealists--Don Quixote, Kilroy, and Lord Byron. Each is tainted (humanized) by the problem of time's meaning; each is dramatized (rather than merely represented) downward to the essence of human existence, forced to examine his problems in the arrested depths of the moment. External reality, the movement of life from point to point, is rejected, for the truth is to be discovered only in context, only in the fusion of past, present, and future: an amalgam of hurts, questions, and no answers. The outcasts (technically they also provide background) elect to ignore time, escaping into drugs and alcohol; for them life is a scavenger hunt "in a bazaar where the human heart is part of the bargain" (II, 452). There is no struggle-- nothing in fact, but the cynical acceptance of things as they are. The sentimental comfort of memories is useless; the satisfaction of appetites is all that remains; and the moral principle is all too clear; indifference to time, to the world, in effect, breeds disaster, self-destruction. To shirk the issue is to end up, as Casanova does, on Skid Row, life hastily collected in a battered portmanteau.

But the decadents, the transients of an expensive tourist hotel, are, like all practicing romantics, terrified of time. Anguished over past glories and present stalemate, their attainment of spiritual freedom (the original reason for their rebellion against the world's order) is movement, flight, escape from the immobility of the Camino. They are morally, however, no better than their counterparts across the plaza. Practicing the same vices, they have more money, but the same fears. And for them to contemplate temporality in human affairs is only to see existence as no more than a series of waystations towards death. With these characters, as we might expect, are posed the play's most serious questions in set speeches of important thematic weight; the chance, as Williams sees it, to play upon his central perception: life is no more than "dim, communal comfort" (II, 527) eroded by change; values are illusory, perpetually in transit. How, in short, is one to live? It is a despair worthy of Beckett, priding itself upon no more than the black honesty of its vision. Neither psychological in origin (as in *Streetcar*) nor diluted with the panacea of the social worker preaching adjustment to the human condition, this despair is metaphysical and profoundly moral. Suspended and viewed in the pity and terror common to all, it is not sentimental; it is artistic, it seems to me, its logic and worth predicated upon the givens of the structure in which it operates. Indeed, in Block Ten, a brief scene between Marguerite and Jacques, Williams drops the theatricalist mask and allows his heroine to proclaim the dilemma correctly:

> What are we sure of? Not even of our existence, dear comforting friend! And whom can we ask the questions that torment us? "What is this place?" "Where are we?" (p. 526)

In the microcosm of the moment all is visible; character, in effect, becomes symbol, the inner life of these people bursts forth, projecting the scope of the play outward to an indictment not only of the world of the play but of a universe equally perverse and corrupt.

The idealists do retain symbols of past achievements (Byron's pen, Kilroy's Golden Gloves, Quixote's blue ribbon), but each chooses, despite the consequences, merely to depart into life against time's ravages. Each makes that deliberate and existential choice by which the self is defined in the world. Yet the promise of self-fulfillment is slight. The Don does forbid Kilroy the pleasures of self-pity, and his only answer to the dilemma is that we must smile, making the best of what we have. To do less is immoral.

Thematically and structurally, then, *Camino* is a most ambitious play; or rather, a scenario, as Williams says, fit only for the "vulgarity of performance" (p. 423). One need not become its apologist to see that its intention and execution are evenly matched. To deprecate it as the triumph of the theatrical over the literary imagination is to miss the most important of matters: its form is its meaning, its central perceptions are stated directly, sincerely, and insistently: a dark message in the garish colors of a circus sideshow.

Tennessee Williams, A Tribute, Ed. Jac Tharpe. Jackson: University Press of Mississippi, 1977. 232-236.

Cat on a Hot Tin Roof (1955)

A Secret Is Half-Told In Fountains of Words
Walter F. Kerr

"Why is it so hard for people to talk?" mutters Ben Gazzara, fondling his fifth or sixth drink and rubbing the back of his neck with a towel, in *Cat on a Hot Tin Roof.* Of course, the people in Tennessee Williams' plays do not really find it hard to talk. They are fountains of speech--blistering, nerve-scraping, recognizable speech.

In the new play at the Morosco, Barbara Bel Geddes stands in her slip on the edge of an apron stage and unleashes a torrent of savage, self-conscious, desperately arch complaint: her husband has refused to sleep with her since the drunken death of his best friend; if she helped to bring about both the drinking and the death with her clumsy suggestion that the friendship was an unnatural one, she has at least tried to tell the truth. The words that tumble over the footlights in panicky profusion are always the right ones: right for the greedy, stubbornly loving girl Miss Bel Geddes is playing.

Burl Ives strides into the spacious, ghost-ridden plantation bedroom, a hard-bitten colossus of the Delta, to bark at the garrulous, gravel-voiced wife who has bored him for forty years, to drive from the premises the insufferable grandchildren who want to present him with a monstrous cake on his sixty-fifth birthday, and to grind from his childless and suspect favorite son a long-overdue confession. Some of the calculated profanity that pours from Mr. Ives is gratuitous, incorporated by the playwright for shock value; most of it has the steamy odor of a long, tough life that has actually been lived.

Wherever Mr. Williams turns his ear and pauses to listen, he hears the exact and expressive inflections of character; in the shrill and selfish pleasantries of a pregnant daughter-in-law (Madeleine Sherwood) who hopes to inherit the plantation; in the genial but obtuse pomposities of a "normal" son (Pat Hingle); in the insistent, rattle-brained vocal scratch of that wife (Mildred Dunnock) who seems to be waiting for Mr. Ives to die of cancer; in the sultry, sneering repetitions of the emotionally paralyzed boy (Ben Gazzara) who cannot forgive or even abide the begging young woman he has married. In *Cat on a Hot Tin Roof* all of these voices are raised in passionate wrangle; the urgent and ugly sounds are unmistakably real.

And in his flawlessly staged production, Elia Kazan has fused these intense, envenomed accents into something like barbarous music. Working in a wide-open, impressively uncluttered setting by Jo Mielziner, he has done more than reproduce the verbal honesties of his author; he has orchestrated them. Early in the second act Burl Ives and Ben Gazzara play a rapid, low-keyed, father-and-son scene of mocking exploration that rolls, rumbles, and treads on its own echoes like an advancing thunderhead.

Again and again the evening's big scenes--these tend to be duologues and even monologues--are fitfully severed by stormy offstage voices, flashes of moody folk music, tumbling flights of children stabbing at the skyline with sparklers and cap pistols. Everything that is intimate is given a place in a larger composition; everything that is mean-spirited and petty is pushed toward theatrical poetry.

Why, then, this curious little feint ("Why is it so hard for people to talk?") on the part of the bitter and bereaved hero, this suggestion that talk is hard to come by? Mr. Williams is naturally not unaware of his own powers; he does not share the contemporary fondness for drawing inarticulate characters; he certainly does not mean to suggest that any one of these people is tongue-tied. The suggestion here is that, behind all of the roaring statement and angry openness of the play, one of the people is soul-tied; he cannot know himself. The boy who has lost a friend and abandoned a wife cannot say what private wounds and secret drives have crippled him.

He is, dramatically speaking, a wholly possible figure. If our interest in him wanes as the evening rages on, if he becomes more and more an impenetrable surface and less and less an unfolding reality, if *Cat on a Hot Tin Roof* gradually acquires an elusive and ambiguous quality that is crippling in its own way, it is not because the tormented Brick cannot read his own heart: it is because we cannot read it.

Is he a homosexual? At one moment he is denouncing "queers," at another describing the way he clasped his friend's hand going to bed at night. Has he loved his wife? She describes him, in some detail, as a good lover because he was a disinterested lover. Listening, we work at the play in an earnest effort to unlock its ultimate dramatic meaning. But the key has been mislaid, or deliberately hidden.

Is it Mr. Williams who, in this instance, "finds it difficult to talk"? How deeply has he cut into the core of his own play? Supposing that he has really unraveled its human mystery, why is he reluctant to give that mystery a name?

It is almost impossible to escape the conclusion that the playwright has been either less than clear or less than candid. He has shown us, with an arresting flourish, a sick young man, he has explored the symptoms in harrowing, unflinching detail; but he has failed--or refused--to isolate the cause of the corruption in Brick, and the play, so far from placing one man's torment in an intelligible relationship to the universe about him, simply catches something of his sickness.

The performance is superb, the language stinging, the substance of the play disturbingly secretive.

New York Herald Tribune, April 3, 1955, sec. 4: 1.

A Cat of Many Colors
John Simon

The American Shakespeare Theater has sensibly chosen to revive one of Tennessee Williams's middle-period plays--not so good as the earlier, vintage Williams, but much better than the plays of the dramatist's long decline, and in need of reassessment. After nineteen years, *Cat on a Hot Tin Roof* reveals itself as a lively, attention-holding, highly theatrical play: worthy commercial fare, but not art. Williams is not sure which of several plays he is writing here. Is it the one about the young wife, Maggie, married to Brick, the ex-football star and sports commentator, who now hobbles on a crutch because of a foolish fracture; Maggie, who went to great lengths to break up Brick's friendship with Skipper--to demonstrate its homosexual coloration--and so, with Brick's half-conscious assistance, drove Skipper to suicide? This Maggie, who has now lost her husband to brooding and boozing, wants him back, so as to have a child by him, so that they can inherit Brick's father's fabulous plantation.

That father, Big Daddy, is dying; and though both he and Big Mama vastly prefer their son Brick to his charmless older brother Gooper and his rather common wife, Mae, the "28,000 acres of the richest land this side of the Valley Nile" may have to go to them; Gooper is a lawyer who has all along concerned himself with the plantation, and Mae is well on her way to a sixth child (repulsive as her brood is), whereas Brick merely drinks and does nothing, least of all procreate. Moreover, there is Big Daddy's personal tragedy: what he now thinks with relief is only a spastic colon is cancer after all--there is no joyous reprieve. Having realized that he disliked his wife, and that there was still time left for some happy womanizing, he soon learns that there is to be no second chance. Is this the play Williams is writing?

If it were merely a question of both Maggie's and Big Daddy's wanting an heir, and of the fight over the inheritance, the two themes could perhaps be made to mesh. But other things, too, are at stake: Brick's agonizing over his guilt--but which guilt? Homosexuality? Or his cowardly concealment of it?

Or just his contributing to Skipper's death? For which of these reasons does he abominate his pretty and passionate wife, and spurn her advances? And Big Daddy: why hasn't he faced up to his connubial loathing until now? Why has he delayed living for so long? And, above all, Maggie: does she truly love Brick and want him, or is it just those thousands of acres? For much of the time it looks like genuine love, but then conception becomes so important that Maggie deprives Brick of the bottle until he impregnates her ("and then I'll bring you liquor, and we'll get drunk together"), which is clearly a ruthless, coercive business proposition.

These strands fly apart. All the more so because Brick, the supposed pivot, is such a nonentity: he hobbles and imbibes, sulks silently, or wearily parries his wife's importuning and his father's probing with evasion or nastiness. When the truth finally erupts from him--disgust with the world's mendacity--it is still a lie. The mendacity, he is made to realize, is his own, his denial of guilt toward Skipper. But here Williams fudges: has Brick betrayed his friend or his homosexuality? It all remains inchoate and obscure. And why all this excitement about "poor, dumb Skipper, a less than average student at 'Ole Miss'"? More to the point, why all this fuss about Brick, who seems to have nothing beyond his good looks to recommend him? He is one of those "weak, beautiful people who give up with such grace," Maggie says, speaking for the author as well, but while we see the giving up plainly enough, where in hell is the grace? Williams has failed to show it, any more than he can show how Maggie can possibly hand his life back to Brick, as she promises to do and Williams at least half implies might happen.

What Brick actually seems to be is a fairly typical figure from the homosexual world: the beautiful but mediocre young man who coasts along on his looks, and drinks because he is beginning to lose them--a golden boy adored by his lovers, often superior, artistic men, who, however, cannot overcome their fatal obsession with mere looks, mere youth, and the indolent passivity that makes their partner perfect as a love object but a failure as a human being. The fanatical passion for Brick that grips Maggie, Big Daddy, and Big Mama has nothing to do with anything we are shown, but hinges on this shied-away-from meaning. Hence, too, the duality with which Maggie is viewed: she is partly the disguised, sentimentalized portrait of the gifted, worldly, passionate homosexual lover frustrated by a shallow beloved; partly the somewhat vindictively drawn sketch of the threatening female who pursues the homosexual with her legally sanctioned but unwanted, burdensome love. (The theme is echoed in Big Daddy's rejection of Big Mama.) *Cat on a Hot Tin Roof,* even in its present, somewhat touched up and improved version, falls short of either cohesion or honesty. Why can't the huge plantation be divided between the two sons? Gooper is not undeserving, merely unattractive, a fault that only a homosexual aesthete--not a father--would penalize with disinheritance.

But there is trouble even with the play's language. Certain words like "mendacity" or "spastic colon," certain phrases like "the richest land this side of the Valley Nile" (why not Nile Valley, by the way?), certain images like that of Maggie as a cat on a hot tin roof, are repeated over and over again, *ad nauseam.* Is Williams yielding to infantile fascination with polysyllables discovered late in life? Is he losing his dramatic control, projecting the weakness on the audience, and assuming they must be repeatedly clobbered with a point in order to get it? Or is it simply that his flagging invention must reuse every ingredient to fill out a play? In his later works, dogged reiteration becomes an omnipresent blight.

The Stratford production is uneven; Michael Kahn, the director, once again moves his principals about adroitly. But the minor characters remain figuratively--sometimes even literally--near-invisible. And he does not pursue emotions very far. The oddly handsome Keir Dullea, whose part all too often reduces him to opaque silence, is allowed to stand there as inexpressive as a Pre-Raphealite saint, though he is actor enough for a better director to coax more significance even out of his silences. And Kahn must in part be blamed for two absolute disasters. Kate Reid is an appalling Big Mama: a coarse, almost demented, busybody, all screechy whining and leaden flutters, her legs always indecently spread apart as though she were about to whelp all over the stage, a posture no Southern woman, however *nouveau riche,* would permit herself. She makes Big Mama far more repugnant than pitiful.

And Fred Gwynne, the Big Daddy, simply isn't an actor, except perhaps in farce. Not only does his tall, gaunt, Lincolnesque frame look beanpolish rather than big, but he cannot even manage a plausible Southern accent or make his implausible one stick for more than a sentence at a time. His demeanor is urban, constricted, taut: he is not the rurally relaxed, sweatily expansive redneck turned millionaire, booming and oozing his way into the farthest crannies of his estate; rather, he is the dryly nasal, buttoned-up New Englander, stiffly contained within the perimeter of his immaculate white suit. But never mind characterization; what about mere acting? The intonations are waywardly barking or meaninglessly strangulated, the eyeballs roll about like a couple of marbles in search of a game, and there is no ease or spontaneity. Above all, Gwynne lacks that unifying breath, that inner rhythm, that steady stream of energy that propels, conjoins, and sustains a true actor's utterances, moods, and movements, and makes him a continuous presence rather than a sequence of disjointed twitches.

The minor characters are unobjectionable, and though John Conklin's set lacks the lived-in quality Williams specifically asks for, Jane Greenwood's costumes are serviceable, if not much more. But above all this towers Elizabeth Ashley's Maggie. I have always considered Miss Ashley talented but rather chilling; here she absorbed me into herself, and made me see Maggie more from inside than from without. Hers is almost more of a juggling act than a performance, keeping grittiness and fragility, a sense of humor and an edge of desperation, sensual coquetry and sexless bitchiness-- and God knows what else--flying around her head like so many complaisant Indian clubs. She is, if anything, too beautiful for the part, but performs with such astonishing, such uncanny precision that not even her heady loveliness distracts us from her acting. Miss this performance at your soul's peril. . . .

New York, 12 August 1974: 48-49.

Turner and Durning in *Cat on a Hot Tin Roof*
Frank Rich

It takes nothing away from Kathleen Turner's radiant Maggie in *Cat on a Hot Tin Roof* to say that Broadway's gripping new production of Tennessee Williams's 1955 play will be most remembered for Charles Durning's Big Daddy. The actor's portrayal of a 65-year-old Mississippi plantation owner in festering extremis is an indelible hybrid of red-neck cutup and aristocratic tragedian, of grasping capitalist and loving patriarch. While *Cat* is not the American *King Lear* its author hoped, this character in this performance is a cracker-barrel Lear and Falstaff in one.

Just try to get the image of Mr. Durning--a dying volcano in final, sputtering eruption under a Delta moon--out of your mind. I can't. *Cat* is a curiously constructed work in which the central but sullen character of Brick, the all-American jock turned booze hound, clings to the action's periphery while Act I belongs to his wife, Maggie, Act II to his Big Daddy and the anti-climactic Act III (of which the author left several variants) to no one. Such is Mr. Durning's force in the second act at the O'Neill that he obliterates all that comes after, despite the emergence of Polly Holliday's poignant Big Mama in the final stretch.

Mr. Durning's Act II tour de force begins with low comedy: the portly, silver-haired actor, dressed in a sagging white suit and wielding a vaudeville comedian's stogie, angrily dismisses his despised, nattering wife and his bratty grandchildren, those cap-gun-toting "no-neck monsters" who would attempt to lure him into a saccharine birthday party. From that hilarious display of W. C. Fields dyspepsia, it is quite a leap to the act's conclusion. By then, Mr. Durning is white with fear, clutching the back of a chair for support, for he has just learned what the audience has long known: Big Daddy is being eaten away by cancer that "has gone past the knife."

In between comes a father-son confrontation that is not only the crux of Mr. Durning's performance but also the troubling heart of a play that is essential, if not first-rank, Williams. Big Daddy loves Brick (Daniel Hugh

Kelly) and would like to favor him when dividing his estate of $10 million and "28,000 acres of the richest land this side of the valley Nile." But there are mysteries to be solved before the writing of the will. Why are Brick and Maggie childless? Why is Brick, once a football hero and later a television sports announcer, now, at 27, intent on throwing away his life as if it were "something disgusting you picked up on the street"? How did Brick break his ankle in the wee hours of the night before?

Mr. Durning will have his answers, even if he has to knock Brick off his crutch to get them. But his Big Daddy, while tough as a billy goat, is not a cartoon tyrant. He wants to talk to his son, not to badger him. He offers Brick understanding and tolerance in exchange for the truth, even if that truth might be Brick's closeted homosexual passion for his best friend and football buddy, Skipper, now dead of drink. All Big Daddy wants is freedom from the lies and hypocrisy of life that have so long disgusted him. Yet Brick, while sharing that disgust, won't surrender his illusions without a fight.

"Mendacity is the system we live in," the son announces. "Liquor is one way out and death's the other." When the truth finally does emerge--and for both men it is more devastating than any sexual revelation--liquor and death do remain the only exits. Life without the crutch of pipe dreams or anesthesia is too much to take. As the lights dim on Act II, Mr. Kelly is isolated in a stupor and Mr. Durning, his jaw distorted by revulsion and rage, is howling like Lear on the heath. Advancing relentlessly into the bowels of his mansion, the old man bellows an epic incantation of "Lying! Dying! Liars!" into the tall shadows of the Southern Gothic night.

Along with the high drama and fine acting--Mr. Kelly's pickled Adonis included--what make the scene so moving is Williams's raw sensitivity to what he called (in his next play, *Orpheus Descending*) man's eternal sentence to solitary confinement. In *Cat,* Maggie probably does love Brick, Big Mama probably does love Big Daddy, and Brick loves Skipper and Big Daddy as surely as they have loved him. Yet the lies separating those who would love are not easily vanquished. In this web of familial, fraternal and marital relationships, Williams finds only psychic ruin, as terminal as Big Daddy's cancer and as inexorable as the greed that is devouring the romantic Old South.

In his revival, Howard Davies, the English director last represented in New York *Les Liaisons Dangereuses,* keeps his eye on that bigger picture: Williams's compassion for all his trapped characters and his desire to make his play "not the solution of one man's psychological problem" but a "snare for the truth of human experience." With the exception of Mae (Debra Jo Rupp), Brick's conniving sister-in-law, everyone on stage is human. The playwright doesn't blame people for what existence does to them. He has empathy for the defeated and admiration for those like Maggie who continue the fight for life and cling to the hot tin roof "even after the dream of life is all over."

From her salt-cured accent to her unabashed (and entirely warranted) delight in her own body heat, Miss Turner is an accomplished Maggie, mesmerizing to watch, comfortable on stage and robustly good-humored. Merely to see this actress put on her nylons, a ritual of exquisitely prolong complexity, is a textbook lesson in what makes a star. Miss Turner is so good as far as she goes that one wishes she'd expose her emotions a shade more-- without compromising her admirable avoidance of a campy star turn. Her Maggie is almost too stubbornly a survivor of marital wars; she lacks the vulnerability of a woman "eaten up with longing" for the man who shuns her bed.

Though somewhat more can be made of Brick--and was by Ian Charleson, in Mr. Davies's previous staging of *Cat* in London--Mr. Kelly captures the detachment of defeat, and later the rage, of a man who buried hope in his best friend's grave. When Brick is finally provoked to stand up for the "one great good true thing" in his life, the actor gives an impassioned hint of the noble figures who inspired worship from all who knew him. But it's a major flaw of *Cat* that this character is underwritten. Williams defines the physique of his golden boy--and Mr. Kelly fleshes that out, too--but leaves the soul opaque.

Since Brick doesn't pull his weight in any of the playwright's third acts for *Cat,* it hardly matters which one is used. Mr. Davies reverts to the unsentimental original draft, which never made it to the stage in Elia Kazan's initial Broadway production. Miss Holliday's Big Mama, an unstrung Amanda Wingfield brought to her own grief by others' mendacity, is a rending figure within the thunderstorm of the denouement. Along with the supporting cast, the designers' vision of a decaying South--from the fading veranda to the intrusion of the latest American innoculation against intimacy, a 1950's console television--thickens the rancid mood of a household where, in Big Mama's words, "such a black thing has come . . . without invitation."

But even in Act III, even offstage, Mr. Durning continues to dominate, and, in a way, he gets the big scene with the star that the script denies him. As Maggie tenaciously clings to her tin roof, Big Daddy can be heard from somewhere deep within, his terrifying screams of pain rattling that roof, threatening even at death's doorstep to blow the lid off life's cruel, incarcerating house of lies.

New York Times, March 22, 1990, sec. 3: 17, 22.

Tennessee Williams: The Playwright as Social Critic
Paul J. Hurley

Now that violently hysterical critical and popular reactions to Tennessee Williams' plays have begun to subside, the moment may have come to offer more sober analyses of his concerns as a dramatist. Williams is, of course, our nation's leading dramatist; and it is unfortunate that concern with his subjects (rape, homosexuality, cannibalism) has obscured attempts to analyze his thematic preoccupations. It may, then, be valuable to begin now to suggest that his plays consistently reveal a continuing interest in values and attitudes which he appears to consider as typically American. I shall even go so far as to suggest that a total understanding of his achievement as a dramatist is impossible without some attempt to relate his plays to recent historical and sociological considerations of American society. Surely we must attach some significance to the fact that Williams almost always places the action of his plays in distinctly American settings, and his major characters are, without exception, Americans. To clarify my point, let me offer here an analysis of one of his best known plays, *Cat on a Hot Tin Roof,* as an example of the way in which interest in American social values pervades--and is even the basis of-- his dramatistic concerns.

I shall approach my subject in a devious manner. As we all realize, one of the problems which has most engaged the attention of critics of our society concerns the relationship between the individual and the group, the person and his society. A question which commentators on our society have raised with alarming insistence concerns the ability of the individual to defend his personal values in the face of a society which demands adherence to group values. The question is certainly as literary as it is sociological. Our failure to recognize that this question is at the heart of *Cat on a Hot Tin Roof* (as well as many other dramas) has impeded critical attempts to understand that play.

We have been informed, with increasing stridency, that in the twentieth century emphasis on the individual has given way to emphasis on the group and the security it can offer. That, at least, seems to be the attitude of William Whyte when he suggests that the challenge which lies before young men today is not to *be* better than their competitors, but to fit in better. Whyte defends the assumption that the individual who hopes to succeed in contemporary American society must be less an individual and more a group man than anyone else. He says that, in the hearts of young men today, "Needless to say, ambition still pulses. . . . It is quite obvious, nevertheless, that [the young businessman] must pursue the main chance in a much more delicate fashion. To get ahead, he must co-operate with the others--but co-operate *better* than they do."[1] Our new attitude, again according to Whyte, is that "while there may be a promotion for the fittest there can be survival for all."[2]

Whyte's words have some relevance to *Cat on a Hot Tin Roof,* a play in which Williams makes use of questions concerning the individual's relation to the values of society as a springboard from which to dive into a more fundamental and far-reaching speculation. That speculation concerns the question of whether life should be continued under any and all circumstances, even if the values which govern life deprive the individual of his dignity as a human being. Most of us accept the proposition that whatever produces life is perforce good and that which hinders it is both wrong and evil. Perhaps none of the beliefs of Western man is more deeply held than the conviction that life, under any circumstances, must continue. It is not unsafe to assume that most Americans share that conviction. Richard Mosier has suggested that the idea insinuated itself most profoundly into the fibre of American life and American institutions because of the impact of Darwinian philosophy in our culture. Speaking of the works of Darwin and Herbert Spencer, he writes,

> There followed, among educated persons, a new critical awareness of man as a biological creature. All the creations of man seemed to reflect an aboriginal force working itself out in his mind and his institutions for the sake of setting up a better in their place. Cosmic philosophies were born which sought to give the title of God to the mysterious dynamic forces at work in the universe, and upon which man so obviously depended for the success of his enterprise. Nature became the scene of a struggle for existence, a battle of the hungry forms, in which triumph emerged for the sake of the continuance of life.
>
> . . . .
>
> Nature had bred a systematic illusion, because the categories of thought and the forms of life were equally doomed by the struggle for existence either to a justification in the service of life or to an ignominious death when they were no longer the instruments of survival.[3]

Whether or not Darwinism is responsible for our belief that some power dictates the necessity for continuing life, it is true that most of us do not seem to question the belief that life is, in and of itself, valuable. But that is one of the questions which Williams asks us to consider in *Cat on a Hot Tin Roof*,[4] a drama which also looks at the threat to individuality posed by the forces of conformity.

The play is concerned with Big Daddy Pollitt and his family: his wife, Big Mama, his son Brick, Brick's older brother Gooper and Gooper's wife Mae, and Brick's wife Maggie, the "cat" of the title. In the first act we learn that Big Daddy, who owns the largest cotton plantation in Mississippi, is dying of cancer. He has been told, however, that he is merely suffering from a spastic colon. Brick's marriage to Maggie is on the rocks; he refuses to sleep with his wife even though she insistently professes her love for him. The only item in their bedroom which is of interest to him is the liquor cabinet, and he abandons himself to the problem of drinking himself into a state of alcoholic torpor. In the course of the play we learn that Brick's drinking started after the death of his close friend Skipper, whom Maggie had accused of being in love with her husband. Brick blames Maggie for Skipper's death and drinks, he says, to escape his disgust with the world's mendacity. The second act is devoted primarily to a scene between Brick and Big Daddy in which the old man tells his son that it is himself, not the world's mendacity, he drinks to escape. Big Daddy reveals that when Skipper had called Brick and tried to confess his love, Brick had refused to listen to him. Infuriated by the accusation, Brick taunts his father with the fact that he too has been victimized by mendacity and finally reveals to Big Daddy that he is dying of cancer. Gooper and Mae, knowing that the old man can't live long, have devoted all their energy to winning his affection in order to gain control of the estate after his death. But they have reckoned without Maggie, who is equally determined to get control of the Pollitt land and money. Realizing Big Daddy's affection for Brick, she knows that presenting him with a grandchild fathered by his favorite son will assure them of a major share of the estate. At the play's end, Maggie announces that she is expecting a child; and then, in order to force Brick to sleep with her, she threatens to keep his liquor away from him unless he helps to make her lie come true. At the final curtain, Brick is about to comply with Maggie's ultimatum.[5]

Most critics assumed that Williams was explicitly concerned with the subject of homosexuality; Richard Vowles has said that "the play is really about that shadowy no-man's-land between hetero-and homosexuality."[6] And Eric Bentley found fault with the drama because the question of Brick's inversion is not resolved:

> One does not, of course demand that he "cure" the boy, only that he present him: he should tell the audience, even if he doesn't tell the boy himself, whether a "cure" is possible, and, if not, whether homosexuality is something this individual can accept as the irrevocable truth about himself. At present, one can only agree with his father that the story is fatally incomplete.[7]

Bentley's conclusion is a curious one, because if Williams were primarily interested in making a literal presentation of the subject of homosexuality, he has proved himself an extraordinarily inept dramatist. The question of Brick's relationship with Skipper is introduced in Act One, is brought up again by Big Daddy in Act Two, and is not even mentioned in Act Three (either version). Bentley presumes that Brick's latent homosexuality is established beyond doubt, but in actuality we never know whether Brick is harboring homosexual impulses more powerful than those which psychologists tell us are common to most men. And Maggie, who seems to have more insight into the relationship between Skipper and Brick than anyone else in the play, says early in the first act, "I know, believe me I know, that it was Skipper that harbored even any *unconscious* desire for anything not perfectly pure between you two!" (p. 42). Furthermore, if Williams intended to deal literally with the subject of sexual aberration, he was guilty of putting his subject and method at odds. As Arthur Miller pointed out,

> As the play was produced, without the surface realism of living-room, bedroom, walls, conventional light--in an atmosphere, instead, of poetic conflict, in a world that is eternal and not merely this world--it provided more evidence that Williams' preoccupation extends beyond the surface realities of the relationships, and beyond the psychiatric connotations of homosexuality and impotence. In every conceivable fashion there was established a goal beyond sheer behavior.[8]

As incisive reading of the play was suggested by those critics who declared that it is concerned with making a statement about truth. "The play dances, thematically, around the problems of truth," William Becker said,[9] and Roger Ashton was insistent that truth, not homosexuality, is the subject of the play:

> Mr. Williams in this play is interested in something far more significant than one man's psychological make-up. He is interested in what may and may not be said about the truth as a motivating force in human life. The play is thus less psychological than moral in orientation.[10]

It seems to me that such an interpretation has many virtues, but it does not go quite far enough in resolving the play's complexities. That insight does, however, offer a convenient path into the concerns of the drama.

Each of the characters in *Cat on a Hot Tin Roof* reveals himself as involved in some kind of lie. Mae and Gooper lie to themselves and to others about Big Daddy's affection for them and theirs for him. Avoiding the obvious fact that Big Daddy has never been fond of Gooper and is disgusted by their five children, they pretend a mutual affection which does not exist, and never has existed, between them. Gooper tells Big Mama, "I've always loved Big Daddy in my own quiet way. I never make a show of it, and I know that Big Daddy has always been fond of me in a quiet way, too, and he never made a show of it neither" (pp. 32-33.). But when Gooper is confronted with the possibility that he may not gain control of Big Daddy's plantation, he reveals the truth about his relationship with his father,

I don't give a goddam if Big Daddy likes me or don't like me or did or
never did or will or will never! I'm just appealing to a sense of common
decency and fair play. I'll tell you the truth. I've resented Big Daddy's
partiality to Brick ever since Brick was born, and the way I've been
treated like I was just barely good enough to spit on and sometimes not
even good enough for that. (pp. 135-136)

Big Mama's lie also concerns Big Daddy. She refuses to accept the fact
that he does not now love her and never has loved her. She finds excuses for
his gross insults, his boorishness and vulgarity. She indulges in every means
of avoiding the truth about their relationship. A revealing exchange occurs
between the two when, at one point, she reprimands Big Daddy for his
language:

BIG MAMA: Big Daddy, I will not allow you to talk that way, not even
           on your birthday, I--
BIG DADDY: I'll talk like I want to on my birthday, Ida, or any other
           goddam day of the year and anybody here that don't like
           it knows what they can do!
BIG MAMA: You don't mean that!
BIG DADDY: What makes you think I don't mean it?
BIG MAMA: I just know you don't mean it.
BIG DADDY: You don't know a goddam thing and you never did!
BIG MAMA: Big Daddy, you don't mean that. (p. 59)

Big Mama is helpless before her husband's brutality; her only defense is to
pretend it doesn't exist. But she, too, is forced to realize the truth even though
it is a truth she always manages to forget.
    Brick's lie, which involves his friendship with Skipper, is more complex.
Their relationship was, for Brick, a symbol of purity in an impure world. He
tells Maggie, "One man has one great good true thing in his life. One great
good thing which is true!--I had friendship with Skipper. . . . Not love with
you, Maggie, but friendship with Skipper was that one great true thing . . . "
(p. 42). When Brick denies imputations of perversion, he is not merely
defending himself against the charge of homosexuality; he is defending an
ideal. As Arthur Miller said,

Brick conceives of his friendship with his dead friend as an idealistic,
even gallant and valorous and somehow morally elevated one, a
relationship in which nothing was demanded, but what was given was
given unasked, beyond the realm of price, of value, even of materiality.
He clings to this image as to a banner of purity to flaunt against the
world . . . .[11]

Thus Brick refuses to face the truth of Skipper's real feeling for him, and in order to preserve his belief he not only rejects Skipper's own admission of the truth but blames Maggie for having implanted the idea in Skipper's mind; he tells Big Daddy,

> She took this time to work on poor dumb Skipper. He was a less than average student at Ole Miss, you know that, don't you!--Poured in his mind the dirty, false idea that what we were, him and me, was a frustrated case of that ole pair of sisters that lived in this room, Jack Straw and Peter Ochello!--He, poor Skipper, went to bed with Maggie to prove it wasn't true, and when it didn't work out, he thought it *was* true!--Skipper broke in two like a rotten stick--nobody ever turned so fast to a lush--or died of it so quick. . . . (p. 107)

We need to recognize that Brick's analysis of his relationship may be quite as valid as Maggie's. The question of Brick's and even Skipper's homosexuality is left purposely ambiguous. Williams offers no answer to that question for reasons which I hope to make clear later. At this point we need realize only that, in order to keep his ideal unsullied, Brick was willing to see destroyed the person who had helped create the ideal. His retreat into alcoholism is not caused by fear that he is latently homosexual. Brick drinks to avoid his sense of guilt at having failed Skipper. As Maggie says of their relationship, "I'm naming is so damn clean that it killed poor Skipper!--You two had something that had to be kept on ice, yes, incorruptible, yes!--and death was the only icebox where you could keep it . . . " (p. 42).

Big Daddy is unimpressed by Brick's explanation that he drinks because of disgust with the world's mendacity: "Hell, you *got* to live with it, there's nothing *else to live* with except mendacity . . . " (p. 93). But Big Daddy is reflecting the fact that he has lived with lies his whole life and has never been particularly disgusted by them. He imagines himself a hard-headed realist willing to face the fact that mendacity is part of the human condition. He recites, at one point during his long conversation with Brick, a litany of the lies which he has endured:

> What do you know about this mendacity thing? Hell! I could write a book on it! Don't you know that? . . . I could write a goddam book on it and still not cover the subject anywhere near enough!!--Think of all the lies I got to put up with!--Pretenses! Ain't that mendacity? Having to pretend stuff you don't think or feel or have any idea of? . . . Big Mama!--I haven't been able to stand the sight, sound, or smell of that woman for forty years now!--even when I *laid* her!--regular as a piston. . . . Pretend to love that son of a bitch of a Gooper and his wife Mae and those five same screechers out there like parrots in a jungle? Jesus!

> Can't stand to look at 'em! Church!--it bores the Bejesus out of me but
> I go!--I go an' sit there and listen to the fool preacher! Clubs!--Elks!
> Masons! Rotary! crap! (p. 92)

It is interesting that Big Daddy's catalogue of mendacity should combine
indiscriminately social concerns (the church and fraternal organizations) with
his most personal family relationships. He counsels Brick that he must learn
to live with lies because Big Daddy himself has never for a moment pondered
the question of whether life might be possible without them. If one is going
to get along and at the same time get ahead, in a society which values
appearance more than reality, living by, for, and with lies becomes instinctive.

We come a step closer to Williams' theme when we recognize that it
seems to be a sense of social obligation rather than any real affection which
has dictated the show of love between the members of the Pollitt family.
Husbands and wives, if they are "respectable," love each other; children, unless
they are unnatural, are devoted to their parents, and parents adore their
children. Thus Big Mama depends on the illusion that Big Daddy loves her;
Mae and Gooper insist on pretending affection for Big Daddy, and Big Daddy
has performed his duty to society by feigning love for his wife and children.[12]

Even Maggie's love for Brick which seems real during most of the play
gradually reveals itself as a perversion of love. In considering Maggie's
character and the particular lie which she tells, it is important to note, we
confront most directly the major concern of Williams' play. For Maggie,
Brick represents primarily the means of getting her hands on Big Daddy's
money. It is that, not Brick's love, she is determined to win. She never
speaks of her love for him in other than sexual terms, and we are led to
believe that what she means by love is merely getting Brick to go to bed with
her. In the course of the play Maggie tells two lies, and both have the same
purpose, to get Big Daddy's money and property. In the first act Maggie
shows Brick a jacket she has bought for Big Daddy's birthday and insists that
he present the jacket as his own gift. She knows, of course, that a gift from
Brick will mean more to Big Daddy than a present from her or anyone else.
Brick easily sees through her scheme and refuses to do his part. But it is her
second lie which is important. In the last act of the play Maggie announces
that she is pregnant, a desperate move to offer Big Daddy what he desires and
to assure herself of a share in his estate.

Maggie knows instinctively that she and Big Daddy share one value in
common, a veneration for life and a belief in the necessity for its continuance.
Big Daddy tells Brick,

> Life is important. There's nothing else to hold on to. A man that drinks
> is throwing his life away. Don't do it, hold onto your life. There's
> nothing else to hold on to. . . . (p. 68)

Later he says to his son,

> --the human animal is a beast that dies and if he's got money he buys
> and buys and buys and I think the reason he buys everything he can buy
> is that in the back of his mind he has the crazy hope that one of his
> purchases will be life everlasting! (p. 73)

Even though Big Daddy dislikes Gooper's wife, he does admire one thing
about her: ". . . Gooper's wife's a good breeder, you got to admit she's fertile"
(p. 64). Mae is a greedy, avaricious woman who wins no sympathy from the
audience. But, as Big Daddy recognizes, she and Maggie are indeed sisters
under the skin; he says to Brick, "That woman of yours has a better shape on
her than Gooper's but somehow or other they got the same look about them"
(p. 63). And Brick explains exactly what it is that gives them that look:

> They're sittin' in the middle of a big piece of land, Big Daddy, twenty-
> eight thousand acres is a pretty big piece of land and so they're squaring
> off on it, each determined to knock off a bigger piece of it than the other.
> . . . (p. 64).

The dominant impression which Maggie's personality makes on us is one
of strength and determination. In contrast to Brick, who Williams tells us has
"that cool air of detachment that people have who have given up the struggle"
(p. 3), Maggie is very much a part of the struggle. As she says of herself,
". . . one thing I don't have is the charm of the defeated, my hat is in the ring,
and I am determined to win" (p. 15). Maggie is undeniably strong, but hers
is a kind of animal strength. She knows that she will win, will survive,
because in the jungle she inhabits, she is one of the fittest of her species. The
real clue to her "love" for Brick is announced both in her character and in her
last speech. Having forced Brick into bed with her, she says to him,

> Oh, you weak people, you weak, beautiful people!--who give up.--What
> you want is some one to--take hold of you.--Gently, gently, with love!
> And--I *do* love you, Brick, I *do!* (pp. 149-150)

Brick answers sadly, "Wouldn't it be funny if that was true?" (p. 150). What
Maggie loves is her husband's weakness; she loves her power over him in the
way a lioness loves its prey.

Maggie's lie about her pregnancy is a manifestation of her determination
to win the power-struggle which is going on in the Pollitt family. It is clearly
calculated to delude and impress Big Daddy. But the most fascinating fact
about Maggie's character and her lie is that American audiences, at least as
represented by the critics, approved quite as much as Big Daddy. The reasons

for their approval are revealing. Maggie's pretense that she is pregnant was called by one reviewer, "a gallant white lie . . . that brings a measure of understanding to the estranged husband and wife."[13] Since the lie is clearly motivated by mercenary self-interest, one wonders why it is called "white," not to mention "gallant." I suspect the answer can be found in a remark by Roger Ashton, who points out that Maggie's announcement of her pregnancy is not really a lie at all since we are led to believe it will come true. Her lie, he says, is really a "desperate truth," that is "the truth which comes to be because it *must* come to be--truth in the service of life."[14] It would seem that any words and actions, no matter how vicious, need only justify themselves as having been committed in order to continue life. Another writer admiringly characterized Maggie as "sturdy, strong, and resilient."[15] No doubt she is, but it is the specific application of those qualities to a particular situation which concerns Williams, and the point of his play, it seems to me, is to place in doubt any certainty we may have that Maggie's characteristics are altogether admirable.

In order to force that doubt on his audience, Williams seems to have taken special care to emphasize Maggie's characteristics by paralleling them to the point of parody in Gooper's wife. Mae, too, is ambitious and determined, but she is much more obvious about her greediness. Mae is pregnant when the play begins, and Maggie is pregnant (or shortly will be) when it ends. The quality of life Mae has produced is hardly admirable; Maggie's first words characterize Mae and Gooper's children as "little no-neck monsters," and our brief glimpses of them on the stage reveal that she does not speak purely out of jealousy. Surely one would stretch optimism about human nature to the point of collapse if he [*sic*] were to intimate that the world is better off for having those additions. Wherein, then, does Maggie differ from Mae? She is surely as ambitious as Gooper's wife and even more determined to win. Can we really believe, given Maggie's characteristics, that her forcing Brick into bed will produce more worthy human beings than those Mae has brought forth? Williams clearly exposes Maggie's vices, and even though her character is in opposition to Mae's, her values are not.

The basic conflict in the play is not between Maggie on the one hand and Gooper and his wife on the other for possession of Big Daddy's land. The actual conflict in which Williams is interested is between differing values. The opposition we are asked to consider is that between Brick's values, as represented in his relationship with Skipper, and those of Maggie and Big Daddy. The values Maggie and Big Daddy live by are, in an ultimate sense, social whereas Brick's are non-(but not necessarily anti-) social. The moral choice the audience is asked to make is given more meaning by the playwright's having endowed Maggie with the power to continue life (and clearly intimating the kind of life she will continue) and having denied that power to Brick and Skipper. I mentioned earlier that the question of homosexual attraction in the relationship between Brick and his friend is purposely unresolved. That ambiguity is appropriate to the play's purpose. The reason for their friendship (or love) is unimportant, but homosexuality dramatically suggests a relationship which is unmistakably not "in the service of life," a relationship which, by its nature, cannot justify itself in those terms. Thus the choice Williams offers us is between a relationship which, as Brick says, represents "the one great true thing" in his life and a marriage which, like that between Mae and Gooper, threatens to pervert the meaning of love but which promises survival for the race. In effect, Williams asks us to consider whether life is, by and for itself, valuable if it is to be characterized by a struggle for power and domination of others. As Arthur Miller has already noted, the ultimate question which hangs over the play is whether a society in which the greed of Mae and Gooper, the vulgarity of Big Daddy and the stupidity of Big Mama are merely individual expressions of larger social truths has any right to perpetuate itself. Miller writes,

> The question here, it seems to me, the ultimate question is the right of society to renew itself when it is, in fact, unworthy. There is, after all, a highly articulated struggle for material power going on here. There is literally and symbolically a world to win or a world to forsake and damn.[16]

Miller feels that the necessary pronouncement never comes. As he says, "There is a moral judgment hanging over this play which never quite comes down."[17] I tend to agree, but I suspect Williams may not have been interested in making that judgment himself but in asking the audience to make it. The point which *Cat on a Hot Tin Roof* seems most concerned to make is not really a condemnation of Maggie and defense of Brick; rather it appears to be concerned with suggesting that in valuing the creation of life, without reference to the kind of life created, man threatens to destroy the "one great true thing" in human relationships.

Richard Vowles has said that ". . . ultimately, the play focuses on the character of Brick . . . his problem is at the heart of the play--even if the desperate vibrancy of Maggie the Cat chiefly absorbs our interest."[18] Brick's problem is indeed at the heart of the drama but not because, as Vowles says, "the play is really about that shadowy no-man's land between hetero- and homosexuality."[19] Brick's problem is not a question of whether he is homosexual or whether he may be cured. His problem is how an individual who has come to respect and understand individual difference may come to terms with a society which refuses to accept such differences. Homosexuality is a metaphor for individual difference, and Brick's ideal, as represented by his friendship with Skipper, seems to be a visionary's dream of an ideal society in which differences are not only tolerated but encouraged and respected. That

Williams is not concerned with a literal presentation of the subject of homosexuality is clear. That he is not even interested in making a plea for social tolerance seems obvious from the fact, ironic enough, that both Maggie and Big Daddy declare, in the course of the play, their tolerance of homosexuals. Brick is more intolerant of overt sexual abnormality than they. One of his most vivid memories is his recollection of what happened to a fraternity brother who, it was discovered, was a homosexual. He says to his father,

> --Don't you know how people *feel* about things like that?   How, *disgusted* they are by things like that? Why, at Ole Miss when it was discovered a pledge to our fraternity, Skipper's and mine, did a, *attempted* to do a unnatural thing with--
> We not only dropped him like a hot rock!--We told him to git off the campus, and he did, he got! (p. 103)

The speech clearly suggests Brick's fear of society's censure, but it is a fear which has acted as a prelude to his questioning of values.

Both Maggie and Big Daddy see Brick as their only hope of renewing themselves, and Brick's alienation from them and the values they represent threatens their renewal just as literal homosexuality is a threat to man's desire to reproduce himself. Thus a difference in values and allegiances forms the basic conflict presented in the play. The victor in that conflict is, of course, Maggie, who succeeds at last in forcing Brick to sleep with her.

Brick loses the battle because, as Maggie knows, he is, finally, weak. He was destined to lose his fight with Maggie because she represents the strength he does not possess, and he had already lost his battle against her when Skipper called and confessed his love. Despite the puzzling fact that most reviewers of the play admired and applauded Maggie, surely Brick deserves some of our sympathy. The man who has held aloft the banner of an ideal only to retreat when it is splattered with mud must appeal to us. Brick's ideal was not, however, anchored in the reality of an understanding of himself and his society. When, through Skipper's confession, his ideal was tested, when Brick was asked in real and specific terms to give understanding and respect to someone who stood outside society, he failed. Symbolically, Brick demanded death in order that he would not be forced to defend his ideal just as Maggie demands life in order to prove the rightness of society's values. Although Williams is interested, as Arthur Miller suggested, in questioning the wisdom of continuing our species, that question is not the play's only concern. What ultimately concerns Williams is spiritual death, the destruction of one's humanity. To deny one's responsibilities to his [sic] fellow men, to abandon ideals because their defense places the defender under suspicion and makes him an outcast from society, is a kind of death. One becomes (as Brick does) a spiritual cripple. (Brick's hobbling about the stage on crutches because of an accident which occurred when he attempted to prove that his youthful vigor--*i.e.,* his idealism--was unimpaired is the reflection of a more significant deficiency than the absence of physical prowess.) Thus, Big Daddy's imminent death and his constant concern with life and death point to the play's final objective. Maggie is alive, and will produce life, because she is faithful to her values, no matter how shoddy those values may be. Brick, under pressure, may have abandoned his values; but Maggie (under different but equal pressure) manages to stand by hers. She possesses life and deserves it; her husband has committed suicide.

In considering *Cat on a Hot Tin Roof* we confront, in a clear light, one of Williams' primary artistic assets, his ability to present fully-rounded, startlingly alive human beings. The shifting, dissolving kaleidoscope of the human personality, in all its complexity of motivation and ambiguity of behavior, confronts us with disturbing reality. One cannot actually dislike Maggie or Big Daddy; they are too human. Big Daddy's coarseness, his rudeness and vulgarity, are more than compensated for by his frankness, his ability to see through the sham world of conventional hypocrisy. He may accept that world and its hypocrisy, but he knows it for what it is. And his love for Brick must win our sympathy. Maggie, too, is attractive. She shares Big Daddy's refusal to be deluded into thinking conventional mores represent an ideal. She may accept society's rules, but at least she sees them for what they are. Her strength, her stubborn refusal to give in, to be weak, arouse (and are intended to arouse) our delighted applause. A fortune is at stake, and surely it is better that she, rather than the insipid Gooper and Mae, win that fortune, if only because Maggie is a human being. Gooper and Mae, though they share Maggie's values as well as her faults, are vicious parodies of human beings.

Interestingly enough, it is Williams' artistry that has most misled his critics. Applauding Maggie and Big Daddy as human beings, comparing them to Mae and Gooper, audiences have forgotten the values they represent.[20] Maggie and Big Daddy may see the world steadily (if not whole), without illusion, but they have also committed the Williamsian sin of having *accepted* that world and its value as final and irrevocable. Brick may be too weak to temper his vision of an ideal world with acceptance and understanding of the real one, but Maggie and Big Daddy refuse even to entertain the possibility of an ideal world or to give much sympathy to those who do. Williams himself has said that, in preparing his play for its Broadway production, following Elia Kazan's suggestions, "Maggie the Cat had become steadily more charming . . . as I worked on her characterization" (p. 152). Kazan, Williams noted, "felt that the character of Margaret, while he understood that I sympathized with her and liked her myself, should be, if possible, more clearly sympathetic to an audience" (p. 152). As readers and viewers we may, indeed should, find Maggie sympathetic and likable, but I doubt that Williams intended for us to admire her or side with her. She is a fascinating human being and a triumph of characterization, but she is also a single-minded, avaricious woman. To applaud her triumph is to applaud her values. Williams seemed to be aware (even if his director was not) of the dangers of making Maggie too sympathetic, and critical reception of the play appears to have justified those fears. Thus, interpretations of Williams' plays have been generally unenlightening because critics have refused to consider the ways in which the playwright's intense concern for American values has pervaded his plays. Until we do face up to that necessity, analyses of his works will continue to be fruitless products of art divorced from life.

NOTES

1. *The Organization Man* (New York, 1956), p. 124.

2. *Ibid.,* p. 123.

3. *The American Temper: Patterns of our intellectual Heritage* (Berkeley, 1952), pp. 233-235.

4. (New York, 1955). Page references to all quotations from the play will be noted in the body of the text and will refer to the edition cited.

5. Williams has written two third acts for the play. He was asked by Elia Kazan, who directed the Broadway production of the drama, to revise the original third act in order to bring Big Daddy back on stage after his second act exit, to make Maggie more sympathetic to the audience, and to show a change in Brick's character. Williams complied with Kazan's advice, but he has expressed a preference for the act as it was originally written. Since there is no basic difference in the plot and since we are concerned here with Williams' insights into American culture rather than dramaturgic problems, I have employed his original version in this study of the play.

6. "Tennessee Williams: The World of His Imagery," *Tulane Drama Review,* III (December, 1958), 54.

7. *What Is Theatre* (New York, 1956), p. 59.

8. "The Shadows of the Gods: A Critical View of the American Theatre," *Harper's,* CCXVII (August, 1958), 42.

9. "Reflections on Three New Plays," *Hudson Review,* VIII (Summer 1955), 271.

10. "Correspondence: Back on a Hot Tin Roof," *New Republic,* CXXXII (April 25, 1955), 23.

11. "The Shadows of the Gods," p. 42.

12. In Hollywood love is even more pervasive. In the movie version of *Cat on a Hot Tin Roof* Gooper and Brick were given a reconciliation scene in which Gooper revealed himself at last as a regular guy who had been misled by his aggressive wife. Thus Hollywood, by forcing even the brothers to love each other, fulfilled its duty to society and by so doing reversed one of the play's major ironies.

13. "Theatre," *Newsweek,* XLV (April 4, 1955), 54.

14. "Correspondence: Back on a Hot Tin Roof," *New Republic,* p. 23.

15. Arthur B. Waters, "Tennessee Williams: 10 Years Later," *Theatre Arts,* XXXIX (July, 1955), 96.

16. "The Shadows of the Gods," p. 42.

17. *Ibid.*

18. "Tennessee Williams: The World of His Imagery," p. 54.

19. *Ibid.*

20. For the most recent, delighted defense of Maggie the Cat, see Benjamin Nelson, *Tennessee Williams: The Man and His Work* (New York, 1961), pp. 198-222.

The Theatre Annual, 21 (1964): 40-56.

Twenty-seven Wagons Full of Cotton (1955)

A Drama, an Opera, and a Dancer*
Richard Watts Jr.

You wouldn't be far wrong if you called *All in One* a crazy, mixed-up evening in the theater. The oddly assorted program that opened last night at the Playhouse consists of an old but characteristic one-act play by Tennessee Williams with the title of *27 Wagons Full of Cotton*, a short satirical opera by Leonard Bernstein known as "Trouble in Tahiti," and a brief dance recital by the talented Paul Draper. We drama critics are being forced to become versatile fellows, but it is quite possible I should have shared the reviewing with my colleagues of music and the dance.

Because it is the item that belongs most securely in my specialized territory, as well as the one which interested me most, I'll begin with Mr. Williams' little contribution, although it is the last number on the bill. I suspect it is among its author's distinctly minor achievements, but it is likewise entirely typical of his mood, manner and spirit. There is in it that disturbing combination of explicit sex and implied sadism which has become his particular preserve. And there is also present that familiar quality of ugly fascination.

27 Wagons Full of Cotton is the rather studiously distasteful tale of a blowzy, half-idiotic child-woman of a wife, her corrupt husband who sets fire to a cotton gin, and the Italian manager of the cotton plantation, who uses his knowledge of the crime to force the husband to accept his seduction of the wife. It is all given over to an unpleasantly gloating observation of the unfortunate woman's imbecilic frailties and her entrapment by the Italian, but I'd be indulging in hypocrisy if I denied that it held my uncomfortable interest throughout.

In large part this fascination is the result of an astonishingly brilliant

*Reprinted with permission from the *New York Post,* April 20, 1955: 72.

performance by Maureen Stapleton as the wife. Miss Stapleton doesn't mind emphasizing the utter foolishness of the woman or the role's leeringly comic aspects, and yet she succeeds in making the part utterly believable, honestly pathetic and even strangely touching. I think it is the finest portrayal I have ever seen this admirable actress give, and one of the season's best. The other roles are well played by Myron McCormick as the husband and Felice Orlandi as the Italian.

Melodrama Isn't Always A Dirty Word
Walter Kerr

Thrice I've thought it this season, and twice I've failed to mention it. But now that I've seen Tennessee Williams's *27 Wagons Full of Cotton* in close conjunction with Sidney Howard's *They Knew What They Wanted,* I've got to pause and praise Williams for a virtue he's not normally credited with. He's a man unafraid of melodrama, and a man who handles it with extraordinary candor and deftness.

This isn't exactly the party-line on Williams. When we acclaim him--as, in this season of revivals, we seem to be doing every week or two--it is mainly for his women and his words. Fair enough. His women are the American theater's best, and so are his words. But if we mention the melodrama that marks the plays at all, it is usually to rue it: what's our finest living dramatist doing mucking about with arson, political violence, gunplay in shady roadhouses? We don't need that sort of thing, in an artist, do we?

In point of fact, we do. Something's got to move the play, propel it dynamically toward wide-open, emotionally revealing scenes, and while of course it needn't be, shouldn't be, cheap, it does have to be vigorous. Watching *Summer and Smoke* a few months ago, I was suddenly struck with how swiftly and economically Williams had brushed in the situation that would lead to a shooting. The sequence, as it happened, was awkwardly and too garishly handled by the Roundabout in performance; even the costuming seemed to make a "B" movie of it. But I went back to the text and there, as I suspected, it's smooth as silk, neither florid nor forced, utterly logical given the habits of the young wastrel-hero we've been following all along.

In *Sweet Bird of Youth* the venal politician and his suavely vicious son are as readily established, plausible in the language first, in their extravagant deeds thereafter. The plotting itself became a kind of poetry as discarded mistresses, ravaged film-stars and end-of-the-road young studs seemed to claw with their nails to keep a grip on a crumbling reality. And now, in the Phoenix Theater's new mounting of the relatively short *27 Wagons* (on a double bill with Arthur Miller's *A Memory of Two Mondays*), almost the first word spat on a Mississippi plantation is "arson."

No bones about it. Mr. Williams is certainly not primarily interested in some sort of whodunit or will-he-get-caught, though he'll use the values as the values serve him; he's interested in temperaments, twisted psyches, people probing one another--sadistically or sensually--to see what brain and flesh can be made to yield. But to get to the portraiture, and to get to it in some depth, he's got to have an occasion, a first pressure. And so, in about two seconds flat, he slips it in, with the ease of a knife-blade. Aging, impoverished Jake Meighan has set fire to a syndicate cotton-gin so that the syndicate will have to come to him to process its waiting wagon-loads. His wife, younger, less than bright but animal-wily, knows what he has done and must be urged to silence: the urging, in the fading light on a front porch from which half the paint has long since peeled, takes the form of brutal, but connubially acceptable, arm-twisting. A battered but pliant girl will be circumspect--or as circumspect as a tongue that outraces thought ever can be.

Pressure applied, we're ready for the play proper. The setup, unblinkingly bold, raw and natural as the Blue Mountain dirt beneath booted feet, has been quickly, quietly arranged. When a young syndicate superintendent comes prying, with caresses for the girl and a riding-crop to brush provocatively against her dress, there are both tension and breathing-space for the dramatist to play with. We can settle down now, locked into the girl's dilemma, to let actress Meryl Streep studiously slap away most believable mosquitoes, splay her legs like a rag doll, twist an evasive but sinuous toe to keep the porch swing rocking rhythmically, count her thoughts on her fingers, clutch her oversize white purse as she weighs inadvertent betrayal against what is happening to her flesh. Tony Musante, as the alternately violent and seductive inquisitor, can take his time, too. Intimacy, the interplay of intelligence and sexual heat, becomes the body of the altogether persuasive piece. Mr. Williams has got the truth of devious, vengeful, vulnerable and calculating human beings out of a situation, an essentially melodramatic situation, faced straightforwardly.

New York Times, February 8, 1976, sec. 2: 5.

Orpheus Descending (1957)

Tennessee Revising
Henry Hewes

One decade and seven years ago the Theatre Guild brought forth in Boston a new playwright. That's as far as they brought him, because *Battle of Angels* was a disastrous flop. But the twenty-five-year-old newcomer protested that had he been given one month to revise his play he could have made it work.

Perhaps he could have--in on month *then*. But returning to it now as a more mature and firmly established playwright Tennessee Williams has not knit his early effort into a well-integrated theatre evening. The new version, titled *Orpheus Descending* is on the surface a story of adultery punished and arson unpunished. Into a Mississippi general store comes Val Xavier, a handsome and poetic young vagrant who is reluctantly hired by Lady, wife of proprietor Gabe [*sic*] Torrance. While Gabe [*sic*] is dying of cancer upstairs Val is leading Lady into love and pregnancy below. Lady is also preparing to open a new "confectionery," which will restore to Two River County the lusty Italian beauty of her late father's grape-arbor, burned down by vicious townspeople because her father had made the mistake of selling a Negro a drink. But just as life inevitably yields to corruption and death, so this rush of vitality and fecundity into a sterile community is horribly stamped out. Chorus to the action is a reckless and jaded nymphomaniac, Carol Cutrere, who rejoices that for a moment at least there is "something wild in the country."

As the bare bones of a tragedy there is nothing wrong with such a plot. Of course, there is a school of thought that maintains sex to be insufficient cause for tragedy, but in this play, as in *The Rose Tattoo,* the playwright has put the emphasis on the sacredness of the life-creating impulse rather than on sex *per se*. This impulse is benign and its product is healthy growth that makes the woman radiant and divine. Opposed to it is the destructive force of corruption and cruelty, symbolized by the malignant cancer that drains Gabe [*sic*] Torrance's flesh of color and his body of substance.

There are times when this play glows with Williams's magnificent awareness of the battle between the forces of life and death. In the last act we hear the calliope hired by Lady to advertise the gala opening of her confectionery tooting gayly in contrast to the anguish of the dying Gabe [*sic*], who turns out to have been the ringleader of the old arson plot. There are speeches as memorable as anything the great playwright ever wrote. Whether it is the comic lament of a woman who finds her sherbet "reduced to juice," or the deeply sad "We're all of us sentenced to solitary confinement inside our skins," it is Tennessee Williams's brand of poetry.

Yet *Orpheus Descending* runs into trouble when it attempts to fly its poetry through a conventional stage atmosphere thick with gossiping old ladies, thefts from the cash register, and Saroyanesque comedy and pathos. The action becomes casual and accidental, a happy ending just as possible as the sad one. Director Harold Clurman has been unable to create an aura out of the forces surrounding the tragedy, an aura which would show men not as villains but as victims. Instead, he seems determined to make the play work on the level of prosaic storytelling, with a bit of comedy here and a bit of melodrama there. Thus, Williams's poetic notions and symbolism tend to emerge as too obvious or too unrelated to the action.

This puts an awful strain on the performers. They find themselves obliged to make momentary responses which do not always arise out of their characters. Maureen Stapleton exhibits such tremendous strength and resourcefulness as Lady that we often lose sight of the desperateness of her position. And we do not feel the intended contrast between a full-blooded Latin temperament and the cold-blooded little foxes who run this southern county. What she does present us with is a woman so hurt by a betrayal in love that she fights her natural romantic instincts. Within this interpretation Miss Stapleton rises to magnificent defiance. When she intolerantly orders the ghost of her past to get out, with "I hold hard feelings," she shows us her raw soul. And Miss Stapleton is second to none in our theatre at the art of allowing the emotion engendered by one situation to erupt into another.

As Val, Cliff Robertson, who took over the role only eight days before the New York opening, gives us a gentle wanderer hardened against women who have always insulted him by using him as a stud horse, but otherwise a blithe and childish spirit. Only the pure in heart could proudly announce as principal qualification for a job, "I can go a whole day without passing water." And in this kind of innocence Mr. Robertson does very well. He makes us believe his story of the blue legless birds who "sleep on the wind" and "never light on this earth but one time, when they die." Perhaps with more time in the role Mr. Robertson will also find a way to make this passive minstrel in a snakeskin jacket more firmly defined without losing the martyr-quality implied by the name Valentine Xavier. (In *Battle of Angels* Mr. Williams hinted at an allegorical similarity between Val and Jesus, and the snakeskin jacket left behind might be an echo of the battle between Michael and his angels against Satan the Serpent and his.)

Lois Smith plays the nymphomaniac Carol Cutrere as a romantic debauched teen-ager, "a benign exhibitionist" who once tried to protest a Jim Crow atrocity. This latter aspect of her character has been spliced to the more grisly Cassandra of the earlier play, and Miss Smith make the most of it. The rest of the cast is handicapped by the brevity of their parts, which tend to intrude on rather than seem one with the story. The playwright may be at fault for overcomplicating his simple tragedy so that the action seems chaotic and arbitrary rather than soul-stirring and inevitable. But isn't this likely to happen to any work revised after such an interval? Every writer feels that he could write his early works better now that he knows so much more about his craft. But the fact is that the writer is no longer the same person. All the experiences that went into arriving at the original work have been rearranged and re-evaluated. This would not be so serious in an objective technician who writes acting pieces. But in an intuitive artist who writes out of a strongly personal view of the human condition, the result is bound to be--as *Orpheus Descending* is--a superimposition of unmatched images.

Saturday Review, March 30, 1957: 26. (Review of Philadelphia production.)

Orpheus Descending In Revival at Gramercy Arts
Judith Crist

Adrian Hall's revival of *Orpheus Descending* provides an interesting demonstration of what can happen to a lesser Tennessee Williams work when it is placed in the hands of a less than inspired cast.

The fire and passion that in its Broadway production made this essay on evil come alive and have meaning, if only for its duration onstage, have disappeared and suddenly one feels that one is listening to a rather clever but overlong take-off on Tennessee Williams. The rhetorical repetitions, the reminiscences of horror, the writhing outcries against the loneliness of living and of dying, the warnings that a slow rot devours us in our corrupt society-- all these stand along without roots, without motivation, in this off-Broadway production. Only the words and the piling on of violence upon violence remain, without a meaning beyond the moment.

It is not easy to discover why this drama of the idealistic guitar-playing wanderer trapped in a mean and degenerate community becomes so superficial on the stage of the Gramercy Arts Theater. Can it be that when John Ramondetta insists repeatedly, "I live in corruption but I am not corrupted," he says it in so sultry a tone, so sophisticated a manner, that it does not ring true for a moment? Is it that Ann Hamilton's Lady Torrance is more a frustrated bundle of nerves than a woman of tragedy, of imprisoned passions that are beyond control? And if Orpheus has lost his innocence and the evil is without root, we remain unmoved in spite of one onstage horror after another.

Diane Ladd's Carol Cutrere emerges as a clownish caricature of the girl who cared but cares no more. Sylvia Davis makes the sheriff's wife a touching figure up to a point and suddenly she too emerges as a caricature. As a result it is the minor characters who spring to life momentarily--Katherine Helmond and Lucille Benson as gossipy townswomen; Frank Lucas as the rotted and dying Jabe Torrance.

It becomes obvious that for this play--which even in its best production was lacking in the complexities, the shadings, the broader implications so clearly defined in earlier Williams works and in the subsequent *Sweet Bird*--perfection of playing is needed.

It is interesting that Mr. Williams reportedly granted permission for the revival on condition that Mr. Hall direct and Miss Hamilton portray Lady. The over-all effect--despite an atmospheric and compact set by Robert Soule--is a strangely remote one. And the addition of original music by Jesusillo de Jerez--producing, for example, some sort of celestial chimes as the lovers retire behind the curtain--adds an uncomfortable and, one hopes, unwittingly satirical note.

New York Herald Tribune, October 6, 1959, sec. 2: 6.

Robert Brustein on Theater: Orpheus Condescending
Robert Brustein

Tennessee Williams's *Orpheus Descending* was originally staged in 1957, 17 years after the failure in Boston of his first commercially produced play, *Battle of Angels.* With the exception of Eliot Norton, who saluted the young author's unusual talent, none of the Boston critics managed to recognize the sound of a new theatrical voice, and *Battle of Angels* abruptly closed, despite Williams's offer to make radical revisions. Williams, who did not take kindly to failure, stubbornly persisted in his desire to rewrite the play: *Orpheus Descending* was the belated result. Produced on Broadway under the direction of Harold Clurman, with Cliff Robertson and Maureen Stapleton in leading roles, the new play failed as well, though for different reasons. By this time Williams's work was being criticized less for unconventionality that for predictability. After a series of well-deserved triumphs, the playwright was beginning to repeat himself.

The major character alteration Williams made in the intervening years was to transform the heroine from a retiring Southern housewife (Miriam Hopkins in *Battle of Angels*) into a lusty Italian virago. The female lead in *Orpheus Descending* was written for Anna Magnani, who wouldn't commit to a stage run but later appeared with Marlon Brando in the film version, *The Fugitive Kind.* Williams kept the subplot involving the sensitive ex-gigolo, Val Xavier, and the neurotic aristocrat, Carol Cutrere (a kissing cousin of Blanche DuBois). And he preserved the melodramatic conflict between the bright angels of sexual freedom and the dark angels of Southern repression. But if, as Williams claimed, 75 percent of the writing was new, most of the additions were fat injections--bloated metaphors regarding the corruption of innocence by the forces of darkness.

These capsize the play. Instead of proceeding from the action, Williams's windy images seem like the burps of literary indigestion. Clearly, *Orpheus Descending* is more about mythmaking that playmaking. Whenever someone is poised to advance the (preposterous) plot, the character stops to describe the significance of snakeskin jackets or the purity of legless birds that never touch the earth. Val Xavier bears the name of two Catholic saints, and is confused by a female visionary with Jesus Christ. (The play takes place just before Easter with Val acting as a surrogate sacrificial object.) Yet this Lawrentian "fox in a chicken coop" is also endowed with the capacity to "burn down a woman," to run a temperature as high as a dog's, to hold his breath for three minutes, to stay awake for 48 hours, and to go a whole day without passing water.

In other words, emblems of Christian renunciation are continually colliding with images of macho muscle-flexing, and all are undermined by the mythological symbolism suggested in the title. In *Battle of Angels,* Val expressed his artistic inclinations by writing a book; in *Orpheus Descending,* he is a musician, toting a 12-string guitar signed by Leadbelly and other blues greats. The analogy with Orpheus's lyre is obvious enough, and Val's descent into the depths of Southern bigotry to redeem the benighted Lady Torannce is designed to mirror Orpheus's descent into Hell to rescue Eurydice.

Yet I suspect that Williams's fascination with the Orpheus myth was stimulated more by a Dionysian variant, described by Robert Graves, where this demigod is pursued by maenads for engaging in homosexual practices. (The maddened women tear him to pieces, then watch his severed head floating down a river singing beautiful songs.) Among the many false things about plays like *Orpheus Descending* is that Williams--like William Inge, and for similar reasons--was not prepared to reveal to a Broadway audience his real theme: the violent fate of the homoerotic artist in an intolerant patrilinear society.

The same kind of reticence marred such plays as *Sweet Bird of Youth* and *Cat on a Hot Tin Roof*--also Oedipal revenge stories weakened by fake phallic posturing and camouflaged references to sexual corruption. Williams' men and women may engage in passionate embraces, but the true heat of his plays is provided by the punishing father figure--Boss Finley or Big Daddy or Jabe Torrance--when he threatens the hero with real or symbolic castration. However melodramatically conceived, this character carries the weight of genuine threat; and it is not until Jabe Torrance lumbers down the stairs in the final scenes of *Orpheus Descending* that the play begins to develop some dramatic tension. It is the same tension described by Freud in *Moses and Monotheism* when he interprets the ritual of circumcision as the father's warning to the potentially incestuous son that if he makes a move on Mom, he'll chop off the rest.

This may explain why, despite the rampant sensuality in his work, Williams almost invariably associates eroticism with mutilation or death: his later plays are only comprehensible as disguised family romances. Williams's habit of pairing off sexually ravenous older women and sexually available young men (this combination appears in at least seven of his plays) may reflect his own unhappy experiences in the markets of rough trade, but it also suggests the courtship of a seductive mother and her mother-fixated son. Which may be why the vindictive Daddy is usually lurking in the wings brandishing his pruning shears.

Peter Hall dredges this unconscious theme to the surface in the final scene when he shows the hapless Val being led naked to his doom by a redneck Sheriff carrying a blow torch. It is one of many Expressionist interpolations in the English production he has restaged at the Neil Simon Theatre. *Orpheus Descending* is hardly a realistic play, but this Freudian nightmare is so supercharged it makes Elia Kazan look like a minimalist. The ominous opening moments are punctuated by pouring rain, barking dogs, and groaning music, as if credits were about to roll for *The Omen* or *The Entity.* Automobile headlights continually rake the windows of the Torrance General Store--is everyone is town using this street for U-turns?--while the electricals change so often you'd think Stanley Kowalski was upstairs getting the colored lights going with Stella. A coterie of prattling women deliver the tedious exposition directly to the audience; characters materialize from corners of the room; and a series of overloaded performances blow the fuses of an already overloaded play.

Vanessa Redgrave, I fear, is the biggest circuit breaker. I wasn't a fan of her Lady Torrance in London, where her accent seemed more Polish than Italian (now it's a combination of Polish, Swedish, and Irish), but by contrast with what she's doing on Broadway, her earlier acting was a model of decorum. There's no quiet in this woman, no sensuality, ultimately no truth; even the breathless radiance of her curtain call struck me as false. I suspect this restless, overwrought performance may be a form of compensation. Rather than swelling the ranks of great Williams heroines, as some have said, she's been seriously miscast. Lady Torrance is juicy, fleshly, curvilinear, passionate, a woman who acts from the groin and the soul; Redgrave is angular, dry, edgy, hoarse, hysterical, a woman who acts from her bones, muscles, and nerves. Redgrave is unafraid to take chances on stage or to look unattractive--in one scene she appears in a hair net, wearing no makeup. But even her risks seem ostentatious. She's always on, always exploding with anger; and the botched accent, rather than being a technical glitch in an otherwise fine performance, is a constant reminder that she's engaged less in a form of acting than a species of impersonation.

The supporting performances represent an unsuccessful effort to sustain a shape in this sandstorm. These are all competent American actors, but few are allowed to stand up to the star. An exception is Tammy Grimes as the Sheriff's goofy wife. Not an actress usually celebrated for restraint or understatement, she has some subtle and powerful moments, especially when, telling a story about holy water, she almost seems internally burned. Another is Marcia Lewis as a mean-spirited nurse. And Anne Twomey, as pasty-faced Carol Cutrere, looks like, though she lacks the power of, Picasso's *Repasseuse.*

But Brad Sullivan, an actor who usually plays weaklings, doesn't capture the brutal Oedipal menace of Jabe Torrance, and Kevin Anderson, though an attractive performer, lacks the experiential weight for Val Xavier. Anderson certainly has more sexual energy than his weak counterpart in London, but he's too innocent for the part, and there's simply no electricity flowing between him and Redgrave. Their relationship is all talk, and without sufficient pressure from a strong male actor, nothing can stop Redgrave from chewing the scenery.

As a result, this *Orpheus Descending* seems to me like a long, tedious circumnavigation of Williams's dream life, with a plot never far removed from gothic soap opera (a spin-off of "General Hospital" called "General Store"). Its endlessly reiterated theme could be compressed within a single sentence: "We are the fugitive kind, tainted with corruption but wild in the country, who want to live, live, live, and fly high above the earth like legless birds in our snakeskin jackets." If you can bear listening to this kind of boozy music for three hours, you'll like the show. But you must weight my dyspeptic response against a critical reception that has been virtually unqualified in praise of the play, production, and leading actress. I didn't like *Batman* either.

The New Republic, October 30, 1989: 25-27.

The Image of Theater in Tennessee Williams's *Orpheus Descending*
Jack E. Wallace

In Tennessee Williams's first major play, *Battle of Angels* (1940), a young vagabond poet named Valentine Xavier wanders into a small Southern town where his sympathy for dispossessed blacks and emotionally starved women gets him in trouble with the citizens. In the end he is framed for murder and lynched with a blowtorch. The play's symbolic system implies that the artist hero is a Christ figure destroyed by the cruelty and commercialism of modern America. Most critics agree with Nancy M. Tischler that Val is meant to be the "archetypal artist" and an "idealized self-portrait" of the playwright.[1] In his preface to *Orpheus Descending* (1957), a later version of *Battle of Angels,* Williams encourages the autobiographical approach to Val's story:

> Why have I stuck so stubbornly to this play? For seventeen years, in fact? Well, nothing is more precious to anybody that the emotional record of his youth, and you will find the trail of my sleeve-worn heart in this completed play that I now call *Orpheus Descending.*[2]

This trail is so well-marked with autobiographical references that the Val of *Orpheus Descending* seems to be a reliable portrait of the fugitive artist. John Gassner, who assumes Val is the hero, says that *Orpheus Descending* is "about the tragic isolation of the artist in the hell of modern society."[3] Donald P. Costello claims that Williams "never fails to make his protagonist a fugitive"[4] in flight from the corrupt earth. And George Niesen argues that Val's insistence on complete freedom represents Williams's belief that "submission to the physical (and therefore corrupt) world demands the destruction of the artistic temperament."[5]

This view of the artist is at odds with Williams's theory of drama and his role in American theater. When Williams calls himself a fugitive, as he often does, we are required to distinguish between his personal loneliness and his public career. As a playwright, Williams adjusted remarkably well to commercial America, and in doing so developed a concept of theater that in *Orpheus Descending* is more nearly reflected in the rebellion of Lady and Carol than in Val's flight from the "corrupt earth." A more immediate difficulty with the Val-centered reading of *Orpheus Descending* is that it ignores the change Williams made during his long revision of the original play. These revisions indicate a significant shift in Williams's concept of the fugitive artist and his relationship to society.

Val has his origins not only in Williams's own experience, but in his early portraits of the artist. In the unpublished plays of the late thirties,

Williams's heroes are writers seeking to help victims of society--coal miners in "Candles in the Dark [*sic*]," tenement dwellers in "The Fugitive Kind," prison convicts in "Not About Nightingales." *Battle of Angels* most nearly resembles the latter play in its violence, imagery, and central action. The heroes, Jim and Val, are both fugitive poets seeking to express the grim and terrible reality of life (which is not about nightingales), and both are trapped in cruel, repressive societies dominated by sadistic powers--the Warden and guards, Jabe and the Klansmen. Jim's immediate aim is to escape and write an exposé that will improve the lot of his fellow inmates, but he is also concerned about their existential loneliness: "There's a wall around ev'ry man in here and outside of here. Ev'ry man is walking around in a cage. He carries it with him wherever he goes and don't let go till he's dead."[6] This vision of universal loneliness eventually causes Williams to abandon the specific solutions recommended in reform theater. His shift from political to psychological drama is partly indicated by his dedications to these two works. "Not About Nightingales" is dedicated to Clarence Darrow, and the first production of *Battle of Angels* is dedicated to D. H. Lawrence, "the brilliant adversary of so many dark angels."[7] And it is primarily in a psychological context that Val repeats Jim's complaint that all men are kept in cages; this is the only passage quoted from Val's book, and it later becomes a key concept in Williams's theory of drama.[8] Neither Jim nor Val ever actually writes a book (Jim probably dies in his escape attempt, and Val certainly does), but this is not important, since in both cases the play itself is the message. In a later version of *Battle of Angels,* Val's book is actually preserved in loose-leaf and called "A Prayer for the Wild in Heart That Are Kept in Cages," a title, Williams says, that might serve for the play itself or any other play he had written.[9]

The key difference between "Not About Nightingales" and *Battle of Angels* is that while the former is mostly concerned with the artist's struggle against social injustice, the latter deals with the artist's inner conflicts. In all versions of *Battle of Angels,* this conflict begins with Val's affair with the Cajun girl. In the earliest completed draft (1939), Val explains that his desire for the Cajun girl created "a struggle inside me, a battle of angels."[10] Williams says in his notes that this line will probably be cut as too obvious, but he goes on to explain that the Cajun girl is the origin of Val's struggle between his "exaggerated sexual desires and his vague but powerful feelings of kinship with God."[11] In this play, Val's sexual desire is consistently treated as an obstacle to artistic vision. Both Ida Mae Whiteside (later Sandra) and Myra tempt Val to violent sexual exertion, and when he tries to escape, they betray him to the Klan. His only hope lies in his pure love for Vee Talbot, a primitive artist who paints him as Jesus on the Cross. In the 1939 version, in which Myra dies at the end of Act II, a long episode is devoted to Val and Vee, who plan to run off and live in some kind of spiritual marriage.[12] But

Val's fear of fire undermines his courage, and he is caught and lynched.

When Williams rewrote the play for the 1940 production in Boston, he minimized Val's spiritual struggle and represented him as a sexually active primitive who was repeatedly victimized by neurotically possessive women. In *Battle of Angels,* Val's affair with the Cajun girl is reduced to an ambiguous bit of erotic nostalgia. His real trouble begins in Waco, Texas, where the wife of his foreman seduces him while he is drunk. The next day he tries to run away, but the infatuated woman insists that he take her with him; when he refuses, she yells into the telephone that he is raping her. Val is thus an actual fugitive when, as the play begins, he wanders into Two Rivers County and takes a job as clerk in Jabe Torrance's Mercantile Store. Again he is drawn into an affair with his employer's wife, a love-starved woman caged with a vicious and diseased old man. At first Myra is treated sympathetically, but when Val tries to leave town without her, she repeats the villainy of the woman from Waco and yells into the telephone that the clerk is robbing the store. Rising from his deathbed, Jabe shoots Myra and blames the murder on Val. The townspeople, already stirred up by the newly arrived woman from Waco, pursue the hero and kill him.

Williams argues that one reason for the play's failure was that the audience thought Val was a "son-of-a-bitch" for deserting the pregnant Myra. In his notes, Williams argues that "the important thing about Val is his wildness (freedom), not anything in his relations with others (creation is lonely)."[13] But the meaning of Val's freedom is not clear. In some respects he seems to be the typical Dionysian artist, embodying the Greenwich Village belief that sexual freedom is essential to artistic expression. Alleged signs of Val's pagan identity are his Indian blood, his birthplace at Witches' Bayou, and especially his snakeskin jacket ("Women will never leave you alone. Not as long as you wear that marvelous jacket."). Williams says in his notes that the jacket symbolizes the "naked unashamed quality of passion."[14] He also equates the jacket with freedom, leading Norman J. Fedder to justify Val's desertion of Myra on the grounds that Williams's ideal artist must "remain wild and unrestricted in all sexual relationships. . . ."[15] In fact, Val's idea of freedom is more Pauline than Dionysian; he leaves Myra not because he wants access to other women, but because he wants to live alone in the desert. But whatever his motive, his desire to escape goes against the play's dominant pattern of expectation. The small-town Southern setting, the poisoned atmosphere of racial hatred and sex envy, the characterization of Jabe as a walking allegory of evil, all suggest that the play's moral imperative is to fight the Klan. Val's real enemy, however, is the woman from Waco and her avatars, Sandra and Myra. Since these women are initially established as sympathetic rebels against the Klan, the resolution is not only unheroic but morally muddled. Williams's problem then, as he saw it, was to improve Val's image--to make him less aggressive in sexual desire, more sympathetic in deserting Myra, and more active in fighting the Klan.

In 1941, Williams revised the play, cutting the cruder sexual episodes and adding a Prologue and Epilogue which sought to give tragic dignity to the lovers' fatal passion. More importantly, he added a new scene in which Val uses his fists and Marxist slogans "The land belongs to the man that works the land!") to defend a Negro arrested for vagrancy. [16] The 1941 version was never produced, but it was published in 1944 with only minor changes and so became the standard text of *Battle of Angels.* Williams was still not satisfied, however, and when it seemed likely that Margo Jones would produce the play in 1946, he made a revision which expanded the brief and irrelevant civil rights scene into what is virtually a new play. [17] In this version, Val comes to Two Rivers to find Jonathan West, a black socialist preacher he had met five years earlier. [18] Val learns that the Klan lynched West with a pack of hounds and disbanded his church, turning the building into Jabe's store. When Val discovers that the old Conjure Man (part Negro, part Indian) has memorized West's sermons, he stays on as a clerk in the store, planning to copy the sermons, study them, and spread the gospel of racial brotherhood.

In the meantime he has his usual sexual adventures, but now his snakeskin jacket has a new meaning. Instead of being a sign of innocent wildness and pagan freedom, it represents the sexual bondage that Val feels he must escape if he is to become a true artist. When he finally takes off the jacket for good, he forgets his fear of the woman from Waco and is able to write with ease and inspiration. As in the 1939 version, he approaches freedom through a spiritual kind of love, the "Jesus kind" embodied in Vee Talbot. Myra also becomes a convert to the higher love and does not complain when Val tells her that he must go alone to the desert. Of course, he does not make it, but he meets his death heroically, now realizing that he must "live up to" the Jesus picture that Vee painted from her "vision." Although Val is torn to pieces by the hounds, his mission is successful. The Conjure Man saves the book, which is later found by the Reporter, who will publish its "indestructible wisdom, the spirit of the two men that hounds could not tear apart." [19]

Although written in 1946, the West version is essentially regressive, a return to the agitprop formulas that Williams had imitated in his early plays. In calling West's church a "socialist club," Williams defines fairly well the accepted role of theater in the thirties, but his own drama had already evolved in another direction. Beginning badly with the 1940 production of *Battle of Angels* and successfully in 1944 with *The Glass Menagerie,* Williams disassociated himself from the literature of social reform and wrote psychological dramas that were essentially lyric rather than realistic, nostalgic rather than utopian. His plays, most of them, were also very violent and very popular--a combination that caused some critics to accuse Williams of commercialism. In defending himself, Williams developed a theory of drama which, while disavowing any claim to social reform, nonetheless fulfilled his old commitment to "those kept in cages." According to Williams, the origin of the poetic impulse is the individuals' sense of being held in solitary confinement. His loneliness seeks an outlet that Williams calls "personal lyricism" and compares to the "outcry of prisoner to prisoner from the cell in solitary where each is confined for the duration of his life."[20] While personal lyricism is, in itself, therapeutic, the writer is not really an artist until he can express his own experience in a way that touches the general audience. Williams says that he feels purged of loneliness and inner violence when he writes a violent play, and he invokes the Aristotelian doctrine of catharsis to argue that when his plays succeed, they have a similar effect on the audience.[21] Unlike reform theatre, which is anticathartic in that it seeks to convert emotions into political action instead of purging them, Williams's theater is essentially popular and cathartic; its aim is to entertain--literally to hold the audience together by stimulating and purging hostility, and by healing, for a few hours at least, the wound of isolation.

Although atypical of Williams's theater, the West version is an important link in the evolution of *Orpheus Descending,* and it solves, in a provisional way, the major problems in *Battle of Angels.* By greatly reducing the influence of the woman from Waco (she is dropped altogether in *Orpheus Descending*), Williams begins to deliver himself from the misogyny that shaped the earlier play. The lynching of Jonathan West now brings Val into heroic opposition with the Klan, an opposition that is represented in the set itself. Williams's alternate title for this play is "The Broken Tower" (after Hart Crane's poem), and Val's motive to change the store back into the church is symbolically realized when, in a final gesture of defiance, he rings the bells in the tower above the store. All these plot elements and symbolic devices are eventually used in *Orpheus Descending,* but in a different form that is closer to Williams's concept of theater. Instead of basing the play on the lynching of Jonathan West and the degradation of his church, Williams bases it on the Klan's murder of the singer Papa Romano and the burning of his wine garden. Williams likewise changes Val from a messianic poet to a popular singer who also will get in trouble with the Klan and be burned alive. It was ten more years, however, before this plot line was finally developed.

After 1946, Williams seems to have suspended his efforts to rewrite *Battle of Angels.* The next typescripts are dated 1953 and are collected under the title "Orpheus Descending." In these drafts, and in the play itself, Val is very different from the hero of the 1940 production. Instead of an unknown writer in flight from a bogus rape charge, the Val of *Orpheus Descending* is a jaded, thirty-year-old nightclub singer in flight from the endemic corruption of modern civilization, in particular the city of New Orleans. Like most critics who see Val as a self-portrait of Williams, Tischler defends his flight from the city as a sign of artistic integrity. In this "part of the portrait," Williams is "apparently chronicling his disillusionment with Bohemia." Val is not giving up his art, says Tischler, but rediscovering its saving power. "Although disgusted with the flesh and the world, Val has found in art a means of cleansing and sanctification. His guitar is his sacred symbol, evidence of an immortality and a transcendence of flesh achievable in art."[22] This is an accurate statement of Val's belief, and perhaps it also expresses one side of Williams's nature, but Val's desire for transcendence is clearly at odds with his own artistic vocation and Williams's actual career. "I found [in New Orleans] the kind of freedom I had always needed," Williams writes. "And the shock of it against the puritanism of my nature has given me a subject, a theme, which I have never ceased exploiting."[23] Unlike Williams, Val gives in, as it were, to the puritanism of his nature and flees the city.

Val's attempt to escape the theater is balanced by Lady's desire to remodel the Torrance Confectionery into a nightclub that resembles the wine garden on Moon Lake. In *Battle of Angels,* Myra's confectionery is a superficial expression of "personal lyricism," a shallow piece of romantic nostalgia. But in *Orpheus Descending,* it replaces Val's book as the central motive of the play. In order to give tragic significance to Lady's motive, Williams adds the character of Papa Romano and the crime in the wine garden--plot elements that are totally absent in *Battle of Angels* and do not appear in the typescripts until the early fifties. This new material is fore-grounded in a Prologue, where we learn that Lady plans to make the confectionery into a replica of her father's garden. This garden, once the only oasis in the County, was destroyed because Papa Romano "made a bad mistake" in selling "liquor to niggers."[24] The local Klan burned the orchard, and Lady's father died fighting the fire. In despair, Lady let herself be married to Jabe Torrance, "a son-of-a-bitch who bought me at a fire sale" (p. 266). What she did not know, does not yet know, is that Jabe, who is now dying of cancer, led the gang that killed her father. The Prologue thus points to the crime in the wine garden as the cause of corruption in Two Rivers, and to the diseased Jabe as the plague bearer. Lady's plan to open the confectionery on the Saturday before Easter announces the main line of action.

As he developed this new plot, Williams completely transformed the character of Jabe's wife. In *Battle of Angels,* Myra was a frail, flighty blond, hysterically romantic and viciously possessive: a replica of the woman from Waco. In the new play, Lady is a voluptuous, down-to-earth Italian who remains faithful to Val and is the most heroic of all those who oppose Jabe and the Klan. One reason for this change was Williams's hope that the Italian actress Anna Magnani would take the part of the heroine.[25] Magnani had been a great success as Serafina in Williams's *The Rose Tattoo,* and in revising the role of Myra, the playwright endowed her with many of Serafina's qualities-- earthy humor, fiery passion, and a Dionysian faith in life.

Besides giving Lady nearly twice as many lines as Val, Williams consistently strengthened her character as he revised the "Orpheus Descending" typescripts. This is especially noticeable in the way Lady resists the weak role assigned her in the Orpheus legend. Ironically, this legend was better suited to the typescripts of the forties, where the women were mostly furies and Val was torn to pieces by dogs. By the time Williams specifically introduced the Orpheus legend, all the women, even Sandra (Carol), were on Val's side, and his death was again by fire. But Williams may have thought the rescue myth would strengthen Val's role and also put Lady in a subordinate position. In his 1952 poem "Orpheus Descending," Eurydice cannot escape from Hades because she is too attached to the "gold of the under kingdom."[26] With the early drafts of *Orpheus Descending,* Williams tried to make the play conform to this legend. In one version Val actually has a wife whom he calls Eurydice.[27] She has had an affair in the past with the Carnival King, Val's employer. When Val caught them together, he castrated the King and fled. As the play begins, he tracks the carnival to Two Rivers and tries to rescue his wife, but she refuses to go with him, preferring a rich eunuch to an impoverished troubadour. Val then has his affair with Myra, the new Eurydice, and the pattern of love and betrayal repeats itself as in *Battle of Angels.* But Williams eventually discarded all drafts in which Myra-Lady betrays Val or brings on the catastrophe by going back to steal Jabe's money. In the final draft, Lady has no interest in money and only a remote interest in escape; her primary motive is to avenge her father and reopen the wine garden. Although Williams kept "Orpheus Descending" as the title, possibly because it was preferred by his agent, Audrey Wood, he eventually dropped every other direct allusion to the legend.[28] By the time the play was produced, Lady was clearly the dominant character, and several of Williams's alternate titles would have been more appropriate: "The Memory of a Garden," "The Gala Opening of the Confectionery," and especially "The Wine Garden of My Father."

Another important artist figure to emerge in *Orpheus Descending* is Carol (formerly Sandra). In most versions she is the worst of the women in Two Rivers, the closest to the woman from Waco. With the 1939 and West versions, she actually betrays Val to the Klan because he will not run away with her and live a free pagan life. In *Orpheus Descending* she wants the same thing, but she is now represented as a sympathetic rebel against the Klan's racism and sexual repression. Early on she had met Val in New Orleans, and assuming that he is still a bohemian, now she invites him to go "jooking" with her. Val refuses: ". . . I'm all through with that route" (p. 246). In a later scene he asks why she makes a "Goddam show" of herself; she says she does it "for the same reason" that he wears his snakeskin jacket and plays the guitar. Again Val tells her: "We don't go the same route . . ." (p. 251). This little quarrel echoes, in dramatic form, a point Williams makes in "Person-to-Person," where he identifies all artists as exhibitionists. Except for the difference in age, Carol resembles the skinny little girl who cries, "[l]ook at me, look at me, look at me!" as she parades in her mother's finery.[29] Unlike the little girl, who immediately falls on her face, successful artists and actresses must learn to keep their balances and hold the audience's attention. The exhibitionist's initial aim may be self-expression and self-therapy, but this compulsion "to be noticed, seen, heard, felt!" (Carol's words, p. 251) is artistically meaningful only when others are entertained (held together) and the dream of community is momentarily realized. Carol is thus confused (and she partly confuses the audience) when she continues to assume that she and Val are two of a kind. Only when they met in New Orleans were they the same types of fugitives--outsiders who nonetheless tried to communicate with others. But Val, as he says repeatedly, has changed. Overwhelmed by a Manichaean vision of incurable loneliness and universal cruelty, he has lost faith in any form of communal action, especially theater. Carol now resembles Val only in that she shares his nostalgia for the lost harmony of the American wilderness. "This country used to be wild, the men and women were wild and there was a wild sort of sweetness in their hearts, for each other, but now it's sick with neon . . . " (p. 327). But Carol differs from Val in her realization that the neon world--the commercial realm of roadhouses, nightclubs, and theaters--is the only human ground between the impossible dream of primal innocence and the unbearable negations inherent in Jabe's absolute rule.

Carol's close association with the Conjure Man further indicates her embattled alliance with wildness, freedom, and racial brotherhood. After Val's death, the Conjure Man brings Carol Val's snakeskin jacket, which she takes as a token "so that the fugitive kind can always follow their kind." In view of Val's persistent rejection of Carol, it seems odd that she should be his successor. Presumably, Val's love for Lady and his martyrdom have restored him to his identity as snakeskin. For the jacket, whatever its sexual and mythical symbolism, is first of all a costume. In a literal sense, it is the costume worn by the actor who plays Val when he first appears on stage. It is also the costume Val wore as the entertainer called Snakeskin. For Carol it represents his New Orleans identity. In a discarded draft, she explains: "Orpheus has his songs, but what did I have but my inexpressible longing to save the singer. And you can save the song but not the singer."[30] And so she saves the jacket, the symbol of song. In explaining the play's "message," Williams says that the "impulse of song . . . breaks out of confinement and goes on despite all order to halt."[31] The play ends with the sheriff calling "Stop!" as Carol runs off with the jacket.

In this way Carol returns to Val to his former identity as Snakeskin, but he has a different desire, one that sets him apart from both Carol and Lady. His main goal was to leave the corrupt earth and find peace in the realm of the legless bird, "a kind of bird that don't have legs so it can't light on nothing but has to stay all its life on its wings in the sky." Because of their blue transparent wings, these birds are invisible against the sky, "and that's why the hawks don't catch them, don't see them up there in the high blue sky near the sun!" When the skeptical and earthbound Lady asks "[h]ow about in gray weather?", Val answers, "[t]hey fly so high in gray weather the goddam hawks would get dizzy" (p. 265). For Val, the real world, the Darwinian order of sex and violence, is completely corrupt; his only hope is to escape to some dream world, a lyric space that lies outside the reach of predatory hawks. In contrast, Lady sees life as a continual struggle between dream and fact, freedom and necessity, death and rebirth. Her aim is not to escape corruption, but to defy it by opening the confectionery. This is her lyric space which stands in opposition to the dark, deathlike atmosphere of the store, just as the wine garden had once stood in opposition to the wasteland of Two Rivers County. There is admittedly nothing very noble about Lady's plan to renew the wine garden, no thought of setting the world right, no real concern for the good of the community. She does not even think it will do her any practical good: "Hell, I don't even want it, it's just necessary, it's just something's got to be done to square things away, to, to, to,--be *not defeated! . . . Just to be not defeated!*" (p. 329). But the existential focus of her tragic passion does not change the audience's conviction that Jabe must be opposed. As an alternate plan of action, Val's flight seems not only impossible (since Two Rivers is the world), but morally untenable, like running from a plague. Val is preserved as the hero only because he gets lynched. If he had escaped, he would have seemed cowardly both as a lover and as an artist. If he and Lady had both escaped and lived happily in the desert, the theme of the artist would have been irrelevant. In short, Val is essentially a portrait of the artist *manqué,* and he is redeemed only by a kind of *deus ex machina* embodied in Carol and the Conjure Man.

The central image in the play, the true sign of theater, is the confection-ery, a lyric space which, like the broken tower in the West version, is located in the set itself. Comparable to the snakeskin jacket, the wine garden is associated with the spirit of wildness. "It was wild and lovely," Lady says, "and lovely wild things are not tolerated." [32] Lady's art is to re-create this "wildness" in the confectionery which, when illuminated, becomes part of the stage setting. Observing this lyric space within the drab "realism" of the store, Lady says: "I feel like an artist. . . . It's the first thing I've done to be proud of in a long time."[33] These lines are somewhat out of character for the unrefined Lady, and Williams cut them in favor of a more colloquial statement. Explaining her determination to open the confectionery, Lady tells a story about a little monkey her father brought with him when he immigrated to Two Rivers. At that time, when Lady herself was "not much bigger than the monkey" (p. 325), Papa made his living by playing a grind organ on street corners. The monkey (another exhibitionist) "had a green velvet suit and a little red cap that it tipped and a tambourine that it passed around for money, . . . " One day the monkey danced too long in the hot sun and fell over dead.

"My Papa, he turned to the people, he made them a bow and he said, 'The show is over, the monkey is dead'" (p. 325). The performance remembered here is a displacement of the "show" Papa later gave in the wine garden, where he played the mandolin and Lady sang Italian love songs. In telling the townswoman the comic tale of the monkey's death, Lady masks her real motive--to avenge her father's murder. She also foretells her own death: "For me the show is not over, the monkey is not dead yet." It is worth noting that this line, in this context, is one of the latest revisions in the play. Originally, the line, "The show is over, the monkey is dead," belonged to Beulah, one of the minor characters, and Williams comments in his notes that it is a "southern saying of inexplicable meaning."[34] In a late revision, he invented an anecdote that gave meaning to the saying and strengthened Lady's role as the principal artist figure.

Val's refusal to help Lady open the confectionery very nearly causes a serious rupture between the two, but his is circumvented by the disclosure that Lady is pregnant (Lady gets this assurance from Jabe's evil nurse--final avatar of the woman from Waco). Knowing that she and Val will be exposed, Lady tells him to take her car and get away (the opposite of her treacherous behavior in *Battle of Angels*). She still hopes to open the confectionery, but her pregnancy is now a more immediate sign that she is "not defeated." Wearing a carnival hat and blowing a paper horn, she dances up the stairs crying, "I've won, I've won Mr. Death, I'm going to bear." In a dying effort, Jabe shoots Lady and calls for the townspeople to lynch Val. Now alone on the stage, Lady rises from the floor and, with a "curious, almost formal dignity," makes her way to "the ghostly radiance" of the "make-believe garden." Entering the confectionery, she looks about at the make-believe audience and repeats her father's line: "The show is over. The monkey is dead." Unfortunately, the show is not really over until Val's death and the passing of the snakeskin jacket, but Lady's final scene is the more fitting completion of the movement announced in the Prologue. Jabe's evil is exposed, and Lady's final gesture re-creates the lyric realm that the Klan tried to destroy when it burned the wine garden. For a moment the dead world of Jabe's store is converted into a stage on which Lady "plays" her own death.

NOTES

1. Nancy M. Tischler, "The Distorted Mirror: Tennessee Williams' Self-Portraits," in *Tennessee Williams: A Collection of Critical Essays,* ed. Stephen S. Stanton (Englewood Cliffs, N.J., 1977), pp. 159 and 158.

2. Tennessee Williams, "The Past, the Present, and the Perhaps," in *The Theatre of Tennessee Williams,* III (New York, 1971), 220.

3. John Gassner, *Theater at the Crossroads* (New York, 1960), pp. 223-225. Esther Merle Jackson also sees Val as protagonist in "[a]nother variation on the 'crucifixion' theme," *The Broken World of Tennessee Williams* (Madison, Wis., 1965), p. 57.

4. Donald P. Costello, "Tennessee Williams' Fugitive Kind," in *Tennessee Williams: A Collection of Critical Essays,* p. 110.

5. George Niesen, "The Artist against the Reality in the Plays of Tennessee Williams," in *Tennessee Williams: A Tribute,* ed. Jac Tharpe (Jackson, Miss., 1977), p. 476.

6. Williams, "Not About Nightingales," TS. in the Humanities Research Center, University of Texas, Austin, p. 46. All typescripts cited hereafter are in this collection.

7. Williams, "Battle of Angels: A Play in Three Acts," TS. dated November 1939. Typescripts, working drafts, and notes for *Battle of Angels* are collected in a single box under eleven call numbers. Typescripts, working drafts, and notes for *Orpheus Descending* are collected in four boxes under fifteen call numbers. Descriptions provided in these notes are not complete, but are adequate for recognition.

8. Val's speech about everyone being "sentenced to solitary confinement inside our own skins" is essentially the same in *Battle of Angels* and in *Orpheus Descending* (Act Two, Scene One in both plays); it is repeated by Williams when he describes the theatre audience in the essay "Person-to-Person," the preface to *Cat on a Hot Tin Roof,* in *The Theatre of Tennessee Williams,* III, 3.

9. Williams first mentions this title in a 1946 version called "The Broken Tower" (TS., "The Battle of Angels," A, T, and Tccms/working notes, and fragments [approx. 75 pp.]). Later, in notes intended as part of a "Foreword to *Orpheus Descending,*" he says the title could serve "possibly for every play I have written" (TS., "Orpheus Descending," Composite T and TCC ts [134 pp.]).

10. "Battle of Angels: A Play in Three Acts," Act Three, Scene Two, pp. 30-31. The play's title comes from Williams's poem "The Legend," where the "battle" is associated with sexual initiation and the loss of innocence (*In the Winter of Cities*) [Norfolk, Conn., 1956], p. 83). But in the play this symbolism is not clearly sustained. On the one hand, the "dark angels" are represented by the sex-starved women (the furies in the Orpheus legend), and on the other, they seem to be the Klansmen, the agents of repression.

11. "The Battle of Angels," TS. (approx. 75 pp.). Williams analyzes Val's character under the heading "Shadow of My Passion," probably an alternate title for the play.

12. "Battle of Angels: A Play in Three Acts," Act Three, Scene Two, p. 46.

13. "The Dismembering Furies," or "Orpheus Descending," of "The Memory of an Orchard: A Play," TS. dated April-May 1954.

14. "Orpheus Descending," TS., unsorted pages of incomplete drafts (about 725 pp.).

15. Norman J. Fedder, *The Influence of D.H. Lawrence on Tennessee Williams* (London, 1966), p. 69.

16. Williams, *Battle of Angels,* in *The Theatre of Tennessee Williams,* I (69).

17. *Tennessee Williams' Letters to Donald Windham 1940-1965,* ed. Donald Windham (New York, 1976), p. 171.

18. "The Battle of Angles: New Outline," TS. (5 pp.).

19. Ibid.

20. "Person-to-Person," in *The Theatre of Tennessee Williams,* III, 3.

21. "Foreword," *Sweet Bird of Youth,* in *The Theatre of Tennessee Williams,* IV, 7.

22. Tischler, pp. 160-161.

23. Benjamin Nelson. *Tennessee Williams: The Man and His Work* (New York, 1961), p. 39.

24. *The Theatre of Tennessee Williams,* III, 232. All page references are to this edition and will appear in the text.

25. Nelson, p. 223.

26. Williams, "Orpheus Descending," in *In the Winter of Cities,* p. 27.

27. In *Battle of Angels,* the woman from Waco is the wife of Val's foreman in the oil fields. In several later drafts, she is the wife of a carnival owner who gave Val a job as musician and hustler. As in *Battle of Angels,* the "carnival woman" pursues Val because he rejects her love. Although the role of the woman is reversed in the Eurydice version, the pattern of betrayal remains the same.

28. "Orpheus Descending," TS. (134 pp.). On the front page, Audrey Wood deletes all titles except *Orpheus Descending.*

29. "Person-to-Person," in *The Theatre of Tennessee Williams,* III, 4.

30. "Orpheus Descending," TS., unsorted pages and incomplete drafts (approx. 725 pp.).

31. "Orpheus Descending," TS. (134 pp.). this explanation of the play's symbolism was intended as part of the "Foreword."

32. Ibid.

33. "Orpheus Descending," TS., unsorted pages and incomplete drafts (appox. 725 pp.).

34. Ibid.

Modern Drama 27.3 (September 1984): 324-35.

Garden District (1958)

Garden District: Short Plays by Tennessee Williams Put On in an Off-Broadway House
Brooks Atkinson

From the point of view of practical producing, an off-Broadway theatre is the proper setting for Tennessee Williams' *Garden District.* The two one-act plays linked under that title are too small for the formality of a large theatre. At the dainty, miniature York Playhouse (First Avenue and Sixty-fourth Street) the proportions of play and theatre are perfectly matched, and the delicate workmanship of *Garden District* is beautifully contained.

Of the two plays, the second, *Suddenly Last Summer,* is the major work. It represents Mr. Williams at the peak of his talent as poet of the damned. It is perfectly contrived; it is written in sensitive prose; it is as the measured sadness of a requiem on purity and love.

Sometimes Mr. Williams' familiar preoccupation with degeneracy and violence is unpalatable; sometimes it seems to be a form of vindictive showmanship, like the last scene in *Orpheus Descending.* In literal terms, *Suddenly Last Summer* is his most devastating statement about corruption in the world, and his most decisive denial of the values by which most people try to live.

His dark values annihilate the basic assumptions of most civilizations. Item: When Sebastian, an epicurean poet, watched the savage, devouring sea birds on a Pacific island tearing away the soft undersides of young sea turtles, his mother, Mrs. Venables [*sic*], reports that he said he had seen God. Item: "We all use each other and that's what we think of as love," says his cousin, Catharine: Item: The grisly conclusion of *Suddenly Last Summer,* with its barbaric fury and its intimations of cannibalism (an extension of the theme of the devouring sea birds) is so terrible that Mr. Williams shies away from being absolutely specific about it.

A playwright cannot be charged with believing everything his characters do and say. They have a life of their own. But, as Mrs. Venables [*sic*] remarks about her dead son, Sebastian: "A poet's life is his work and his work is his life." And the frequency with which this joyless, nihilistic point of view turns up in Mr. Williams' plays (*Camino Real, Cat on a Hot Tin Roof, Orpheus Descending*) suggests that it represents his experience and belief. It is not a theatrical pose; it conveys his sense of reality.

In *Suddenly Last Summer* it is less shocking than it has been in previous plays because the lyrical writing expresses responsibility and sincerity. Since Mr. Williams is solely concerned with putting into moving words the hopeless things he believes, *Suddenly Last Summer* is a triumphant piece of dramatic literature.

The story concerns Mrs. Venables [*sic*], a rich, venomous widow of New Orleans, and her niece, Catharine. They are engaged in a merciless conflict over the reputation of Sebastian Venables [*sic*], the poet, who is dead before the play begins. Catharine had gone abroad with him the last summer, and has come home with the story of his hideous death in Cabeza de Lobo at the hands of a mob of wild, rapacious street urchins. Since the story destroys Mrs. Venables' [*sic*] legend of her son as a sublime genius, she is determined to destroy Catharine's sanity.

Almost nothing happens in *Suddenly Last Summer* except that words are spoken. They are spoken with extraordinary perception by admirable actors in a meticulously directed performance. But to read the play is to realize that its dramatic vitality derives from the script directly.

Mr. Williams has imagined everything that the production reveals. Robert Soule's setting of a rankly luxuriant garden (like Henri Rousseau's painting, "The Jungle and the Lion") is carefully described in the stage directions: "The set is unrealistic like the décor of a dramatic ballet," and the personality of the flowers is carefully specified. Lee Watson's heavy, sickening lighting is also described: "The colors of this jungle garden are violent, especially since it is steaming with heat after rain."

Everything in the written play evokes in dramatic movement the central mood of evil, decadent luxury, cruelty, voracity, tropical degeneracy. The sensuousness of the phrasing and imagery (sunlight in Cabeza de Lobo "looked as if a hugh white bone had caught fire in the sky") and the immaculate, rose-perfumed description of Sebastian's mutilated corpse are evocative pieces of sheer writing. Believing in the validity of what he is saying, Mr. Williams has made art out of malignance and maleficence, like Rémy de Gourmont or Baudelaire.

The performance, staged for rhythm and mood by Herbert Machiz and giving an impression of effortlessness and spontaneity, perfectly communicates the controlled wildness of the theme. As Catharine, Anne Meacham has to deliver a very long, climactic speech that is the core of the play. It contains the viciousness of the present situation as well as the remembrance of the horrors of Sebastian's death. Miss Meacham plays the part with a technical virtuosity and a personal force that are hypnotic.

As Mrs. Venables [*sic*], Hortense Alden is also excellent--casually vindictive, aloof in manner, pitiless in her relation to the other characters, a cultivated lady who is without remorse or scruple. Miss Alden has caught all aspects of the character. The other five parts are played with taste and lucidity by Robert Lansing, Donna Cameron, Eleanor Phelps, Alan Mixon and Nanon-Kiam.

What Mr. Williams has to say is in essence repugnant. But he says it with awareness, sentience, musical grace and conviction; he believes it. He is bemused with death.

As flies to wanton boys, are we to the gods,
They kill us for their sport.

New York Times, January 19, 1958, sec. 2: 1.

Accelerando
Tom F. Driver

If theater were to be judged solely in terms of emotional effect, Tennessee Williams' latest creation, *Garden District,* would rate exceptionally high honors. Through the sheer force of words the second play of this double bill, called *Suddenly Last Summer,* reaches a well-nigh exhausting peak of frenzy. Mr. Williams is nothing if not vivid, and here, in a story of sordid death told by a psychotic girl under the spell of a truth drug, he has worked his vividness into an accelerating crescendo which must turn audiences loose on the street either stunned or in a state of mania. He moves his listeners from one shock to another on the beat of a pagan rhythm. When the excitement is at its height, he closes the curtain, with pulses pounding.

No theater in a state of health, however, is to be judged solely in terms of emotional effect. Preoccupation with or overreliance upon that one aspect to the exclusion of others spells death for the theater as an art form. The Roman theater and the Jacobean were both destroyed by it; or at least it marked the last phase of those theaters, which perhaps were already weary of the fullness of life.

In the past, Tennessee Williams has not asked us to judge his work solely in terms of emotional effect. As recently as *Cat on a Hot Tin Roof* he was, by his manner of writing, asking us to look beyond the surface shock to consider the effect of mendacity upon human relationships and the relation of truth to the will and to action. In the past, Williams' poetry has served as a means whereby he cold criticize, and cause his audience to question, the surface representation on the stage. He was able to reflect the tension in the human spirit over the difference between the way things are and intimations of the way they ought to be. This tension was communicated not so much in the characters themselves as in the playwright's attitude to the characters and in the actions of which they were a part. It was a product of Williams' poetic approach to common and sordid realities.

That same quality is not entirely lacking in *Suddenly Last Summer,* especially in the early part of it. The curtain rises on the semi-tropical garden of the wealthy Mrs. Venable in the Garden District of New Orleans. The garden (beautifully set by Robert Soule) is overly luxuriant, already an unspoken critique of the hothouse atmosphere in which Mrs. Venable reared her poet son. The latter, in her eyes a chaste genius but in fact a thoroughgoing voluptuary, died abroad "suddenly last summer." His mother is eager to stop the sordid story of his death which her niece, a mental patient, who witnessed the scene, has been telling. Assembled to hear the story from the girl's own lips are her mother and brother, afraid of losing an inheritance, a brain surgeon, who wants truth and diagnosis; and the poet's mother, who wants to guard her son's reputation.

As the cloud of the girl's story--truth or hallucination?--moves closer in the first half of the play, Mr. Williams hints at the exploration of genuine questions. "My son was searching for God," explains the mother; "he wanted more than anything to see God." "Sebastian said that we are all children in a vast kindergarten," says the niece, "trying to spell the name of God with the wrong alphabet blocks." Later she cries "It's the truth! I can't change the truth! I don't believe even God can change the truth."

All this is, as I say, in the early part of the play when we are still interested not only in the story the girl will tell but also in its effect on various characters and in its relation to truth, action, love and hate. But once the truth drug has taken over and the story of Sebastian's death begins to come out, Mr. Williams sacrifices everything to the sheer bizarreness of his tale. He seems to have been carried away with the very emotions he was generating. The girl's narrative of blood, death and sensuality sweeps everything else out of the way.

I once had a playwriting instructor who spoke of the "neurotic curtain" in the contemporary theater--the tendency to bring down the final curtain early, so that the action is arrested very close to the climax. It is *so* titillating. *Suddenly Last Summer* has the most "neurotic curtain" I have ever seen. It reveals that the play as a whole is too nervous to make a dramatic statement and must settle for a sensual wallop.

Tennessee Williams is now at a point in his career where a very important choice must be made. Either he must push further with the kind of poetic exploration of basic questions of existence that he dealt with in *The Glass Menagerie, A Streetcar Named Desire, Camino Real* and *Cat on a Hot Tin Roof*; or else he must settle for the kind of shock material he has given us recently, material better suited to the more lurid pages of *Esquire* than to the serious stage. To judge from last season's *Orpheus Descending* and from *Suddenly Last Summer,* he is making the easier choice, the one that demands less in terms of observation and intellect while it feeds more on private phantasmagoria. In this way it will not be difficult for him to lose the high stature in our theater which his earlier plays so deservedly earned for him. He is still a master at effect. A play of his is still an exhilarating event. But he once was more, and no doubt could be so again.

I must pay tribute to the acting of Anne Meacham in the role of the disturbed niece and of Hortense Alden as the poet's mother. The direction of Herbert Machiz is carefully restrained, a blessing in a play of such intensity.

The opening play in *Garden District* is frightfully dull and mercifully short. It is called *Something Unspoken* and had better be left so.

Christian Century, 29 January 1958: 136-37.

Sweet Bird of Youth (1959)

Sex, Sin, and Brimstone In Tennessee Williams
Sylvia Gassel

It was enlightening to learn from a story in the *New York Times* that Tennessee Williams writes out of the frictions of rage. Let us hope that newer and younger playwrights will take example and light their own flames of rage against Tennessee Williams himself and his ultra-conservative view of life. For it is growing increasingly irksome to have brimstone and hellfire hurled at our heads by an exhortative writer-preacher who uses his stage as a pulpit and the theatre as an old-fashioned revivalist meeting.

It is droll to see a playwright, seeped in erotic sensationalism, receiving easy acceptance by critic and audience alike, when one thinks of Havelock Ellis, Lawrence, Joyce, and others. It is not in the least strange, however, when one realizes that Mr. Williams, like all good shouters for repentance, is merely following in the familiar tracks of those who whip up forbidding and tempting concoctions of vice in direct proportion to the wages of sin and flames of hell for those who transgress. Mr. Williams is a dyed-in-the-wool Puritan, Southern variety, and as such does nothing at all to disturb our conventional attitude toward sex: it's sinful, but oh you kid!

Witness the fate which awaits many or most of Mr. Williams' female characters. A woman, it would seem, exists for this playwright only in her amazing capacity to produce children in wedlock. In any other role she is a whore, a nymphomaniac, a monster, a man-devourer. Any sexual activity outside the bounds of matrimony leads to 1) disease or infection by a male (*Sweet Bird*); 2) illicit pregnancy, which means abortion (*Sweet Bird*), or possible death in childbirth (*Orpheus*); 3) whoredom (*Streetcar, Summer and Smoke*); 4) loss of her only justification for being, the ability to bear children (*Sweet Bird*); 5) corruption and misanthropy (*Sweet Bird*).

Now most women will probably recognize the time-worn warnings passed on to female youngsters as they attain to sexual maturity. Any rash, passionate members of that sex will burn in more ways than one before the end.

Marriage with intention to bear children (*Streetcar, Rose Tattoo*) is the only safety zone.

As for the men, once they have lost their innocence, or their purity, they may become diseased (*Sweet Bird*); they will be punished in orthodox fashion by having a highly effective instrument removed (*Orpheus, Sweet Bird*); if engaged in an extra-marital affair, they will lose their potency (*Sweet Bird*); and if --white or colored--they sleep with anybody's sister . . . well!

In short, if they abuse themselves in any manner whatsoever, they may become corrupt and inefficient. Unless, like Stanley Kowalski (*Streetcar*), they are married with intent to bear children, in which case they triumph, but are rather thick in the head as well. Most men will recognize here the early interdictions against sexual activity with which they were introduced to the intricate life of man and woman. If nothing else, they can ruin some fair young thing for life (*Sweet Bird, Rose Tattoo*).

And it is in precisely this area that Tennessee Williams' own fallacy is exposed. The difference between people, he wisely points out, lies in the difference between those who know pleasure and those who do not. At the same time he tries to persuade us that Pleasure abides only in the demon urges: in drink, in drugs, in deliberate cruelty, in debauchery, in congress with the devil. But a subtle imp in Mr. Williams' own psyche torments him with the possibility that these very devices lead us directly away from pleasure. Needing to support his faulty logic, he distracts us by placing *true* pleasure unassailably in the realm of innocence, the Garden of Eden, faith. As in Eden, it is dat ol' dabbil sex which always begins the pitiless unwinding of cruel fate.

It is hardly necessary to point out that there are many forms of pleasure in life, not all of them born of innocence. Knowledge and knowledgeability are frequently of enormous assistance. Physical sensation alone has never yet fascinated anyone but infants.

The rage which Mr. Williams feels is directed at the roots--or the facts-- of life: the manner in which we are born. Original sin. It is what man and woman do together which astonishes and perplexes him. He stamps his foot in rage and does not realize that he is thereby marking time. In that fixed position, he can surely witness time crossing his universe from east to west like the sun, but he cannot stop its course. From such a point of view it would indeed seem that time corrupts and takes away. But it is not the movement of time which causes this effect: it is stagnation. Inertia. Change is movement in man, and a simultaneous action between man and time creates growth. Everything dies when one stands still. Which is why, for all his dreams of the heroic, only sorrowful, angry children grace Mr. Williams's world.

The time is sweet for Mr. Williams' bird to leave the nest. Otherwise, the true admirers of Mr. Williams' genius will know beforehand that he can continue to produce only extravagant erotic fantasies in which abound the puritan backwaters of a conservative mentality.

The Village Voice, June 24, 1959: 8-9.

Williams' Nebulous Nightmare
Robert Brustein

In *Sweet Bird of Youth,* Tennessee Williams seems less concerned with dramatic verisimilitude than with communicating some hazy notions about such disparate items as Sex, Youth, Time, Corruption, Purity, Castration, Politics and The South. As a result, the action of the play is patently untrue, the language is flat and circumlocutory, the form disjointed and rambling, and the characters--possessing little coherence of their own--function only as a thin dressing for these bare thematic bones. Cavorting through the forest of his own unconscious, Williams has taken to playing hide-and-go-seek with reality in a manner which he does not always control. *Sweet Bird of Youth,* in consequence, contains the author's most disappointing writing since *Battle of Angels,* and frequently looks less like art than like some kind of confession and apology.

Even so, the confession might have assumed the dimensions of art if it were not so clearly that of a solipsist. About to be castrated, the play's hero, Chance Wayne, turns to the audience to ask for "the recognition of me in you, and the enemy, time, in us all!" Since Chance has had about as much universality as a character in an animated cartoon, to regard his experience as an illuminating reflection of the human condition is a notion which borders on the grotesque. For *Sweet Bird of Youth* is a highly private neurotic fantasy which takes place in a Terra Incognita quite remote from the terrain of the waking world. There all events have a mechanically sexual construction, everyone is caught up in extravagant depravity, success and failure alternate with astonishing swiftness, letters are sent but never delivered, and people not only get threatened with castration but have this threat executed and do nothing to avoid it when it actually comes. That this world is to be regarded as real or meaningful is a surprise sprung too often to promote much confidence in the author's vision.

The production, too, shakes one's confidence for it bakes the play in a gallimaufry of styles, part real, part fantastic. The acting, except for a splendid caricature by Geraldine Page (of a character generally peripheral to the action) is uncertain, and the direction, by Elia Kazan, is surprisingly mannered and hollow. Uncomfortably suspended between his traditional realism and a new theatricalism he is experimenting with, Kazan has underlined rather than disguised the play's defects. People act against each other as if alone in a room, but they also aim their remarks at the audience. Some of the business is pantomimed, and some is executed with real props. There is a phone on the stage but it is not attached by any wires, and the sets include real furniture but no walls. Thus Kazan unwittingly confirms a suspicion that the play, written in a predominantly realistic style, contains something disturbingly unreal; if Kazan's suspicion has been a conviction, it might have had more fortunate results. For, in the world of this play, it is no use pretending that time and space exist. The phone on the set is purely gratuitous when you have only to think bad thoughts in order to be heard, and all those thoughts are known anyway to the dark forces which plot your destruction.

In other words, the play is a nightmare, the disconcerting thing being that Williams is confusing his bad dreams with objective truth. The nightmarish element in Williams' recent drama has been fitfully apparent but his pretense at documenting reality has hitherto been less insistent. In *Garden District,* for example, one could ignore the occasional fib that the action was "a true story of our time and the world we live in" and enjoy the play as an extended sick joke (actualizing a homosexual metaphor--the invert hero of the narrative is literally "eaten" by the Spanish boys he has been seducing). But *Garden District* was mainly cast as a monologue, a Guignol horror tale told in the first person by a woman whose sanity is at least open to question. *Sweet Bird of Youth,* on the other hand, despite a few subjective soliloquies in the first act, is not narrated but dramatized and, consequently, is colored less by the fantasies of the characters than of the author. But if the play is a nightmare, the author does not always know he is asleep. In Strindberg's *Dream Play,* the artist took precedence over the sufferer and objectified the torment; in *Sweet Bird of Youth,* the sufferer's neurosis is dictating the play.

Thus Williams' nightmare does not, like Strindberg's, penetrate to a deeper subjective reality so much as distort, disfigure and disguise objective reality for its own purposes. The fantastic nature of the external action demonstrates this clearly. The play concerns a handsome blond gigolo of twenty-nine who has been exiled from his southern home town for some time through the machinations of the local political boss. Having now returned to St. Cloud in company with his latest keeper--an aging glamor queen named Ariadne Del Lago who keeps alive on a nourishing diet of sex, hashish, benzedrine and pure oxygen--Chance Wayne is greeted with antagonism and ominous warnings which he ignores. By an ostentatious display of borrowed wealth, Chance hopes to regain the hand of Heavenly, Boss Finley's daughter, who had been his mistress and true love at the age of fifteen. Since his "corruption" began only after Finley broke off the match, the recapturing of his "purity" and youth is contingent on her response to him; but he soon learns that Heavenly has had her organs removed after he unwittingly infected her with venereal disease some years ago. Rather than flee the town with the movie queen (who, in a twist of the plot, has staged a dramatic comeback), he remains to be castrated by the henchmen of Boss Finley.

The illogicalities of this plot suggest that, as in most dreams, the external action is only a metaphor providing clues to the hidden action. The play is about only two things consistently: time and emasculation. Four people lose their procreative organs: Chance is castrated, and so is a Negro mentioned casually in the second act; Heavenly undergoes a hysterectomy; and Ariadne Del Lago speaks of the castrating effect of age on women of her condition. Since emasculation for Ariadne Del Lago is figurative, a symbolic representation of sexual impotency, it probably has symbolic values for Chance Wayne too--after all, it is he who speaks most often of "the enemy, time." Yet, he can hardly be referring to impotency for he has not even reached thirty. That Chance's castration is metaphorical is clear but the difficulty lies in determining precisely what this metaphor is.

In a Christian context, the violence done to Chance is a punishment for his "corruption." Chance is unsuccessfully striving to return to his "clean, unashamed youth," a time when according to a number of characters, he was the "sweetest," "finest," "cleanest," "most decent boy" in town. With Time and Boss Finley having worked manifold variations on his sexual purity, Chance has now emerged, in the full flush of original sin, as a "monster" and a contaminating influence on everything he touches. The corrupting agent, then, is experience, even life itself, and the sweet bird of youth is that same fowl mentioned in *Orpheus Descending:* an image of childhood innocence and grace before the fall which, by staying always in the sky, remains free from the corruptions of the earth. Since Chance, in his present fall from grace, has committed a grave offense against the bird, the removal of his sexual organs can be regarded as a form of poetic justice. Chance is guilty as charged and his punishment is deserved.

Unfortunately, this interpretation cannot be squared with the pagan implications of the play. The bird not only represents purity but--through a pun common in most Latin languages and even in children's English--the male sexual organ. If the bird is a phallic image, then Chance's sweetness and youth are associated with sexuality, not innocence, and his purity is terminated only when he is castrated, not when he turns to more perverse pleasures. Thus, it is Boss Finley who has offended against the bird; Chance has only advanced its pagan doctrine. In a non-Christian interpretation, Chance's fate is undeserved and reflects not Chance's guilt but the anti-sensual sadism of the man who perpetrated the violence.

These are not ambiguities but direct contradictions. They cannot be reconciled for they stem from Williams' irrepressible tendency to utter sexual affirmations through a Calvinist larynx. In more objectified plays, Williams could have it both ways by creating two characters each of whom embodied one aspect of sexuality: usually, a Christian-spiritual heroine and a pagan-physical hero. As his plays grow more personal, however, these elements become confused, and in *Sweet Bird of Youth* his central character buckles under both constructions of sexual behavior. At the same time that Chance Wayne sees himself as the apotheosis of depravity, he is the heroic rebel proudly articulating his contempt for the system. Thus, soon after he flagellates himself for corruption, he congratulates himself for his dedication to "love-making" in a world consumed by hate. Speaking in that circuitous mode peculiar to everyone in the play, he says:

> The greatest difference between people in this world is not between the rich and the poor or the good and the evil; the biggest of all differences in this world is between the ones that had or have pleasure in love and those who haven't and hadn't pleasure in love, but just watched it with envy--sick envy.

Since no one at this point bellows "Liar," we may take the statement as a theme, especially when we later learn than Chance's castration, apart from a punishment, is a sign that everyone is envious of his sexual powers.[1] Furthermore, Chance's dubious profession--a sign of his corruption--also indicates his sweetness of character: he claims he brought appreciation, understanding and tolerance to many lonely women. Chance, then, is the deformed Vulcan, the sensual Tristan, and the innocent Parsifal, and all at the same time. Depending on whether Williams is viewing sex as salvation or sin, Chance is represented alternately as both the purest and most depraved character in the play, and there is even a suggestion, though some fancy Easter Sunday symbolism borrowed from *Orpheus Descending,* that he is to be identified with Christ!

Sweet Bird of Youth, in short, is the kind of work Graham Greene might have produced if he tried to write like D. H. Lawrence: it embodies Chance's confession of guilt, his apology for it, and his exaltation of it. The pagan element in the play, however, seems to me the spurious one, a literary smoke screen spread over the dream to hide its true content. Let us examine the action from a different perspective to explain some of its contradictions.

It is significant that Williams labors hard to exculpate Chance; he is made to bear little responsibility for his situation. When Chance maneuvered the fifteen year old Heavenly into a Pullman car, it was he who said "no," she who said "yes." More important, Chance was completely free from taint until Boss Finley's villainous prohibitions forced him into a life of lust. In an earlier draft of the play--published in *Esquire*--he is even innocent of infecting Heavenly since she contracted syphilis after participating (against *her* will!) in an orgy which Chance did not attend. Chance is surely a peculiarly blameless sinner, but a sinner he is nevertheless--punished for having engaged in a forbidden act of sexuality.

It is interesting that most of Williams' heroes and heroines, also more sinned against than sinning, have been visited with physical and mental mutilations as a reward for their sexual transgressions. Declaring their innocence to the end, they have been lamed, eaten alive, burned, threatened with lobotomies and driven mad. The hero to whom Chance Wayne bears the closest resemblance--Val Xavier in *Orpheus Descending*--is set upon by dogs and torn apart after reluctantly having been seduced by the villain's wife.

Williams's central theme, then, concerns a hero (or heroine)--once "pure," now "corrupted" by the dark masculine forces of society--who gets involved sexually with a willing and sometimes aggressive female (or male). As a result of this encounter, the central character is mutilated or destroyed by an avenging and sadistic male, usually a relative. If we regard these mutilations as symbolic castrations and make the obvious substitutions, the theme emerges as a Freudian melodrama embodying the classical Oedipal situation: Big Daddy punishes his sensitive child for lusting after abnormal delights. Although these perversions are variously suggested--as nymphomania, male prostitution, homosexuality, adultery and sodomy--these too are metaphors. For Freud, the castration fantasy was invariably a punishment for incestuous desires. It is Williams' obsessive fascination and horror over this theme that accounts, I think, for the alternating defiance and self-hatred of his heroes--and for his desire to exonerate them at the very moment they are proven guilty. In the Freudian fantasy, every man is both innocent and guilty of the crimes for which he imagines himself punished, since the wish is always confounded with the deed.

If the play were simply a Freudian fantasy, and straightforwardly offered as such, it might have achieved some of that universality that Williams claims for it now. For if the dreamer, Chance, is--as one character calls him--an innocent lost in the "bean-stalk country," it follows that Boss Finley is the "flesh-hungry, blood-thirsty ogre" who pursues him. In the sex nightmare, the evil father is frequently black and threatening, and one can accept an antagonist as starkly one-dimensional as the villainous figure Sidney Blackmer gropes to find a character for on the stage.[2]

But in confusing his nightmare with actuality, Williams has created a wholly fraudulent conflict. To make Boss Finley anything as substantial as a segregationist is to wrap a neurotic fantasy in a social document. The repressive, castrating father can, if he is generalized enough, represent all conventional authority and morality, as he often does in Expressionist drama. But with Boss Finley as a racist, the conflict is specified in a topical manner calculated to win approval from a liberal audience which otherwise might have some reluctance to accept the sexual conflict underneath. Boss Finley is a device to divert the spectator's attention from the fact that *his* morality is being criticized by playing on certain of his prepared responses towards the South.

It doesn't work. The segregationist themes emerge as mindless and unreal, and Boss Finley bears no resemblance to anything on land or sea. Granted that the South is the one area in America which most resembles ogre country--the one area where castration is likely to take place--it simply would never happen to a white man, especially one in "the genteel tradition." For Finley to have any coherence as a racist, Chance would have to be a Negro and Williams would have been forced to write another play.[3] As it now stands, the contemporary southern setting of the play is a trick to insure a Broadway success by enlisting the audience's sympathy on the safe side of a conflict which has no basis in truth.

But it is useless to document any further the evasions and contradictions of this inferior work. If it has a single virtue, it is in its uniqueness--no one but Williams could have created it. But the wild and fertile imagination which conceives has far outstripped the mind which shapes. With his fancy leading him into areas which he does not seem completely able to enter or leave, Williams is losing his ability to examine either the internal or external worlds with any real penetration. Williams has been often criticized for his sensationalism, but I find him still not sensational enough, for there is nothing more daring that the truth. He continues to disguise his true sexual concerns much as Miller obscures his political themes; and O'Neill remains the only American dramatist who has doggedly pursued his furies to their lair. There is a place in our drama for the nightmare and no one seems more qualified than Williams to write a good one. But his work will founder in formlessness, incoherence and dishonesty if he does not soon prove himself the master of his dreams.

NOTES

1. When the Negro is castrated, Chance identifies with him: "Sex-envy is what that is, and the revenge for sex-envy which is a widespread disease that I have run into personally too often for me to doubt its existence. . . . For some reason hate-makin' is easier than love-makin'." In addition, Boss Finley's villainies are partly attributed to the fact that he is now "too old to cut the mustard."

2. Aside from his penchant for castrating everyone in sight, Boss Finley has raped his own wife, displays incestuous desire for his daughter, and possesses fantastic delusions of grandeur.

3. Parts of that other play are scattered through this one, for Williams sometimes seems to realize that Chance makes no sense as a white. Why did Finley break off his match with Heavenly when Chance was once the town's white-haired boy? Why is there a parallel--and irrelevant--castration of a Negro in the course of the play? What do Finley's frequently uttered fears about "the threat of desegregation to white woman's chastity in the South" have to do with Chance and Heavenly? And, finally, why does Finley say that the Supreme Court would find a "handsome young criminal degenerate like Chance Wayne . . . the mental an' moral equal of any white man in the country."

Even a racist wouldn't say this if Chance were not a Negro. Clearly, the sexual and social plots bear very little relation to each other.

Hudson Review, 12.2 (Summer 1959): 255-260.

Theatre
Harold Clurman

"I don't ask for your pity but just for your understanding--not even that--no. Just for your recognition of me in you." The young man who makes this request of us in Tennessee Williams's *Sweet Bird of Youth,* recently presented anew at the Brooklyn Academy of Music, has been a gigolo, has infected his sweetheart with a venereal disease and tried to blackmail an aging movie star in the hope that he may land a job for himself in Hollywood. He is hellbent for success and his only other characteristic is his scorn of the mean, little business employees--former schoolmates--of his native Southern town and for their vile boss.   Then, too, his central conviction is that imparting and receiving pleasure in love-making is the supreme benefit of life. So, when he pleaded for my recognition of myself in him, I felt like shouting back, "I'll be damned if I do," and thought the audience might join me in unison. Our sins are less lurid than his, but far more meaningful.

I did not like the play when it was first produced in 1959 and I like it much less now. The best I can say for it at this point is that it has all the marks of a best-seller. It is colorfully and fluently written, with moments of pungent talk; it is anti-Establishment; it has suspense, violence, and implies larger issues. But it is mushy in thought, sensational in attitude and vibrantly banal in juvenile rebelliousness.

There would be little point in going into all this now if it were not to consider the acting in Edwin Sherin's well-directed production. Irene Worth, as the monstrously pitiful movie star, has rather less humor than Geraldine Page did in the original production, but--more strikingly than ever--she displays great power and command. I find her extremely effective perfor- mance . . . a *performance.* Its source is in will, intelligence and craft. Here her powers are at their height. Still, "She don't make me shiver none."

Christopher Walken plays the horrendous "hero" for all *he* is worth, matching savagery with savagery. There is in everything he does a cold, energetic resentment with a strong admixture of superciliousness that fits the part all too well. Only Matthew Cowles, who plays one of the "villains" of the piece, the hate-filled brother of the girl whom the protagonist defiled, stirred me. Cowles managed to convey the acute pain which may be mixed in the flesh of murderous vindictiveness. I pitied this killer more than his victim, not on any moral grounds but because Cowles infused his part with a hot, albeit morbid, humanity.

The temper of acting in a particular period reflects something of its cultural climate. Paul Newman, who played the "lead" in the earlier production of *Sweet Bird,* did not repel me (though the part did), not only because he is endowed with a particularly wholesome personality but because he seemed representative of a less hysterical time than ours. John Garfield, in his day, conveyed something of the crude but hearty optimism of the fervent 1930s. Earlier still, Fredric March was typical of the quiet, sturdy dignity of the decent citizen in the days of greater security. For the most part, our moment produces bitter herbs in acting as in other fields. I have mentioned Christopher Walken's wrathful disdain, but I think also of George Scott's sovereign contempt, Rip Torn's venom, the sometimes sad Al Pacino who is frequently frightening, and Dustin Hoffman who suggests a despair that has moved on to a semblance of oddball indifference or tired mockery.

Nation, December 27, 1975: 700-01.

Sweet Bird of Youth: Williams' Redemptive Ethic
William M. Roulet

The moral aspect of Tennessee Williams' dramas has provoked perhaps more commentary than any other phase of that writer's material. Much has been written about it, and that quite heatedly. In many quarters playwright Williams is viewed as an apostle of pessimism who is intent upon convincing us that down deep, where it really matters, we are rotten. Voices have not infrequently been heard protesting that the dramatist should not waste his talent writing the sordid things he does when there are so many nice things with which he might deal:

> If Tennessee Williams writes about a tree on a hillside, invariably the tree is old and twisted. The background is starkly desolate. While that is an accurate report, why forget the same scene in the spring when God's miracle of rebirth graces the same tree with tiny flowers and the background becomes appealingly green? Or why not describe the third stage, when the magnificently robed tree is bearing apples or cherries?[1]

To evaluate a writer's contribution in such terms, to ask "When will Mr. Williams write as cogently of the spirit as of the flesh?"[2] is to overlook entirely the purpose of critical examination. It is to quarrel with the artist's right to choose his material rather than question his manner of expression.

Arthur Ganz realizes a more distanced, disinterested and objective viewpoint when he incisively notes:

Moralist . . . may seem a perverse appellation for a playwright whose works concern rape, castration, cannibalism and other bizarre activities, but in examining the work of Tennessee Williams it is exactly this point-- that he is a moralist, not a psychologist--that should be borne in mind . . . Admittedly Williams's morality is not the morality of most men, but it is a consistent ethic, giving him a point of view from which he can judge the actions of people.[3]

The substance of the Ganz article is not to be reduced to a startling revelation that Williams is the great moralist of the modern theatre, a sort of "angel unaware." This would be as great an error as that which categorically damns him to the sordidness and degeneracy--and chunky royalties--of Erskine Caldwell's "little acre." However, it does suggest that each of the playwright's works is worthy of careful analysis. Indeed, such an approach to the dramas will reveal that they possess in varying degree positive attitudes--if not statements--about life. If *Summer and Smoke* presents an end of innocence through the moral disintegration of Alma, her fall specifically colors the regeneration of the young doctor who has seduced her and testifies to the fact that virtue triumphs only in the hearts of the sincere--saint or sinner. The heroine's destruction is the dramatist's inverted ethic at work challenging false respectability and hypocritical restraint in the face of overt excess. *The Rose Tattoo,* seeming to revel in the earthy and the vulgar, proclaims the joy, vigor and healthy lust for life and love which dominate and fulfill the uninhibited Serafina delle Rose. *Camino Real* philosophizes in the "curtain line" that "the violets in the mountains have broken the rocks!" Tenderness and love, positive manifestations of natural feeling, thereby reveal themselves as powerful forces in man's struggle for survival in a world indifferent to his agonies. *Cat on a Hot Tin Roof* focuses upon the evil inherent in the stifling of sexual expression which for Williams remains one of the few means which poor, fallible, perhaps doomed man recognizes as an escape from the bonds of self.

The dramatist's two major works, *The Glass Menagerie* and *A Streetcar Named Desire* touch similarly upon the theme of acceptance. Laura, the young crippled girl of *Menagerie,* is separated from the world by reason of her extreme sensibility; she is much too delicate for the world and is, therefore, cast aside. She does not act positively against the demands of life, but her inability to respond, to descend as it were, effects her ultimate return to the little glass animals. Blanche Du-Bois of *A Streetcar Named Desire* also suffers because of her failure to accept or understand some phase of reality. Violently rejecting the sexual perversion of her husband, Blanche dismisses the display of basically positive emotion--generally the normal moral ethic for a Williams character. It is this denial, actually a neurotic denial in light of her own promiscuity, which propels Blanche toward destruction.

Sweet Bird of Youth deals with a more explicitly orthodox morality than any of the previously named dramas. It considers the question of individual guilt and responsibility in a most uncompromising manner. The play reflects the predicament of two people who no longer are of any use to the world: Ariadne Del Lago, a retired film actress, has fled from the reality of age by seeking refuge in a procession of pretty young men intersperses with "hash" binges; Chance Wayne, as his name suggests, is a not-so-young "young man" attempting to trade upon his youth and looks while they remain negotiable items. Youth with its promises and dreams has vanished; in its place are the sadness and futility of what once was or almost was. Of the two characters, Chance is the more pitiable and despicable because he stills clings to the hopes and deceptions of younger days. Together in their room in an old-fashioned hotel in the Gulf Coast town of Saint Cloud, he and Ariadne discuss the possibilities of her giving him, or making arrangements for, a screen test. Chance is certain that this is, at last, the big opportunity; his companion, embittered realist that she is, sees however that the young man is obviously untalented and not particularly bright. Her cynicism played against his fatuous optimism creates an interesting variation on the theme of despair. The "lost" quality which pervades so much of the dialogue is effectively underscored by Williams' utilization of specific dramatic devices. Shadows of gulls sweep across the window blind of the room when Chance learns of his mother's death; the passage of the birds, graceful yet somehow final, helps to clarify the truth which heretofore only the hairs in his comb told Chance. Further, a Lament, a vaguely sorrowful musical theme, is introduced to add dimension to the impact of the sight of these souls in transit between two worlds, the real one and the safe one. The Lament captures and sustains the futility of lost youth. Ariadne explains her motivations as it moans in the background:

> Well, sooner or later, at some point in your life, the thing that you lived for is lost or abandoned, and then (*Lament in palm garden*) you die, or you find something else. (*She takes the lighted "stick" from him.*) This is my something else. Act I, Scene 1.[4]

Similarly, Chance begins his self-analysis to the accompaniment of the dirge:

> I've had more chances that I cold count on my fingers, and made the grade almost, but not quite, every time. Something always blocks me . . . terror! Otherwise would I be your goddam caretaker, hauling you across country? Picking you up when you fall? Well, would I? Except for that block? Be anything less than a star? Act I, Scene 1.

Having established the frustration and lack of fulfillment which haunt his characters, Williams develops the monologues and dialogues from scenes of self-analysis and projection to moments of self-recognition. The process is a slow one, but the air of inevitability is clear. A moment of truth comes for Ariadne when she searches frantically for Chance after has been gone for the entire evening; finding him in the cocktail lounge of the hotel, she tells him breathlessly:

> Chance, I have a wonderful thing to tell you. Will you let me tell you? Will you listen to me? I knew when I saw you driving under the window with your head held high with that terrible stiff-necked pride of the defeated which I know so well--I knew that your comeback has been a failure like mine. And I felt something in my heart for you; that's a miracle, Chance. That's the wonderful thing that happened to me, I felt something for someone besides myself. That means my heart's still alive, at least some part of it is, not all of my heart is dead yet. Part's alive still. (Act II, Scene 3 [*sic*].

In this speech Ariadne relinquishes the haven of self-pity which her fears created for her. Sorrow is gradually losing itself in Charity; a reconciliation to the realities of life is underway. It is the first phase of her redemption. Eventually, Chance, too, comes faces to face with the ugly fact that is his life:

> I didn't know there was a clock in this room . . . It goes tick-tick, it's quieter than your heart beat, but it's slow dynamite, a gradual explosion, blasting the world we live in to burnt out pieces . . . Time! Who could beat it, who could defeat it, ever? Must be some saints and heroes, but not Chance Wayne. I lived on something that--time? yes--time gnawed away like a rat gnaws off its own foot caught in a trap, and then with its foot gnawed off and the rest set free, couldn't run, couldn't go, bled and died . . . Act III.

In this manner, then, does the young man note and confront the incongruity evident between his youthful aspirations and the present truth of things. Seeing the success of old friends in Saint Cloud, his home town, Chance begins to realize all that he is and is not; he recognizes the phoney in himself. By the decision to remain at the hotel, Chance makes articulate the desire to redeem what remains of his life. With full purpose of amendment, he elects to submit to the symbolic death of which George Scudder, a former acquaintance, has warned him:

> This is a thing that Boss Finley wanted for you ever since he found out you'd corrupted his daughter, and that was a long time ago. He said you

should be castrated. And I think I agree with him, now. You better think about that: that would deprive you of all you've got to get by on.

This voluntary mutilation, it should be stressed, becomes in the context of the play a gesture of repentance rather than the sensational curtain which rings down the drama. Crude though it may be, Chances's submission to such a fate has a touching simplicity that seems to capture perfectly the mentality of his character.

Sweet Bird of Youth employs, as has been noted earlier, a less esoteric code of values than some of Williams' other plays--although the dramatis personae more than compensate for any seeming concession to convention. One of the more stabilizing features of the drama is the time setting. This story of "spiritual odyssey" occurs on Easter Sunday, a traditional symbol of renewal and regeneration. While there is nothing in the day itself, as conceived by Williams in the course of events, to explain the conversions of Ariadne and Chance, nevertheless, consciousness of the transformative quality inherent in the feast is suggested in Boss Finley's messianic campaign speech:

Last Friday, which was Good Friday! Last Friday, Good Friday, I seen a horrible thing on the campus of our great State University, which I built for the State. A hideous straw-stuffed effigy of myself, Tom Finley, was hung and set fire to in the main quadrangle of the college I built. This outrage was inspired--*inspired*--by Nawthun radical press! However, that was Good Friday! Today is Easter! Today my sacred mission is burning brighter than the straw effigy burned in the quadrangle of the great State College that I erected to the white youth of this State. I say today is Easter and I'm in Saint Cloud . . . Act II, Scene 3.

The change which has taken place between Good Friday and Easter Sunday in Boss Finley's experience finds a parallel in the transformation of Ariadne and Chance. Ironically, their new lives lack the glory of Finley's Easter exultation, although their Good Friday involved, unlike his, a complete oblation: her decision to return to the temporary security of a shaky and doomed film career confident that new hope will inspire new strength for the lonely years ahead; Chance's resolution to accept failure and make amends through the promised mutilation. Despite the tragic implications of these moments, the protagonists manifest a serenity in the face of sorrow which is far closer to the spirit of Easter Day than the pseudo-prophetic gibberish of the politician. The redemptive pattern of Easter is vaguely sketched in the fabric of Williams' two major characters.

The conversions, of course, remain on the natural level. Nothing of the spirit is actually treated here. God does not actually become a moral force in the events of the drama for Williams' concept of God, as expressed in the play, is basically deistic. A heckler has been paid to upset Boss Finley's polemics at a political rally. In reply to Miss Lucy, Finley's mistress, who tells the man that the Boss actually believes he is the voice of God, the Heckler cries:

> I don't believe it. I believe that the silence of God, the absolute speechlessness of Him, is a long, long and awful thing that the whole world is lost because of; I think it's yet to be broken by any man . . .

Against this theological background, the struggles of Chance and Ariadne become memorable testimonies to the resilience and basic goodness of human nature. The stage directions which appear near the conclusion of the play seem to express these same concepts at work in Williams' own vision and understanding of the conversion and triumph of Ariadne and Chance:

> Note: in this area it is very important that Chance's attitude should be self-recognition but not self-pity--a sort of deathbed dignity and honesty apparent in it. In both Chance and the princess, we should return to the huddling-together of the lost, but not with sentiment, which is false, but with whatever is truthful in the moments when people share doom, face firing squads together. Because the Princess is really equally doomed. She can't turn back the clock any more than can Chance, and the clock is equally relentless to them both. For the Princess [Ariadne]: a little very temporary, return to, recapture of, the spurious glory . . . She makes this instinctive admission to herself when she sits down by Chance on the bed, facing the audience. Both are faced with castration, and in her heart she knows it . . . Oh, one thing more. Chance stayed. He wasn't driven out of the town he was born in.

One might quarrel with Tennessee Williams' moral code, but not about it; it cannot be denied that he has one operative--a very straightforward one it is, too: the acceptance of life on its own terms. Each of his dramas details the flight of a character or characters from some reality; the degree to which their retreat is successful marks the extent of their tragedy. The acceptance of life involves for Williams many things: the shaking off of the dream world, the return to the real, ugly, dirty one which his characters know; the freedom of sexual expression; any manifestation of man's humanity. Whether this acceptance involves what may be socially displeasing to many is not a concern of the dramatist. His interest and emphasis is upon the great need for affirmation in a basically negativistic world. In Williams, the "here and now" are given eloquent defense; they are made important, not as a delusory means of escape, but as the only certainties, the opportunities for goodness in a precarious world. His is a hard ethic, but it is there.

NOTES

1. Oscar Hammerstein II as quoted in Jerry Cotter, "The Crisis on Broadway," *The Sign* (December, 1960), pp. 22ff [*sic*].

2. Euphemia Van Rensselaer Wyatt, Review of *Sweet Bird of Youth, Catholic World* (May, 1959), pp. 158-159.

3. Arthur S. Ganz, "The Desperate Morality of the Plays of Tennessee Williams," *The American Scholar* (Spring, 1962), pp. 278-294.

4. [This and] all [subsequent] references to the play are taken from Tennessee Williams, *Sweet Bird of Youth,* New York: New Directions Books, 1959. Also published in *Esquire* (April, 1959), pp. 114-155.

Cithara, 3.2 (May 1964): 31-36.

I Rise in Flame, Cried the Phoenix (1959)

Tenstrikes
Henry Hewes

I Rise in Flame, Cried the Phoenix is Tennessee Williams's purest piece of dramatic writing. Indeed it is so pure that the playwright, when he wrote it in 1949, did not believe that it could be performed in the theatre. Happily, the short play's public unveiling on the New York Chapter of ANTA's Matinee Theatre Series proves Mr. Williams wrong in this particular estimate of his own work and suggests in general that the great playwright should have more faith that audiences will learn to appreciate what he finds most valuable in his own writing.

For played without alteration by a trio of actors dedicated to the author's inspired vision, this play distills the beauty of D. H. Lawrence's life into a brief death scene. It does not stick to the literal facts of that last day at Vence, but rather attempts to fashion the poetic truth of Lawrence's spirit as it might have been revealed in the final critical moment. The mortal shell burned out by inner fire at its hottest.

To do this he has invented a visit by Dorothy Brett, a woman who seems to love the poet in a colder and more repressed way than did Lawrence's wife, Frieda. Before Brett arrives we hear Lawrence tell his wife, "I have a nightmarish feeling that while I'm dying I'll be surrounded by women. They'll burst in the door and the windows the moment I lose the strength to push them away. They'll moan and they'll flutter like doves round the burnt-out phoenix. They'll cover my face and my hands with filmy kisses and little trickling tears."

Lawrence makes Frieda promise him to let him die alone fiercely and cleanly like some old animal. Alfred Ryder plays the role as a dying man but wonderfully fierce, angry, and prophetic. He can make such an unpleasant act as spitting up blood into a bowl beautiful and poetic. He achieves a lovely sadness when he says weakly, "People are damn complicated and yet there's nothing much to them."

And in a speech reminiscent of Dylan Thomas's "And Death Shall Have No Dominion," Mr. Ryder's Lawrence exits gloriously with "The sun's going down. He's seduced by the harlot of darkness. Now she has got him, they're copulating together! The sun is exhausted, the harlot has taken his strength and now she will start to destroy him. She's eating him up . . . Oh, but he won't stay down. He'll climb back out of her belly and there will be light . . . there will always be light."

As Frieda, Viveca Lindfors gives an earthy performance that is quickly responsive and ever changing. One moment she is vengeful, the next protective. She taunts her sick husband but is distraught when the resultant anger takes him closer to death. In the end she triumphs when the dying Lawrence calls her to him.

The other woman, Brett, is played by Nan Martin who is delightful when she plays childish games with Lawrence as a sex-substitute. Miss Martin makes her role a waltz of celibacy in contrast with Miss Linfors visceral symphony.

That *I Rise in Flame, Cried the Phoenix* should have waited ten years for its New York première is hard to understand, but it could hardly have waited for a better production. Is Mr. Williams' espousal of Off-Broadway a sign of a growing playwrights' and performers' revolt against Broadway producing conditions that dictate they must do everything, everything, everything to meet the shallowest wishes of undiscriminating audiences? Support for such a speculation would seem to be provided by several other theatre events last week.

Saturday Review, April 25, 1959: 23.

The Purification (1959)

The Purification by Williams Is Staged
Arthur Gelb

The ANTA Matinee Series did itself proud yesterday with a stunning production of Tennessee Williams' long one-act verse play, *The Purification*.

The play, staged by Tom Brennan at the Theatre de Lys, is a lyrical tone poem, set a century ago in the Spanish ranchlands of the Southwest.

The production has realized the mood of the play with near perfection. Underscored by the haunting music of a guitar and the dolorous chanting of a chorus, it has a somber unity and beauty that soar beyond the limits of most of our earthbound contemporary theatre.

Mr. Williams' protagonists are gathered to hear the details of a murder of a rancher's daughter. The guilty are present, and are expected to sit in judgment upon themselves.

Slowly, with gathering violence, the classically tragic story emerges. The murdered girl and her brother have been lovers; the girl's husband, half-crazed by her refusal to grant him his marital rights, has discovered the lovers and slain the girl with an axe.

The girl appears in a vision to her brother and her husband, as each tells his story before the judge. Finally, each having confessed his crime, the brother and husband achieve purification by taking their own lives. As the tortured brother in whose veins runs the bad blood--"sangre mala"--of his proud and ingrown Spanish ancestors, Ted van Griethuysen is profoundly moving. John Braden achieves a beautiful balance as the humbler, less eloquent but equally tormented husband.

As the judge who knows his verdict will be superfluous, John Cunningham is a model of firmness and restraint. Mary Hara and Stan Kahn portray the boy's parents with dignity and strangled passion, and Eva Stern is lovely in her brief appearance as the ghost of their murdered daughter. Sunja Svendsen, as a malevolent Indian servant, rounds out the roster of superior players.

One reservation: The effectiveness of the chorus was weakened by its appearance of physical immaturity; sterner-visaged--perhaps almost mask-like-- faces would have been more in keeping with the mood of the play.

New York Times, December 9, 1959: 57.

The Stage: *Purification:* Williams's Only Verse Play Given in SoHo
Mel Gussow

In the summer of 1940, as he recalls in his *Memoirs,* in "ecstasy" over a romance and with "a premonition of [the] doom" of the affair, Tennessee Williams wrote *Purification,* his only verse play.

Ecstasy and doom--the two ride like horsemen over the cobblestones of this one-act play. In many ways, the short work--it runs less than one hour in performance--presages the later, full-length *Out Cry.*

The scene is a desert town. Aridity is pervasive. The characters long for rain, just as they search for purification. A brother and a sister have been as close as two halves of one spirit. Were the two bound in "innocent rapture," as their mother insists, or was it incest?

A court has been convened to investigate the death of the sister. The identity of the killer is not in doubt. He is a rancher who was married to the girl. The brother, we learn, has been a catalyst to the crime; his passion has driven the rancher to his deed.

As the characters testify, they bear witness to their ingrown jealousies and rivalries. "The tainted spring is bubbling," intones an Indian servant as chorus. Finally that spring boils over. Purification is death by suicide; only sacrifice can purge the sin. In common with the boy's unquenchable love and the rancher's act of violence, the play is a burst of passion. It is lofty and at times eloquent.

Clearly, it is difficult to perform. How can you act a rhapsody without acting up a storm? Paul Kielar's production at Theater at Mama Gails (an intimate and most hospitable dinner-theater in SoHo is fortunate in its choice of leading actors: Todd Drexel as the rancher, Marie Puma as the sister and, especially, Peter Kingsley as the brother. They prove themselves well equipped to use poetic language to illuminate anguish. The others in the cast are not on their level.

The staging is simple: actors in Southwestern costumes, wooden stools, a shimmering, usually crimson, backdrop against which appears a vision of the dead girl.

Since the play is short, it is preceded by a "Prelude." Certainly *Purification* could be counterpointed by dance or music, or a fiesta could be presented as a curtain-raiser, with the play itself staged as a masque. There are aspects of all this in the prelude, but none of it seems necessary. The fiesta is self-consciously hearty; Bruce Pomahac's songs, dully strummed on a guitar, are mundane. And the choreography is awkward.

The play can--and does--survive on its own merit. The appreciative audience at the performance I attended included the playwright. This was the first time that he had ever seen a production of *Purification*. At the end of the play, Mr. Williams's enthusiasm was abundant--and justified.

New York Times, December 10, 1975: 56.

Period of Adjustment (1960)

The Broadway Scene
John Griffin

If a theatregoer conversant with Broadway fare of the last decade were to be brought in from the hinterlands, taken to see *Period of Adjustment,* now playing at the Helen Hayes, and asked the name of the author, that gentleman's name being withheld from him, he would reply, "William Inge, of course." Sex talk in a small Southern town. The inability of people to communicate on an intellectual or physical basis. The unconscious comedy in the small talk of the middle class. The happy ending: "Turn out the lights; everything's going to be all right." But of course our Broadway visitor would have to be told the awful truth. Tennessee Williams wrote this play. Then perhaps he would go back the next night to see the work again, and he would realize that this is indeed Williams, only in a minor key. On the first night he was so busy chuckling at the wryly humorous lines ("She's brought up that boy of mine to be a sissy: I'll bet he even rides his rocking horse side saddle.") and experiencing that warm glow that often occurs when actors thoroughly ingratiate themselves with an audience, that he scarcely had time to reflect that Mr. Williams hasn't really changed so very much.

Period of Adjustment is the story of two couples. Ralph Bates is living in a suburban house on High Point that is slowly sinking into an underground cavern. His wife has left him, taking their baby son, on Christmas Eve. He is visited by an old war time buddy who has just taken unto himself a bride. They have been married twenty-four hours but the union has not yet been consummated. George Haverstick has a mysterious case of the "shakes" that inwardly makes him timid of his virgin bride but outwardly he shows the braggadocio of the most accomplished Lothario. Both he and his newly-taken wife, a former nurse, have lost their jobs. Ralph's recently departed wife, whom he married in order to secure a promotion in her father's dairy, was the unfortunate possessor of buck teeth, a nose in need of plastic surgery, and general homeliness. Also, she put Vicks Vaporub on her chest at night. These young, or not so young, people have problems. At curtainfall the audience is encouraged to go out into 46th Street fairly secure in the knowledge that the problems will be solved. The two men are going to West Texas to start a ranch where they will breed Texas Long Horns and buffalo for T.V. Westerns. As the curtain descends it is made apparent that the Goddess Venus is watching over this house and that by the time coffee is perking in the "sweet little kitchen" at daybreak all, or most, of the couples' sexual inhibitions will have disappeared and they will slumber in nightly connubial bliss for ever after. Really!

It seems that neither Mr. Williams nor his director, George Roy Hill, has been entirely honest about this play. The direction consistently stresses, emphasizes, and reiterates the humor of the play, while totally disregarding what must surely be Mr. Williams' real message: spiritual and physical love between a man and a woman is a very difficult, very tenuous thing. So difficult and tenuous in fact that Mr. Williams slyly mocks it for nine-tenths of the evening, then tries to make everything right by that final curtain. There's a great deal of despair, even desperation, lurking behind the bright facade of this "serious comedy"; it will be interesting to see the play directed from an entirely different viewpoint, as a scathing commentary on current American sexual mores. Perhaps off-Broadway in 1965.

Of the actors, the distaff side definitely come off best. Neither James Daly nor Robert Webber strikes one as a particularly resourceful actor. Mr. Daly's warm good humor seems a little forced and Robert Webber is a bit too much the back-slapping old war buddy. Miss Barbara Baxley has the difficult job of sustaining her timorous but gallant virgin bride amid the bravura shouting and cavorting of the two war buddies. That she manages many quiet moments of dignity and compassion is greatly to her credit. Miss Rosemary Murphy has the short but demanding role of the homely spouse. Her performance is deeply moving without being pathetic. Dignity is a homely person can be very touching, particularly when the actress concerned rejects any suggestion of the maudlin. Perhaps Mr. Williams himself is going through a "period of adjustment" as a playwright; his latest play, as presented on Broadway is neither funny enough to be a comedy, nor serious enough to merit close attention as a psychological drama. It is one of his minor works.

The Theatre, December 1960: 18, 45.

The Night of the Iguana (1961)

A Little Night Music
Robert Brustein

In *The Night of the Iguana,* Tennessee Williams has composed a little nocturnal mood music for muted strings, beautifully performed by some superb instrumentalists, but much too aimless, leisurely, and formless to satisfy the attentive ear.   I should add that I prefer these Lydian measures to the unmelodious banalities of his *Period of Adjustment* or the strident masochistic dissonances of *Sweet Bird of Youth*; for his new materials are handled with relative sincerity, the dialogue has a wistful, graceful, humorous warmth, the characters are almost recognizable as human beings, and the atmosphere is lush and fruity without being outrageously unreal (no Venus flytraps snapping at your fingers).   With this play, Williams has returned once again to the primeval jungle, where--around a ramshackle resort hotel near Acapulco--the steaming tropical underbrush is meant to evoke the terrors of existence. But he has explored this territory too many times before--the play seems tired, unadventurous, and self-derivative. Furthermore, the author's compulsion to express himself on the subjects of fleshly corruption, time and old age, the malevolence of God, and the maiming of the sensitive by life has now become so strong that he no longer bothers to provide a substructure of action to support his vision. *The Night of the Iguana* enjoys no organizing principle whatsoever; and except for some perfunctory gestures towards the end, it is very short on plot, pattern, or theme.

One trouble is that while Williams has fully imagined his *personae,* he has not sufficiently conceived them in relation to one another, so that the movement of the work is backwards towards revelation of character rather than forwards towards significant conflict. "The going to pieces of T. Lawrence Shannon," a phrase from the play, might be its more appropriate title, for it focuses mainly on the degradation and breakdown of its central character--a crapulous and slightly psychotic Episcopalian minister, very similar to the alcoholic Consul in Malcolm Lowry's *Under the Volcano*. Thrown out of his church for "fornication and heresy"--after having been seduced by a teen-age parishioner, he refused to offer prayers to a "senile delinquent"--Shannon now conducts guided tours in Mexico, sleeping with underage girls, coping with hysterical female Baptists, and finding evidence of God in thunder, in the vivisection of dogs, and in starving children, scrabbling among dungheaps in their search for food. Other characters brush by this broken heretic, but they hardly connect with him, except to uncover his psychosexual history and to expose their own: The Patrona of the hotel, a hearty lecherous widow with two Mexican consorts, out of *Sweet Bird of Youth*; Hannah Jelkes, a virgin spinster with a compassionate nature, out of *Summer and Smoke*; and Nonno, her father, a ninety-seven-year-old poet--deaf, cackling, and comatose--out of *Krapp's Last Tape*. The substance of the play is the exchange, by Hannah and Shannon, of mutual confidences about their sexual failures, while the Patrona shoots him hot glances and the poet labors to complete his last poem. When Shannon goes berserk, and is tied down on a hammock and harassed by some German tourists, the iguana is hastily introduced to give this action some larger symbolic relevance: the lizard has been tied under the house, to be fattened, eaten, and to have its eyes poked out by native boys. Persuaded by Hannah to be kinder than God, Shannon eventually frees the iguana, tying its rope around his own neck when he goes off, another Chance Wayne, to become one of the Patrona's lovers. But though Shannon is captured, Nonno is freed. Having completed his poem about "the earth's obscene corrupting love," he has found release from such corruptions in death.

The materials, while resolved without sensationalism or sentiment, are all perfectly familiar: the defeated perverse central character, punished for his perversity; the Strindbergian identification of the human body with excrement and defilement; the obsessively sexual determination of every character. But by keeping his usual excesses to a minimum, Williams has provided the occasion for some striking performances. Margaret Leighton, especially, has endowed the stainless Hannah with extraordinary sensibility and tenderness, plumbing depths which Williams himself has been unable to reach since his earliest work. Bette Davis, playing the Patrona in flaming red hair and blue jeans, bats her pendulous lids on her laugh lines and is always on the surface of her part, but she is still a strongly felt personality; Alan Webb's Nonno is humorously senescent; and Patrick O'Neal plays Shannon with suppressed hysteria and a nagging, relentless drive which sometimes reminds one of Fredric March. Always on hand to produce rain on the stage, Oliver Smith has stifled his passion for opulence in the setting, within which this gifted ensemble seems to find its way without directorial eyes (Frank Corsaro's name is still on the program but I detect his influence only in a couple of Method Mexican extras).

For all its virtues, though, the play is decidedly a minor opus. A rich atmosphere, a series of languid scenes, and some interesting character sketches are more than Williams has offered us in some time, but they are still not enough to sustain our interest through a full evening. Perhaps Williams, identifying with Nonno, has decided to think of himself as only "a minor league poet with a major league spirit," and there is enough fatigue in the play to suggest that, again like Nonno, he feels like "the oldest living and practicing poet in the world." But even a minor poet fashions his work with more care and coherence that this; even an aged eagle occasionally spreads its wings. I am inclined to persist in my heresy that there is at least one more genuine work of art left in Williams, which will emerge when he has finally been able to objectify his personal problems and to shape them into a suitable myth. Meanwhile, let us put down *The Night of the Iguana* as another of his innumerable exercises in marking time.

The New Republic, January 22, 1962: 20, 22-23.

Williams, *Iguana*, Chamberlain*
Martin Gottfried

There are three distinct phases in the Tennessee Williams career to date. The first phase, which ended in 1953, was the time of his creative outburst and richest artistic achievement: *The Glass Menagerie, A Streetcar Named Desire* and *The Rose Tattoo*. Come what may, those plays have established him as American's finest playwright. Even the flawed *Summer and Smoke* displays the rich poetry and soulfulness of this Williams.

The second phase was one of distinct commercialism, some self-parody and an apparent uncertainty about the direction in which his work should go. His past concern with fragile, sensitive, artistic souls began to wane. His poetry turned florid. This phase began with *Cat on a Hot Tin Roof* in 1955, included *Suddenly Last Summer, Sweet Bird of Youth* and *Period of Adjustment* and ended in 1961 with *The Night of the Iguana*.

The latest phase has continued ever since he abandoned his special blend of poetic naturalism for the absurdist caricature of *The Milk Train Doesn't Stop Here Anymore* in 1962. Since then, Williams has wavered between similar misguided attempts to modernize his style, as with *Gnadiges Fraulein* or *In the Bar of a Tokyo Hotel* or *The Seven Descents of Myrtle* or *Out Cry,*

*Reprinted with permission from the *New York Post,* December 17, 1976: 31, 39.

and vain stabs at recovering the old realism as in *Small Craft Warnings.* Incoherence plagued him.

It has been a long and dry spell for this great playwright, surely an agonizing one of artistic and commercial frustration. So the revival of *Iguana* that opened last night at the Circle in the Square, is of particular interest. It was the last hit Williams had and one hopes to find in it a key to the change in his fortunes. What did he do afterward--was there a hint of it in this play-- that turned his work unsatisfying?

There are some clues. I don't think *Night of the Iguana* would be the popular success today that it was 14 years ago and I certainly should think not the critical success. It is a vague play, uneven dialogue. Unlike the works to follow, its characters and setting are realistic and there is a comprehensible sequence of conversation and event. Yet, its exaggeration and uncontrolled flights of symbolic poetry promise the stylized, unreasonable plays to come. Its religious concerns certainly predict the oncoming work.

Iguana is set in a small Mexican resort hotel that is run by a tough, sexed-up woman named Maxine. It is the off-season when she entertains friends and one of them is the Reverend T. Lawrence Shannon. Shannon was locked out of his church for heresy and a sex scandal (he is attracted to teenage girls), but it is important to Williams' religious theme that he wasn't defrocked. Shannon is religious in a personal way, presumably nature's way, and the iguana of the title represents him. The author's choice of an animal that most people find repellent is significant were one to psychoanalyze the play.

Shannon earns his living by guiding tourists through Mexico and he has left his current busload to cool their heels while he visits Maxine at the hotel. There he meets an attractive, spinster who cares for her senile father, a poet. Shannon is attracted to her, much to Maxine's jealousy, but the spinster is sexless.

When he loses his job for mistreating the tourists, he nearly breaks down and must, like the iguana, be restrained, but Williams has him arbitrarily regain both his freedom and his senses and the play ends with a rambling, droning speech. Despite all the religious and philosophical references, the play seems no more than a passive triangle involving three nervous people.

None of this is particularly dramatic and it is interesting mainly in reference to Williams' other works. The spinster Hannah would seem cast in the mold of the classic heroines on [*sic*] the playwright's past, but the character is only an outline. It is the Rev. Shannon who is actually closer to those world-lost artist figures.

Playing this character, Richard Chamberlain is making an impressive New York debut. Chamberlain is not a pretty movie actor hoping to cash in on his name. For several years now he has been doing serious plays, even Shakespeare's, abroad and on the West Coast. He has proved to have surprising technical equipment but an odd, unreal presence, as if still on a movie screen. This performance, however is superb. He has masked his extraordinary good looks with a seediness that goes to the character's burnt-out soul. He presents a man who is frayed physically and emotionally. His recollection of a past, gentility, real or imagined, is as heartbreaking as Blanche's in *Streetcar*.

Dorothy McGuire an actress I've long admired, gives too quiet and reserved a performance as the spinster. There is a considerable difference between that and playing a quiet, reserved woman. One cannot so understate on the stage. Miss McGuire's energy level is too low, a problem that affects Joseph Hardy's overall direction. This is a production--McGuire, Chamberlain, Hardy--that has essentially been transported from Los Angeles and I cannot imagine how it carried the cavernous Ahmanson Theater there.

Otherwise, Hardy staged the play satisfactorily, even making the German tourists on the premises believable though there is no compelling reason for their being in the play at all. But why in earth he cast Sylvia Miles as Maxine, the hotel owner, is incomprehensible. Miss Miles is earthy enough, but her accent is almost a lampoon of New Yorkese and she comes through as so gross it is inconceivable that Chamberlain's or McGuire's character, would even deal with her.

On the other hand, Allison Argo, is excellent as the minister's jail bait of the moment and most of the company is satisfactory. The overall performance is so competent, in fact, that the play itself can be seen for what it is. And what it is is Williams getting by on popular reputation while heading plainly and inexorably for artistic crisis.

God, Man, & The Lizard*
Clive Barnes

Presumably it is simply a coincidence that America's two indisputable playwrights--O'Neill and Williams--were both men pursued by demons, writing out of pain, and revising out of misery.

The Night of the Iguana, by Tennessee Williams--the last of that playwright's critical and public successes--is a play that looks at religion and life, sex, and sensuality, and the compromises of survival through a mist of pained compassion.

Compassion is the quality that instantly separates Williams from O'Neill, for while O'Neill suffered corrosively for himself, Williams suffered noisily for the world. And Williams forgave, while O'Neill simply remembered.

*Reprinted with permission from the *New York Post,* June 27, 1988: 29.

This season we have the Yale Repertory Theater's centennial production of O'Neill's "family" plays on Broadway, while Circle-in-the-Square is staging a Williams retrospective which started with a revisionist *Streetcar,* has proceeded with *The Night of the Iguana,* opening last night, and will conclude with a third Williams play yet to be named.

Iguana, first produced in 1961 with Patrick O'Neill [*sic*], Margaret Leighton, and Bette Davis, has never enjoyed the general acclaim of *Streetcar, Menagerie,* or even *Cat,* but in its day it had a decent, if backstage-troubled, Broadway run, and, in the final love-fest with his critics, won Williams his last New York Drama Critics' Best Play Award.

Made into a modestly successful movie by John Huston, even with Richard Burton delivering a desultory performance as Shannon, the defrocked priest hero, it's only major theatrical revival was also by the Circle-in-the-Square, in 1976, this time round starring Richard Chamberlain as the agonized Shannon.

It is a great play--destined eventually, perhaps not right now, to find a high place in the Williams canon. Of all the major Williams plays, it is the one--with the exception of *Milk Train,* the Williams work with which it has most in common--that is thematically the least clear and most dense.

For one thing it seems to be about sex, and sexual repression, when it is really about salvation, poetry, and God. And getting through the night and the night after.

Shannon, described so wonderfully by Williams as a "man of God--on vacation," unquestionably has his sexual problems, stemming from a mixture of attractiveness and instability, but these are symptomatic of his inability to center his life or secure it some kind of purpose.

In comparison the people Williams places around Shannon--Maxine, the sensual, newly widowed owner of the cheap Mexican hotel where it all takes place; Hannah Jelkes, the New England spinster, for whom Shannon has an emotional surge of energy; and Nonno, Hannah's old and dying minor poet of a grandfather--all know vaguely what they want and instinctively what they need.

Only Shannon is undetermined, rootless, deserted by the God he has himself deserted, unfitted for the only life he can find, unable to reshape himself in terms of character or circumstance. A man, not unlike Tennessee Williams himself, quite perfectly doomed.

For, again like O'Neill, Williams only had one subject: himself and his life. And both playwrights busied themselves writing about the way these were, or should, or could, have been.

In *The Night of the Iguana* it is the iguana, a lizard, one of God's creatures, captured for death and struggling in the dark for blind survival, who is the ultimate hero.

At the end the iguana is released, the old poet dies--with the final ecstacy of having composed what he feels to be his finest poem--and his granddaughter and, of course, the world-smart widow, settle down to survival.

But Shannon, who has released the iguana, is himself tethered, settling for a future once more not of his making.

This new production, staged by Theodore Mann, has a lot going for it, including a setting by Zack Brown of considerable beauty and with the realism of a film set, and at least one beautifully judged performance.

Yet in the final count it lacks something in urgency and anxiety--partly because of the conventionally distraught but essentially bland portrayal given by Nicolas Surovy as Shannon.

Surovy is far from inadequate, and in his big scene with Hannah (given by Maria Tucci with a consummate mixture of chicanery, spirituality, and prissiness--for this is another view of Williams himself) he does indeed rise to the dusty occasion.

Yet he never dominates the play with his indecision or colors it with his pain. Also Jane Alexander, charmingly earthy, does not make the most of the widow Maxine, and at the end you feel she might even try to reform Shannon rather than take him to the final corruption.

This is still a play in search of its ultimate definition--a definition that cannot come, oddly enough, until a great and perhaps bizarre actor (it would be a wonderful role for a man like Jonathan Pryce) shows us how the play can really work.

Meanwhile this is a production worth your attention, partly for Williams's writing, which here is both spare and luxuriant all at once, exaggerated yet direct, also to a degree the performances, especially Miss Tucci's tenderly judged an exquisite Hannah, and finally to Brown's expansive setting.

Not a complete success, the production demonstrates that *The Night of the Iguana* still deserves another day in court.

The Subterranean World of *The Night of the Iguana*
Glenn Embrey

Most of Tennessee Williams' characters eventually discover there is no fate worse than sex; desire maims and kills, often in the most violent fashion. Val Xavier is burnt to death, Blanche DuBois is raped and driven insane, Chance Wayne waits to be castrated, and Sebastian Venable is torn apart and devoured by children--all because of sexual drives. Many other characters in Williams' plays are destroyed by their passions, only in less physical and sensationalistic ways.

The idea that sex is fatal is not always easy to catch in the plays, for it is usually not developed explicitly. Instead, it lurks in the background, like a vague but persistent nightmare that affects the shape of whatever else the plays have to say. Also, it contradicts some of the popular notions about Williams. After all, his heroes and heroines often openly revel in their sexual exploits. He is considered the champion of the promiscuous, the passionate, the deviant. When these characters are destroyed, they appear to be the victims of an insensitive or sadistic world that will not tolerate their differences, especially their sexual differences; they seem to be brutalized not by their own desires, but by cruel, external forces. Blanche DuBois, for example, is assailed by a crude society that has no room for her sensitivity, her ideals, or her need to find comfort in sexual encounters. But this view of Blanche is only half true. There is in *Streetcar* what Shannon would call a "subterranean" or "fantastic" level. On this level, the play is really a dramatization of how Blanche and her delicate nature are devastated by the promiscuous behavior her sexual nature drives her to, a fate paralleling the way her family's plantation was lost through the "epic fornication" of their ancestors. When Stanley ravages her mind and body at the end of the play, he is not so much an agent of the real world as he is a symbol of the sexual drives that have ravaged her throughout her life.

The main character of *The Night of the Iguana* seems to escape the violent fate usually in store for Williams' heroes. True, desire has been ruining Shannon's life for the past ten years, but at the climax of the play he manages to form what promises to be a lasting sexual relationship with a mature woman. This optimistic ending appears to make *Iguana* very different from the serious plays that precede it; for the first time hope breaks across Williams' bleak world. But appearances are deceptive, for there is a "subterranean" world within *Iguana,* as there is in *Streetcar,* and this world makes *Iguana's* optimism naive and unjustified, and makes the play just another variation on the theme that haunts all of Williams' works--that sex kills, that it is disgusting and dangerous. The conflict that exists between the different levels of *Iguana* is also typical of the playwright's works, and the play provides a clear example of how they collapse into confusion because unacknowledged fears of sexuality undermine their more overt and positive levels.

Shannon arrives onstage in the condition of the typical Williams hero--on the verge of going to pieces. Emotionally, physically, psychologically, financially, in almost every possible way, he is at the end of his rope, just like the frantic iguana. The play provides a surfeit of explanations for his imminent breakdown. One is simply his bizarre lifestyle: he roams about the world, towing his unsuspecting tour groups after him, in search of the most horrifying and disgusting scenes he can find. The understandable complaints posted by his parties, along with his seduction of the youngest ladies of the groups, get him fired from one travel agency after another. He is currently employed by the sleaziest of the agencies, and none is left to hire him if he is fired again.

Another reason for his collapse is that he is so preoccupied with himself he is cut off from everyone else. Despite his busloads of companions, some more intimate than others, he is abjectly lonely. In his conversation with Hannah during the second act he explains what has led to his miserable way of life. Ten years before, his brief career as a minister ended after he committed both fornication and heresy in the same week. A young Sunday school teacher had come to the rectory and wildly declared she loved him. When he knelt with her to pray for guidance, they suddenly found themselves making love. Afterwards, he slapped her and called her a tramp; when she went home she tried to commit suicide. On the following Sunday, facing a congregation expecting an explanation and apologies, he suddenly threw away his prepared remarks and shouted an impromptu sermon that drove the people from the church. The gist of his outburst was that he refused to conduct services for the kind of God he felt they believed in: a *"senile delinquent,"* "a bad-tempered childish old, old, sick, peevish man" (IV, 303-4).

He was locked out of his church and committed to an asylum to recover from his apparent nervous breakdown. When released he became a tour guide, and his itineraries show he never fully recovered from whatever had possessed him. On each of his tours he clearly reenacts the dual sin of fornication and heresy. He seduces one or more of the youngest members of the party, afterwards treating them as abusively as he did the Sunday school teacher. The tours themselves are a continuation of his heretical sermon, for on them, he tells Hannah, he is trying to "collect evidence" of his own "personal idea of God" (p. 304), evidence that attacks his congregation's notion of God. And the results are just the same: he is fired by his tour groups as he was fired by his congregation.

Shannon's concept of God needs some explaining for it seems at odds with the kind of evidence he gathers. He is primarily interested in examples of the disgusting misery of human life. The story that Hannah finds nauseating about the aged filthy natives crawling about a mound of excrement looking for bits of undigested food to eat epitomizes what Shannon collects. So does the iguana. Jerking about desperately and uselessly against its noose, destined to become Maxine's dinner, the iguana is a metaphor not only for the major characters of the play but also for all human beings, creatures made grotesque by suffering and terror, frequently forced to live in the mode degrading of conditions.

Shannon's God provides quite a contrast to these images. He is personified as a "terrific electric storm"; he is the "God of Lightning and Thunder" and of blazing, apocalyptic sunsets. Shannon's descriptions recall the Old Testament God of overwhelming majesty and righteous wrath. And although this is the kind of God he really believes in, he overtly rejects the idea by arguing that his God is in no way interested in punishment or suffering.

The key term in Shannon's theology is "oblivious"; when he points out the nearing thunderstorm to Hannah, he says, "That's him! There he is now! . . . His oblivious majesty" (p. 305). According to Shannon traditional theologies see suffering as purposely sanctioned by God as an opportunity for men to atone for their sins and rise to him, but Shannon feels that suffering is simply the result of the world's "faults in construction." They are architectural imperfections, God's accidents, and men do suffer because of them; but no divine plan lies behind the misery. To claim design, as Western theologies do, says Shannon, makes God either a cruel child or a sadist; Shannon refused to conduct services for such a God. The logic connecting human degradation and divine majesty is somewhat tenuous. Apparently Shannon's twisted thinking runs along these lines: God is awesome, powerful majestic (this idea is a product of his childhood, and he never seems to question it; it is a given). But a God who is all these things could not possibly be aware of man's extreme misery and let it continue to exist; therefore God must be unaware of it. Thus, the more examples of suffering Shannon can collect, the more he is demonstrating that God is oblivious, and consequently the more he is proving God's majesty.

Williams takes the explanations of Shannon's crack-up a step further in the third act, when Maxine uncovers the psychically damaging events that eventually led to the eruption of Shannon's double offense. She recounts to Shannon, surely for the audience's sake rather than his, what she once heard him telling her deceased husband. His problems supposedly began when his mother caught him masturbating; after spanking him she said his behavior made God even angrier than it made her and that if she did not punish him, God would, and much more severely. Maxine continues, "You said you loved God and Mama and so you quit it to please them, but it was your secret pleasure and you harbored a secret resentment against Mama and God for making you give it up. And so you got back at God by preaching atheistical sermons and you got back at Mama by starting to lay young girls" (p. 329). A simplistic psychological explanation, to be sure, but one that Williams apparently intends us to take seriously, for none of the characters or Shannon's actions contradict it. On the contrary, his theology and behavior are perfectly in tune with it. It reveals, for example, the origin of his belief that God is awesome, threatening, and by extension, majestic; this is his adult version of his mother's warning that God was angry and ready to punish him severely. It also explains why fornication is always linked with heresy. He was told that he would have to suffer for his sexual pleasure; thus, to ward off the punishment he has earned whenever he indulges his sexual desire, he must immediately assert that God is actually oblivious to mankind. Sex becomes safe if he can deny his mother's idea of God, so he tries to collect evidence for this denial.

Maxine's comments also explain the sudden, powerful emergence of his sexuality that occurred that day on the rectory floor. Fear of punishment caused the young Shannon to repress his sexual nature; the consequences of his repression are the same as those suffered by other Williams characters. Driven underground for whatever reason, sexual urges grow more powerful and more threatening. The vicious circle in which repression causes a strengthening of the desire repressed, which in turn causes renewed effort to repress, can end only disastrously when desire breaks through its restraints. By this time it has grown so powerful that it is virtually uncontrollable and blasts away the character's former life. This pattern appears in the lives of Blanche in *Streetcar* and Alma in *Summer and Smoke.* The dangerous energy that repressed desire takes on is manifest in Stanley Kowalski and John Buchanan, menacing sexual supermen who are really the women's alter egos. Since that first incident, Shannon has learned what Blanche and Alma learned. Initially he was able to smother his sexual nature so thoroughly that he became not only a minister of the God who opposed his sensual pleasure; he also became what he calls "the goddamnedest prig" imaginable. Desire burst free while he was kneeling with the Sunday school teacher and has remained irrepressible ever since. His continual seductions are not so much a way of getting back at his mother, as Maxine suggests; they are something he is driven to, in spite of his conscious reluctance, by his voracious sexual appetite.

And he obviously has a great deal of reluctance. I have said that his initial trauma explains Shannon's wanting to make God oblivious and unvengeful, but it should be clear by now that all his efforts in this direction are a case of his protesting too much. Shannon is afraid that God is full of righteous wrath, and naturally he is terrified about what his uncontrollable passion will bring down upon him. His panic and anxiety are very understandable in this light. No doubt even his feeble efforts to avoid God's wrath by preaching about a different kind of God aggravate his guilt and fear--he is aware rebellion will not escape notice or punishment.

There is plenty of evidence that Shannon still believes in the God he pretends to dismiss. We have his latest lover's word that he continues to feel as guilty about sex as he did after his first transgression: "I remember that after making love to me," Charlotte tells him, "you hit me, ... you struck me in the face, and you twisted my arm to make me kneel on the floor and pray with you for forgiveness" (p. 298). An oblivious God would hardly be interested in forgiveness. Shannon's continuing fantasy that he will write to his former bishop and be reinstated as a minister suggests how ineffectual his efforts have been to break away from the God his mother warned him about. He dreams of giving up his heretical and sexual offenses and being forgiven by one of God's agents. In effect, he wants to become a good boy again.

Shannon's parody of Christ's crucifixion is the most blatant evidence of his failure to get free from this God. He is so far from truly believing that

God is oblivious to suffering and atonement that he plays at being God's son. In the third act when he finally cracked up, Maxine has him tied in a hammock to keep him from drowning himself. He struggles melodramatically against the rope, and Hannah, a quick-sketch artist who specializes in accurate psychological portraits, accuses him of being a perverse Christ figure engaged in a self-indulgent passion play: "There's something almost voluptuous in the way that you twist and groan in that hammock--no nails, no blood, no death. Isn't that a comparatively comfortable, almost voluptuous kind of crucifixion to suffer for the guilt of the world, Mr. Shannon?" (p. 344). How useless all his evidence has been. Afraid of being punished for his sins, he tried to stave off God's wrath by "suffering" like Christ, to atone for his offenses. Ironically, he is never totally free from either his dread of God or his sensual nature; each aspect of his personality corrodes the other. His guilt and fear keep him from ever enjoying sex fully, and his sexual instincts manage to corrupt his attempts to suffer for his sins since he derives sensual pleasure even from his suffering.

Caught between his sexual drives and his religious fears, between his need to deny God and his yearning for forgiveness, Shannon can find momentary relief from this tension, from his "spook," only in periodic crack-ups. During such times he loses control of himself and can no longer be held accountable for his sins.

Williams captures Shannon's predicament brilliantly in a brief and wordless scene in act three, after Shannon has lost the last vestiges of control over his touring party. He stands onstage wearing a few pieces of his ministerial garb; suddenly, he "with an animal outcry beings to pull at the chain suspending the gold cross about his neck" (p. 340). He jerks savagely back and forth on it, slashing himself. His actions illustrate how he is tied to his warped theology, just as the iguana is tied to the stake. He shows how his religious beliefs make him suffer, how his efforts to free himself from them are useless and only make him suffer the more. And he shows how willingly he punishes himself.

This masochistic pantomime ends in a very significant way, and this is where *Iguana* begins to differ from Williams' prior works. Hannah rushes over to help him and soon frees him from his chain and his self-laceration. During the rest of the play, she will accomplish in actuality what she does here symbolically--she frees him from his obsessive, self-destructive notions so that he can move completely out of the previous pattern of his life, find a measure of peace, and establish a healthy sexual relationship. To underline Hannah's triumph, at the end of the play Williams has Shannon give his cross and chain to her.

Hannah begins her therapy by pointing out to him how self-indulgent and voluptuous his struggles actually are. Then she focuses on the problem of his miserable loneliness. He has been so obsessed with himself and his fears, she tells him, that he hasn't been able to see that people might help him. Even his sexual escapades have been cold and lonely, she says, and isolate rather than connect him with others. Her initial advice echoes Big Mama's plea in *Cat*: "we just got to love each other an' stay together" (III, 157). Hannah tells Shannon he needs to find relief in "Broken gates between people so they can reach each other, even if it's just for one night only . . . communication . . . A little understanding exchanged between them, a wanting to help each other through nights like this" (IV, p. 352). People must struggle to break through the walls that keep them apart and come together, even if only momentarily, with understanding, kindness, and sympathy. Hannah reinforces her advice by becoming an example of what she is talking about. She reaches out to him with compassion and respect. And her advice and example are very effective; he is finally able to put aside his obsessions and establish a healthy connection with another human being, Maxine.

Hannah also makes two other important suggestions. She tells him he must learn simply to endure the tension and terror that are part of his life. Later she advises him to go beyond endurance to acceptance; after recounting the two bizarre incidents that comprise her "lovelife," she tells him "the moral is Oriental. Accept whatever situation you cannot improve" (p. 363). It's no accident that "the moral is Oriental" for the play creates a definite contrast between East and West, in which the Eastern attitudes of stoicism and fatalism are offered as a positive alternative to the Western preoccupations with guilt and suffering.

Iguana conveys the superiority of East over West in a number of ways. For example, near the end of the play Hannah tells Shannon how moved she was by the peaceful deaths of the poor in Shanghai: their "eyes looked up with their last dim life left in them as clear as the stars in the Southern Cross. . . . Nothing I've ever seen has seemed as beautiful to me" (p. 356). In this respect, Nonno's calm resignation before death is "Oriental," as Hannah makes clear, and is in stark contrast to the terror and hysteria the approach of death usually evokes in Williams' characters. The East-West theme is also established visually. Close to the beginning of the third act Hannah puts on a Japanese Kabuki robe, so that when she later manages to free Shannon from his cross and chain her exotic Eastern attire makes her look a world apart from the neurotic minister. She wears the robe throughout the act, reminding us of the source of her compassionate advice.

The Fahrenkopfs provide an even more vivid contrast to the Oriental Hannah. In their Rubensesque proportions and Wagnerian exuberance they represent the culmination of Western civilization. Their boisterousness and frenetic activity counterpoint Hannah's demeanor, and as Nazis they epitomize the cruelty and violence of the Western world.

Williams even manages to have Maxine reinforce the theme--in her characteristically crude way. Early in the third act, in an effort to soothe

Shannon's nerves, she tells him her cook's philosophy of life, one she appears to share: "The Chinaman in the kitchen says, 'No sweat.' . . . 'No sweat.' . . . All the Chinese philosophy in three words, 'Mei yoo guanchi'--which is Chinese for 'No sweat'" (p. 330). And at the very end of the play, in a surprising transformation, Maxine *becomes* Oriental; in a stage direction Williams writes: "It is apparent that the night's progress has mellowed her spirit: her face wears a faint smile which is suggestive of those cool, impersonal all-comprehending smiles on the carved heads of Egyptian or Oriental deities" (p. 373). No doubt the metamorphosis is a major reason Shannon can accept her at the climax of the play.

This climax sets *Iguana* apart from Williams' other serious works. Shannon survives. He attains some measure of peace. He is neither returning to the ministry nor continuing his rebellion against it and his mother. Instead, he has been led beside the "still waters" of the Costa Verde Hotel. Much more than this, he enters what is apparently a healthy sexual relationship. Other Williams characters have found momentary stays against despair in brief, casual encounters with strangers, but Shannon seems to be entering into something more lasting with Maxine. His decision to stay with her fulfills both parts of Hannah's advice: he is finally reaching outside of himself, and he has decided to accept Maxine and his present situation. He leaves the play chuckling happily, with Maxine "half leading half supporting him" (p. 374). Anyone familiar with the bulk of Williams' work can appreciate how unusual, how positive this description of their relationship is.

Shannon's loosing the iguana at the end of the play is obviously a symbol of the optimistic resolutions that are simultaneously occurring. The lizard is set free at the same time Nonno is set free from his poem and his life, at the same time Hannah is unburdened of her dying grandfather, and at the same time Shannon escapes from his God, his mother, and his loneliness.

Unfortunately, the ending isn't as believable as it is formally pleasing and optimistic. Even according to the overt level of the drama, the ending sounds suspiciously like the product of wishful thinking. For one thing, it comes rather suddenly and unexpectedly; an hour's exposure to human compassion, a cup of poppy tea, and a bit of Oriental wisdom hardly seem sufficient to eradicate habits and attitudes hardened over the past ten years. For another, the advice Hannah gives him doesn't really speak to the main sources of his problems: terrible guilt, fear of God, and an overpowering sex drive. The two characters never mention these things, much less work through them during their conversation. Hannah could conceivably convince him that human contact is worthwhile, but she never points out or tells him how to combat those feelings that have made human contact so difficult for him. The optimistic conclusion simply ignores the psychological portrait Williams works out so carefully during the course of the play.

And if the ending isn't entirely convincing on the overt level, it is completely incompatible with some less explicit, subterranean elements which work like an undertow to suck the mood of the play back into bleakness and despair. The difference between acceptance and endurance is a key to the nature of the shadow side of the play. Acceptance is a more positive notion. A person is able to accept an undesirable situation by putting aside his own needs or expectations and seeing beyond the negative aspects to find something positive he can embrace. Endurance is more pessimistic. It implies that the unsatisfactory situation remains exactly as it seems--painful, destructive, threatening, or whatever. Nothing redeeming is to be found in it. Maggie in *Cat* provides an example of this notion. Tense and frustrated by her husband's physical and emotional rejection of her, she wonders what victory a person who feels like "a cat on a hot tin roof" can achieve; she decides, "Just staying on it, I guess, as long as she can . . . " (III, 31). Endurance implies that the roof never cools down; the cat merely grins fiercely and bears it. This is the implication of Hannah's remarks when she tells Shannon she showed her own spook "that I could endure him and I made him respect my endurance." Shannon asks how and she replies, "Just by, just by . . . enduring" (p. 353). Though she will later speak of *acceptance,* much in the play makes this concept out of the question for Shannon and indicates he is in a situation he can barely endure.

In a way, we have Williams' own word for this point. In an interview during the rehearsals for *Iguana* he said the theme of the play is "how to live beyond despair and still live" (Funke and Booth, p. 72). The context makes clear that *beyond* means not *without* but *in a state worse than* (despair). Many elements of the play itself reinforce this feeling of utter bleakness. Nonno's poem, his best, coming as it does at the climax, is a poetic commentary on what the play is about. Implicit pessimism in the first stanza is emphasized because the penultimate stanza is almost identical:

How calmly does the orange branch
Observe the sky begin to blanch
Without a cry, without a prayer,
With no betrayal of despair (p. 371).

The implication is clearly that there is a great deal of despair--however, the tree heroically refuses to give any sign of it, much as Hannah tries to keep hers under control with her deep breathing.

But what is it that can only be endured, that is the cause of this vast despair? The poem suggests initially that it is death, or the ageing or ripening accompanying it. But the fourth stanza carries a much more important idea. According to the poem, when the fruit grows ripe it falls to the earth where it must suffer

An intercourse not well designed
For beings of a golden kind
Whose native green must arch above
The earth's obscene, corrupting love.

This is an accurate description of the basic dilemma of most of Williams' major characters: they are sensitive idealists forced to indulge in sexual activity, which they find corrosive and obscene. The assumption that sex is disgusting and threatening is the real motive for Shannon's behavior; in fact, the play itself seems to foster the same feelings about sex. It is this underlying fear that makes Shannon's final situation at best only endurable.

What makes this attitude hard for the audience or reader to catch is that it is never explicitly discussed by any of the characters, much less identified as the basis of Shannon's problems. As we've seen, all three main characters offer a variety of other plausible explanations, and these keep us from seeing this one clearly. It is a very real part of the play, nonetheless, and makes itself felt in a number of ways. We sense, for example, that much more than either guilt or rebellion accounts for Shannon's sexual behavior. At the end of the play he speaks of "Always seducing a lady or two, or three or four or five ladies in the party, but really ravaging her first by pointing out to her the-- what?--horrors? Yes, horrors!--of the tropical country being conducted a tour through" (p. 369). It is as if for a select few the last stop on his repulsive itinerary is his own bedroom. Sex for him is on a par with the other raving horrors he subjects himself and his tours to.

His penchant for the very youngest ladies suggests that he is afraid of more mature women. His attitude toward Maxine reinforces this idea and reveals his feelings of disgust as well. Whenever she makes sexual advances, he draws away vehemently, uncomfortably, or cruelly. At the beginning of the play, he disgustedly tells her she looks as if she's "been having it" and then pleads with her to button up her blouse so she will look decent. Later he suggests she has turned into a pig. At another point he says she is "bigger than life and twice as unnatural" (p. 270). His fear of her is apparent in his calling her a "bright widow spider" (p. 317), referring to an insect that proverbially devours her mate after intercourse. The audience itself tends to see her in much the same way. Nothing whatever in the play suggests that Shannon is incorrect about her, that his feelings are a product of his demented imagination. On the contrary, the playwright seems at pains to validate his vision of Maxine. In a stage direction at the beginning she is described as "rapaciously lusty" (p. 255). We are quickly made aware to what excess her sexual appetite runs--she has hired not one but two young Mexicans to serve her desires. Williams' description of her constantly recurring laugh emphasizes her animallike nature: "*Maxine* always laughs with a single harsh, loud bark, opening her mouth like a seal expecting a fish to be thrown to it" (p. 255).

Throughout the play she is coarse and suggestive, and at one point she tells Shannon that her interest in him is primarily sexual: "I know the difference between loving someone and just sleeping with someone--even I know about that. We've both reached a point where we've got to settle for something that works for us in our lives--even if it isn't on the highest kind of level" (p. 329). Even her name, Maxine Faulk, is unattractive: her first name suggests that she is manlike, aggressive, and her last name is a crude pun. Given all this, the audience has little chance of regarding her in a way fundamentally different from Shannon's.

The central symbol of the play also points up the frightening nature of Maxine's desires. The iguana scrambling frantically at the end of its rope represents all the main characters, but it has a special affinity with Shannon. Not by coincidence is it supposed to become Maxine's dinner--its intended fate reinforces Shannon's fears that she will devour him, too. He may free the lizard at the end of the play, but he himself is tied more closely than ever to the "bright widow spider." The director of the original Broadway production must have sensed how inappropriate optimism is in the conclusion, for when Shannon returned to the stage after cutting the iguana loose, he was wearing the rope around his own neck (see Adler, *"Night,"* p. 63).

No wonder, then, that Shannon feels threatened by Maxine, this female version of Big Daddy Pollitt. The wonder is that at the end of the play she can abruptly change, somehow, somewhere offstage, into a mellow Oriental goddess. To be believable such a radical transformation requires much more than the stage-direction and the few lines of dialogue Williams supplies. As it stands, the ending comes as quite a jolt. A character we have been forced to see as vulgar, aggressive, and menacing suddenly acquires alluringly soft edges. More than this, throughout the play Shannon has drawn away from the rapacious widow in apprehension, an apprehension the play helps the audience to share; now in a bizarre about-face he willingly agrees to live with her. Blanche DuBois might as easily become more receptive to the sexual overtures of a Stanley who has become suddenly more gentle and solicitous. (The arrangement Shannon and Maxine come to at the very end makes the conclusion even more outrageous. He agrees not only to live with Maxine but also to cater to the sexual needs of the female guests of the hotel. Incredibly, he "chuckles happily" at the thought--this from a man who previously has been obsessively guilty about, disgusted by, and terrified of sex. Their interchange-- at least his response--violates the seriousness of the play and of Shannon's problems. This interchange ought to be dismissed simply as a momentary lapse, or as one of the occasions on which the playwright falls victim to his popular reputation of being obscene and shocking.)

Even Hannah, the most positive and sympathetic of the main characters, contributes to the underlying feeling that sex is dangerous or dirty. In stage directions, Williams describes her as appearing "androgynous" (p. 266) and as having "a fastidiousness, a reluctance, toward intimate physical contact" (p. 348), a description made concrete when she hesitates to touch Shannon to find his cigarettes. She admits to Shannon that sex is definitely not a part of the "broken gates" between people that she sees as an antidote to loneliness. She has clearly never accepted or enjoyed her own sexuality. Her lovelife consists of two pathetic incidents in which she was hardly a willing participant and which, in spite of her protest to the contrary, add to the suspicion that sex is degrading. The only lasting relationship she has formed is the very safe, asexual one with her grandfather. She quickly and surely squelches Shannon's suggestion that the two of them travel together, even after they have grown close through their compassionate nighttime exchange. There is obviously a very definite boundary to her willingness to communicate and share: it comes to a complete halt this side of the physical. In effect, Hannah creates in the audience the impression that withdrawing from sex is positive or healthy, since we tend to see all the behavior of an admirable character as admirable, unless something indicates we should feel otherwise. And nothing in this play indicates that her sexual reluctance is a problem.

Hannah's attitude, however, adds to the improbability of Shannon's final decision. Why would his feelings toward the sexually voracious Maxine turn around after a conversation with this sexless spinster? In fact, it seems likely that a major reason he is able to communicate with Hannah to any degree is that she *is* sexless; since she does not arouse his desires, he does not have to be afraid of her. In this regard *Iguana* reflects a pattern typical of Williams' works: a character can offer or find either love or sex, but not both. The underlying attitude toward sex explains why this dichotomy occurs: love is an ideal, something only "beings of a golden kind" can attain; sex is obscene and corrupting and so must be kept separate from the ideal. Thus Hannah can give Shannon a momentary glimpse of what it means to love only by being asexual; and Maxine's sexual drives keep her from being able to offer him real love.

A glance at the play as a whole shows how everyone in it contributes to the feeling that human desire is obscene and fearful. Not a single sexually healthy character appears; no figure can define for the others (or for the audience) what sexual normalcy is, or give any hope that such a state can even be attained. (Where in any of Williams' work is such a figure?) Miss Fellowes is more than a strident castrating woman who reduces Shannon to feebly demonstrating his manhood by urinating on the luggage; she is a butch lesbian. Her protégée, Charlotte Goodall, flings herself hysterically, masochistically at Shannon "like a teen-age Medea" (p. 294). Both women make celibacy attractive. The Fahrenkopfs may be the most telling of all. No one could be more exuberantly physical and sexual than these caricatures who charge in and out of the drama bulging out of their scant swimming suits, clutching at one another, swilling beer, and booming out marching songs. It is no accident that these gross honeymooners are also part of the most monstrous political machine in Western civilization. The most overtly sexual characters, they are also the most grotesque, dangerous, and genuinely obscene.

Clearly, then, some less explicit elements in *Iguana* make its optimistic conclusion untenable. Considering the subterranean aspects of the play, Shannon's staying with Maxine means he is putting himself in the maw of a devouring monster. Obviously he cannot do so optimistically or happily. In effect, the different levels of the play pull the audience in opposite directions, an uncomfortable feeling created even in Williams' best works. *Cat* is another example. Overtly, the play demonstrates that Brick's extreme idealism, his refusal to grow up or old, is unhealthy and damaging, presaging death rather than life. But the abundant animal imagery and the behavior of the other characters graphically support his attitude toward reality and sex: human beings are mean, greedy, pathetic, cruel, and beastlike, and when they make love they are no different from, or better than, "two cats on a--fence humping" (III, 123). As in *Iguana* we are made to think one way and feel another.

What is usually at the heart of the internal conflict in Williams' works is a disgust with and terrible fear of the sexual act. As I mentioned at the outset, these ideas are not always easy to discern. They are contrary to his general reputation as a sexual libertine, in his life and works; and though his plays are obviously about sex and violence, critics and reviewers usually do not recognize that sex itself, not the brutal world, causes the violence. The fundamental rejection of sexuality is hard to see also because sex usually is made to bear a heavy and confusing burden. A character may behave at various times as if sex is an immensely pleasurable activity, as an assertion of life in the face of death, a mean of staying young, a degrading or bestial act, a source of guilt, and a means of expiating this guilt. Add to them the feeling that sex is dangerous and obscene, a feeling that is the more insidious because it is not explicit, and the works add up to a welter of confusion about how to regard human sexuality. It is not as if sex is presented as a complex phenomenon; rather, the characters act, at successive moments, as if one particular attitude is true and all the others are nonexistent. The plays themselves reinforce this problem by providing nothing or no one to point out that at these moments the characters are confused, incorrect, or self-contradictory.

Iguana may look like a new kind of play for Williams, but it is not. What makes it more of the same, despite its surface optimism, are the feelings about sex that emerge from the subterranean world of the play. Early in his career Williams captured vividly the nature of these feelings in the short story "Desire and the Black Masseur." It is a grotesque and violent tale of a helpless little man who puts himself in the hands of huge black man. The masseur beats him repeatedly and cruelly and at the climax of the story, after beating him to death, eats him. Desire, the story suggests, *is* the black masseur, is a gigantic dark force that batters human beings and finally devours them. *The Night of the Iguana* shows that thirteen years after the publication of the story, this fear of sex is still a part of Williams' work and undermines whatever positive values the playwright consciously wishes to attribute to human relations.

Tennessee Williams: A Tribute, Ed. Jac Tharpe. Jackson: University Press of Mississippi, 1977. 65-80.

The Milk Train Doesn't Stop Here Anymore (1963)

One Milk Train, One Scandal
Anthony West

For an uncomfortably long time after the curtain has gone up on Mr. Tennessee Williams' new play, *The Milk Train Doesn't Stop Here Anymore,* the playgoer is left in tormenting doubt as to whether he is in the right theater or not. There in front of him is, to put it mildly, a vulgar old bag on a stage set of quite extraordinary vulgarity busily at work on her memoirs. She talks about these in a coarse and rapid manner, which shows that she is a tasteless fool, and when she dictates what are supposed to be passages from them, they, too, turn out to be sickeningly vulgar. Can it be, the playgoer wonders, that he has got to *Little Me* by mistake and is to spend a second evening in the company of Mr. Dennis' Belle Poitrine? This is not the case, though he is to have the misfortune, having come in the expectation of seeing and hearing something worthy of Mr. Williams, to spend the rest of the evening on the level of Mr. Dennis' imagination. What has happened? There is a sad moment in the career of an artist of the second rank, a point of no return, beyond which his work ceases to develop. The artist loses his gift for selecting viable new material and begins to go through his old material all over again, reproducing it this time with its salient feature exaggerated in involuntary self-parody.

The offstage episode of the young gentleman from New Orleans who was eaten by his ill-chosen playmates in that jolly little one-acter *Suddenly, Last Summer* held in its grotesque and humorless enormity a hint that Mr. Williams might be approaching this horrid milestone, and that he might, possibly, not be going to sail on triumphantly past it. The reports coming from the Two Worlds Festival at Spoleto last summer, after *The Milk Train Doesn't Stop Here Anymore* had been given its first performances, were guarded but ominous; they hinted that the play was a very silly one, but they gave no warning of the extent of Mr. Williams' collapse. It is the first time he has produced a play with no dramatic substance and with nothing in the way of significant experience behind it. Mr. Williams' plays in the past have been to the last degree substantial. His characters, too, have always seemed to be condemned from birth to the situations in which he placed them and to be inescapably what they were because they occupied specific places in space and time which could not, conceivably, allow them to be anything else. His plays, at any rate until now, have been made by, and made from, his obsession with a specific way of life, knowledge of which was in Mr. Williams' bones as a Southerner. Now we get an anecdote of foreign travel which concerns people who belong to that mobile group of international insiders who have as their main concern in life the business of being in the right company at the right place at the right time.

The location of the action, significantly enough, isn't in any place where people live and work, but in a phrase out of a tourist agency's brochure, "Italy's Divina Costeria." Nor is there any compelling reason for the characters to have assembled there rather than anywhere else. Their motivations go no deeper than the twitterings among the chorus which used to prelude a change of scene in the old style musical comedies: "Flora says she knows a divine place, a little island near Capri, let's all go there!" There is not logical reason why Mr. Williams should not take his cast to Capri, or to Formosa, if he wants to do so, but it just happens that the world of the arbitrary, in which things happen as they do simply because someone feels like having them happen that way, is, so far as literature and the theater is concerned, the world of the trivial and the unimportant. People, like quotations, have a way of losing most of their meaning out of context. But even allowing for all that, it soon becomes apparent not only that Mr. Williams' characters don't belong anywhere in particular, but also that they are mere chance acquaintances. He doesn't know them very well.

His heroine is called Flora Goforth, and he tells us that she has had a gift for making rich men marry her which has enabled her to make marriage, as the women's magazines say, a rewarding career. She appears to have been married six times, five times for profit and once for love. Mr. Williams has, it becomes evident, no clear idea of what such a record as this means. He seems to imagine that it could be done of the basis of a certain sexual bounciness by a woman who took no trouble to conceal the fact that she was a vulgar harpy. What makes such women as Flora Goforth attractive to men is evidently a mystery to him, and he clearly has no idea that to operate in this field successfully the last thing Flora Goforth can possibly be is demanding, much less sexually rapacious in a blatant or threatening way. Comfort and an easy time are her strong points. She must spend much of her time bolstering up the male ego, and she must be not only seen to be warmer and more reassuring, but also more amusing and more charming than most women. Nobody succeeds in that line of business by being a manifest threat to male virility. Flora Goforth, as Mr. Williams portrays her, is that above all, and when she announces that she intends to take a lover she does so in a manner which suggests that she intends to cook and eat him rather than to go to bed with him. When a suitable young man appears she makes a bizarre assault upon him, taking no trouble whatever to suggest that a liaison with her would be either pleasurable or profitable, but simply making it plain that he won't get anything to eat in her house until he has been to bed with her and done his stuff.

The victim of this attempted rape by starvation is a young man called Christopher Flanders who is by way of being a professional sponger, of what used to be called a gigolo. He gets his room and board from old ladies by being charming to them and carrying out the functions of a valet and companion, fetching and carrying parcels and steamer rugs and getting tickets and reservations. To glamorize a dingy situation, Mr. Flanders affects to be a poet, an artist (he has a little bagful of mobiles he has tinkered up) and a spiritual healer of a kind familiar to readers of Mr. Maugham's novel *The Razor's Edge*. He also affects the possession of integrity, and the action of the play turns on the question of how far he is willing to go to get Flora Goforth to keep him. Not, it turns out, so far as to go to bed with her--though there is some doubt on this score. There is an ambiguity in the action which makes it possible to think that Flora would have got what she had worked so hard for if her interfering secretary hadn't at a late stage slipped the poor boy a bottle of milk and a box lunch. Saved from a fate worse than death by this gift, Christopher hangs up one of his mobiles and escapes. And that, believe it or not, is the end of the evening's proceedings. Mr. Williams has never before tried to get away with such a thin brew, and he seems guiltily aware that he is letting himself down. Nothing but a strong sense of guilt can account for the amount of padding that he has put into the play, in which he achieves what is another first for him: the creation of an entirely superfluous character whose sole function is to fill up some vacant running time.

Mr. Williams has never done that before, and it is sad to see him doing it now, even though the existence of the character gives Mildred Dunnock a place in the play which she turns to the fullest account. The saddest thing of all, however, is that as time runs out on the play and all the gimmicks fail, one after another, one hears Mr. Williams more and more frequently rattling the dry bones of old speeches from old plays together to try to strike a spark. Flora Goforth is less and less a woman as the evening goes on, and more and more a medium from whose lips comes the passionate resentments and fears of Big Daddy, while Christopher Flanders begins to sound more and more like the young men of the old plays who really stood for something as the incarnations of poetry and lyricism lost, dumb and blind in a society busy with other things. But the arguments for abstentionism and revolt which were appropriate on their lips, as men who really had the divine fire in their souls, are hollow and contemptible in the mouth of a man for whom poetry and the arts are means to an end--the end being breakfast in bed and first-class staterooms on ocean liners.

The final curtain falls on a peculiarly dismal stage trick, with Flora Goforth in the beginning of her death agony standing enraptured in contemplation of the little mobile which Christopher Flanders has hung up for her. The mobile has competition: a staggering view of the two loveliest islands in the Mediterranean, a wide expanse of moving sea and beyond that the Italian coast fading into soft twilight. Mr. Williams used to stand for the imaginative vision of the world, the heightened awareness, the waking state of the spirit to which poetry is the key: his "white" people had it; their dark enemies, the killers of the spirit, denied it. He must know, very precisely, how fraudulent this moment of pseudotriumph for pseudo-art is and just how much ice that trashy little mobile would cut with any woman or man *in articulo mortis,* who was about to leave all the mixed joys, pains and splendors of the world behind forever.

Of the acting of this aberration of Mr. Williams, there is not much to be said. Hermione Baddeley gives a tremendously enjoyable performance as a lecherous retired vaudeville star, common as dirt, tough as old boots and, particularly when claiming to be just an old Georgia swamp-bitch, British as the flag; Paul Roebling plays Mr. Flanders as if he had been sandbagged, his concussed manner presumably indicting otherworldliness; and Ann Williams resolutely refuses to be beaten by the boringly written and unplayable part of Flora Goforth's secretary. Her lines include some of the worst that Mr. Williams has ever allowed himself to write, and he owes her a lot for preventing the audience at the Morosco from noticing how wooden and pathetic they are. . . .

Show, 3.4 (April 1963): 40-41.

Still on Wrong Track
John McClain

An interesting experiment was conducted last night at the Brooks Atkinson Theatre: it was to determine whether or not a play once rejected on Broadway could be rewritten, recast, remounted and regenerated. The opinion from here is that it cannot long endure.

The property in question is Tennessee Williams' *The Milk Train Doesn't Stop Here Any More* [sic]. It opened last season and bit the dust. Thereafter the author rewrote portions of it, employed a different director and a fresh cast, and took another shot at it.

This was a noble endeavor, and I believe everybody hoped it would come off as a famous "first." It would have given solace to the many people who write plays and live through flops with the feeling that if they had only had a different set of players and a more sympathetic director they would have had a hit.

What it proves, conversely I'm afraid, is that once the milk train has stopped there is almost nothing you can do to get it started again. Mr. Williams is said to have written the play for Talullah Bankhead, but settled for Hermione Baddeley in the earlier effort because she had done it with some success at Spoleto, Italy, in a Summer festival try-out. He thereupon opened it in New York with Miss Baddeley and it didn't work. Now he has Miss Bankhead in the lead, and in my opinion it still doesn't score.

There is something wrong with the play; it is not fundamentally a drama with the importance or depth of most of Mr. Williams' better achievements, and the business of warming it over, with the addition of some visual and vocal paprika, plus the services of the captivating Miss Bankhead, are still not enough to bring it to life.

The current production has been stylized into a single Japanese-type set, by Rouben Ter-Artunian, and employs a couple of Oriental-looking characters labeled as stage assistants who move props and also take part in the proceedings. There is strange music and sound effects which I found more intrusive than captivating; in fact, very little to suggest the climate of the Divina Costiera, Italy, where the scrimmage is said to take place. How did the Far East get into the act? Even the hero appears unexpectedly in a Japanese robe and Samurai sword. The characters explain that this is an old device borrowed from Japan for the occasion, but I found it only ostentatious and highly confusing.

Miss Bankhead cannot be anything less that great, any more than Mr. Williams can write a dreary play, but last night she seemed to rush some of her early speeches to the point that they were barely audible. Later, in the more casual moments of repartee, she was her magnificent self--lending added lust to some of the dialogue at which the author excels.

There are some reservations about the casting of Tab Hunter as the Angel of Death, as he is laughingly called; he seemed to be a good college player suddenly thrust into a pro backfield. But Ruth Ford was fine and so were Marian Seldes and Ralph Roberts.

I don't know about this new direction by Tony Richardson. It was different, but it wasn't enough different to make me care about his tired diva, interrupted in dictating the events of her squalid life.

I think Mr. Williams should have torn up *The Milk Train Doesn't Stop Here Any More* [*sic*] and started all over. Hopefully with a shorter title.

New York Journal American, January 2, 1964: 2.

Train Wreck
Mimi Kramer

The Milk Train Doesn't Stop Here Anymore, currently being revived at the WPA Theatre, is Tennessee Williams' play about a handsome young man who arrives mysteriously at an Italian villa and gets all the women there very excited. Set in 1962, it chiefly concerns Flora Goforth, an aging actress who has come to the Divina Costiera to write her memoirs. A former Follies girl who has lost six husbands, Mrs. Goforth--known as Sissy--is now dying herself, though of what is not entirely clear. (At times, such as when Mrs. Goforth has herself injected with morphine, it seems to be cancer. At other times, such as when she coughs blood, it seems to be tuberculosis--though, as far as I know, tuberculosis was not a big problem in 1962, so perhaps it is cancer after all.) Living with Mrs. Goforth and helping her to organize the story of her life and loves is her personal secretary, Frances Black--known as Blackie--whom she alternately abuses and exploits. Also drifting in and out of the villa is Mrs. Goforth's friend Vera Ridgeway Condotti, another wealthy and faded widow who is known, for no discernible reason, as the Witch of Capri.

Christopher Flanders, the new arrival, is the pivotal figure in the play. A jack-of-all-trades--part parasite, part visionary--he constructs mobiles, dabbles in literary translation, and travels around Europe making his home with rich women of advanced years. He's also a poet, also an erstwhile ski instructor--though sadly out of shape, for, winded (apparently) by the mountainous terrain and the long climb up to the villa, he falls asleep immediately on arrival and is put to bed. When Vera, a fierce gossip, tells Mrs. Goforth over drinks that night that Chris's reputation as a compassion to dying women has earned him the nickname the Angel of Death, she is horrified. Haglike, the two women go in to ogle Chris, thinking him still asleep. On rising later, he describes the incident to Blackie, who, having taken a liking to the young man, goes to bed with him. The following day, Mrs. Goforth attempts to humiliate Chris, first by withholding food and then by offering herself to him. When he rebuffs her, explaining the he'd hoped to bring spiritual, not physical, comfort, Mrs. Goforth flies into a rage and sends him away. The play ends with Chris starting back down the mountain and Mrs.Goforth weakly imploring Blackie to bring him back.

The first Broadway production of *Milk Train* (with Hermione Baddeley in the role of Sissy Goforth) opened in January of 1963 and ran for sixty-nine performances. The following year, a revised version of the play opened on Broadway on New Year's Day and closed four nights later. The present revival, which features Elizabeth Ashley as Flora Goforth, Amanda Plummer as Blackie, and Marian Seldes as Vera Ridgeway Condotti, is strictly for those who feel either than Williams can do no wrong or that no wrong can be done him. That it seems so traumatizingly long and boring--and productions like it have been known to make mutes scream--may be partly due to the presence of three actresses of such disparate extravagant tendencies. All three overact dreadfully, but in such different ways that the result is fascinating, though ultimately exhausting. Miss Ashley favors old-fashioned Method realism, Miss Seldes old-fashioned mannerism. Playing Mrs. Goforth with the rough, gravelly voice of a Texas jukebox mama, Miss Ashley sounds like a lower-class version of Tallulah Bankhead, who played the role in the second Broadway production. Miss Seldes, for her part, is putting her all into getting across the message that the Witch of Capri is a comic character; she does funny things with her mouth, and tilts her body toward or away from the audience, and dangles her absurdly long-seeming arms loose from the elbow. If we've seen these tricks once, we've seen them a thousand times, and if we've seen Miss Seldes in *Painting Churches* we've seen her as Vera Ridgeway Condotti. Amanda Plummer, meanwhile, is doing her own thing in her own special way. It's not the Method hamming that Miss Ashley is engaged in or the grand-actress hamming of Miss Seldes but something newfangled and unique to Plummer--"unnaturalism," I suppose you might call it. As Blackie, a character who is likened at one point to "a Brownie den mother," Miss Plummer works hard to seem disengaged from whatever is happening onstage. Wrapped up in her own unholy thoughts, she takes on the aspect of a slightly disturbed adolescent: she's always looking off somewhere, as though she were seeing Hamlet's father's ghost. Seemingly incapable of delivering a line without affectation, she speaks now with a Bryn Mawr accent, now in baby talk, now as though English were her second language. To a simple observation-- "There's no wind"--she brings a whole casebook of interesting subtextual meanings.

For the record, it's only fair to point out the difference between Miss Ashley's performance and the performances of Miss Plummer and Miss Seldes. There is, after all, such a thing as honest acting that fails. In Elizabeth Ashley's Mrs. Goforth I found not a shred of authenticity, but her performance had a kind of honest bravado. What's going on with Plummer and Seldes is something quite different--a kind of passive upstaging not often encountered in the professional theatre. Both actresses appear unable to go out of focus, as it were--to watch or listen to another character without seeming to want to attract attention to themselves. They radiate a kind of narcissistic energy, which--when bad acting vies with bad acting on the few occasions when the two of them share the stage--becomes a psychic wrestling match. Watching Seldes and Ashley two-step staggeringly about the stage with drinks in their hands, watching Plummer lurk broodingly, I was struck by the utter impossibility of three such actresses wringing any kind of pathos out of this material.

The character of Blackie in *Milk Train* is a bit of an anomaly. Alone of the central figures in the play, she fails to fit into a Tennessee Williams mold.

Mrs. Goforth comes from a long line of desperate older women--like Blanche DuBois and Amanda Wingfield, like Alexandra del Lago in *Sweet Bird of Youth* and Big Mama in *Cat on a Hot Tin Roof*--who either live on illusions and dreams of their fairer past or are unable to face death head on. Young Flanders comes from a long line of poet-parasites. He's one of that crowd of proud, beautiful young men in Williams' work who--like Val in *Orpheus Descending,* Chance Wayne in *Sweet Bird of Youth,* and the young man in *The Roman Spring of Mrs. Stone*--are vagrants and freeloaders yet always, somehow, more spiritually attuned than the women they prey on, and reluctant (though wryly willing) to be sexually used. Even the bitchy Vera is a Williams type. Yet for Blackie, who is neither greatly overwritten nor sentimentalized, who occasionally employs sarcasm (rare in Williams) and who has some rudimentary capacity for judging those around her, I can find no precursor--unless, perhaps, it is Tom in *The Glass Menagerie.* A college girl, sharp and blunt, Blackie is somewhat less stagy than most Williams creations: not realistic, exactly, but cinematic, Williams couldn't help daubing her slightly with the too-deep-for-tears mystique of suffering with which he imbued so many of his characters. (Blackie comes to Mrs. Goforth, for instance, "fresh from the deathbed of [her] young husband.") Still, she's made up of Hollywood, rather than Broadway, clichés. And, standing, like Tom Wingfield, midway between an ethereal spirit and a delusionary, she's the closest thing the play has to a moral norm.

To cast in such a role an actress like Miss Plummer, who specializes in the abnormal--the possessed (*Agnes of God*), the withdrawn (*The Glass Menagerie*), the brain-damaged (*A Lie of the Mind*), the mad (*Daniel*)--seems inordinately perverse. Equally perverse is the performance that the director, Kevin Conway, has elicited from Stephen McHattie as Flanders. Mr. McHattie, who has proved himself able enough in situations where he can play for the broadest possible comedy--he was a good Hector Hushabye in the Circle in the Square revival of *Heartbreak House*--here delivers his lines in funereal tones, like a dying prophet or a psychopath. He overacts so badly in silence that we're bored before he opens his mouth.

Other aspects of the production are equally inexplicable. Candice Donnelly's costumes are alternately shopworn and anachronistic. Miss Plummer and Miss Ashley both wear eighties hair styles throughout the production, and Miss Plummer wears eighties clothes. (In Act I, she wears slacks and the same kind of striped man-tailored blouse that Ellen Barkin looked so terrific in this summer in *The Big Easy*.) At one point, Miss Ashley appears wearing non-matching earrings--a long, dangling feather and a rhinestone post. Miss Seldes is got up in a costume that any self-respecting child would refuse to wear to a Halloween party: a gown of grimy-looking chiffon--turquoise and spring green--awash with rhinestones, and set off by silver dime-store shoes. Mr. Conway's direction is a bouillabaisse of mistaken assumptions about what can and cannot be accomplished with non-realistic staging. He has characters glancing at one another through stone walls and Miss Seldes fishing an olive out of her cocktail with gloved fingers. Even the set, by far the most pleasant aspect of the production, proves ultimately unworkable. Designed by Edward T. Gianfrancesco and lighted by Craig Evans, its bright stonework, laced with marble and white bougainvillea, is pretty to look at but requires areas that have been vividly defined as exterior spaces to double as interiors. There isn't much scenery left, in any case, by the time the cast gets through with it.

New Yorker, December 7, 1987: 165-66, 169-70.

Slapstick Tragedy (1966)

Theatre
Harold Clurman

Tennessee Williams did himself an injustice by having his two one-act plays, collectively entitled *Slapstick Tragedy,* produced on Broadway. They might have gained considerable esteem had they been given in a more modest manner. Their closing was announced after six performances.

A second injustice, almost as great, is the plays' critical reception. *Slapstick Tragedy* is not the author's "top-drawer" work, but he has struck a new note in at least the second of the two plays and both have a peculiarly personal stamp that merits attention.

The plays are melancholy but masked avowals. The first, called *The Mutilated,* might be described as a freakish Christmas Carol. Two whores--the first has had one of her breasts removed, the other has just been released from a short-term jail sentence for shoplifting--become reconciled in wretched companionship one Christmas Eve, because although they have reviled each other through corrupt professional rivalry, they realize that they have only their mutual deprivation, and the understanding of it, to give them solace in their common exile from respectable society.

As in certain of his former plays, Williams in *The Mutilated* reveals his compassion--more, his sense of identification--with the insulted and the injured, the misfits and the maimed. But while the earlier plays were soft in sentiment, *The Mutilated* is savage.

Its "slapstick" consists of deliberate bitchiness. Even the final moments in which the two whores induce a vision in themselves of the Blessed Virgin who will forgive and heal them are bitterly ironic. (This is Williams' squint-eyed flirtation with mysticism.) The intention is to make us see that the two women, one stupidly infantile, the other horribly stricken with shame at her affliction, are as absurd as they are pitiable. Williams refuses to gush over them; they are meant to be both grotesque and ridiculous, and these qualities themselves are to lend the women all the commiseration they need to make them kin to us. They play requires its jokes to be horrible; its horror funny.

To make clear how *The Mutilated* differs from other Williams plays the production should not dodge the play's cruelty. Perhaps the director (Alan Schneider) and the author felt that an emphasis on its savagery would alienate an "uptown" audience.

Margaret Leighton, whose voice touches the heart and who is blessed with the very appealing look of a Pre-Raphaelite beauty in anguish, never for a moment suggests anything but noble sorrow. She doesn't seem to have a bitchy bone in her body. Kate Reid, a gusty and essentially good-natured actress, is amusing but hardly conveys anything soiled or mean. The result is that the play strikes us as a minor repetition of an old Williams theme, when it is really an acid variation.

The second slapstick tragedy, *The Gnadiges Fraulein,* is more interesting in several ways than the first. It is a stylized essay in farcical fantasy altogether new for Williams. It is filled with sardonic mirth at the plight of the artist applauded and glamorized in his triumphs and then repudiated and derided when he fails. The "artiste" in the play is a once celebrated middle-European *chanteuse,* but the inner motivation for the personage is Williams' projection of his present situation. He attempt to ward off self-pity through self-mockery, avenging himself on the "enemy" with satiric lunacy.

The Fraulein earns her keep in a God-forsaken boarding house at the seaboard of the southernmost point of our States by fighting to catch fish in the waters whipped by the hurricanes which harass the place. The difficulty of bringing in the fish (prestige, status, success) is compounded by the jealousy and competition of a bird of prey, the Cocaloony, who not only snatches the fish from the Fraulein's grip but pecks out her eyes in the process.

The play abounds in symbols. The Cocaloony may represent the Critics. The public becomes a Permanent Transient at the boarding house. Certain aspects of the Press appear in the person of Polly, a madcap society reporter who combines impregnable complacency with malice. The clownish lady who runs the boarding house may stand for managerial powers, producers, editors, publishers and the like. There is also a blood Indian who steals and makes a banquet of the fish which the Fraulein has struggled and lost her eyes to catch. Is this meant to stand for one of Williams' directors?

However we interpret this nightmare it is written in an odd but effective mixture of gallows humor and Rabelaisian zest. On opening night the audience laughed uproariously at the broad-stroked slapdash language, but though I was able to appreciate the style I could not bring myself to smile. I was too conscious that its author was in pain.

The outstanding performance in *The Gnadiges Fraulein* was that of Zoe Caldwell as Polly, a truly remarkable creation, all venom and sugar, risible and appalling. Both plays are sure to be seen and acclaimed in future productions at universities, community theatres and on foreign stages.

Nation, March 14, 1966: 309.

Kingdom of Earth (The Seven Descents of Myrtle) (1968)

The Name of the Game Is Blame
Walter Kerr

Like the characters in Tennessee Williams's *The Seven Descents of Myrtle* who were prepared to cling to the roof for dear life while flood waters rose through the house, I was prepared to cling to the play. Whatever the rising winds may have been doing to three people trapped in a shaky relic of a homestead, the prevailing theatrical winds were right. Mr. Williams had stopped trying nervously to imitate the absurdist fantasies of the generation nipping at his heels and was neck-deep in materials he had mastered before: all the fears and frustrations and violent invasions of privacy that come of lust and pride in tandem. There was always the chance--it seemed a very good chance--that our finest playwright would for the 9th or 10th time declare himself.

And so, in the process of clinging, I began to play a little game of Blame. Things were subtly off, gestures tended to pull back before they could be quite completed, shadows roamed the downstairs kitchen and the rickety stairway restlessly without asserting themselves as more than shadows. Who's to blame here, I asked myself sharply, aware that the writing had some attractive overtones, the situation a sharp initial interest. I settled on director José Quintero first.

Why had Mr. Quintero been so careless as to permit a whole first faraway shouting match to be played unintelligibly? At curtain rise, a swarthy, hip-booted Chicken (Harry Guardino) is doing his chores under an overcast sky. Neighbors pass in a car off stage, pause to scream at him. All we really need to know is that they are not truly friendly, that Chicken is in some sense a loner. But we scarcely get to know that much in the vocal screech over the wind, we are forced to deduce it for ourselves when the roar has subsided and Chicken has gone surly to his quarters, there to nuzzle a photographed nude with oversize breasts. (The flood waters may or may not stand for sexual energy, but that is a matter for later.) The evening has begun insecurely, its emphases and even its words unformed, and Mr. Quintero could easily have fixed that.

When Chicken's half brother (by a "very different" mother) arrives in the person of Brian Bedford, bleached hair reaching to his shoulders, to display a silly goose of a girl he's just taken for a bride, our curiosity comes thoroughly awake. Mr. Bedford seems fonder of the faded parlor than he does of his bride ("These drapes are velvet drapes, neglected lately"). He is quick to remember how to clean the pendants of a chandelier (his mother taught him how), he is eager for his wife to misrepresent him to his brother as a "strong lover." We watch him, alert and puzzled. What has a bride to do with this evasive frond of a fellow, pursing his lips as though they could defend him from a world coming too close? More than that. Young, why does he seem to get around on an old man's bones?

Halfway through the first act he takes a sudden tumble, crashing to the floor between kitchen and parlor, unable to rise by himself. If we are surprised, we are not surprised properly. There was no rhythm to make us ready for the fall. We'd heard Mr. Bedford, we'd seen him walk like an ache, and we still hadn't come with him to the topple. In a flash, a single thought fills our heads. Kazan should have directed the play. He'd either have paved the way to the moment for us or hit us hard with its shock value. Quintero has left us between, disbelieving. And surely Mr. Quintero has *asked* designer Jo Mielziner for these cramped acting spaces: a parlor in which no one can move on impulse, an upstairs bedroom tiny and remote as a pop-up greeting card, a crucial staircase squeezed into place so treacherously that it seems made of crumpled paper and plainly cannot be negotiated with any sort of dramatic force. Yes, the fault is in the staging.

But still. Listening to the addlepated, slightly past-it bride chatter on about her onetime companions--all dead or deranged now--in a tawdry show-biz act, watching her ignore the accumulating truths about her new and virtually unknown husband (when Mr. Bedford asks not to be hated for having concealed the extent of his illness, she blandly replies, "When I love I don't hate"), we become aware that something other than the physical façade is out of sync.

In my own game of Blame, I turned my attention to Estelle Parsons, fussing about as the new bride. And in fact it is as easy to rebel against Miss Parsons' performance as it is to be half-taken with it. The role is extremely well written. This girl--motherly, vulgar, vulnerable, pathetically confident of her own blowsy charms and yet frightened of using them--belongs, or nearly belongs, in the Williams canon of rattled women. You can overhear Blanche DuBois or Alma Winemiller anytime you care to strain enough; you can also overhear the differences, the little traits of cheapness and loyalty that distinguish her and insist on a personal identity card.

But the part won't come whole, won't rise out of the echoes to say, "No, listen to *me!*", won't detach itself from the green-and-white-striped wallpaper to stand and move as a cohesive shape formed of many shades. It is bleached. We see the good things Miss Parsons is doing. This bride is at last told that though her husband owns the house and would like to leave it to her, he has weakly deeded it to his brother. She is to retrieve the deed, by any means; that is what he has married her for. As the actress decks herself out in the come-on finery of her vaudeville act, a preposterous failure in feathers, to stalk her prey in terror and on unsteady spiked heels, she indicates in severe outline all of the erratic responses that are meant to move us. Awkwardly parading herself like soiled merchandise, gasping and sputtering as asthma and fear contract her courage, stammering into vacant bursts of silent laughter, crouching helplessly beside a trap door that may drop her into the waters below if the man standing over her decides that she should be dropped, Miss Parsons provides us with a complete and most accomplished catalogue of Attitudes to Admire. We do not forget how good she was in *Bonnie and Clyde*.

At the same time we are aware--and appalled--at what her voice is doing to us and to the part. Miss Parsons has elected to play the entire play at the shrill, colorless, fake nightclub pitch she uses when she is screeching her way, deliberately tinny, into a half chorus of "Cuddle Up a Little Closer, Baby Mine." It is as though a complex woman, hurled into every sort of bizarre posture, were being funneled to us through the nasal single-note of Adelaide in *Guys and Dolls*. Coloration vanishes, crisis piles on crisis without any shift of sound, identity itself becomes blurred under the constant calliope of pressure. What would this girl be like, how rich might she seems, if she ever changed key? We are forced to filter a graphic performance through an earache.

In the end, though, the dodges won't wash. Mr. Quintero might have helped more, Miss Parsons might have tried less hard. But the play is not filling its own outline, isn't coming up like the flood that is so constantly threatening. There is a reluctance about it, a caution about possibly saying too much too soon that rather resembles Mr. Guardino's reluctance to enter the action. For most of the play, Mr. Guardino simply prowls the lower back room of the house, uninsistent, sneering when approached but without the moral force to initiate the next confrontation, hiding out.

I suspect that this hesitation is more Mr. Williams's than the characters', and it may very well come from an apprehension about stirring memories. Aware that a faint Blanche DuBois halo hovers about the girl in the case, Mr. Williams may have drawn his hand back from prodding his potentially explosive Chicken too much. He might have turned out to be Stanley Kowalski. In any case, the author avoids him, lets him stew on his own terms without telling us what those terms are, postpones and postpones him until it is too late for him to affect the vital movement of the play. The play goes all one-sided as a result: everything that happens happens tentatively from upstairs. The passive characters must carry the action--and carry it to a man not wholly present.

And it is difficult for Mr. Williams's girl to assume so heavy a burden because she is not herself moving from one clear pole to another. The play ends with the assertion of Chicken as life force; only a sexual partner can save Miss Parsons from the flood. She must join it to endure it, leaving her impotent "husband" behind. But if this is to seem a kind of advance or even change, and if Miss Parson's terror in approaching it is to be emotionally justified, the girl must begin at some other point on the fever chart. She must be frigid, or sick of sex, or in some way desperately committed to neutrality. She isn't. It isn't clear what she is, or where she stands, in relation to the last-minute scurry toward sexual safety and a possible future. If anything, she seems to be promiscuous from the outset; various perfectly good jokes are made about her just happening to be standing "on a street in Memphis, for no particular reason." Thus there is no troubling transition to be got through: You feel that Mr. Guardino could wrap up the play whenever he wanted to, simply by snatching the girl's wrist. One end of the play's lifeline is unanchored.

The Seven Descents of Myrtle, then, is unfinished, not so much ill-conceived as unrealized. With some luck and some openness and some urgency, it is possible that it could be finished. Mr. Williams has rewritten plays before, including--as in the case of *Summer and Smoke*--some that didn't need the careful afterthought. There are things to be salvaged here: an environment, a provocative symbolic structure, a girl of idiot but actual quality, effective contrasts (Mr. Bedford, by the way, is very good as the enfeebled manipulator, of sturdier destinies), whole blocs [*sic*] of language that are teasing in the familiar--and unfailingly fresh--Williams way. I'd hate to see them lost, flood or no flood.

New York Times, April 7, 1968, sec. 2: 1-3.

Sleeping with Caliban: The Politics of Race in Tennessee Williams's *Kingdom of Earth*
Philip C. Kolin

Kingdom of Earth (earlier entitled *Seven Descents of Myrtle*) is the only Tennessee Williams work where a character of color--Chicken Ravenstock--plays a major role. In other Williams plays where people of color are present, they are often seen as the supernumeraries of Southern patriarchy as in *Sweet Bird of Youth* or pursued victims of racial bigotry as in *Orpheus Descending.* Though only one of three characters in *Kingdom of Earth,* Chicken is the most dynamic and resourceful. But he has been frequently minimized in theatre history and critical commentary alike. Of all Williams's full-length plays, *Kingdom of Earth* is perhaps the least well known and the most infrequently performed. Its Broadway premier in 1968 lasted only 29 performances, and since then surprisingly few national premiers or revivals have been mounted as compared with other Williams plays. As I shall argue, because Chicken's racial/ethnic presence lies outside the performative experience of a dominant culture, he has been marginalized in a play in which he should rightfully dominate. A dominant white critical establishment has illegitimatized Chicken through a culturally imbalanced discourse aimed at the play itself. Views of him and the play need to be profitably reformulated in light of post-colonial discourse. Chicken has a right to be heard, and, in the phrase coined by Homi Bhabha, a "right to signify."

I

Much of the criticism--theatrical as well as textual--has labeled *Kingdom of Earth* a parody of Williams's earlier work, especially *A Streetcar Named Desire*. For Judith Thompson, *Kingdom of Earth* is a "comic revision of *Streetcar's* predominant tragic mode" (195). More bitterly, Chauncey Howell quipped, "The Old Pretender has brought us a play that is in nearly every respect a parody and travesty of his great works of the past." The never-gentle John Simon likewise pronounced that *Kingdom of Earth* was "stale self-plagiarism, self-parody, all self-flagellation" (*Hudson Review*). British sentiment was remarkably similar about the 1984 London premiere. Dick Vosburgh bristled, "No parodist could write up a more wicked send-up of Tennessee Williams than did Williams himself in *Kingdom of Earth*."

With few exceptions the character of Chicken has fared no better than the play itself. He has been branded the "other," the "misfit," the "outsider." His stature has been minimized through the taint of parody, too. For Albert Kalson, Chicken is a parody of the Laurentian hero whom Williams once admired (91); for Jerrold Phillips, he is "a muddled hybrid like Stanley Kowalski" (353); and for Vosburgh, Chicken is the "brutish embittered Stanley Kowalski-esque." Besting other critics in their denouncements, Craig Clinton dismisses Chicken as a perverse parody of Orpheus, claiming that his cowardice, stupidity, and "overwhelming desire to possess" make Chicken "no less abhorrent that death itself" (32).

Criticism has further minimized Chicken by structurally disempowering him. Walter Kerr, for example, accused Williams of intentionally sequestering Chicken:

For most of the play Mr. Guardino [who played Chicken in the Broadway premiere] simply prowls the lower back room of the house, uninsistent, sneering when approached but without the moral force to initiate the next confrontation, hiding out. . . . In any case the author avoids him, lets him stew on his own terms without telling us what those terms are, postpones and postpones him until it is too late for him to affect the vital movement of the play.

Since Chicken is denied an opportunity to function, it becomes easy to brand his actions as "subhuman" (Kalson 92) and "grotesque and mindless" (Derounian 156), "single-minded, ape-like" (Nelsen), and to compartmentalize him as a prime specimen of "primeval animality" (Phillips 351).

2

The critics' negative response to Chicken emanates from a refusal to grant the script an overriding political message. This is wrongheaded, since a strong social voice is heard in almost every one of Williams's plays. Reviewing the off-Broadway production by the Staircase Theater Company at the Impossible Ragtime Theatre (IRT) in June-July 1976, Bonnie Marranca spoke for many critics who denied Williams the status of a political thinker: "As a major American playwright, it is somewhat to Williams's disfavor that he has failed to take the great metaphysical or political questions--as the greatest world dramatists do--but has instead reworked themes on elemental passions in a few stock character situations." When Williams is granted the power to make political comments, he is too glibly dismissed as a "Southern gothicist or the mordant poet of dissolution and despair," as C. W. E. Bigsby has so accurately summarized this misleading characterization of Williams himself (36). Speaking of *Kingdom* in particular, Foster Hirsch typifies yet another distorted opinion of Williams as political thinker: "The decaying house, and the corresponding dilapidation of the characters, constitute Williams' lament for the South's blighted heritage . . . " (11). But the presentation of the South in Williams's canon, and especially Mississippi in *Kingdom,* is far more complex and radical than the nostalgia Hirsch's observation seizes on.

Bill Bankes-Jones, the director of the 1991 *Kingdom* at the Redgrave Theatre in Farnham, was in sympathy with Williams's social message: "Williams's sense of place is equally important: *Kingdom of Earth* is one of the many plays set in the fictitious Two River County. Behind the surface backwardness of an area where alcohol is still prohibited and blacks are not only exploited but disenfranchised. . . . " ("An Introduction"). Yet ultimately, for Bankes-Jones, Williams "belongs firmly in the tradition of the gay playwright . . . " and so lets Williams's sexual orientation overshadow the political/social message in *Kingdom.*

Williams repeatedly emphasized that all of his plays "have a social consciousness." Paradoxically enough, the social messages embedded in his scripts foreshadow their more public disclosures. For example, the 1975 revival of *Cat on a Hot Tin Roof* emphasized the "political corruptions of Watergate and had restored its concern with mendacity to its central role in the drama" (Bigsby 58). Commenting on *Orpheus Descending,* Bigsby similarly notes: "Written before the Civil Rights movement made such a resolute condemnation of Southern bigotry and racism fashionable, the play is sharply political as anything Williams had written since his days with the Mummers in St. Louis . . . " (60). Not just nostalgic laments or lyrical, personal tragedies, Williams's plays incorporate many troubling social events and the alarming consequences of their not being remediated.

The premier of *Kingdom of Earth* in March 1968 could not have been more propitious for articulating the social and political messages this Williams play centered on. The spring of 1968 saw the assassination of two of the most influential leaders of the civil rights movement in the United States--Martin Luther King, Jr. and Robert F. Kennedy. That spring also witnessed the Vietnam War in full swing, spawning virulent protest movements against its alleged colonizing goals. Williams himself made several public appearances denouncing the war. Not surprisingly, racial inequities and the ravages of colonization, crucial issues for the 1960s, lie at the heart of *Kingdom of Earth.* As many Williams's dramas do, *Kingdom of Earth* contextualizes American history, for the script is a complex matrix of many colonial criticisms from which an audience dare not disassociate itself. In essence, then, *Kingdom* is less about the parodying of William's early work that it is about the danger of investing in any racial hegemony as a precondition for authority.

Williams repeatedly deplores racism, one of the essential colonial targets *Kingdom* aims at. As C. W. E. Bigsby has observed, "Although, in stark contrast to Faulkner, scarcely a black face is to be seen in Williams's South; [yet] in *Orpheus Descending* and *Sweet Bird of Youth* he made clear his contempt for the racist, his association of bigotry with sterility and death" (37). I maintain that even more than in these two plays *Kingdom of Earth* is insistently occupied with the politics of racial identity. Speaking of his own identity as a writer and a loner, Williams perceptively confessed: "I always thought I was black" (Rasky, caption for photograph inset following page 10).

It is significant that Williams changed Chicken's racial identity from a Cherokee Indian in the short story "Kingdom of Earth" (1954) that preceded the play *Kingdom of Earth* to a "mixed breed" or, as Gill stated, "a bastard with a tincture of Negro blood." Chicken is by his own admission a "woods colt," "someone with colored blood." His "very different" mother had some black blood while he and Lot had the same father. Though the white Lot's half brother, Chicken does not share in a privileged patrimony. Instead, he is repeatedly associated with blacks in the repressive colonial culture of Williams's Two River County, Mississippi. Chicken is fixed as the quintessential black man; he cannot buy liquor, is forbidden to have relations with white women, and is dismissed as "untutored." He is treated as the animalistic Caliban who must be contained or, better yet, dispossessed. Appropriately, the play begins as white people, fleeing the flood, inform chicken "Sorry we don't have room for you in the car" (126).

But *Kingdom* privileges honest biology over corrupt racial politics. Chicken may inhabit the world of the Other, yet he is emancipated in and empowered through the liminal world of the script. His appearance challenges colonial notions about racial stereotypes. "*He is a strange good looking young man but also remarkably good looking with his very light eyes in darker than olive skin and the power and male grace of his body*" (126). As he tells Myrtle, Lot's new wife: "My mother had colored blood in her. She wasn't black but she wasn't white neither and that's why I'm dark complected with freckled eyes." His looks, like his behavior, resist easy categorization. Incredulous that Chicken has black blood, Myrtle acknowledges that he is a handsome man (182). *Kingdom* thus trivializes power bases built upon racial differences as it valorizes anthropological claims that it is nearly impossible to identify racial traits by origin. That is the focal point of the script as it challenges race ideology by destabilizing the "either/or" economy of colonialism and demoralizes such mythologies upon which racial stereotypes are grounded. In the spring of 1968 these mythologies were tested in the fires of the streets, and at the Ethel Barrymore Theatre where Williams's play premiered.

Through Chicken *Kingdom of Earth* initially raises all the stereotypes that have debased people of color in a colonial economy but reverses each of these damaging mythologies by standing them on their head and mocking their validation through irony, reversal, and even assaultive forays against conventional white-only wisdom. *Kingdom* validates Karen Malpede's belief that "It's the playwrights' role to deal with what society can't deal with" (Kramer 53).

3

Kingdom's short stage history reflects the critics' inability or reluctance to see Williams as a political thinker. Such distorted opinions of Williams blind them to the reasons for Chicken's role. What critics have labeled as ineptitudes of productions may be less the result of flawed stage history than of the critics' failure to give Williams and Chicken their political due. As can be seen in the following survey of the critics' opinions of various productions of *Kingdom,* the critics are just not used to thinking of Williams in political terms. They deny his political engagement at all. For them he is just doing some perverted, Gothic thing that does not quite come off.

Casting a person of color to play Chicken would unquestionably allow the script to foreground the social anxieties of a dominant white culture. But unfortunately, in the three main premieres of the play--in New York (1968), Moscow/Leningrad (1977), and London (1984)--actors of color have not been cast in the part. And, in fact, several critics have discredited attempts by white actors to play Chicken as a man of color. In the New York premiere, Richard P. Cooke was disappointed with Harry Guardino's honesty as Chicken: "Mr. Guardino . . . is again the exponent of heterosexual vitality, but he seems somewhat too articulate and too much in command of his grammar for an uneducated outcast. . . ." Brendan Gill similarly faulted attempts to make the first white Chicken look black: "Guardino has his skin implausibly darkened by something that looks like Man Tan." . . . The critics cannot acknowledge Chicken as being "white" nor will they allow a white actor to portray him as a person of color.

In the three British productions of *Kingdom* to date--at the New Vic, Bristol, 1978; the Hampstead Theatre, London, 1984; and the Redgrave, Farnham, 1991--Chicken was also played by white actors. Peter Postlethwaite's Chicken in the British premiere at the New Vic was criticized for the difficulty of his "Deep South accent" (Chaillet) and for portraying Chicken as "hyper-sensitive to a suspicion of coloured blood that has kept him out of society . . ." (Young). Alluding to Postlethwaite's make-up, Ian Stewart condescendingly called him a "bronzed farmhand."

Overall, the critics of the London *Kingdom* similarly echoed those in New York in giving the play mixed to unfavorable reviews, but, more relevant for this inquiry, they revealed as a whole a colonialist attitude in assessing Chicken. For example, Jack Tinker referred to Chicken as Lot's "brutish half caste half brother"; for Milton Shulman, Chicken was Lot's "half brother who is the bastard son a black woman"; and for Giles Gordon, Lot's half brother was a "brutish, embittered Stanley Kowalski-esque quadroon."

Actor Stephen Rea fared slightly better in the critics' eyes than the character he played, though Rea's "glowering hulk" made the act of sex even more "brutal" for Francis King. But what is most disturbing, culturally speaking, is that several of the London critics attacked Chicken by insidiously discussing Rea's performance in terms of the distorted mannerisms of white actors, another way of subjugating the role and effectiveness of Chicken through parody. For example, King maintained that "Stephen Rea's Chicken, though sounding sometimes like Brando in the *Missouri Breaks,* effortlessly exudes taciturn dangerous virility" and Milton Shulman even more caustically jabbed: "Stephen Rea seems at times to be doing an imitation of Jimmy Cagney as he bullies and threatens the other two." John Barker, however, faulted Rea for not being colored enough: "Stephen Rea should show signs of the Negro strain which so troubled Chicken, but otherwise was convincing as is probably possible as the combined stud, bully, and pariah." Clearly London critics were unwilling to recognize or concede an underlying social angst and plea in the script. The same kind of cross-racial stereotyping occurred earlier in the off-Broadway revival at the IRT, where another white actor Will Patton (the son of director Bill Patton) was cast as Chicken. Emphasizing the actor's white roots, Mel Gussow remarked that Patton "plays Chicken somewhat in the manner of Rip Torn."

From a post-colonial standpoint, the most significant production of *Kingdom* to date was at Princeton's McCarter Theater from 6 March to 16 March 1975, directed by Garland Wright. Initially, black actor Scott Thurston . . . was cast as Chicken but he was replaced during rehearsals by another black actor David Pendleton . . . who had appeared in such daytime television series as *Edge of Night, The Doctors,* and *Guiding Light.* Pendleton marvelously represented Chicken's liminal status that, as we saw, was grounded in Williams's stage direction. Casting an actor of color as Chicken was a major vindication of the script's post-colonial sympathies.

Disappointingly, however, few of the forty or more reviews the McCarter production received from New Jersey, Pennsylvania, and New York critics acknowledged or agreed with *Kingdom's* revolutionary social message. One that did was by Fred Porter who writes: "*Kingdom* is a picture of the anti-massar caste system still prevalent in the deep South in 1960." More often, though, reviewers sided with Mirko Tuma who voiced the stale opinion of Williams's political sympathies: "Williams writes almost exclusively about the disintegration of southern gentility and about aesthetics and grace being raped by the brutal forces of man's modern quest." Or, most pessimistically, critics sided with Colleen Zirnite's attack on Williams's thinking in general. "Williams's message or purpose is nebulous. It is almost as if the author lost his way, forgot where he was going and groped for the nearest exit." Refusing to see Williams's provocative social message in this production made the McCarter critics more myopic than other reviewers. Williams himself had especially revised the script for the McCarter production and doubtless had approved the casting of actors of color--Thurston and then Pendleton--to play Chicken, thus realistically embodying the postcolonial sentiments the play advances.

Pendleton garnered lots of praise for his work: his performance was hailed as "superb" and "terrifying." Sympathetically, Jean Ogden recognized that "Chicken's mean and tough. He's been fighting being black and a bastard all his life," an observation made even more poignant thanks to Pendleton's acting. Still, the critics assailed Chicken for being the "other," perhaps because of Pendleton's racial background. Rubincam maintained that Chicken has "the sexual appetite of a satyr," and Makin characterized him as a "brutish angry mulatto." Linda Holt castigated Chicken as Lot's "bestial half brother" and then added: "There's a scruffy Neanderthalism about him that's quite fetching, and a mercurial sense of humor." According to Ernest Albrecht, Chicken was the dreaded fulfillment of Blanche's admonition to Stella: "Myrtle must turn back (to the apes as it were) and cast her lot with the brother,

Chicken, which suggests a variation on the animal imagery."

Ironically, as Harry Guardino was rebuked for not being and acting black enough in the New York production, David Pendleton was criticized for being too unracially eloquent. Nanci Heller's comments are apropos:

Chicken, the part Negro half-brother of Lot, is fighting to inherit the farm where he has toiled all his life. He is the Stanley Kowalski figure of the play. Played with ample terror by David Pendleton, he is convincing until he starts philosophizing--"Life is hard, a man gotta be hard too," or "There's nothing in this world, in this whole kingdom of earth [a phrase overly stressed] that can compare with one thing, what happens between a man and a woman." All of a sudden, our brutish animal-man has become eloquent--and totally out of character.

Finally a fairly recent production of *Kingdom* in Boston demands comparison with the McCarter *Kingdom* by privileging Chicken's role through a minority actor playing the past. The Boston Post Road Stage cast Hispanic actor--Ramiro Carrillo--in the role in 1991. . . . While it may have been more textually appropriate to find a black actor to play Chicken, director James Luse is to be applauded for incorporating the ethnic presence of a traditionally marginalized group in the play through Carrillo's Chicken. To accommodate Carrillo's Hispanic ancestry Luse conveniently and consistently made Chicken's mother Hispanic as well. "Carrillo's own built-in Hispanic accent works, since his character is supposed to have had a Mexican mother" (Backalenick). Critic David Rosenberg, however, remarked negatively on Carrillo's accent: "Carrillo says Chicken's lines as if translating them into English as he goes along, mishandling even easy gags . . ." But, closer to the truth, it seems Carrillo, like David Pendleton, facilitates the decolonizing agenda in *Kingdom*; he is a minority voice within that script and thus incorporates ideas of emancipation motivating it. Future revivals of *Kingdom* need to cast actors of color--black, Asian, and Hispanic--in the role of Chicken.

4

The actual staging of *Kingdom of Earth* represents as it undercuts racial ideologies. The *mise en scene* of *Kingdom* is a polarized playing area. "*This back wall of the house, except for the doorway, is represented by a scrim that will lift when the house is entered. Then the interior will be exposed: a kitchen stage right, a mysterious little 'parlor' stage left, a narrow dark hall between them* . . ." (126). Jo Mielziner's see-through set similarly allows an audience to watch Chicken in the kitchen while simultaneously observing Lot in the bedroom upstairs (160). The ideologies of color are lodged in, and separated by, these two opposing locations: a white parlor and a black servant's kitchen, Lot vs. Chicken. A white colonial/critical culture likewise misguidedly structures the world of Williams's play by relegating Chicken to the kitchen. It links him with cooking, subservience, and the shadows of the dark kitchen. Critics and audiences have fallen into the philosophically naive trap of "either/or" suggested by, but really demoralized through, *Kingdom's* original set. Critics such as Walter Kerr and John Simon want to keep Chicken in the kitchen world of Caliban, to control him by ostracizing him. They grow restive when Chicken comes into the white world of the parlor with his muddy hip boots and arrogant attitudes.

But Chicken is punished even when he stays in the kitchen. His focal position in the kitchen, however, is anything but subservient. Black playwright Suzan-Lou Parks appropriately remarked, "I think that people from the minority culture know a lot about the majority culture because we have to watch to survive." This is just what Chicken does. In the kitchen he watches, examines documents that might be used against him, and interrogates Myrtle who has become the pawn of the white master Lot. Yet while seemingly typifying the stereotype of the black by hiding in the kitchen, Chicken deconstructs such a role by uncovering the weakness and foolishness of the white power structure enfied in the parlor. When Chicken as Caliban triumphantly enters the parlor, he vindicates the times when blacks were denied such forceful entrances. The Ravenstock's black maid Clara could not enter Miss Lottie's parlor and was expressly forbidden to touch the chandelier. When, near the end of the play, Chicken comes into the parlor before the flood, asserting his mastery of the estate, he self-assuredly turns the chandelier off. Quite literally, Chicken changes the color of the parlor, reversing the hold colonial dominance had on people of color.

5

As *Kingdom* shows, such a hold has deep economic and legal roots. In an oppressive colonial economy, people of color are victimized by contracts that deny their property rights from working the land. The play unfolds through a series of injustices relating to agreements, contracts, deals, and nuptials. More particularly, the plot of *Kingdom of Earth* is energized by the (il)legal deceptions the lily white Lot attempts to use against his half brother, Chicken. By calling attention to these injustices, *Kingdom of Earth* raises our cultural consciousness about the rights of the dispossessed. Debates about ownership of America and individual rights were seething in the late 1960s--when *Kingdom* was first performed--as militant black groups challenged the prejudicial authority of the white industrial-military complex. Lot and the colonial establishment he represents are determined to deny Chicken his fair share of America. In the play, the Ravenstock farm becomes a microcosm for that America.

Land traditionally confers power, and those who own the land control the power. Substantiating the legitimacy of rival claims to that land is Lot's and Chicken's central occupation. As a man of color, Chicken is free to work the land but not free to inherit it. He claims that "[I] live the life of a dawg that nobody owns and owns nothing" (205). Upholding the exclusive values of colonialism, Lot cannot fathom Chicken being empowered through land: "I hate and despise him with such a passion that if this place or anything on this place became his property . . . " (178). In fact, Chicken's status as a likely claimant offends Lot. The Ravenstock prejudice is ingrained. Miss Lottie, Lot's mother "dismissed me off this place, and she said to me 'Chicken, I don't want my son to be known as half brother to a nigra'" (206). Paradoxically, though, people of color sustained a colonial economy. "I work out in the fields and Lot just lays in bed" (140), protests Chicken.

Chicken is repeatedly associated with the land he tills; "he is the rude earth with all its sustaining vitality" (Clurman). Appropriately enough, Chicken characterizes his relationship to the earth in racial terms: "Feel the calluses on 'em? I got those calluses on my hands from a life of hard work on this . . . . place, worked like a nigger and got nothing' for it but bed and the bed was a cot in the kitchen and the board was not better than slops in the trough of a sow" (198). Sharing the experience of people of color in a colonial society, Chicken is paid a paltry wage to cancel his birthright to the land: "A hired man on a place always does what pleases the lady and the bossman" (181)--he says of himself denouncing his unjust inheritance. Institutional critics who chastise Chicken for greed or fault him for his obsession with acquiring the farm (e.g., Clinton 33) fail to recognize, in Bhabha's phrase, Chicken's "right to signify." Chicken's right resides in having a legitimate claim to the Ravenstock property through birth, hard work, and legal enfranchisement. He is Caliban rebelling against the dominance of a decadent Prospero/Lot. The script of *Kingdom of Earth* thus proclaims the entitlements of minorities as it legitimizes the grievances of an oppressed counterculture.

The strong social message of entitlement is foregrounded by having Chicken outsmart Lot through the very legal system that his white half brother marshals against him. Motivated by hate, Lot believes that disinheriting Chicken is the only right thing to do to preserve the purity of white ownership. Recognizing that he cannot run the farm by himself, Lot asks the dispossessed Chicken to return after the death of Miss Lottie. Finding work easily elsewhere, Chicken has taken a job in a sawmill in Meridian, and it is there that Lot sends several messages promising Chicken the right of inheritance if he will come back (187). The fact that Chicken has emigrated from the farm is historically significant. Like pervious people of color who have left the land, Chicken seeks employment in a quasi-technical industry in an urban area.

Not that Meridian, Mississippi is Detroit or Chicago, but at least Chicken has established his independence.   Lot, however, needs Chicken as much as Prospero does Caliban to do manual work.   Interestingly, Chicken and Caliban are both cast as workers in wood.

6

The script of *Kingdom* presents colonial prejudice as a disease.   Fearing an imbalance in the colonial dichotomy of white power/black usurpation, Lot succumbs to internal turmoil.   The Boston Post Road Stage's production fittingly captured the errant sickness and imminent demise of Lot's white supremacy.   As played by Daniel Nathan Spector, Lot represents a decaying and decadent social order.   The "spectral Lot [was] an Oscar Wilde figure in a white suit, purple shirt, and brocade vest, orchid corsage and flowing hankie" (Rosenberg).   Plymath McDermott likewise characterized Spector's Lot as a "completely mannered, foppish creep with dyed white hair and white costume to match. . . ."   Lot is the spoiled aristocrat, governed by revenge signaled by a chatty and diseased rancor.   Similarly, V. Belovolsky's Lot in the Leningrad *Kingdom* of 1977 dies from a fatal bout of racism.   Irene Shaland appropriately translates Russian drama critic Komissarzhevsky's sociological assessment of Lot's character:

> Why is Lot dying? . . . Because of tuberculosis or because of the metastases of his greed and racial hatred?   Lot does not have to demonstrate his physical sickness but to overcome it.   Only then will his diseased attitude be revealed; the refined prince turns into an ordinary racist.   The role, that is static now, has to be put in motion. (78-79)

In *Kingdom's* criticism of colonialism, Lot is eaten up as much by racial arrogance and hatred as he is by a physical malady.

   To his further damnation, Lot would turn over the family estate to a white woman he has known barely a few days, a woman he later denigrates as a "whore," rather than see his colored half brother inherit the farm.   Urging Myrtle to join his revenge plot against Chicken, Lot plays upon her own socioeconomic status and prejudices.   "Have you ever owned much of anything in your life," he taunts, enlisting Myrtle's aid in defrauding Chicken.   His plan for her to swindle Chicken bears the stench of all colonializing white men who tried to enslave through giving liquor to oppressed people: "Get Chicken drunk but get drunk yourself, and when he passes out, get this legal paper out of his wallet, tear it to bits and pieces and burn 'em up."   If Myrtle does this, "Then as my wife, when I die, the place will be yours, go to you. Valuable property" (168).   If guile does not work, Myrtle needs to be violent: "If you can't make him pass out to get that paper, knock him out with a hammer that's in the drawer of the kitchen table, and don't come up here again without that paper" (180). Lot's plotting may seem melodramatic, but it is historically consistent with the clash of cultures depicted in *Kingdom*.

If the script presents Lot as shady, it invites audiences to see Chicken as honorable, something few mainstream critics concede. While Lot is busy subverting contracts and laws, Chicken tests their validity so he can act legally and properly. Chicken's tactics must be seen as legal because the documents he introduces are bona fide contracts admissible in court to protect Chicken's rights as agreed to through the "deal" he made with Lot and that Lot made with him. Beyond doubt, Chicken has honored his part of the bargain by returning to work the farm. For Chicken, this agreement with Lot is his *magna carta,* his right to signify; Chicken believes he is honor-bound to adhere to it. Even the cynical Lot confesses that to Chicken such an agreement is "sacred" (178). As the script of *Kingdom* protests loudly, Chicken is not the rebellious outsider threatening disorder but, rather, a consummate man of the law an audience is urged to support in his quest to regain possessions a dominant white culture would steal.

Justifying his case, Chicken carefully explains the details of the "legal set up" to Myrtle, since she has become Lot's dupe to strip him of his inheritance. "I ain't about to leave here. You know we got this agreement. Have you forgotten about this agreement we signed between us" (140). He later expands on the terms of the agreement he has reached with his brother Lot to convince Myrtle of the futility of acting on Lot's behalf: "There's no future for you. You remember that agreement between us, witnessed, signed, notarized, giving the place to me when you take the one-way trip to the kingdom of heaven? I never have that paper out of my wallet here" (151).

Chicken also astutely plumbs the truth behind Lot and Myrtle's marriage contract. When she informs him that they were married on a television program, Chicken questions the validity of such a marriage and scoffs at the license: " . . . you can buy those things for two bits in a novelty store to show in a motel where you brought a woman to lay" (147). He later characterizes the marriage as "make-believe," but Myrtle insists the license is "genuine." Ironically, Chicken perceptively doubts the legality of a marriage between the lily white Lot and Myrtle and, in questioning it, analogizes the white couple's status to that of the dispossessed Clara and "her unmarried husband," the "unmarried couple of niggers" as Myrtle refers to them (131).

Late in the play, when he learns of Lot's plot and Myrtle's participation in it, Chicken forces her to make out a quit claim deed. Afraid of Chicken, Myrtle admits that the marriage license is "no good . . . the thing is fake" (197) peppered with bogus signatures to make it look real. "I'm not Lot's widow, I mean I won't be his widow if he dies, 'cause we ain't married" (193). Rightfully skeptical, Chicken dictates the terms of the quit claim deed to Myrtle: "Me, Mrs. Lot Ravenstock, give up and deny all claims when my husband is dead. Because this place goes to Chicken, all Chicken's, when Lot Ravenstock dies and also if I die too because of river in flood, a natural act of God" (200).

Chicken is valorized in the script as the catalyst for correction. The script empowers Chicken into ethics, and he indemnifies himself against dispossession by legitimately inheriting the land when Lot dies at the end of the play. It is fitting that before Chicken can reap what he as sown, the land must be washed clean by the flood of Lot's corruption and duplicity. "Floods make the land richer" (183), affirms Chicken. Properly speaking, Chicken wins the recompense deserving of disenfranchised people of color. Foster Hirsch, it seems to me, senses only part of Williams's message by missing the central point about Chicken's legal tactics: "Since Lot dies before the flood, the approach of the orgasmic flood coincides with Chicken's inheritance of the land. The flood symbolizes the full release of the 'lust body,' and Williams celebrates this release through the impure, but vital character of Chicken" (12).

7

Chicken justly inherits through two institutions that sustain a while colonial culture--property and marriage. Benefiting from the second institution, Chicken, a man of color, inherits through his sexual bonding with Myrtle, the prejudiced white woman. Yet Chicken's sexual behavior has been consistently undermined and ferociously attacked. His carving lewd words into the kitchen table; his looking at the picture of a nude woman; and his receiving fellatio from Myrtle have infuriated establishment critics who conclude that his sexuality is tainted. Kathryn Derounian, for example, finds that "Chicken parodies the virile male whose sexuality is a fulfilling, liberating, life-force" and so "his sexual development is retarded" (155). Jack Kroll claimed that Chicken "cannibalizes Myrtle on the kitchen table." And Susan Todd misjudged that "In *Kingdom of Earth* Tennessee Williams wittily invites us to consider the terrifying proposition that average, usual thoughtless heterosexual relations are morally and spiritually horrifying. . . . Chicken has a stupefying confidence rooted in facts no more remarkable than he can physically . . . terrorize a woman." Thus critics have marginalized Chicken sexually as well as politically.

Again, the critics' objections should be seen against their refusal to acknowledge the strong anti-colonialism in the script. Sexual economy in a colonial world is intimately connected to and controlled by racial issues, a message *Kingdom* repeatedly proclaims. Sex and race are two sides of the same prejudice that exclude and stigmatize Chicken because his is "dark-complected" (126). By denying Chicken a healthy sexuality, the society of Two River County can easily forbid his assimilation into white society and his entrance into power it promises. Because of his colored ancestry, Chicken is not allowed to have sex with white women; in fact one of the local trollops prefers cruel treatment from a white man to Chicken's courteous entreaties. Chicken has been recreated in the image of Caliban. In fact, he himself alludes to the Calibanesque status forced upon him after his sexual contact with Myrtle: "You moved your chair back from the table like a monster was on it. Move your chair back" (205). If the forces of regeneration Williams built into the role are to be liberated in American society, the epithets "unnatural" and "brutal" need to be removed from a description of Chicken's sexual behavior.

Even if Chicken may not be the most likeable character in the Williams canon, his sincerity in sexual matters is far superior to that of the racist community which the Ravenstocks are empowered. Chicken is unashamedly priapic with his hip hugging boots and overt sexual gestures. At one point Chicken *"consciously or not drops one of his large, dusky hands over his crotch, which is emphasized, pushed out by his hip boots"* (144). But being a subject in a script means being a sexual being, as Julia Kristeva, Jacques Lacan, and Jacques Derrida have repeatedly stressed, and Chicken constructively fulfills all the qualities of subjecthood. His passion is forthright and generative unlike that of Lot who offers only the *"sexless passion of the transvestite"* (212). Lot is the epitome of a debauched colonial master whose perverse pleasures--dressing in his mother's clothes--are kept hidden within the sanctuary of the white-only parlor.

If Chicken is honest about his own sexuality, he is brutally honest about that of others, too. He knows about women and can see right through Mytrle's sham modesty as he interrogates her about her own sexual background. Though crassly expressed, Chicken's assessment of her past is accurate: "Yes, I bet. You kick with the right leg, you kick with the left leg, and between your legs you make your living" (147). Even so, he woos Myrtle in his own honest fashion with a song from his repertoire--"Stars Fell on Alabama" (173); recall that Chicken's mother was from that state. And he even performs a wooer's trick for Myrtle by dropping the cat down the trap door. The critics who worry that Chicken broadcasts infernal associations by this action forget that Lot is linked more intentionally to the sexually satanic--"*Lot remains in the wicker chair, still smoking with his mother's ivory holder and wearing now her white silk wrapper. His 'Mona Lisa' smile is more sardonic and the violet shadows about his eyes are deeper*" (177).

Chicken's most problematic sexual action occurs a few minutes before *Kingdom* ends. Between Act 2, scene 2 and Act 2, scene 3--on a darkened stage--Myrtle, seated on a chair, and Chicken, on the table, engage in fellatio. This act is the central stumbling block to appropriating Chicken into the boudoir of Williams's acceptable romantic lovers. The critics are livid. Perhaps the most damning accusation of Chicken's sexuality comes from Albert Kalson who maintains that "Clearly *Kingdom of Earth* is an extended dramatic metaphor for an act of fellatio which becomes in itself a metaphor for any brutal degrading, sterile relationship between a man and a woman" (92). Even Thomas P. Adler, an otherwise sensitive reader of Williams, concludes that while in Williams's other plays sex acts "are performed with unselfish compassion towards the needs of others, here [in *Kingdom*] the sexuality seems bitter and cynical, devoid of any positive value, almost a puritan disgust for the body and over-reaction against what had perhaps before been a too tolerant attitude towards fleshly acts as a saving grace" (6).

I do not see Chicken's lovemaking as bitter or lifeless. His ideas about sex as well as his sexual presence ultimately are salutary and positive. For within this palpable scene of physicality lies a source of hope for decolonization and reconciliation, an agenda in the play abhorrent to many critics. Even those who do spy some hope here give qualified praise to Chicken and Myrtle's lovemaking. Irene Backalenick, for instance, claims that "the lovers do have a tender, moving scene, but one waits for too long for that moment." And while Irene Shaland perceptively observes, "Genuinely desiring Chicken, [Myrtle] hoped to find with him re-birth through love and maternal compassion (76), she avoids mentioning the twin critical/cultural taboos of miscegenation and fellatio in her discussion.

The so-called perverse act between Myrtle and Chicken takes on almost a religious quality rather than something unnatural, revolting, or suspicious. Sex becomes a means of salvation for Chicken and Myrtle. Their lovemaking is the *summum bonum* for a postlapsarian world, the only thing approaching perfection. As Chicken says,

> I'll tell you how I look at life in my life, or in any man's life. There's nothing in the world, in the whole kingdom of earth, that can compare with one thing, and that one thing is what's able to happen between a man and a woman, just that thing, nothing more, is perfect. The rest is crap, all of the rest is almost nothing but crap. (211)

The way Myrtle's response is described in one stage direction speaks volumes about a comedic conclusion: "*Myrtle is still on a chair so close to the table that's she's between his boots, and she looks as if she had undergone an experience of exceptional nature and manipulation*" (203). She has had an epiphany thanks to Chicken, who subsequently becomes her savior/protector. Craig Clinton is surely misguided to suggest that Chicken will leave Myrtle below to drown when the floods come (35). Darkness between the scenes is replaced with light, emphasizing the script's message about a new relationship being born. The first words out of Chicken's mouth after the sex act are "Let there be light."

Within and through this sexual act the script quarrels with prejudicial myths about sex between the races. An expression of one of those myths came from Henry Hewes: "Because Myrtle has been brought up with all the old-fashioned racial prejudices, this last descent for her is most traumatic." As Myrtle's doubt about Chicken's intentions dissolve, she succumbs to the magic of his presence, a magic that has a great many political as well as sexual implications for an audience, too. From this initial sexual act will come a new sexual revolution overturning race barriers and leading to a new decolonized union. Chicken's sexual victory should be seen in light of the ideological struggle of a decadent empire versus a healthy emergent nation. The sexual contract between Myrtle and Chicken marks the demise of Lot's colonial reign and the beginning of a new order, for Chicken has legally inherited the estate which Myrtle has co-opted with him. A man of color, freed from the ravages of an oppressive legal and social order, Chicken can now enter freely into building a more diverse and healthy society. This new society will be blessed, unlike that fabricated by Lot and Myrtle, with children. As Chicken exults: "Always wanted a child from an all-white woman" (214). *Kingdom* most ambitiously redefines the American national identity as it exposes the sexual-political blind spots of a conventional and colonial ideology. In advocating a new nationalism through Myrtle and Chicken, *Kingdom* demands that an audience understand what forces for good can be unleashed in a post-1968, post-colonial America. *Kingdom's* social message in 1968 was prophetic. Twenty-five years later, the culturally high-brow *New Yorker* changed a decades-old policy on cover design to show a Hasidic man receiving a passionate kiss from a black woman (Feb. 15, 1993).

Critics who bemoan *Kingdom of Earth* as Williams's darkest play, his "bleakest statement," miss the emerging promise woven into this last scene. Paradoxically, the whore for Chicken will become the new Eve, the mother of succeeding generations of Ravenstocks who will own property as men and women of color. The white sexual and legal duplicity of Lot and his mother has ended; and the sexual secrecy to which Chicken was consigned and in which Lot perversely gloried are also ended. Long live Caliban!

WORKS CITED

Adler, Thomas P. "Two Plays for Puritans." *Tennessee Williams Newsletter* 1.1 (Spring 1979): 5-7.

Albrecht, Ernest. "Williams Digs More Bones of Old Glories." *Home News* [New Brunswick, NJ] 7 Mar. 1975.

Backalenick, Irene. "Post Road's *Kingdom* Drowns in Flood." *Westport News* [CT] 3 Apr. 1991.

Bankes-Jones, Bill. "An Introduction to the Play. . . Redgrave Playbill, Farnham, U.K. 1991.

Barker, John. "A Minor Play by a Major Poet." *Daily Telegraph* [London] 30 Apr. 1984.

Barnes, Clive. Review. *New York Times* 28 Mar. 1968: 54. Rpt. *New York Theatre Critics' Reviews* 29 (1968): 313.

Bhabha, Homi. *SCT [School of Criticism and Theory*--Dartmouth] *Newsletter* 7, no. 1 (Dec. 1992): 2.

Bigsby, C. W. E. *Modern American Drama, 1945-1990.* Cambridge: Cambridge UP, 1992.

Billington, Michael. Review. *Guardian* 28 May 1984. Rpt. *London Theatre Record* 4 (1984): 350.

Bruce, Alan N. Review. *Christian Science Monitor* 9 Apr. 1968: 6.

Chaillet, Ned. "*Kingdom of Earth,* New Vic, Bristol." *Times* [London] 22 Feb. 1978.

Chapman, John. Review. *New York Daily News* 28 Mar. 1968, sec. 5: 3. Rpt. *New York Theatre Critics' Reviews* 29 (1968): 313.

Chawick, Bruce. "By Any Name, Williams Play Smells as Bad." *New York Daily News* 11 May 1975.

Clinton, Craig D. "Tennessee Williams's *Kingdom of Earth:* The Orpheus Myth Revisited." *Theatre Annual* 33 (1977): 25-37.

Clurman, Harold. Review. *Nation* 206 (15 Apr. 1968): 516-17.

Cooke, Richard F. Review. *Wall Street Journal* 29 Mar. 1968. Rpt. *New York Theatre Critics' Reviews* 29 (1968): 315.

Derounian, Kathryn Zabelle. "'Kingdom of Earth and *Kingdom of Earth* (*The Seven Descents of Myrtle*): Tennessee Williams' Parody." *University of Mississippi Studies in English* 4 (1983): 150-58.

Gill, Brendan. Review. *New Yorker* 6 Apr. 1968: 109-10.

Gordon, Giles. Review. *Spectator* 5 May 1984. Rpt. *London Theatre Record* 4 (1984): 356.

Gussow, Mel. "*Kingdom of Earth* by Williams at IRT." *New York Times* 27 July 1976: 19.

Heinemann, Elaine P. "Williams' Play Another Triumph for McCarter." *Princeton Packet* 12 Mar. 1975: 23.

Heller, Nanci. "Undeniably Williams." *The Daily Princetonian* 10 Mar. 1975

Hewes, Henry. Review. *Saturday Review* 13 Apr. 1968: 30.

Hirsch, Foster. "Sexual Imagery in Tennessee Williams' *Kingdom of Earth.*" *Notes on Contemporary Literature* 1.2 (1971): 10-13.

Hirschhorn, Clive. Review. *London Sunday Express* 6 May 1984. Rpt. *London Theatre Record* 4 (1984): 355.

Holt, Linda. "Little Good in *Kingdom.*" *The Trentonian* [NJ] 11 Mar. 1975.

Howell, Chauncey. Review. *Women's Wear Daily* 28 Mar. 1968. Rpt. *New York Theatre Critics' Reviews* 29 (1984): 316.

Hurren, Kenneth. Review. *London Mail on Sunday* 6 May 1984. Rpt. *London Theatre Record* 4 (1984): 355.

Kalson, Albert E. "Tennessee Williams' *Kingdom of Earth:* A Sterile Promontory." *Drama and Theatre* [Purdue U] 8 (Winter 1969-70): 90-93.

Kerr, Walter. Review. *New York Times* 7 Apr. 1968, sec. 2: 1, 3. Rpt. *Thirty Plays Hath November . . .* (New York: Simon, 1968): 224-30.

King, Francis. Review. *London Sunday Telegraph* 6 May 1984. Rpt. *London Theatre Record* 4 (1984): 350, 355.

Kramer, Richard E. "An Interview with Karen Malpede." *Studies in American Drama, 1945-Present* 8 (1993): 45-60.

Kroll, Jack. Review. *Newsweek* 8 Apr. 1968: 131.

Makin, Rich. "Tennessee Williams Premier Puzzling." *Asbury Park Press* [NJ] 10 Mar. 1975: A6.

Marranca, Bonnie. "*Kingdom of Earth:* Not Mirth, Not Worth." *The Soho Weekly News* [NY] 15 July 1976: 26.

McDermott, Plymath. "Twiss Irresistible at Boston Stage." *Norwalk Hour* [CT] Apr. 1991.

Neslen [*sic*], Don. "Myrtle's Last Descent." *New York Daily News* 15 July 1976: 77.

Ogden, Jean. "Tennessee Williams Revival: Chicken on a Cold Wet Roof." *Messenger Gazette* [Somerset, NJ] 13 Mar. 1975.

Parks, Suzan-Lou. "Writing Home." *American Theatre* Oct. 1991: 38.

"Pendleton Joins Company for Williams Comedy." *Princeton Packet* 26 Feb. 1975: 18.

Phillips, Jerrold A. "*Kingdom of Earth:* Some Approaches." *Tennessee Williams: A Tribute.* Ed. Jac Tharpe. Jackson: UP of Mississippi, 1977. 349-53.

Porter, Fred. "Theatre: Town and Country: *Kingdom of Earth. Store News* [Dunellen, NJ] 12 Mar. 1975.

Radin, Victoria. Review. *London Observer* 6 May 1984. Rpt. *London Theatre Record* 4 (1984): 350.

Rasky, Harry. *Tennessee Williams: A Portrait in Laughter and Lamentation.* New York: Dodd, Mead, 1986.

Rosenberg, David. "Tennessee Descending." *Fairpress* [Norwalk, CT] 4 Apr. 1991: D2.

Rubincam, Don. "Compelling Performances Mark Revival of Williams' 'Comedy.'" *Courier News* [Plainfield, NJ] 7 Mar. 1975.

Shaland, Irene. *Tennessee Williams on the Soviet Stage.* Lanham, MD: UP of America, 1987.

Sheed, Wilfred. Review. *Life* 27 Apr. 1968: 18.

Shulman, Milton. Review. *London Standard* 2 May 1984. Rpt. *London Theatre Record* 4 (1984): 355.

Simon, John. Review. *Commonweal* 88 (3 May 1968): 209-9.

-----. Review. *Hudson Review* 21 (July 1968): 322-24.

Stewart, Ian. "Dark Corner of the Deep South." *Country Life* 9 Mar. 1978: 612.

Tinker, Jack. Review. *London Daily Mail* 10 May 1984. Rpt. *London Theatre Record* 4 (1984): 350.

Todd, Susan. Review. *New Statesman* 4 May 1984: 32. Rpt. *London Theatre Record* 4 (1984): 350.

Tuma, Mirko. "Williams Revision Opens at McCarter." *News Tribune* [Woodbridge, NJ] 4 Mar. 1975.

Vosburgh, Dick. Review. *Punch* 9 May 1984. Rpt. *London Theatre Record* 4 (1984): 356.

Watts, Richard, Jr. Review. *New York Post* 28 Mar. 1968: 67. Rpt. *New York Theatre Critics' Reviews* 29: 316.

Williams, Tennessee. *Kingdom of Earth.* In *Theatre of Tennessee Williams,* Volume 5. New York: New Directions, 1976.

Young, B. A. *Kingdom of Earth. Financial Times* 23 Feb. 1978.

Zirnite, Colleen. "Tennessee Williams Rewrite: Poor Play with a Good Cast." *The Democrat* [Flemington, NJ] 11 Mar. 1975.

Studies in American Drama, 8.2 (1993): 140-62.

In the Bar of a Tokyo Hotel (1969)

Tennessee's Quest
Henry Hewes

Like Eugene O'Neill before him, Tennessee Williams in his later period appears to be turning to more personal material. His most recent work, *In the Bar of a Tokyo Hotel,* seems concerned with expressing Williams's agony both at the difficult process of artistic creation and at the specter of old age, waning sexual magnetism, and death.

The play's protagonists, who may be a composite of two sides of the playwright's personality, are a woman named Miriam and her husband, Mark. Miriam is a boldly lecherous operator, obsessed with the physical attractiveness of younger men. She sees her pursuit of her compulsion as a necessary affirmation of her vitality. She is resolved to go on with it until the time when her age makes the process of disgraceful behavior and rebuff too painful. Then she will kill herself with a little pill she carries around in a Regency snuffbox.

Her husband, Mark, is a famous painter who has become a nervous wreck, and who may be suffering from a brain tumor. But the source of his anguish is more complicated. First of all, he complains that he is no longer able to maintain a separation between himself and what he is creating. Perhaps his moving to a new style has caused "a loss of momentum," and he needs to recognize that to doubt his own talent is a necessary part of the creative transition. Whatever the reason, his new paintings have apparently degenerated into what Miriam calls "circus-colored mud pies."

While he, the artist, is coming apart, she, the life-force is sanguinely at work trying to seduce the young barman, and making plans to ship her sick husband back to the United States, while she continues her amorous odyssey around the world.

Since the play is really happening inside Miriam and Mark, and since they are given little opportunity to face each other down, the action is not very dramatic. It is too indirect, too inconclusive, too full of unfinished sentences and awkward attempts at inconsequential humor and abrupt sexual candor. Yet, there are occasional flashes of recognizable Williams poetic dialogue. And the play's ending indicates a concept which, if fulfilled, might have made a fine play. In it, Miriam voices a religious belief that in this life we must all stay within the "circle of light," which is the approving eye of God. And she adds that her husband's error was that he thought that he could create his own circle of light. From his mistake, she apparently realizes that to continue her lustful life is also a foredoomed attempt to create her own circle, and rather than face her husband's fate, she gives up.

Anne Meacham plays Miriam with an intense concentration that always holds our interest. And possibly it is not her fault that we don't find her as pitiable or tragic as we should. Donald Madden moves us more as Mark, who demonstrates his agony in limited appearances. But even here, the playwright has made him less eloquent about his state than we would have liked.

The failure of *In the Bar of a Tokyo Hotel* is unimportant compared with our concern for its author. Tennessee Williams need never write another line to be assured of his supremacy as a playwright. And he can afford to write as many unsuccessful works as he wishes. His quest for the creation of his own circle of light may be painful, but we will rejoice in his determination to follow it.

Saturday Review, May 31, 1969: 18.

Small Craft Warnings (1972)

The Deathday Party
Henry Hewes

Tennessee Williams's latest work, called *Small Craft Warnings,* is currently playing at Off-Broadway's Truck and Warehouse Theatre. Across the street the La Mama Experimental Theatre Club on East 4th Street is offering *Persia, A Desert Cheapie* (the most expensive production ever staged there), which is a product of John Vaccaro and the Playhouse of the Ridiculous. The coincidental juxtaposition is most appropriate. The theatergoer can now proceed almost instantly from the ridiculous to the sublime.

Sublime is a word that can be applied to everything that Williams writes, and that quality, plus his passionate concern for the dispossessed people who live on the border line of despair, is again evident in *Small Craft Warnings,* a revision of a play originally known as *Confessional.*

This new theater piece is less a play that it is a series of personal self-revelations offered by seven of the play's nine characters. These seven souls face increasingly shabby existences. They are not large enough to be true derelicts. They are tiny abandoned vessels. And they are threatened by nothing so magnificent as a great storm. What they face is the kind of disturbance that endangers only small craft.

Five of the seven lost souls are presented sketchily. Violet, an inefficient prostitute whose urgent need for a place to stay (she has lost her no-water flat above the amusement arcade) sets the play in motion, is the only one whose problem is resolved at the end. She weeps easily and is happiest when she is eating a hamburger called a "Whopper" or when she is fondling men's genitals under the table with what is described as a "religious" ecstasy. Steve, her regular boy friend between sailors, accepts with anguish his humiliating relationship with her because, as a forty-seven-year-old short-order cook, he has two choices--very little, or nothing at all. And Doc, an alcoholic doctor who has lost his license to practice and ekes out a living by performing abortions, is haunted by what his profession has done to reduce the dignity and size of the two holy mysteries, birth and death. He describes these mysteries as "dark as the face of God whose face is dark because it is the face of a black man . . . a negro miner in the pit of a lightless coal mine, obscured completely by the irrelevancies and irreverences of public worship."

The bartender-proprietor, Monk, has a heart condition that may be fatally tested before the night is over, but he is completely reconciled to serving his troubled and troublesome clientele. He lives on their news and considers his life justified because one of them once left him $250 in his will. And Bill McCorkle is a stud, who uses his sexual assets shamelessly in order to live without working. Most recently, he has been kept in a deluxe trailer by its owner, Leona Dawson. But Leona has kicked McCorkle out because she feels she has lost his respect, and we see him revert to becoming trade for cruising homosexuals.

One such homosexual, Quentin, is drawn most profoundly. He describes the deadening coarseness in the unchanging pattern of homosexual experiences, and more significantly, he explores the tragedy of any person who has repeated emotional relationships to the point where he is no longer capable of being surprised by anything. His long poetic soliloquy suggests a whole other play that might be written.

However, the major character in this play is Leona. We meet her drunk, mourning the "deathday" of her younger brother, an anemic homosexual violinist who had the gift of making people capable of emotions beyond themselves, and who died young. The memory of his companionship and violin playing is the one beautiful thing that saves Leona from corruption. She explains, "Without one beautiful thing in the course of a lifetime, it's all a death-time." Like Quentin, she is aware that her life now is in danger of becoming a repetition of pickup relationships. But she has the capacity to look at the good in each and to move on when disrespect sets in.

This character revelation lays all the groundwork for dramatic confrontation. Yet the form of *Small Craft Warnings* is to substitute revelation for action. There is no anticipated event and no apparent theme.

Whatever conflict there is seems accidental, with most of the meaningful dialogue spoken by characters frozen in a spotlight and unheard by the others. It is true that this is a deathday party, but since only one person knows or cares about the dearly departed it cannot tie everyone together the way it does in Edward Albee's *All Over*.

Perhaps, as in his *The Seven Descents of Myrtle,* Williams intended to have the outside elements of nature as the antagonist. The sea and the fog build to a crescendo, threatening to destroy the barroom drifters, and then diminish to a temporary calm in which the man-made sound of Violet taking a shower in preparation for a pleasant night of love with Monk reassures us that the small craft will remain afloat. But this is a difficult mood to sustain on a stage, and the drama must therefore be preserved on a moment-by-moment basis by the performers' ability to make the characters interesting.

Under Richard Altman's direction they succeed only to a limited extent. As Leona, Helena Carroll offers an Irish vitality that is not incompatible with the character's wild swings from toughness to sentimentality. Alan Mixon is compellingly true in Quentin's one long soliloquy. William Hickey manages to make Steve convincing with very little dialogue. And Cherry Davis is all watery weakness as the vulnerable Violet.

Fred Voelpel's setting catches the flavor of a southern California coastal town by constructing the bar's walls out of slats, through which gaps the outside street is visible. One wonders if these slats might have made possible the walls of encroaching fog stipulated by the author. Though such an effect might have been expensive and distracting, the play could have used more nonrealistic atmosphere than it has here. It could also have used some piece of music more overpoweringly effective than the thin violin solo heard faintly from the jukebox.

Small Craft Warnings is, by design, a play about small people, who, unlike the impressive sailfish mounted over the bar, have never sailed an inch in their lives. And its location is less a bar than that point in life where each of these minnows must make peace with comparative insignificance and bleakness of outlook. However, as in *Camino Real,* Williams includes one quixotic character, in this case a young homosexual who rides blithely off on his bicycle to brave the uncertainties of Mexico by himself. Unfortunately, this good example doesn't seem to affect the others. Instead, we are left with a bunch of people who have already come to terms with their smallness and who manage to survive some to-be-expected setbacks for just one more night.

Saturday Review, April 22, 1972: 22-24.

Out Cry (The Two-Character Play) (1973)

Honest or merely disarming?
Julius Novick

Shadowy, crepuscular, green-tinted space, the stage of the "State Theatre of a state unknown." Felice and Clare, brother and sister, are actors, leading their company on a world tour. It is almost curtain-time, but much of their scenery has not arrived. The spiral staircase onstage goes nowhere, as Clare points out--it just stops in space. Worse yet: their fellow-actors have deserted them, leaving Felice a telegram saying, "Your sister and you are insane. Signed--the company." There is only one thing left for Felice and Clare to do: they must perform "The Two Character Play," in which Felice plays the part of Felice, and Clare plays the part of Clare, who are brother and sister, and frightened, and mad. The play itself, the "real" play, the play that the *real* audience has come to watch, used to be called also *The Two Character Play*. It is now called *Out Cry* and David Merrick is presenting it on Broadway, but it still has only two characters, and the author is still Tennessee Williams. It is an annoying, pretentious, slightly maudlin piece of work, but I found it impossible to dismiss it entirely: there is something haunting about it.

"I think this is some sort of dramatic metaphor," says Clare. No doubt. It is quite evidently, first of all, a metaphor for Mr. Williams's own well-known recent and long-standing sorrows, with Clare representing his impulse to collapse under the strain, and Felice standing for his determination to go on. But like any work of Romantic art (perhaps like any work of art at all), *Out Cry* is ultimately an attempt to make of the writer's personal experience a more or less universal metaphor. In spite of it obvious borrowings from Pirandello and Beckett, no one can deny that the play is deeply felt, that Mr. Williams is wrestling with his demons as desperately as Eugene O'Neill used to do. But this kind of wrestling can easily lead toward obsessiveness and away from discipline and craft. This happened often to O'Neill, and in this play it has happened--not for the first time--to Mr. Williams (though Mr. Williams will never be able to write as badly as O'Neill did at his worst). Mr.

Williams loves his sorrows, but he cannot at this time quite make us shere [*sic*] his sense of how important and precious they are, precisely, perhaps, *because* he loves them so much.

He is aware of the problem: "I sometimes wonder," says Clare about "The Two Character Play," "if it isn't a little too special, too personal, for most audiences." But is it open honesty for him to admit to this fear, or just a fearful attempt to forestall our reaction? And when does a writer's open honesty about his agonies turn into an annoying insistence on showing them off? It is a sadly difficult line to gauge, but in his late plays Mr. Williams crosses it frequently in the wrong direction. It is a matter of skill and tact, I suppose; a writer can do anything, in this direction as in any other, if only he does it well enough (Cf. that true and great masterpiece of the confessional, *Long Day's Journey into Night.*) Or is that begging the question? At any rate I wish Mr. Williams could avoid plucking at our sleeves to beg for mercy, as he does when he has Clare say, "You know, Felice, artists put so much into their work that they have a very little left over for acting like other people."

Out Cry is a repetitive, ever-insistent piece of work. Felice is forever trying to persuade Clare to *do* something, to help him to take arms against their sea of troubles. Felice persuading Clare, in the play-within-the-play, to come with him to the grocery store to demand that their credit be restored (a motif, incidentally, from *The Glass Menagerie*) sounds all too much like Felice persuading Clare to play the play-within-the-play in the first place. Mr. Williams has been talking a good deal lately about the importance of humor in his work; this play needs more of it--or of some kind of variation. Near the end, there is a moment of friendliness and comparative relaxation between brother and sister; it is welcome, but very brief. They spend virtually the whole play at the end of their respective tethers, and the play is not short enough or concentrated enough or unified enough to make its consistency of emotion a virtue. Monotony is the danger that is not entirely avoided: monotony, and a certain lack of progression. Desperation is evoked, but not explored.

The play is both over-explicit and vague. Mr. Williams has not quite mastered the technique of Pirandello and Beckett, the technique of planned confusion, of withholding information in order to achieve greater precision, not less. Certain specific metaphors, moreover, fail of their impact--what *about* those giant sunflowers which surround the house of Felice and Clare in the play-within-the-play? Enough is said about them--but what are they a metaphor *for?* And the great trauma that haunts Felice and Clare within-the play--their father was a mad mystic who killed their mother and himself--is this functional, or is it, as it seems, a gratuitously Gothic piece of horror?

Peter Glenville has directed *Out Cry* with sympathy for its Romantic extravagance--and the flamboyant gestures that Mr. Williams writes *must* be played to the hilt, or there is no play. But Mr. Glenville might have found, or made, more of the variations in feeling that the play needs. In particular, he has not made clear the shock and horror of those moments when Felice or Clare falls out of his or her part in the play-within-the-play. "The show must go on" is an imperative that we have almost in our blood; we feel primevally, as so many dreams tell us, that this is one appearance the [*sic*] must be kept up at all costs. To fail to maintain the performance is somehow a terrifying thing; Mr. Williams seems interested in this terror, but Mr. Glenville does not.

Jo Mielziner, the designer, has made a mistake, I think, in enclosing the stage with large, neutral drops; they enable him to do things with projections, but his projections are somewhat timid, and he loses some of the eerie magic of a deserted, empty stage. His lighting, however--elaborate even to follow-spots--seemed to me successfully bold in its dramatization of the performers in space.

The acting: Michael York is a very competent Felice, but conventional and unsurprising: Cara Duff-MacCormick as Clare is a notably more exotic and arresting presence. Miss Duff-MacCormick first appeared in New York last year, in the still-lamented *Moon-children,* as the funny, gurgling, gawkward [*sic*] little hippie waif who spent most of her time sitting under tables; now she flings a white fur collar around her neck with authority, she has somehow become tall, her voice is husky and elegant, and she is impressively racked by the anxieties and fears that female flesh is heir to in the world of Mr. Williams. Miss Duff-MacCormick has range, imagination, intensity; if she does not become an important American actress, it will be our loss as well as hers.

And Mr. Williams himself, like his Southern heroines, is still, somehow, bravely himself, even in reduced circumstances. And this play is better than some of his later, sadder ones. It has its crippling faults (as I believe I have suggested [*sic*]--and they are of course Mr. Williams's familiar faults, but though they are much in evidence, they are *less* in evidence than in *Milk Train* or *The Seven Descents of Myrtle. Out Cry* is Mr. Williams's farthest departure from specific time and place since that beautiful dramatic poem, *Camino Real,* and I think the departure has done him some good. He borrows from Pirandello and Beckett, but the borrowings are not excessive or abject, and do not diminish his own flavor. *Out Cry* has some fine lines--"Fear: the fierce little man with a drum inside the rib-cage"--and it does distill a certain poetry or music of mood. Desperation is not explored, but it is, at moments, feelingly evoked. The night-mare quality of the play's basic situation--being onstage without being able to sustain a performance--counts for something. And the possibility raises itself that *Out Cry* might reveal further riches if given further study, or another production, or merely another look.

Mr. Williams has not recaptured the mysterious thing he lost after *Night of the Iguana,* but *Out Cry* (in spite of the sleeve-plucking title, and in spite of much else) makes it possible, at least, for this well-wishers to believe that he may have found the beginning of the right road back.

Village Voice, March 8, 1973: 58.

Stage: Williams's *2 Character Play*
Lawrence Van Gelder

When a playwright writes about actors and acting and sets his play amid the clutter of a decrepit theater, the temptation arises to cast his metaphors aside and deal with the possibility that the work at hand is the product of a desperate rummaging for material.

The suspicion may be valid, but it is not always fair. Certainly not in the case of Pirandello, and although recent times have not been wholly kind, not to Tennessee Williams either.

Through next Wednesday, with the exception of Monday, Mr. Williams is being represented Off Off Broadway with a production of *The Two-Character Play.* This work at the Quaigh Theater, 808 Lexington Avenue, near 62nd Street, is another version of the play presented on Broadway two years ago under the title *Out Cry.*

Before that, it was presented in Chicago, and before that, in London. Demonic, ghost-ridden, elliptical, it endures--and is appeals. Not to all tastes, not for all times, and certainly not because it bears the name of a distinguished playwright. It endures because of the assurance of its craftsmanship, and it appeals because it plays to what bedevils us all--fear.

But it is not an entertainment. And, as directed by Bill Lentsch, it is a play for players--a darkly passionate salute to the heroism of performers and, by extension, to all who go on and go forward despite terror at what lies ahead and in the recognition of the impossibility of turning back.

Yes, Mr. Williams has set his play in a chill, decrepit theater. Two actors, a brother and a sister, various ravaged, abandoned on grounds of nonpayment and lunacy by their troupe, are waiting to go on in a play called *The Two Character Play.*

It is set in the sunny South, in a house increasingly inhospitable to life, and the two characters are a deranged brother and sister, fearful of venturing out of the home where their father killed their mother and then himself--even if the neighbors suspect otherwise.

And so they perform until "in a state theater of an unknown state," they find there is no audience, and the theater, if it is that, is locked, and confinement, the most unspeakable of states, threatens them.

As the brother, Felice, and the sister, Clare, Robert Stattel and Maryellen Flynn, give performances that at their best invest the play with tension and at worst strip it briefly of its poetic qualities. But Miss Flynn, with her disordered hive of honeyed hair, her furrowed brown, sagging cheeks and bowstring torso, speaks a poetic body language, and with a voice that resonates and weakens and a broad face, and expressive mouth, Mr. Stattel seems the proper model for the masks of comedy and tragedy.

New York Times, August 22, 1975: 16.

The Later Career of Tennessee Williams
Albert J. Devlin

Only a few American writers, including Twain, Frost, Hemingway, and, I suspect, Tennessee Williams, can be said to have "entered" the national consciousness to any measurable depth. The shape of their careers is distinctively American, for they illustrate unique national pressures exerted by fame, mass appeal, early success, and a fierce competition, which is turned obsessively against the self. Tennessee Williams in particular has seemed to concentrate these pressures. The uniqueness of his plays is often blurred as a consequence, and the career itself becomes a rigid enactment of the writer's legendary fate. The later career of Williams has suffered the most acute effects of this mythologizing process. Its profusion of texts, with such grim, forbidding titles as *The Gnadiges Fraulein* (1966), describes only a curve of personal and artistic decline after *The Night of the Iguana* (1961)--the last play widely deemed successful. Through it all, Williams exploits his apparently inexhaustible store of fame to retain the perennial celebrity. Ironically, defenders of the later career often conspire with this view by focusing upon the man rather than the work. They recall in effect Flannery O'Connor's blunt question of Norman Mailer, who also elaborated a public persona: "Why doesn't he let his work speak for itself . . . doesn't he think it would?"

One play in particular can speak for itself and help to reveal a deeper intention in the later career. In the *Memoirs* (1975), Tennessee Williams attached great personal and artistic importance to *The Two-Character Play* (1967-75). On the whole, it disappointed audiences in London, New York, and Chicago, but this exceedingly personal drama has a surge of objectivity that dispels any notion of doddering or opportunistic conception. In *The Two-Character Play,* Williams confronted his own notorious "decline" by reflecting upon the most intimate dynamics of his singular career. Perhaps this study became more urgent after *The Night of the Iguana,* but Williams' examination of the modern literary life is a constant and evolutionary signature of his writing rather than a desperate apocalypse of the later career. What Tennessee Williams knew, or hoped to learn, in writing *The Two-Character Play* confounds any paradigmatic view of his distinguished life in letters. To probe this knowledge is to read instead the inner story of Williams's career: his constant struggle to renew the artistic motive amid nearly overwhelming personal and professional adversity.

In *The Two-Character Play,* Felice, "the male star" of an acting company on tour, is "a playwright, as well as [a] player" whose "sensibilities [are] perhaps a little deranged." The stage directions indicate further that his "total effect" is to be "theatrical and a bit narcissan" (2). Felice's sister Clare is also a player, but her condition, at least at the outset, is the more precarious: "Stoned," she alternates between a "grand theatre manner" and "something startlingly coarse" (3). In their tics, mannerisms, and idiosyncrasies of speech, in their personal and artistic despair, Felice and Clare portray the self in extremis that Williams exhibited during the 1960s and the 70s. *The Two-Character Play,* as Tennessee Williams claimed in 1976, "depicts the interior landscape of the most terrible period of my life" (qtd. in Leverich 20).

The Two-Character Play is formally designed as a play-within-a play. The outer frame is described in the stage directions as "an evening in an unspecified" theater "before and after the performance" (ix). A "dusky violet light" obscures the backstage area, which is cluttered with "unassembled set pieces." The strain of theater life, as well as its peculiar magic, is conveyed by the "statue of a giant, pedestaled," with "a sinister look," that haunts the shadowy background of the stage. The inner play is performed within "a widely angled V-shape" set, which contains "the incomplete interior of a living room in Southern summer." The stage-right flat "contains a door, the other a large window looking out upon . . . a thick growth of tall sunflowers." Interior furnishings include "an old upright piano" and "various tokens of the vocation of an astrologer" (1). The present action begins after Felice and Clare have been deserted by the rest of the road company who think them insane! (14). Only at Felice's desperate urging does Clare agree to perform the claustrophobic little drama, "The Two-Character Play," set on "a nice afternoon in a deep Southern town called New Bethesda" (ix).

Williams's innovation in this play is less radical than first impressions may indicate, but it points nonetheless to his precarious literary situation in the 1960s and thereafter. For much of that time, Williams was preoccupied with revising and mounting one or another version of *The Two-Character Play*--in London in 1967; in Chicago in 1971, as *Out Cry*; on Broadway two years later, under the same new title; and then again in New York in 1975, but off-Broadway and with the original title restored. Showcase versions appeared in San Francisco and Los Angeles in 1976 and 1977. Throughout this ordeal, Williams was always a practical man of the theater; he deeply cut *The Two-Character Play* to remove obscurity and make the piece more accessible to restive audiences.   "It gets better as it gets shorter," he quipped with an interviewer in 1975 ("Showcase Interview").   In part at least, Williams employed the same practicality to gauge his relation to the changing theater of the 1960s.   Often he felt himself to be as much a stranger there as did Lillian Hellman and William Inge.

Shortly before *The Night of the Iguana* opened on Broadway in 1961, Williams confessed to having "suffered certain attritions of time and energies" in his quarter century of playwriting (*Conversations with Tennessee Williams* 101).   In particular, he sensed that his "kind of literary and pseudo-literary style of writing" was "on its way out" (Conversations 99).   Williams may echo here the lingering fashion of presentation, environments, and happenings--the "other theater" of the 1950s and 60s, as Gerald Weales has described it--but he was more attentive to the lessons, and certainly the prominence, of dramatists whom he loosely grouped as "new wave" writers.   Williams was "enthralled" by Beckett, Albee, and Pinter--especially by *The Caretaker,* which he thought a "fabulous" play (*Conversations* 98).   But his awe was tinged with sadness and regret as well.   The acclaim of Pinter's play and others like it taught Williams the brevity of unassailed leadership in the theater.

The Two-Character Play bears the imprint of contemporary absurdist theater--a term that Williams regarded warily if at all (*Conversations* 118). The play is governed by the same spatial image that Harold Pinter described in 1960 as the inspiration for his own sparse drama.   "Two people in a room. . . . . The curtain goes up on the stage, and I see it as a very potent question: What is going to happen to these two people in the room? . . . Obviously they are scared of what is outside the room.   Outside . . . there is a world bearing upon them which is frightening" (qtd. in Esslin 232).   This is the setting and situation of Felice and Clare in the inner play.   Nearly all of their movement is choreographed as abortive passage through door and window into a world whose harsh reality is symbolized by Mr. Grossman.   While waiting, Felice and Clare give phrase to a host of familiar absurdist themes: a nameless fear that underlies all experience, the frightening prospect of communication, the plentitude of time coupled with its nullity, and, of course, waiting.   In *The Two-Character Play* all of this is stated not in the familiar Williams arias, but in a language stripped of fustian and hyperbole, and of much poetry too.

As recently as 1983, Williams was described as having ransacked the absurdist literature in *The Two-Character Play.*   "When he lost contact with his roots," the artist Vassilis Voglis claimed, "he turned to others' roots and to their work for inspiration" (qtd. in Spoto 267).   Williams's attention to this literature is undeniable, but the absurdist themes cited above did not appear suddenly in 1960 or thereabouts.   Williams correctly saw himself and Pinter as "fellow" observers of the "terrifying ambiguous" nature of human relations (*Conversations* 98).   Nor do these common themes imply any philosophic agreement with the postulates of "the absurd."   In 1949 in the famous

"Dialogues" with Georges Duthuit, Samuel Beckett spoke of an art commensurate with the "void": it would be one that was "unresentful of its insuperable indigence and too proud for the farce of giving and receiving." It could never be "a rallying," he agreed with Georges Duthuit, "among the things of time that pass and hurry us away, towards a time that endures and gives increase" (18-19). Tennessee Williams's own conception of the "void" never quite exceeded his romantic faith in transcendence, if only the "banner" of a gallantry raised in defeat.

Williams's engagement with contemporary drama is better understood as recognition of his own precarious literary situation. Donald Spoto has accurately traced Williams' deepening self-doubt to the production of *Orpheus Descending* in 1957. The brief run and poor notices of this revision of *Battle of Angels,* the notorious failure that inaugurated Williams's career, brought to a climax the personal and artistic problems that besieged Williams throughout the decade. With *Orpheus Descending,* he felt he "was no longer acceptable to the theatre public" (qtd. in Spoto 213). Undoubtedly, the acclaim of Pinter and other innovative writers exacerbated this judgment and created for Williams a moment of poignant self-examination. His identity as one who had transformed the postwar theater virtually required that he restore his prestige as a experimenter in dramatic form. Instinctively, he turned to his own "roots," instead of "others," and in *The Two-Character Play* created a unique testament to the artist's vocation. Although the so-called "new wave" writers and especially Pirandello helped to shape the design and intention of *The Two-Character Play,* Williams needed little assistance in feeling the "inspiration" of his materials.

The inner drama, which is set in "Southern summer" and played on a cold stage in an "unspecified" theater, is an amalgam of personal, professional, and artistic instances that comprise the Williams identity. A memory play, the inner drama is charged with family strife that leads to a night of murder and suicide. Clare's mother, a "frigid," loquacious woman "given to little fears and superstitions," is finally silenced as she speaks to her daughter through "a soundless fountain of blood." Father, a man of "mystical powers," goes "to the window where he fire[s] again." Among the properties required by the inner play is the revolver used on this "accident night" (20-21), as Clare evasively calls it. Its lure for each is to repeat their father's murder and suicide. A wooden spool and a bowl of soapsuds are more idyllic properties that connote the innocence of childhood. But its signature is naturally delicate and precarious, and it does not tolerate well the world's rough handling. "Soap bubbles floating out of the parlor window would not indicate to the world that we are in full possession of our senses" (33), Felice reasons. The "warm amber light" that floods the inner stage is an apt medium for Felice and Clare to test their relationship. By turns they dare, taunt, unmask, injure, and console each other, but their relations center around the fear of confinement.

For Clare, this word is "prohibited," and Felice is a perverse monster (31) to speak it in the evolving script of "The Two-Character Play." In the most bitter moment of the inner drama, Felice abandons Clare when she refuses to go with him to Mr. Grossman's market. "When I go out of this house I'll never come back. I'll walk and walk, I'll go and go!" "I'll wait!" (45), Clare replies.

This much seems clear in Williams's plotting of the inner drama: in depicting family strife, lost innocence, and the confinement of a beloved sister to whom he was inextricably bound, he has evoked the constants of his personal-literary history and in effect, as Ruby Cohn points out, composed another "typical" Williams play: Southern, familiar, violent, and bittersweet in resolution (337). What is less clear, if assorted reviews and notices for the play are any indication, is Williams' intention in restoring his distinctive "menagerie."

This intention begins to clarify when the inner drama is seen in relation to the frame, which is a metaphor for the magic of authorship. The inner plot reconstructs Tennessee Williams's personal-literary history as it was rendered in the prototypical play *The Glass Menagerie.* But his wish is not to trade on the brilliance of an early work, as reviewers often supposed; rather it is to reclaim authorship and endow characters who "crave life." Citing Pirandello's preface to *Six Characters in Search of an Author* is not without relevance. In the first published version of *The Two-Character Play* (1969), Clare asks, "Are we doing the Pirandello tonight?" (4). She takes her cue from a papier-mache giant on stage which in all probability recalls Pirandello's unfinished play, *The Mountain Giants* (Cohn 338). The allusion is dropped in later versions, but the phrase itself, "crave life" (369), suggests both the design and intention of *The Two-Character Play.* Williams's inner drama is set in motion by a creativity that Pirandello had likened, in the preface to *Six Characters,* to the "miracle . . . of the saint who sets his own statue in motion: it is neither wood nor stone at such a moment" (373). Williams's forbidding statue of "a giant, pedestaled" implicitly states the premise that "Going back's reversing a law of--Nature" (58). But such a reversal, or renewing of the past, is precisely the logic of the play "within."

A "C-sharp struck on the piano . . . means a cut's coming at you" (17), Clare warns at the outset of "The Two-Character Play." Thereafter the "script" follows an unforeseen course, re-imagining the past, playing one hypothetical scene within another, not knowing "what to do next," improvising, trying out alternate endings--in short, "destroying the play" (27), as Felice ruefully puts it. Within this fluid, self-reflexive medium, Felice-Tennessee-Tom and Clare-Rose-Laura reenact the author's prototypical drama of love and guilt. The "endings" proposed in the 1976 text, as well as those contained in earlier versions of *The Two-Character Play,* argue that Williams resisted sentiment and wishful thinking in treating these exceedingly personal issues. But while their intimacy is well known, I doubt that Williams's aesthetic motive has ever been adequately understood. *The Two-Character Play* reflects the complex dynamic of Tennessee Williams's literary career-specifically, the fear, tension, and ambiguity occasioned by his compact with the commercial theater. In effect, *The Two-Character Play* makes a fundamental contribution to Williams's examination of the modern literary life. Well before he suffered his first great success on Broadway, Williams anticipated this theme, if not the artistic form that it would finally take.

In an early correspondence, Tennessee Williams foresaw the challenge of his impending career. On September 3, 1940, he wrote to his friend, Joe Hazan, from New York City. He was convinced that a supreme "endurance" would be required of the artist to guard his "one ineluctable gift." This ability "to project himself beyond time and space through grasp and communion with eternal values" was the vision of "beauty" that the artist instinctively served. Several weeks later, Williams wrote to the same friend from the Hotel Costa Verde in Acapulco, where he lived for the remainder of September. In anticipation of the Theatre Guild production of *Battle of Angels,* Williams confessed feeling drawn like "a moth" to the "excitement" of Broadway, although he knew that is would soon pall and he would flee to some such remote place as Acapulco. Of one thing he was certain, however: "Everyone shrinks in New York" (Collection).

Before his first major production, Tennessee Williams had accurately gauged the allure of the commercial theater, as well as his own susceptibility to its "glitter and excitement." The "endurance" that he valued above all bespoke not only the resolve of his apprentice years but also the greater courage required by an advancing career. By endurance, by periodic retreat from the confinement of Broadway, Williams would guard the "ineluctable gift" of the artist and the "beauty" he served. This is an important manifesto, but neither the envisioned shape nor tension of the literary career is unique to Tennessee Williams. He has described instead the definitive situation of modernism, and it is one that might have been derived from the careers of D. H. Lawrence or Hart Crane, or Lord Byron, for that matter--Williams's most cherished antecedents. But the experience of this career was unique to Williams, and it gradually became for him the subjective center of his dramaturgy. What Tennessee Williams made of this center is, however, a daunting question: did it permit "self-justification," rather than "self-dramatization," as some have claimed; or is there a more critical, disinterested thread running through the later career that leads inevitably, say to *The Two-Character Play*? If so, it is a threat that has origins in one of the more hopeful periods of Williams's career, when he looked ahead in 1940 to the struggle and fulfillment of the literary life.

Williams's artistic theme is well known and requires only brief summary here. In *Camino Real* (1953), in the historic spectre of Lord Byron, Williams assembled for the first time the constituent parts of the modern literary life.

Byron's fame is coincident with the betrayal of his "gift" amid "glittering salons" and "huge shadowy courts." But in his final testament to the "poet's vocation," Byron resolves to court "the old pure music" once again: "Make voyages!--Attempt them!--there's nothing else" (Block Eight), he says, in annunciation to each of Williams's succeeding artists. In *Suddenly Last Summer* (1958) Sebastian Venable's grisly demise at Cabeza de Lobo metaphorically expresses the conjunction of the poet's failure to write and his absorption into a "savage nature" of sexual cannibalism. A similar conjunction in *Sweet Bird of Youth* (1959) binds the aging film actress Alexandra Del Lago to Chance Wayne. "Forge the legend that I was and the ruin of that legend," she warns, explaining to Chance the terms of his "employment" (1.1). Perhaps one reason why *The Night of the Iguana* (1961) is often cited as a watershed text is that it seems to release the accruing tension of the artist's vocation. By completing his "last poem," the aged Nonno defeats the "spooks and blue devils" (as his granddaughter Hannah describes them) that have terrified Williams's protagonists. His courageous literary performance is precisely the vindication of the artist's "ineluctable gift" that Tennessee Williams foresaw at the beginning of his career.

"The Gnadiges Fraulein" (1966) and *In the Bar of a Tokyo Hotel* (1969) further dramatize the artistic theme, but these later plays do not alter the core of Williams' thinking about the life of the artist. "The work of a poet is the life of a poet," Mrs. Venable proclaimed with unmistakable authority in *Suddenly Last Summer* (sc. 1). this equation became for Williams the durable center of his dramaturgy, but it was not a passive or static condition of artistic perception, as the thread leading from *Camino Real* to *The Night of the Iguana* would seem to imply. Rather it was an evolutionary theme that drew Williams into a deeper and more profound relation with his artistic environment and creative self. That same evolution, or unfolding, I would like to think continued to play a formative role in the design and intention of *The Two-Character Play.*

Williams's gravitation to Pirandello in designing *The Two-Character Play* was not an accident or a crass borrowing. In his famous play, Pirandello rejects the drama of his importuning "characters" and consigns them instead to search eternally for authorship. The consolation they seek in vain is artistic form. Its "particular value," as Pirandello notes in the preface to *Six Characters,* is to relieve "the inherent tragic conflict between life (which is always moving and changing) and form (which fixes it, immutable)" (367). Only "the work of art," which is born anew with each performance, can elude this tragic dictation: it "lives forever in so far as it is form" (372).

"Stale Pirandellicatessen," as one reviewer said in 1973, is a glib judgment of the quality of *The Two-Character Play* and of Williams's presumably famished appropriation of a much greater work of art (rept. to Gagnard by Leverich). Such a skewing of influence is regrettable because it diminishes a complex literary relationship. Tennessee Williams was led by Pirandello into a deeper appreciation of the artistic theme. From *Camino Real* to *The Night of the Iguana,* Williams had examined the environment of art. His artist figures lived uneasily with adulation, rejection, or obscurity, the triad of judgments of a mass culture that sees artistic performance as commodity. As a corollary of this environment, time itself became an attenuating medium in which artistic energy, vision, and self-discipline suffered "the fatigue of years," as Williams said in 1950 ("A Writer's Quest" 33). With *The Two-Character Play,* Williams became more concerned with the nature of literary form itself. The dual structure of *Six Characters in Search of an Author* provided Williams with a vehicle for restaging his quintessential drama and at the same time reaffirming his devotion to the world of art.

In performing "The Two Character Play," Felice and Clare hope to allay their painful experience. Their failure, which commits them to the same endless search as Pirandello's characters," [*sic*] is wholly consonant with Tennessee Williams's vision of life as ceaseless struggle: "The heart of man, his body and his brain, are forged in a white-hot furnace for the purpose of conflict" ("On A Streetcar Named Success" 21). No doubt Williams found in Pirandello a reflection of his own existential values. Williams's attraction to the artistic theme in *Six Characters* is somewhat more complex, but it is related to his conception of the artist's "one ineluctable gift."

Ironically, the Mother, the least knowing of Pirandello's "strange family" of characters, proclaims the efficacy of art. To the Manager who assumes that her suffering has ended, she answers, "No, it's happening now, it's happening always! My torture is not a pretense, signore! . . . [I]t is renewed, alive and present, always!" (371). An improbable "character," the Mother nonetheless states the miracle of artistic form--"a form which does not delimit or destroy its own life and which life does not consume" (372). This is the same renewal of experience that Williams sought in *The Two-Character Play.* Felice and Clare do not gain the consolation of artistic form, but as "characters" in the Pirandellian sense they reaffirm its creative potential. The first performance of "The Two-Character Play" is a "disaster" that points to the murder and the suicide of Felice and Clare. Gradually, though, the lure of the playhouse, though now chill and empty, inspires a second performance that centers again on the deadly property. Their father's revolver has "always" been there, but in the present enactment neither Felice nor Clare can pull the trigger. As "The Character Play" [*sic*] ends, they embrace in the darkness, their faces showing "a tender admission of defeat" (62-63). By conventional standards, their faith is meager; Felice and Clare, and the author as well, reject the usual "alternatives" of a deity or "Citizens Relief" and advance the progression of the play itself. To her brother's statement that the "The Two-Character Play" seems without end, Clare replies, mockingly, "I didn't know you believed in the everlasting" (53).

Felice might have spoken for Tennessee Williams in saying "our home is a theatre anywhere that there is one" (8), but Williams, knew at the beginning of his career that this would be a difficult habitation and that he would often flee its confining effect. This dynamic of attraction and resistance eventuated quite naturally, even inevitably, in the lengthy thread of Williams's artistic theme. Its farthest extension, which led him to dramatize the nature of artistic form, is a manifestation as well of the corrosive environment of art. In *The Theater and Its Double* (1938), Antonin Artaud stated that "the idolatry of fixed masterpieces is one of the aspects of bourgeois conformism" (76). I do not know that Williams read Artaud, but he came to realize the truth of this assertion. The long shadows cast by his early masterpieces were lengthened and darkened by a theater establishment that often maneuvered Williams into competition with himself. Calls that he repeat his early success, both in kind and degree, invariably attended revivals of his most famous plays in the 1950s and 60s. Williams, it seems, had never been so poignant or affecting as in *The Glass Menagerie* and *A Streetcar Named Desire,* or so the bittersweet notices opined (Spoto 208-209). Exasperated, Williams replied in the late 1970s: "I have done my operas--now I want the privilege of doing my chamber works" (rept. to Gagnard by Leverich). But the better answer to such calls was *The Two-Character Play* itself. By restaging his quintessential drama, Williams attempted to reclaim it from the box-office tag "Masterpiece" and restore it to the superior plane of art. His success, no doubt, was limited, but his intention was wholly faithful to the poet's "one ineluctable gift."

Study of *The Two-Character Play* reveals that during the last two decades of his life, Tennessee Williams wrote with much the same divided attention that marks the more celebrated period of the 1940s and 50s. On one plane, his writing was wholly personal and self-absorbed; on the other, he seldom lost sight of the politics and fashions of the contemporary theater. At no time did these planes exist in anything but strain and tension. The degree varies, of course, but the inner structure or story of Tennessee William's literary life remained unchanged for nearly five decades of writing.

This continuity, however painful to Williams is a more reliable starting point for study of his later career than the prevailing thesis of "decline and fall." For Williams, the writer's "gift" was "ineluctable," and hence his life and work (as Violet Venable proclaimed) could scarcely be separated. His study of the artist was a natural expression of this core, and as we have seen, it encompassed virtually all of his important writing. To equate this theme with "self-justification," as a fair number do, simply palls in relation to the magnitude and duration of Williams's career. *The Two-Character Play* contributes fundamentally to his long-standing aesthetic concerns by dramatizing the nature of literary form itself. The incorruptible design that he wished to project in *The Two-Character Play* was a final vindication of the artist's mission to reach "beyond time and space through grasp and communion with eternal values" (Collection).

There is ample reason for thinking that the later Williams is much same conscientious writer that produced the great "operas" of the 1940s and 50s. To make rigid divisions in the canon, with *The Night of the Iguana* usually serving as a watershed text, is to obscure this presence and insert artificial elements into the natural expression of Tennessee Williams's literary life. Such a spurious conception of the career not only diminishes the faithful practice of his craft, but it also seals away from judgment and appreciation too the curious, inviting works of the later Williams. In the present critical climate, this authentic, self-interpreting voice sounds as "faint with distance" as the Varsouviana in *A Streetcar Named Desire.*

WORKS CITED

Arnaud, Antonin. *The Theater and Its Double.* Trans. Mary C. Richards. 1938. New York: Grove Press, 1958.

Beckett, Samuel and Georges Duthuit. "Three Dialogues: (1949), in *Samuel Beckett: A Collection of Critical Essays.* Ed. Martin Esslin. Englewood Cliffs, NJ: Prentice-Hall, 1965.

Cohn, Ruby. "Late Tennessee Williams." *Modern Drama* 27 (1984): 336-344.

Esslin, Martin. *The Theatre of the Absurd.* 1961. New York: Anchor Books, 1969.

Gagnard, Frank "An 'Authorized' Portrait of Williams." *New Orleans Times-Picayune.* Lagniappe sec. 3 April 1987: 6.

Leverich, Lyle. "*The Two-Character Play:* A Producer's View." *Tennessee Williams Newsletter* 1 (1979): 20-23.

Pirandello, Luigi. Preface (1925) to *Six Characters in Search of an Author,* in *Naked Masks: Five Plays.* Ed. and trans. Eric Bentley. New York: Dutton, 1952.

Spoto, Donald. *The Kindness of Strangers: The Life of Tennessee Williams.* Boston: Little, Brown, 1985.

Weales, Gerald C. *The Jumping Off Place: American Drama in the 1960's.* New York: Macmillan, 1969.

Williams, Tennessee. Collection. Humanities Research Center, University of Texas at Austin.

_____, *Conversations with Tennessee Williams.* Ed. Albert J. Devlin. Jackson: University Press of Mississippi, 1986.

_____, "On a Streetcar Named Success" (1947), in *Where I Live: Selected Essays.* Ed. Christine R. Day and Bob Woods. New York: New Directions, 1978.

_____, "The Showcase Interview." With Gene Anceri. San Francisco, 20 October 1976. Videocassette.

_____, *The Two-Character Play,* New York: New Directions, 1969.

_____, *The Two-Character Play,* New York: New Directions, 1976.

_____, "A Writer's Quest for a Parnassus" (1950), in *Where I Live.*

The Eccentricities of a Nightingale (1976)

Stage: Williams's *Eccentricities*
Clive Barnes

Perhaps the most eccentric thing about Tennessee Williams' new (yes new) and pungently atmospheric play *The Eccentricities of a Nightingale* is its provenance. It opened at the Morosco Theater last night and, I suspect like most people, I had been expecting a rewrite of *Summer and Smoke*. It is really no such thing, but a different play with different characters and even a different theme.

The story of how the play came to be written is interesting. It started as a rewrite for the London production of *Summer and Smoke,* obviously a radical rewrite. But that production was already deep into rehearsal when Mr. Williams arrived with his revised script. This was put away and did not emerge until years later. Now Mr. Williams has worked further on the script-- one speech, I understand was actually added over this last weekend--and the resultant new play has precious little to do with *Summer and Smoke.*

On the face of it, that may seem an exaggeration. The central characters are still there with the same names living in the same Southern small town just before World War I. The heroine is still a frustrated vocal teacher living with her minister father and crazy mother, and while the doctor hero may have lost a father, he has gained a mother. Some scenes have gone completely, others have been left vestigially but entirely rewritten, and, in some, even whole patches of dialogue have been retained, including most of the final scene.

Yet this is now of interest only to scholars, for the new work effectively knocks *Summer and Smoke* off the map, except as a literary curiosity. The old play contrasted man's soul and his body, and pointed out, with fairly heavy symbolism, the dangers of dividing the two. The new play is a straightforward conflict of two people--one hot and one cold, a woman at base nervously confident, and a man at base confidently nervous.

These two characters, the warm-hearted ugly duckling and the gentle, reserved mother's boy are far more complex and credible than their counterparts in the earlier play, and the resolution of their conflict is far neater and more satisfying. It is as if a rather suaver Gentleman Caller from *The Glass Menagerie* had met a rather younger Blanche DuBois before she finally became Blanche Dubois.

The atmosphere of the lonely town, with its fears and frustrations, is beautifully conveyed, and in the character of Alma, who courageously takes fate in her own hands, and personally finds her own nature is lovingly drawn. (In the earlier play, Alma makes something of the same discovery about herself but in a far less convincing fashion.) John, the glittering young doctor, straight from Johns Hopkins, something of a prig, but not an unlikable prig. If he could get away from his clinging, cloying adoring mother there might still be hope for him.

The play started life earlier this season in Neal Du Brock's Studio Arena Theater in Buffalo. Theoni V. Aldredge's costumes are attractively apt, but William Ritman's permanent setting, while ingenious, is spare almost to the point of skimpiness. Something more lush for this play would have been appropriate--a shoestring can only be made to stretch so far before it breaks.

Edwin Sherin's direction makes the most of Mr. Williams's speed of action, with its almost cinematically encapsulated scenes, and the performances had depth and perception to them.

Betsy Palmer is hardly the wall-flower type, and this makes her initial task rather difficult. But her frantic gaucheness and her frenetic fears soon make sense and she is magnificent in her untidy passion and painful sincerity. David Selby, easy-mannered and good-looking, is perfect as John, chaffing at his mother's attentions, yet meekly complying with them. Of the others, Nan Martin glitters like a bejeweled snake as the awful mother. Shepperd Strudwick is dependably grufff [*sic*] as the minister and Grace Carney is pleasantly daffy as his deranged wife.

This is a warm, rich play full of that compassion and understanding and that simple poetry of the heart that is Mr. Williams at his shining, gentle best. It may be an eccentric nightingale but its tune is still sweet.

New York Times, November 24, 1976: 23.

Vieux Carré (1977)

A Touch of the Poet Isn't Enough to Sustain Williams's Latest Play
Walter Kerr

What is so particularly painful about Tennessee Williams's *Vieux Carré* is that, if you listen carefully enough to penetrate the appalling stage direction that has been imposed upon it, and if you disregard totally the monstrously shabby physical design that is supposed to represent a rooming house in New Orleans, and if--beyond these things--you are willing to tolerate the aimlessness of the playwright's own structure, you can hear his voice.

Tennessee Williams's voice is the most distinctively poetic, the most ideosyncratically [*sic*] moving, and as the same time the most firmly dramatic to have come the American theater's way--ever. No point in calling the man our best living playwright. He is out best playwright, and let qualifications go hang. In fact, he has already given us such a substantial body of successful work that there is really no need to continue demanding that he live up to himself, that he produce more, more, more, and all masterpieces. We could take some casuals and just tuck them into the portfolio, gratefully, as small dividends.

All the more disturbing, then, to have to fight so hard to pick up vagrant echoes of the Williams manner, and the Williams method, at the St. James. You do of course see what he's getting at, from time to time and through a glass darkly. If a group of gushing tourists, doing the French Quarter dutifully, stare up at the handsome facade of a decayed building that has been cut into cubicles for stray borders and devoutly murmur "It's like a dream," while *we* know that behind that facade a girl dying of leukemia is desperately trying to make contact with her drugged stud of a lover, the intended irony can scarcely escape us. If the girl, ash blonde to begin with and freshly pale with fear, rebukes her sodden man for his "choice of employment" and for "using my place as a repository for stolen goods," the syllables fall from her lips-- ever so precisely--with the fastidious ripple that long ago made Alma Winemiller, Blanche du Bois, and Amanda Wingfield the women they were.

The sound is there, the sound defines character, the sound is music.

But two things are wrong, one of them with the play proper. *Vieux Carré* very much means to be a "memory" play in the style of *Glass Menagerie*. A boyish narrator, standing in for Williams himself, picks up where the lad of *Menagerie* left off: he has finally fled the exasperations of life at home in St. Louis and, in his New Orleans attic room, is in process of becoming both a writer and homosexual. He plays scenes with ghosts of the past: a salty slattern of a landlady (Sylvia Sidney), an aging and tubercular homosexual who seduces him (Tom Aldredge), the heterosexual stud and plaintive blonde who live across the hall (John William Reilly, Diane Kagan). There is even a genuine ghost, a dead grandmother who appears now and again in a blue spotlight, much as the absent father of the boy in *Menagerie* turned up regularly courtesy of a lighted photograph on the wall. When the present lad isn't crossing paths with his troubled neighbors, on the stairwell, in the kitchen, he is addressing us. "If I excused myself or withdrew, this scene would be incomplete," he remarks, redirecting our attention to two Dickensian crones, one wearing a headpiece that looks like an explosion of tulle, who have invaded the kitchen in search of a sip of newly made gumbo.

The remark, unhappily, goes directly to the heart of the problem. The crones aren't really playing a scene. They are only chittering, in a kind of near-senile birdsong Williams remembers. The boy is not needed to complete it, it would stand as the fragment it is without him. There is, in fact, nothing in the entire evening that *requires* completion, by the boy or by anyone else. *Glass Menagerie* had two tremendously powerful forces at work in it, two hard-driving wills determined on satisfaction: mother Amanda, leaving her son no peace until he found a gentleman-caller for his sister; and the son himself, in a fury of a hurry to escape Amanda's clutches. There were urgencies to be dramatized and they were conflicting urgencies. The play, for all its smokey aura of reminiscence, moved angrily, sorrowfully, grippingly.

Here there are no such energies at work. The tubercular painter will cough his life away and simply disappear from the play. The girl will be unable to penetrate the stupor of her man. The others will go their noisy or flighty rounds, glimpsed in passing, ephemeral, irrelevant. Echoes have been recorded; no dynamic pattern has been arranged to house them. And this much must be laid to Williams's charge.

What is truly unthinkable, though, is that the genuine perceptions, the characteristic and characteristically tantalizing inflections we do overhear, should be so disgracefully served. The young writer, for instance, has a habit of referring to his grandmother as "the mother of my mother." That is a quite possible character trait (let's say that the boy's mother has, whether he likes it or not, become the center of his universe and all other relationships must derive from *her*); it is a way of speaking that could easily intrigue us. As novice Richard Alfieri mouths the phrase, it comes out hopelessly stilted, no more than ink on a page, merely and stubbornly quirky. Mr. Alfieri does not act, he recites. When he agrees, during a discussion of loneliness, that "Yes, it's an affliction," or when he addresses his landlady with "May I sit down a moment? Eviction presents a problem," we can scarcely detect the traces of genuine Williams that actually inhabit the lines, we can only suppose that this absurd youngster has been reading bad translations from the Norwegian and has become mired in them.

Because other actors who are good actors (Mr. Aldredge, Miss Kagan) suffer similarly, blame has got to be passed on to Director Arthur Allan Seidelman. Miss Kagan should not get the disbelieving laugh that stirs in the auditorium with her "I have been betrayed by a sensual streak in my nature," and Mr. Aldredge--subject to coughing spells or no--should certainly not be unintelligible during his early approaches to the boy under the rafters. The physical staging is, if anything, worse: the moment there are more than two people on stage, the performers seem to be making certain that they are standing exactly where they have been told to stand without having any notion whatsoever of which colleague they should be listening to. From all of this, by the way, Miss Sidney must be exempted: pattering about in her fluffy, dirty mules, cackling over gossip and rasping out the nonexistent rules of the house, she is animated, full-bodied, exemplary.

I wish there were not need to continue this bill of complaints. But how is one to overlook the further serious disservice done the play by designer James Tilton's setting? If a "memory" play wants anything, it wants atmosphere. What it gets is a front scrim that would seem to have done service for the fifth road company of *Blossom Time* and grown mangier in a warehouse ever since, and, once the scrim has gone away, a junkpile of wood and beaverboard that does not so much suggest a run-down residence as it does a residence that has never been run up. It's as though some carpenters had started work without a ground-plan and, growing baffled, walked away after a couple of hour's work.

Inside, one of the setting's oddities quite distracted me from the effort to get through to Mr. Williams's text for a few moments. The rafters that shape the attic in which both Mr. Alfieri and Mr. Aldredge reside are nakedly exposed to the sky; they are, however, festooned with heavy spotlights that look uncannily like big black bats. Fairly early in the evening a housemaid comes on with a broom, explaining that she's just been swatting at a bull bat she'd trapped somewhere (not in the attic). This promptly set me to wondering whether Mr. Tilton had deliberately arranged his spotlights to suggest that there were bats in the house or whether Mr. Williams had added the housekeeper's gratuitous line later to explain away the curious look of the roof. Time wasted, time wasted. I should have been concentrating on searching out the nuances of language and portraiture that were being so ruthlessly masked by an irresponsible production.

Someone will try the play again. They won't have anything inherently dramatic to work with, but they'll have more than meets the ear at the moment. I'm game for a second go.

New York Times, May 22, 1977, sec. 2: 5, 30.

A Lovely Sunday for Creve Coeur (1979)

Tennessee's Waltz: Familiar Williams Themes
Gerald Weales

The final image in *The Glass Menagerie* is that of Laura, alone, illuminated by the candles which, for all that they are the Gentleman Caller's "favorite kind of light," will bring no warmth to the girl. Tom finishes his last speech; Laura blows out the candles; the play ends in darkness. The quiet, almost sentimental quality of that final speech, of the play as a whole, masks the fact that *Menagerie* ends with the starkest picture of loneliness in the Williams canon. The heroines who follow tend to have more Amanda than Laura in them. The specter of separateness haunts them too, but, whether lyric victims or comic grotesques, beset by violence or desperation or plain indifference, they manage a kind of vitality which insists that they try to escape, to outsmart, to smother the loneliness that Williams sees as central to the human condition.

Now, almost thirty-five years after Laura's disappearance into darkness, Williams is back with a quartet of women coping with or succumbing to the perennial Williams problem. *A Lovely Sunday for Creve Coeur,* which was first performed at the Spoleto Festival USA last year, is in a showcase production at the Hudson Guild, presumably--like its characters--looking for a more permanent home. The *Creve Coeur* of the title is not simply the heartbreak of Dorothea, the leading character but an amusement park to which her roommate, Bodey, regularly goes with her twin brother for Sunday picnics. Williams has always been partial to that kind of playful serious title (*A Streetcar Named Desire, Camino Real*), and what little plot the play has carries Dorothea beyond her *crève-coeur* to the amusement park, to an acceptance of life in which one settles for what one can get instead of what one wants. Dorothea is a school teacher (civics), a foolish, pretty blonde woman, running to plumpness and shortness of breath, who expects a romantic marriage to the handsome, socially prominent principal of the school where she teaches and who finally, this lovely Sunday, learns that her dream man has become engaged to a girl in what a 1930s comedy (the play takes place in 1935) would have called "his own set." She pulls herself together and goes off to join the picnic, to acquiesce in the courtship that Bodey has been engineering with her fat, cigar-smoking, beer-drinking St. Louis German brother, the antithesis of the now inaccessible principal. Before she goes, she stops long enough to quiet the hysterical German girl from upstairs, to give her coffee and crullers and compassion, to recognize--as she has refused to do before--that the girl's fear of being alone in the apartment where her mother died is only an extension of what all the characters feel.

Both Bodey and Helena, the schoolteacher who expects Dorothea to share an apartment, want to use her--not quite as the principal did, on the reclining seat of his brand-new Reo touring car--as a defense against loneliness. Bodey, who knows that she will never have children of her own, envisions a marriage which will make her an aunt, give her a surrogate family which might bring meaning to her preoccupation with the kitchen. Helena, who somehow confuses the history of art with tea sandwiches and contract bridge, needs Dorothea financially (to pay for the expensive apartment she covets), but her brief soliloquy on eating alone indicates that Dorothea's presence is as important as her money. Both Bodey's blowzy cheerfulness and Helena's thin-lipped bitchiness (she has most of the good lines) are forms of desperation, but Dorothea's decision to ally herself with Bodey suggests that warm vulgarity is more desirable than waspish correctness, although even that warmth is cold comfort.

Familiar Williams theme then, relentlessly explicit, and characters that bring echoes of so many Williams women who have gone before, but how are we to take the play? Shirley Knight does Dorothea in a voice that suggests Marie Wilson as much as the traditional Southern belle--a comic voice, one might assume, had Knight not used a similar one when she played Blanche a few seasons ago in Princeton and Philadelphia in a production that wrecked the rhythm of *Streetcar*. She manages to get through the voice to the character by the end of the play, but Peg Murray (as Bodey) and Charlotte Moore (as Helena) are never more than the vaudeville antagonists Williams has written and Jane Lowry's suicidal Miss Gluck is a travesty character as well as an unlikely Hiss Happiness. Add that each act opens with a tinny victrola grinding out "Alone" and that the lines are so full of the names of products, places, people that they seem a parody of Blanche DuBois's fondness for the specific.

Perhaps a comic variation on the familiar Williams theme is intended (remember *Slapstick Tragedy*), but the mention of Blanche in this context is a reminder that Williams has always used comedy in his serious plays--particularly verbal comedy (think of Amanda on the telephone, Blanche's conjuring "Mr. Edgar Allan Poe" to describe Stella's apartment). The four women in *Creve Coeur* lack the urgency of the early Williams heroines and, contrariwise, the comedy fails to penetrate the surface and set up shop in the viscera of the characters. The problem, I suspect, is that there is an idea rather than dramatic substance at the heart of their speeches--conversation and soliloquy alike--and it takes more than the proclamation of *crève coeur* to provide a substantial theatrical picnic.

Commonweal, March 16, 1979: 146-47.

Clothes for a Summer Hotel (1980)

Damsels Inducing Distress
John Simon

" . . . Tennessee Williams's Zelda is yet another precious lost soul, driven by her frustrations into lyrically foulmouthed dementia . . ."

With *Clothes for a Summer Hotel,* Tennessee Williams has finally written a play that, unlike its eight or ten predecessors, is not embarrassing. Neither, however, is it good. It starts out promisingly enough, as an overworked Scott Fitzgerald, himself in precarious health, comes from Hollywood to call on his allegedly cured wife--soon to die in a fire--at an Asheville mental institution. The asylum is atop a windswept hill and guarded by ominous German nuns in Draculaesque capes. But soon we switch to the overillustrative reminiscences of one or the other tormented mind, to the wheezing symbolism of fire and salamander tropes, and hindsight-burdened colloquies in limbo between omniscient ghosts. A program note by Williams calls this "a ghost play," and adds defensively: "In a sense all plays are ghost plays." Especially, I daresay, when written by ghost playwrights.

Sadder--as well as duller--as it gets with each repetition, it has to be said yet again: Williams has long since written himself out, and this unfocused, meandering, unnecessary play--for all that it is a short step up--merely reconfirms the obvious. *Clothes* shuttles not so much between Scott's and Zelda's fantasies and recollections as between two already published works: Nancy Milford's *Zelda* and Hemingway's *A Moveable Feast.* Almost everything of interest and value in the play is contained in one of those books, and is better in its original form.

I reiterate: There is nothing necessary about this ghost play, nothing that needed saying in *this* world. Williams's Zelda is yet another precious lost soul, driven by her frustrations into lyrically foulmouthed dementia--just like all those other Tennessean Ophelias, e.g., Alma (Winemiller), Blanche (DuBois), and Catherine [*sic*] (Holly) from the standard Williams ABC. As for Scott, he functions mostly as a straight man to Zelda, except in a scene with Hemingway, where both his straightness and his talent are questioned by a callous competitor who protests too much. The remaining roles are indeed disembodied wraiths, and it does seem rather a pity to haul in Gerald and Sara Murphy, Mrs. Pat Campbell, and several others as little more than window dressing for an undertaker's parlor. It takes a lot more living than these characters do to make even a funeral home.

There is, moreover, a curious textbook quality about much of the writing. Thus Scott will say things like " . . . My novel, *The Last Tycoon,* which I must live to complete," to which Zelda responds with "You have your notes, and Bunny Wilson will complete it--not quite in your style, of course." Be is said for Williams that he has no one interject, "Bunny? Oh, you mean *Edmund Wilson*"; he does, however, give us such anachronistic language as "counter-productive" and "a meaningful conversation." If, as he puts it in the play, "words are the love acts of writers," he is clearly suffering form lovelessness, if not impotence.

Occasionally a bit of the old Williams wit resurfaces. When Edouard, the dashing French flyer who has just had sex with Zelda in a cheap hotel and is worried that Scott may have tracked them down, exclaims, "He may have recognized your cries," Zelda answers, "How could he have, having never heard them before?" The clever old hand reasserts itself, but the ear is failing; surely no one between any sheets except those of a book would use that participial construction, especially with "have" and "having" clumsily jostling each other. But perhaps the play is merely a first draft for a screenplay in the Hollywood that Williams (through Fitzgerald) describes as a place where "people pretend to feel, but . . . don't feel at all."

Under the circumstances, José Quintero's direction does whatever flesh and blood can do for a ghost play, and Oliver Smith's scenery is nicely evocative--creepy or nostalgic, as the particular scene requires. Theoni V. Aldredge's costumes and Marilyn Rennagel's lighting discharge the flashy demands made on them, and Anna Sokolow's "dance consulting" gets the cast to sashay around appropriately to Michael Valenti's suitably unoriginal "original music." But, perhaps understandably, the acting falters.

Kenneth Haigh does intelligent, conscientious work as Scott (although no writer would turn "plagiarize" into four-syllable word), in an underwritten part for which he is not quite suited physically or vocally. Still, this is nothing to be ashamed of--which is more than I can say for Geraldine Page's Zelda. Miss Page gives what she has doubtless been encouraged to view as a virtuoso performance oozing technique from every syllable, movement, and pore. But technique--particularly when it is of the affected kind--can be that multitude of trees for which one cannot see the forest. Consider the sheer inhumanity of her voice, which here sounds mostly like the meowings of a sick cat gallantly trying to be coquettish. The mannerisms never abate--not even in the scenes in which Zelda is supposed to be anything but mad. Thus, time after time, Miss Page builds to a major outburst, only to peter out at the last moment into a dying fall. Quite effective once or twice, but not when it is as recurrent as the design in wallpaper. And all that making like a sculpture gallery with the body--truly, we are left in a daze of whines and poses.

Yet if Miss Page has turned an act into a jag, the blame must be shared by the director, who must also be castigated for casting David Canary and Marilyn Rockafellow in key roles that they manage to trivialize. Especially unsatisfactory is Robert Black's (physically right) Hemingway--with whom, incidentally, Williams practices his typical gossip-mongering approach when he has someone remark on (I haven't got this down verbatim) "Ernest's somewhat too carefully calculated cultivation of the prizefight, the bull ring, and the man-to-man attitude derived from Gertrude Stein." There is, however, very sound work from Michael Connolly as Gerald Murphy, from Mary Doyle as a lesser madwoman, and (though she is miscast) from Josephine Nichols as Mrs. Campbell.

In one scene, Williams articulates the not entirely novel notion that Fitzgerald jealously sabotaged what might have turned out to be his wife's superior talent for writing. If that had been the main thrust of the play, the result might have been, however unfounded as literary criticism, something of greater dramatic and human interest.

New York, April 7, 1980: 82, 84.

Tennessee Williams's Next-to-Final Finale
Wilborn Hampton

At the top of the second act of *Clothes for a Summer Hotel,* Tennessee Williams's rueful rumination on the disillusions of life as mirrored through Zelda and F. Scott Fitzgerald, Zelda has a brief, torrid affair with a young French aviator named Edouard. As the lovers part, Zelda postulates that the pilot will leave her arms and die in a fiery plane crash. It doesn't happen, of course. As the flier points out, he doesn't crash his plane. He just grows old. Williams suffered the same disappointment.

Clothes for a Summer Hotel was Williams's last, futile attempt to kindle one more dramatic blaze on Broadway. Although he had another, final play a year later (*Something Cloudy, Something Clear* far off Broadway, at the Bouwerie Lane Theater), the failure of *Clothes* in 1981 devastated Williams. The York Theater Company is currently staging a revival that, while a game effort, hardly transforms a play that such talents as José Quintero and

Geraldine Page failed to salvage.

The main, and by no means small, satisfaction the York revival affords is the reminder that while Williams may have become lax in his craft as a playwright, the poet in him had not been stricken dumb. If the thunder of his dramatic storms had rolled off-stage, there were still occasional flashes of poetic lightning.

It is easy to see how Williams drew inspiration from the Fitzgeralds' troubled lives. The play is straightforward biography, taking as a starting point a one-day visit Scott paid Zelda at the Highland Hospital in Asheville, N.C. (and in his haste, bringing the wrong clothes), and then resorting to flashbacks as a sort of grand tour of their marriage.

The biggest weakness in the play is that most of the emotional conflicts are described rather than played out. There are references to Scott's thwarting Zelda's own talents as a writer, to Scott's drinking and to Zelda's addictions and madness. "Zelda's a crazy and Scott's a rummy," Hemingway tells their mutual friend Gerald Murphy in one scene. But we never see Zelda behave "like a lunatic on the street," or Scott more than slightly tipsy. "His whole life has been a drunken disturbance," Zelda says of her husband, but you would never know it from the play. The most disagreeable behavior Scott displays is at a party when he cannot find anyone to mourn the death of Joseph Conrad with him.

Some of the writing is facile and some of it heavy, as though the tedium of plotting and construction no longer interested the playwright. In one scene, in which Scott and Hemingway challenge one another's masculinity, Hemingway fast-forwards to his own end, explaining his suicide. Even some poetic allusions seem tired, with Scott calling Zelda a Cassandra and Zelda's frequent references to a salamander.

But some scenes are vibrant with the passion of new love that Williams always understood, like the tender yet ultimately disappointing assignation between Zelda and Edouard, in which Zelda for once can "cry out in the arms of a man married to the sky," or poignant with the sorrow of lost hope. "What happened to expectation?" Zelda asks at one point, and observes later, "As we grow older, losses accumulate." Unlike Zelda's aviator, neither of the Fitzgeralds grew old. Maybe by the time of his writing about them, Williams simply envied them their fiery crash.

The York production has had some setbacks as well. The director and the actress playing Zelda left the show shortly before the scheduled opening. The company hired a new director and cast, and decided to go ahead with the opening. At a performance on Tuesday, the new cast played with scripts in hand. As a result, characterizations have not been fully developed. Diane Kagan as Zelda seems to be closest. On Tuesday, she had most of her lines off and gave a credible reading that was seemingly on its way to a fine, haunting interpretation. Robert Lupone has more work to do on Scott. Robert

Duncan is already solid doubling as Edouard and a hospital intern, and Tony Giordano's direction would appear to be on target.

New York Times, April 21, 1995: C30.

Something Cloudy, Something Clear (1981)

Tennessee Revisited
Dan Isaac

CAROLINE: *How can you expect a man that lives at the "Y" to write a play for me?*

MAURICE: *Playwrights are spawned in tenements and bordellos, then they graduate to the YMCA, then they graduate suddenly to Park Avenue apartments and grand hotels and they lose everything but their taste for booze and their outraged outrageous egos, and finally, usually, they die in Bowery gutters from delirium tremens or an overdose of narcotics. We have to remember this cycle and make allowances for them.*

Tennessee Williams
Something Cloudy, Something Clear

The failure--whatever that commercial concept may finally come to mean --of Tennessee Williams' most recent plays, represents a significant chapter in the creative odyssey of America's greatest living playwright. And it has become smart and popular to talk about his flagging talent.

Yet, history and culture have a way of recovering works that a wasteful, spend-fast age would overlook. Think of how long neglected were the poems of John Donne and the rough treatment *Camino Real* received the first time around.

Sooner or later, I am convinced, theater culture will recover for its permanent repertory such idiosyncratic works as *The Milk Train Doesn't Stop Here Anymore*--waiting only for an aging *grande dame* of the theater to make its central character Mrs. Goforth as much a legend as Norma Desmond--or simply the right program notes for *A Bar in a Tokyo Hotel* [*sic*] to take its proper and respected place in the Williams canon.

Meanwhile, there is one such, *Something Cloudy, Something Clear*, reopening in repertory at the Bouwerie Lane after the first of the year. Whatever the problems of this play, it is surely worth more consideration than the critics gave it when the Jean Cocteau Repertory first opened it this past fall.

Something Cloudy, Something Clear is a perfect title for Tennessee Williams' new play. More autobiographical than anything the playwright has written since *The Glass Menagerie,* the cloudy-clear reference is to a cataract condition in one of the playwright's eyes that produced an embarrassing flux as well as a blurry view of the world.

The title could just as easily represent the uneven quality of the play itself, a fragmented work that comes into beautiful focus under the sensitive and reverent direction of Eve Adamson. One senses a gentleness, a special kind of purity here, a Zen-like concentration--part Williams, part Adamson-- and the result is a unique ambiance, a special world for the characters to live and breathe in.

The time of *Something Cloudy, Something Clear* is 1940. A playwright named August--alias Tennessee Williams--is still hanging out on the beach after the summer is over. August lives in a broken-apart hut by the sea that requires a tarpaulin when it rains, a clear metaphor for the insubstantial nature of his life.

Possessed of only a silver victrola and a typewriter, August is trying desperately to rewrite his second act for the producer who has optioned his play for a promised Boston tryout prior to a Broadway opening. The situation recalls *Battle of Angels,* Tennessee Williams' first play to receive a profession-al production. It opened in Boston under the auspices of the Theatre Guild, starring Miriam Hopkins, on December 30, 1940 and closed *precipitously* January 11, 1941, the Broadway premier canceled. Years later Williams rewrote this play and called it *Orpheus Descending.*

Something Cloudy, Something Clear describes that precise moment of pressure and expectation for a playwright who believes he is about to make it if he can only please both the prestigious producer and the essential star with his new second act. At the very beginning August lets you know how he feels about this situation. When a young girl apologizes for interrupting his work, August claims to be glad for the interruption: "You did me a favor for that. I was about to make a concession to the taste of someone else, a powerful man with practically no taste."

The reference is to Lawrence Langner, founding producer of the Theatre Guild. And at the end of act one, Williams brings him on stage in the person of Maurice Fiddler, along with his wife and the famous Hollywood star. The result is a crackling confrontation between the impoverished playwright and the slimy, money-grubbing producer who claims to know what it feels like to be an artist because, he says, he is one, too. A knockout scene, this is vintage Williams, indeed a new, tougher, crustier Williams, the best piece of writing the master has done in some time.

The victory of August over the money-lenders who control the fame and fortune of frail playwrights is a stirring, albeit comic cartoon triumph. More complicated, and the real heart of the play, is August's dealings with two, young beachcombers who turn out to be even more vulnerable and waif-like than *even* our would-be playwright.

Clare and Kip--partners in crime, mutual protection, and perverse affection--have staked out young August as their last best hope for a hustle that will get them through the winter. The particular problems and infirmities of Clare and Kip make Tennessee/August look like the best bet in town for health and longevity, cataract and all.

Kip, in spite of the impression created by his Nijinsky-like body, is dying of brain cancer. Clare, a diabetic living on half a kidney--"everyone lives on half of something," she tells us--is in need of insulin and hospital care. When she observes August getting the hots for Kip, she decides to encourage the affair. Maybe August will be so happy with Kip that he will decide to keep both of them for the winter. With a big producer about to visit, this guy with the typewriter and silver victrola looks like a good long shot.

So this play is mostly about a triad of desperate people maneuvering and hustling to get what they want, with some insight into the price they will have to pay in terms of integrity and self-image.

Williams is unsparing of himself. When Clare gets beaten up by a hit-man mobster who was her former lover, August's cowardice makes us cringe as he turns his back and walks away. When August introduces the frightened and reluctant Kip to homosexual love, we begin to raise uncomfortable questions about the protagonist's integrity.

From a moral point of view, there is much that is cloudy here; clearly Williams means is to be that way. Moral ambiguity is his business.

Something Cloudy, Something Clear is layered over with double exposures, disparate memories from the past that appear to be pasted on at first glance. It is precisely this aspect of the play that tends to drive critics to astigmatic distraction. August the writer is also a narrator who steps outside the action from time to time in order to view things from the sad heights of omniscience. At one point he tell us: "Life is all--it's just one time, it finally seems to occur all at once."

The dramaturgy does appear to get off track with the inclusion of several scenes that record the final days of friends helplessly dying, alone in hospitals. With two of these characters--Frank Merlo, Tennessee Williams' long-term lover and live-in companion, and Tallulah Bankhead--Williams doesn't even bother to change the names. The inability to link these isolated interludes into a central plot makes this material appear to be a piece of undisciplined sentimental pleading, a slippage into a closed circuit of webbed associations that inevitably return to death and dying. But one does finally perceive a thematic relevance to the situation of Kip who is dying of a malignant brain tumor. This rhetoric is real.

Craig Smith's portrayal of the shy Southern playwright is a gentle, beautifully attenuated performance that is dangerously on the edge of imitation. Considering that Williams was present for much of the rehearsal period, writing and rewriting, one sympathizes with the immense difficulties and problematic choices for an actor playing the very playwright who is sitting out there in the dark watching you try to build a character. *His* character!

I asked Craig Smith about this and he claims to have strenuously tried to avoid an imitation. But Craig did recall that he said to Williams at the beginning of the rehearsal period, "I've played you twice now." (The reference was to Craig Smith's performance in the Cocteau Repertory's premier production of Tennessee Williams' "Kirche, Kuche, and [sic] Kinder"; presented in 1979 at the Bouwerie Lane as "an experimental work in progress.") Williams' response to Craig's remark was: "No, baby! In the other play you played my vulgarity."

There was one significant occasion when the playwright did correct the current portrayal of himself. "You're getting too poetic," Tennessee Williams told Craig Smith. "Don't fall in love with the language!"

As to the other performers, Dominique Cierci and Elton Cormier, as Clare and Kip, are very much the beautiful aggressive children that the playwright had in mind. Ms. Cierci handles the role of Clare with gamin savvy, showing us how an outcast from the upper class can turn into a tough little cookie. Elton Cormier has the tougher job with Kip because his role is not simply underwritten, but *unwritten.* Why did Williams make Kip so passive, so empty--a *tabula rasa* for someone else to write on? It would have been good to have heard from Kip how he felt about his first night with August.*

John Schmerling, Phyllis Deitschel, and Meg Fisher play the producer, his wife, and the attendant Hollywood star with a proper mix of bravado, arrogance, and casual contempt. The result is one of those scenes that you remember and talk about ten years later.

Douglas McKeown and Giles Hoyga are to be congratulated for the set and lighting, creating the sense of a bright spacious beach on the small stage of the Bouwerie Lane.

Something Cloudy, Something Clear is a poignant, witty portrait of the playwright as a young beach-bum, still a few years away from the intoxication

---

*In the summer of 1994, while continuing research on unpublished versions and fragments of Tennessee Williams plays, I found several pages of dialogue that perfectly answer my complaint: dialogue put in the mouth of Kip to Clare, describing in some detail August's style of love-making, which could be characterized as selfish and cruel. We are left to ponder what structural concerns or accident of misplaced pages caused the playwright to leave this material out of a final redaction.

of an illustrious career. For the first time Williams has put himself on stage center. And for the first time he creates a protagonist who is a homosexual scrounging around for a little love, security and affection.

A work that deserves to live, *Something Cloudy, Something Clear* is an important play in the ongoing and continued development of America's greatest playwright. Whatever dramaturgic misdemeanors Mr. Williams may have committed this play contains the poetic beauty and hard-earned ironic insight that we associate with the best of Tennessee Williams.

One wonders why all of New York has not journeyed down to the Bouwerie Theatre to see this fine and rare production.

Other Stages, December 17, 1981: 6, 8.

*Finally, *Something Cloudy, Something Clear* was published in the Fall of 1995. According to New Directions Vice President, Peggy Fox, Tennessee Williams' executrix, the late Lady Maria St. Just, did not want this play in print because she believed it would call attention to the playwright's homosexuality and adversely effect his reputation.

A House Not Meant to Stand (1982)

A House Not Meant to Stand
Albert E. Karlson

Stung by the adverse critical reception of *Clothes for a Summer Hotel* on Broadway in 1980, Tennessee Williams has retreated to the Midwest to form an association with Chicago's Goodman Theatre. The association has been a useful one for both theatre and playwright, culminating in a major full-length production of *A House Not Meant to Stand*. Williams's new play developed out of the one-act, "Some Problems for the Moose Lodge" which was performed as part of a program of short plays billed as *Tennessee Laughs* in the Goodman's tiny Studio Theatre in November 1980. The first expanded version of the play with its present title took shape soon after in the Studio in March 1981. Williams, as has been his habit, tinkered considerably with the play in preparing it for Goodman's main stage, but he has not yet solved its many problems. Under the direction of Andre Ernotte, a not-yet-polished performance by some imported actors from New York has not strengthened the fragile, unfocused work, which the author labels "a Gothic spook sonata."

On viewing the set, a dilapidated living-room with a raised dining area at the rear, a playgoer is immediately reminded of *The Glass Menagerie*. The walls are made of scrim and melt away as Bella McCorkle, an obese Amanda Wingfield, loses touch with the present and romanticizes her past. Late in the play an omnipresent storm even causes a power failure. Not a St. Louis apartment this time, the play is set in Williams's more familiar Mississippi Delta country, a house in Pascagoola.

The other characters, too, are reminiscent of *Menagerie,* except that the missing father of the early play is very much present here (named Cornelius, Williams's own father's name). The brother and sister of *Menagerie* are constantly present in their parent's thoughts, materializing as children only at the end of the play as Bella withdraws from reality. Their daughter Joanie, earthier than the delicate Laura, is about to be committed to a state asylum, while Chips, a homosexual, with the soul of an artist like Tom, has succumbed to alcoholism in Memphis. The play begins as the McCorkles return home from his funeral.

Bella (Williams grandmother's name was Isabel [*sic*]) tries to account for the tragedy which has befallen her family as Cornelius, always at odds with her, plots to find her family's money hidden somewhere in the house. Never much concerned with his disappointing offspring, his thoughts are focused on a coming election and, like Williams's own brother Dakin, is obsessed with capturing public office. At home they find their other son, the ne'er-do-well Charlie, and his pregnant fiancée, Stacey, a born-again Christian with an unquenchable evangelical calling. The family is frequently interrupted by visits from their neighbors, the Sykes. Mrs. Sykes, who is about to have her husband committed, has found rejuvenation through cosmetic surgery, while Mr. Sykes spends his time planning outlandish deals, such as the building of the Night O'Glory Motel. Finally ridding herself of her husband, Mrs. Sykes attempts to steal the money herself, which brings on Bella's fatal attack. As she dies, Bella imagines herself with her children as a scrim dissolves to reveal an upstairs room containing some toys and a crib.

Once again Williams has concocted a play which may be too personal for his audience. In its shorter version there were violent shifts of mood punctuated by grotesque moments of farce. The farcical material is now oddly compressed into the final act, and the first act has little more than grim reminders of man's mortality. If the original one-act seemed at times a pointless exercise in self-parody, it was vastly entertaining. A wildly comic description of Bella sneaking Danish pastries at an airport lunch counter has been cut, and Joanie's sadly amusing letter describing her plight now that her black boyfriend has deserted her occurs too late. The account of Chips's high school days when he was voted the prettiest girl in the class has lost the edge of barbed wit it once had; only Stacey's evangelical fervor brightens the full-length version.

Perhaps Williams realized that the expansion into a longer work necessitated theme, and the theme is now clearly the coming to grips with advancing age. Bella refuses and regresses, Cornelius flails about in politics, Mr. Sykes still sees some point in planning for a future through business, and Mrs. Sykes thinks she has found the age-old solution--sex. But time, as Williams has been reminding us since *Sweet Bird of Youth,* wins out in the end.

The experience of watching the play develop over the months has been a unique one for faithful Goodman audiences, but *A House Not Meant to Stand* remains minor Williams, soon to be relegated to his growing pile of unworkable later plays.

Theatre Journal, 34.4 (December 1982): 539-41. (Review of Chicago production.)

Selected Bibliography

Works by Tennessee Williams

Plays and Screenplays

The Glass Menagerie. New York: Random House, 1945.

27 Wagons Full of Cotton and Other One-Act Plays. New York: New Directions, 1946.

You Touched Me! New York: Samuel French, 1947.

A Streetcar Named Desire. New York: New Directions, 1947.

American Blues. New York: Dramatists Play Service, 1948.

Summer and Smoke. New York: New Directions, 1948.

The Rose Tattoo. New York: New Directions, 1951.

I Rise in Flame, Cried the Phoenix. New York: New Directions, 1952.

Camino Real. New York: New Directions, 1953.

Lord Byron's Love Letter. New York: Ricordi, 1955.

Cat on a Hot Tin Roof. New York: New Directions, 1955.

Baby Doll: The Script for the Film by Tennessee Williams Incorporating the Two One-Act Plays Which Suggested It. New York: New Directions, 1956.

Orpheus Descending with Battle of Angels. New York: New Directions, 1958.

Suddenly Last Summer. New York: New Directions, 1958.

Sweet Bird of Youth. New York: New Directions, 1959.

Period of Adjustment. New York: New Directions, 1960.

A Perfect Analysis Given by a Parrot. New York: Dramatists Play Service, 1961.

The Night of the Iguana. New York: New Directions, 1962.

The Milk Train Doesn't Stop Here Anymore. New York: New Directions, 1964.

The Eccentricities of a Nightingale and Summer and Smoke. New York: New
    Directions: 1965.
The Gnadiges Fraulein. New York: Dramatists Play Service, 1967.
The Mutilated. New York: Dramatists Play Service, 1967.
Kingdom of Earth (The Seven Descents of Myrtle). New York: New
    Directions, 1968.
In the Bar of a Tokyo Hotel. New York: Dramatists Play Service, 1969.
The Two-Character Play. New York: New Directions, 1969.
Dragon Country. New York: New Directions, 1970.
The Theatre of Tennessee Williams. New York: New Directions. 8 vols.
    1971-1992.
Small Craft Warnings. New Directions, 1972.
Out Cry. New York: New Directions, 1973.
Vieux Carré. New York: New Directions, 1979.
A Lovely Sunday for Creve Coeur. New York: New Directions, 1980.
Steps Must Be Gentle. New York: Targ Editions, 1980.
Clothes for a Summer Hotel. New York: New Directions, 1983.
The Remarkable Rooming House of Mme. Le Monde. New York: Albondocani
    Press, 1984.
Stopped Rocking and Other Screenplays. New York: New Directions, 1984.
The Red Devil Battery Sign. New York: New Directions, 1988.
Baby Doll and Tiger Tail. New York: New Directions, 1991.
Something Cloudy, Something Clear. New York: New Directions, 1995.

Short Stories

One Arm and Other Stories. New York: New Directions, 1949.
Hard Candy: A Book of Stories. New York: New Directions, 1954.
Three Players of a Summer Game and Other Stories. London: Secker &
    Warburg, 1960.
The Knightly Quest: A Novella and Four Short Stories. New York: New
    Directions, 1967.
Eight Mortal Ladies Possessed. New York: New Directions, 1974.
It Happened the Day the Sun Rose. Los Angeles: Sylvester & Orphanos,
    1981.
Collected Stories. New York: New Directions, 1985.

Novels

The Roman Spring of Mrs. Stone. New York: New Directions, 1950.
Moise and the World of Reason. New York: Simon & Schuster, 1975.

Poetry

In the Winter of Cities. New York: New Directions, 1956.
Androgyne, Mon Amour. New York: New Directions, 1977.

Essays

Where I Live: Selected Essays. Eds. Christine R. Day and Bob Woods.
New York: New Directions, 1978.

Autobiography and Interviews

Memoirs. Garden City, New York: Doubleday & Company, 1975.
Devlin, Albert J., ed. *Conversations with Tennessee Williams.* Jackson: UP
of Mississippi, 1985.

Letters

Tennessee Williams' Letters to Donald Windham, 1940-1965. Ed. Donald
Windham. New York: Holt, Rinehart and Winston, 1977.
*Five O'Clock Angel: Letters of Tennessee Williams to Maria St. Just,
1948-1982.* New York: Knopf, 1990.

Works about Tennessee Williams

Bibliographies

Arnott, Catherine, comp. *Tennessee Williams on File.* London: Methuen,
1985.
Crandell, George W. *Tennessee Williams: A Descriptive Bibliography.*
Pittsburgh Ser. in Bibliography. Pittsburgh: U of Pittsburgh P, 1995.
Gunn, Drewey Wayne. *Tennessee Williams: A Bibliography.* Scarecrow
Author Bibliographies. 89. Metuchen, N.J.: Scarecrow P, 1991.
McCann, John S. *The Critical Reputation of Tennessee Williams: A
Reference Guide.* A Reference Guide to Literature. Boston: G. K.
Hall, 1983.

Biographies

Falk, Signi. *Tennessee Williams.* 2nd ed. Twayne's United States Author
   Ser. 10. Boston: Twayne, 1978.
Leverich, Lyle. *Tom: The Unknown Tennessee Williams.* New York:
   Crown, 1995.
Spoto, Donald. *The Kindness of Strangers: The Life of Tennessee Williams.*
   Boston: Little, Brown, 1985.
Van Antwerp, Margaret A. and Sally Johns, eds. *Tennessee Williams.*
   Detroit: Gale, 1984. Vol. 4 of *Dictionary of Literary Biography.*
   Documentary Series: An Illustrated Chronicle. 12 vols. 1982-94.
Williams, Dakin and Shepherd Mead. *Tennessee Williams: An Intimate
   Biography.* New York: Arbor House, 1983.
Williams, Edwina Dakin and Lucy Freeman. *Remember Me to Tom.* New
   York: Putnam's, 1963.

Books

Adler, Thomas P. *A Streetcar Named Desire: The Moth and the Lantern.*
   Twayne's Masterwork Studies. 47. Boston: Twayne, 1990.
Bigsby, C. W. E. *Tennessee Williams, Arthur Miller, Edward Albee.*
   Cambridge: Cambridge UP, 1982. Vol. 2 of *A Critical Introduction
   to Twentieth-Century American Drama.* 3 vols. 1982-85.
Boxill, Roger. *Tennessee Williams.* Macmillan Modern Dramatists. New
   York: Macmillan, 1987.
Fedder, Norman. J. *The Influence of D. H. Lawrence on Tennessee
   Williams.* Studies in American Literature. 5. London: Mouton,
   1966.
Griffin, Alice. *Understanding Tennessee Williams.* Understanding
   Contemporary American Literature. Columbia: U of South Carolina
   P, 1995.
Hirsch, Foster. *A Portrait of the Artist: The Plays of Tennessee Williams.*
   Port Washington, N.Y.: Kennikat P, 1979.
Jackson, Ester Merle. *The Broken World of Tennessee Williams.* Madison:
   U of Wisconsin P, 1965.
Murphy, Brenda. *Tennessee Williams and Elia Kazan: A Collaboration in
   the Theatre.* Cambridge: Cambridge UP, 1992.
Tischler, Nancy. *Tennessee Williams: Rebellious Puritan.* New York: Citadel
   P, 1961.
Vanatta, Dennis. *Tennessee Williams: A Study of the Short Fiction.*
   Twayne's Studies in Short Fiction Ser. 4. Boston: Twayne, 1988.
Weales, Gerald. *Tennessee Williams.* Minneapolis: U of Minnesota P,
   1965.

Chapters in Books

Inge, M. Thomas. "The South, Tragedy, and Comedy in Tennessee Williams's *Cat on a Hot Tin Roof. The United States South: Regionalism and Identity.* Eds. Valeria Gennaro Lerda and Tjebbe Westendorp. Rome: Bulzoni, 1991. 157-65.

Kazan, Elia. "Notebook for *A Streetcar Named Desire." Directing the Play: A Source Book of Stagecraft.* Eds. Toby Cole and Helen Krich Chinoy. Indianapolis: Bobbs-Merrill, 1953. 296-310.

Lant, Kathleen Margaret. "A Streetcar Named Misogyny." *Violence in Drama.* Ed. James Redmond. Themes in Drama. 13. Cambridge: Cambridge UP, 1991. 225-38.

Miller, Jordan Y. "*Camino Real." The Fifties: Fiction, Poetry, Drama.* Ed. Warren French. DeLand, Florida: Everett / Edwards, 1970. 241-48.

Collections of Essays

Bloom, Harold, ed. *Tennessee Williams.* Modern Critical Views. New York: Chelsea, 1987.

_____. *Tennessee Williams's A Streetcar Named Desire.* Modern Critical Interpretations. New York: Chelsea House, 1988.

_____. *Tennessee Williams's The Glass Menagerie.* Modern Critical Interpretations. New York: Chelsea House, 1988.

Kolin, Philip C., ed. *Confronting Tennessee Williams's A Streetcar Named Desire: Essays in Cultural Pluralism.* Westport, Connecticut: Greenwood P, 1993.

Miller, Jordan Y., ed. *Twentieth Century Interpretations of A Streetcar Named Desire: A Collection of Critical Essays.* Twentieth Century Interpretations. Englewood Cliffs, N.J.: Prentice-Hall, 1971.

Parker, R. B., ed. *The Glass Menagerie: A Collection of Critical Essays.* Twentieth Century Interpretations. Englewood Cliffs, N.J.: Prentice-Hall, 1983.

Presley, Delma E. *The Glass Menagerie: An American Memory.* Twayne's Masterworks Studies. 43. Boston: Twayne, 1990.

Stanton, Stephen S. *Tennessee Williams: A Collection of Critical Essays.* Twentieth Century Views. Englewood Cliffs, N.J.: Prentice-Hall, 1977.

Tharpe, Jac., ed. *Tennessee Williams: A Tribute.* Jackson: U of Mississippi P, 1977.

Critical Articles

Adler, Jacob. *"Night of the Iguana:* A New Tennessee Williams?"
    Ramparts 1.3 (1962): 59-68.
Adler, Thomas P. "The Dialogue of Incompletion: Language in Tennessee
    Williams's Later Plays." *Quarterly Journal of Speech* 61 (1975): 48-
    58.
_____. "The Search for God in the Plays of Tennessee Williams."
    Renascence 26 (1973): 48-56.
Bak, John S. "'Celebrate Her with Strings': Leitmotifs and the Multifaceted
    'Strings' in Williams's *The Glass Menagerie." Notes on Mississippi
    Writers* 24 (1992): 81-87.
Berkowitz, Gerald. "The 'Other World' of *The Glass Menagerie." Players*
    48 (1973): 150-53.
Beaurline, Lester A. *"The Glass Menagerie:* From Story to Play." *Modern
    Drama* 8 (1965): 142-49.
Blackwelder, James Ray. "The Human Extremities of Emotion in *Cat on a
    Hot Tin Roof." Research Studies* 38 (1970): 13-21.
Blackwell, Louise. "Tennessee Williams and the Predicament of Women."
    South Atlantic Bulletin 35.2 (1970): 9-14.
Bluefarb, Sam. *"The Glass Menagerie:* Three Visions of Time." *College
    English* 24 (1963): 513-18.
Brooking, Jack. "Directing *Summer and Smoke:* An Existential Approach."
    Modern Drama 2 (1960): 377-85.
Bruhm, Steven. "Blackmailed by Sex: Tennessee Williams and the
    Economics of Desire." *Modern Drama* 34 (1991): 528-37.
Brustein, Robert. "America's New Culture Hero: Feelings without Words."
    Commentary 25 (1958): 123-29.
Buell, John. "The Evil Images of Tennessee Williams." *Thought* 38
    (1963): 167-89.
Callahan, Edward F. "Tennessee Williams' Two Worlds." *North Dakota
    Quarterly* 25 (1957): 61-67.
Campbell, Michael L. "The Theme of Persecution in Tennessee Williams'
    Camino Real." Notes on Mississippi Writers 6 (1973): 35-40.
Chesler, S. Alan. *"A Streetcar Named Desire:* Twenty-five Years of
    Criticism." *Notes on Mississippi Writers* 7 (1974): 44-53.
Cless, Downing. "Alienation and Contradiction in *Camino Real:* A Conver-
    gence of Williams and Brecht." *Theatre Journal* 35 (1983): 41-50.
Clinton, Craig D. "Tennessee Williams' *Kingdom of Earth:* The Orpheus
    Myth Revisited." *Theatre Annual* 33 (1977): 25-37.

Clum, John M. "*Something Cloudy, Something Clear:* Homophobic Discourse in Tennessee Williams." *South Atlantic Quarterly* 88 (1989): 161-79.

Corrigan, Mary Ann. "Memory, Dream, and Myth in the Plays of Tennessee Williams." *Renascence* 28 (1976): 155-67.

Downer, Alan S. "Experience of Heroes: Notes on the New York Theatre, 1961-62." *Quarterly Journal of Speech* 48 (1962): 261-70.

Dukore, Bernard F. "The Cat Has Nine Lives." *Tulane Drama Review* 8.1 (1963): 95-100.

Durham, Frank. "Tennessee Williams, Theatre Poet in Prose." *South Atlantic Bulletin* 36.2 (1971): 3-16.

Falk, Signi. "The Profitable World of Tennessee Williams." *Modern Drama* 1 (1958): 172-80.

Fritscher, John J. "Some Attitudes and a Posture: Religious Metaphor and Ritual in Tennessee Williams' Query of the American God." *Modern Drama* 13 (1970): 201-15.

Gunn, Drewey Wayne. "The Troubled Flight of Tennessee Williams's *Sweet Bird:* From Manuscript through Published Texts." *Modern Drama* 24 (1981): 26-35.

Hainsworth, J. D. "Tennessee Williams: Playwright on a Hot Tin Roof?" *Etudes Anglaises* 20 (1967): 225-32.

Hanks, Pamela Anne. "Must We Acknowledge What We Mean? The Viewer's Role in Filmed Versions of *A Streetcar Named Desire.*" *Journal of Popular Film and Television* 14 (1986): 114-22.

Hays, Peter L. "Arthur Miller and Tennessee Williams." *Essays in Literature* 4 (1977): 239-49.

_____. "Tennessee Williams' Use of Myth in *Sweet Bird of Youth.*" *Educational Theatre Journal* 18 (1966): 255-58.

Hendrick, George. "Jesus and the Osiris-Isis Myth: Lawrence's *The Man Who Died* and Williams's *The Night of the Iguana.*" *Anglia* 84 (1966): 398-406.

Hill, Francis A. "The Disaster of Ideals in *Camino Real* by Tennessee Williams." *Notes on Mississippi Writers* 1 (1969): 100-09.

Howell, Elmo. "The Function of Gentlemen Callers: A Note on Tennessee Williams' *The Glass Menagerie.*" *Notes on Mississippi Writers* 2 (1970): 83-90.

Hurley, Paul J. "*Suddenly Last Summer* as Morality Play." *Modern Drama* 8 (1966): 392-402.

Hyman, Stanley Edgar. "Some Notes on the Albertine Strategy." *Hudson Review* 6 (1953): 417-22.

King, Kimball. "The Rebirth of *Orpheus Descending.*" *Tennessee Williams Literary Journal* 1.2 (1989-90): 19-53.

King, Thomas L. "Irony and Distance in *The Glass Menagerie.*" *Educational Theatre Journal* 25 (1973): 207-14.

Kolin, Philip C. "The First Critical Assessments of *A Streetcar Named Desire:* The *Streetcar* Tryouts and the Reviewers." *Journal of Dramatic Theory and Criticism* 6 (1991): 45-67.

_____. "Obstacles to Communication in *Cat on a Hot Tin Roof.*" *Western Speech Communication* 39 (1975): 74-80.

_____. "*A Streetcar Named Desire:* A Playwright's Forum." *Michigan Quarterly Review* 29 (1990): 173-203.

Lee, M. Owen. "Orpheus and Eurydice: Some Modern Versions." *Classical Journal* 56 (1961): 307-13.

Lees, Daniel E. "*The Glass Menagerie:* A Black 'Cinderella.'" *Unisa English Studies* 11.1 (1973): 30-34.

Leibman, Nina C. "Sexual Misdemeanor / Psychoanalytic Felony." *Cinema Journal* 26.2 (1987): 27-38.

Leon, Ferdinand. "Time, Fantasy, and Reality in *Night of the Iguana.*" *Modern Drama* 11 (1968): 87-96.

Levy, Eric, P. "'Through Soundproof Glass': The Prison of Self-Consciousness in *The Glass Menagerie.*" *Modern Drama* 36 (1993): 529-37.

Magid, Marion. "The Innocence of Tennessee Williams." *Commentary* 35 (1963): 35-43.

Mansur, R. M. "The Two *Cats* on the Tin Roof: A Study of Tennessee Williams's *Cat on a Hot Tin Roof.*" *Journal of the Karnatak University-Humanities* 14 (1970): 150-58.

Mayberry, Susan Neal. "A Study of Illusion and the Grotesque in Tennessee Williams' *Cat on a Hot Tin Roof.*" *Southern Studies* 22 (1983): 359-65.

Melman, Lindy. "A Captive Maid: Blanche Dubois in *A Streetcar Named Desire.*" *Dutch Quarterly Review of Anglo-American Literature* 16 (1986): 125-44.

Miller, Arthur. "The Shadows of the Gods: A Critical View of the American Theater." *Harper's Magazine* (Aug. 1958): 35-43.

Miller, Jordan Y. "The Three Halves of Tennessee Williams's World." *Studies in the Literary Imagination* 21.2 (1988): 83-95.

Moritz, Helen E. "Apparent Sophoclean Echoes in Tennessee Williams's *Night of the Iguana.*" *Classical and Modern Literature: A Quarterly* 5 (1985): 305-14.

Morrow, Laura and Edward Morrow. "Humpty-Dumpty Lives!: Complexity Theory as an Alternative to the Omelet Scenario in *The Glass Menagerie.*" *Studies in American Drama, 1945-Present* 8.2 (1993): 127-39.

Napieralski, Edmund A. "Tennessee Williams' *The Glass Menagerie:* The Dramatic Metaphor." *Southern Quarterly* 16 (1977): 1-12.

Pagan, Nicholas O. "Tennessee Williams' Out Cry in *The Two-Character Play.*" *Notes on Mississippi Writers* 24.2 (1992): 67-79.

Parker, Brian. "The Composition of *The Glass Menagerie:* An Argument for Complexity." *Modern Drama* 25 (1982): 409-22.

Parker, R. B. "The Circle Closed: A Psychological Reading of *The Glass Menagerie* and *The Two-Character Play.*" *Modern Drama* 28 (1985): 517-34.

Peterson, William. "Williams, Kazan, and the Two Cats." *New Theatre Magazine* 7 (1967): 14-20.

Popkin, Henry. "The Plays of Tennessee Williams." *Tulane Drama Review* 4.3 (1960): 45-64.

Presley, Delma Eugene. "The Search for Hope in the Plays of Tennessee Williams." *Mississippi Quarterly* 25 (1971-72): 31-43.

Quirino, Leonard. "Tennessee Williams' Persistent *Battle of Angels.*" *Modern Drama* 11 (1968): 27-39.

Renaux, Sigrid. "The Real and the Royal in Tennessee Williams' *Camino Real.*" *Ilha do Desterro* 3.7 (1982): 43-66.

Riddel, Joseph N. "*A Streetcar Named Desire*--Nietzsche Descending." *Modern Drama* 5 (1963): 421-30.

Sacksteder, William. "The Three Cats: A Study in Dramatic Structure." *Drama Survey* 5 (1966-67): 252-66.

Satterfield, John. "Williams's *Suddenly Last Summer:* The Eye of the Needle." *Markham Review* 6 (1977): 27-33.

Savran, David. "'By coming suddenly into a room that I thought was empty': Mapping the Closet with Tennessee Williams." *Studies in the Literary Imagination* 24.2 (1991): 57-74.

Schleuter, June. "Imitating an Icon: John Erman's Remake of Tennessee Williams's *A Streetcar Named Desire.*" *Modern Drama* 28 (1985): 139-47.

Simon, John. "Brothers Under the Skin: O'Neill and Williams." *Hudson Review* 39 (1987): 553-565.

Spector, Susan. "Alternative Visions of Blanche DuBois: Uta Hagen and Jessica Tandy in *A Streetcar Named Desire.*" *Modern Drama* 32 (1989): 545-60.

Starnes, Leland. "The Grotesque Children of *The Rose Tattoo.*" *Modern Drama* 12 (1970): 357-69.

Stavrou, Constantine N. "The Neurotic Heroine in Tennessee Williams." *Literature and Psychology* 5 (1955): 26-34.

Traubitz, Nancy Baker. "Myth as a Basis of Dramatic Structure in *Orpheus Descending.*" *Modern Drama* 19 (1976): 57-66.

Vlasopolous, Anca. "Authorizing History: Victimization in *A Streetcar Named Desire.*" *Theatre Journal* 38 (1986): 322-38.

Von Szeliski, "Tennessee Williams and the Tragedy of Sensitivity."
    Western Humanities Review 20 (1966): 203-11.
Weldon, Roberta F. *"The Rose Tattoo:* A Modern Version of *The Scarlet
    Letter." Interpretations* 15.1 (1983): 70-77.
Young, Vernon. "Social Drama and Big Daddy." *Southwest Review* 16
    (1956): 194-97.

Index

About the Editor

GEORGE W. CRANDELL is associate professor of English at Auburn University. He is the author of *Tennessee Williams: A Descriptive Bibliography* (1995) and *Ogden Nash: A Descriptive Bibliography* (1991). His articles on American literature have appeared in *Studies in American Humor* and *The Library Chronicle*.